"America's leading source of self-help legal information." ★★★★

—Yahoo!

LEGAL INFORMATION ONLINE ANYTIME

24 hours a day

www.nolo.com

AT THE NOLO.COM SELF-HELP LAW CENTER, YOU'LL FIND

- Nolo's comprehensive Legal Encyclopedia filled with plain-English information on a variety of legal topics
- Nolo's Law Dictionary—legal terms <u>without</u> the legalese
- Auntie Nolo—if you've got questions, Auntie's got answers
- The Law Store—over 250 self-help legal products including: Downloadable Software, Books, Form Kits and eGuides
- Legal and product updates
- Frequently Asked Questions
- NoloBriefs, our free monthly email newsletter
- Legal Research Center, for access to state and federal statutes
- Our ever-popular lawyer jokes

Quality LAW BOOKS & SOFTWARE FOR EVERYONE

Nolo's user-friendly products are consistently first-rate. Here's why:

- A dozen in-house legal editors, working with highly skilled authors, ensure that our products are accurate, up-to-date and easy to use
- We continually update every book and software program to keep up with changes in the law
- Our commitment to a more democratic legal system informs all of our work
- We appreciate & listen to your feedback. Please fill out and return the card at the back of this book.

OUR "NO-HASSLE" GUARANTEE

Return anything you buy directly from Nolo for any reason and we'll cheerfully refund your purchase price. No ifs, ands or buts.

An Important Message to Our Readers

This product provides information and general advice about the law. But laws and procedures change frequently, and they can be interpreted differently by different people. For specific advice geared to your specific situation, consult an expert. No book, software or other published material is a substitute for personalized advice from a knowledgeable lawyer licensed to practice law in your state.

First edition

Creating Your Own Retirement Plan

A Guide to Keoghs & IRAs for the Self-Employed

by Twila Slesnick, PhD, Enrolled Agent
& Attorney John C. Suttle, CPA

NOLO

Keeping Up to Date

To keep its books up-to-date, Nolo issues new printings and new editions periodically. New printings reflect minor legal changes and technical corrections. New editions contain major legal changes, major text additions or major reorganizations. To find out if a later printing or edition of any Nolo book is available, call Nolo at 510-549-1976 or check our website at http://www.nolo.com.

To stay current, follow the "Update" service at our website at http://www.nolo.com/update. In another effort to help you use Nolo's latest materials, we offer a 35% discount off the purchase of the new edition of your Nolo book when you turn in the cover of an earlier edition. (See the "Special Upgrade Offer" in the back of the book.)

This book was last revised in: **February 2001.**

First Edition	FEBRUARY 2001
Editor	AMY DELPO
Illustrations	MARI STEIN
Cover Design	TONI IHARA
Book Design	TERRI HEARSH
Production	SARAH HINMAN
Proofreading	ROBERT WELLS
Index	ELLEN DAVENPORT
Printing	BERTELSMANN SERVICES, INC.

Slesnick, Twila.
    Creating Your Own Retirement Plan: a Guide to Keoghs & IRAs for the Self-Employed / by Twila Slesnick and John C. Suttle.
        p. cm.
    Includes index.
    ISBN 0-87337-592-0
    1. Individual retirement accounts--Law and legislation--United States--Popular works.
    2. Keogh plans--Law and legislation--United States--Popular works. 3. Pension trusts--Taxation--Law and legislation--United States--Popular works. I. Title:
    Creating your own retirement plan: a guide to Keoghs and IRAs for the self-employed.
II. Suttle, John C. III. Title.

KF3510.Z9 S55 2000
332.024'01--dc21   00-033252

Acknowledgments

Many thanks for many things to Nolo's Amy DelPo. An editor with her skill and tact must surely be a national treasure.

Our thanks and admiration also go to attorney Barbara Creed of Trucker Huss in San Francisco. Her expertise in the defined benefit plan arena is unmatched.

We also want to express special thanks to Marilynn Krause of Inline Plans in San Francisco, for reading numerous chapters and offering important and useful suggestions.

Thanks also to Tisha Findeison at The Vanguard Group for her cheerful cooperation and good nature.

Finally, we'd like to express our appreciation to The Vanguard Group itself for allowing us to reprint a number of its retirement plan documents.

Table of Contents

I Introduction

1 Retirement Plans for the Self-Employed: An Overview

A. Why Establish a Retirement Plan? 1/2

B. Choosing a Plan 1/6

C. Putting the Plan in Place 1/26

D. Maintaining the Plan 1/28

2 Comparing Plans

A. Employer Plans 2/3

B. Individual Plans: Traditional IRAs and Roth IRAs 2/10

3 SIMPLE IRAs

A. What Is a SIMPLE IRA 3/3

B. How to Establish a SIMPLE IRA 3/6

C. Contributions 3/8

D. Ongoing Administration 3/15

E. Distributions 3/16

F. Penalties 3/23

G. Terminating Your SIMPLE IRA 3/30

H. Multiple Employer Plans 3/31

I. Adding a Traditional or Roth IRA to Your SIMPLE IRA 3/34

J. Filling Out the Forms 3/34

4 SEPs

A. What Is a SEP? 4/3

B. How to Establish a SEP 4/6

C. Contributions 4/8

D. Ongoing Administration 4/12

E. Distributions 4/13

F. Penalties 4/18

G. Terminating Your SEP 4/27

H. Multiple Employer Plans 4/27

I. Adding a Traditional or Roth IRA to Your SEP 4/32

J. Filling Out the Forms 4/33

5 Profit Sharing Plans

A. What Is a Profit Sharing Plan? 5/3

B. How to Establish a Profit Sharing Plan 5/6

C. Contributions 5/11

D. Ongoing Administration 5/17

E. Distributions 5/19

F. Penalties 5/26

G. Terminating Your Profit Sharing Plan 5/31

H. Multiple Employer Plans 5/33

I. Adding a Traditional or Roth IRA to Your Profit Sharing Plan 5/39

J. Filling Out the Forms 5/39

6 Money Purchase Pension Plans

A. What Is a Money Purchase Pension Plan? 6/3

B. How to Establish a Money Purchase Pension Plan 6/6

C. Contributions 6/10

D. Ongoing Administration 6/17

E. Distributions 6/19

F. Penalties 6/25

G. Terminating Your Money Purchase Pension Plan 6/31

H. Multiple Employer Plans 6/33

I. Adding a Traditional or Roth IRA to Your
Money Purchase Pension Plan 6/38

J. Filling Out the Forms 6/39

7 Defined Benefit Plans

A. What is a Defined Benefit Plan? 7/3

B. How to Establish a Defined Benefit Plan 7/6

C. Contributions 7/10

D. Ongoing Administration 7/15

E. Distributions 7/18

F. Penalties 7/23

G. Terminating Your Defined Benefit Plan 7/30

H. Multiple Employer Plans 7/32

I. Adding a Traditional or Roth IRA to Your
Defined Benefit Plan 7/35

8 Traditional IRAs

    A. What Is a Traditional IRA? 8/3

    B. How to Establish a Traditional IRA 8/5

    C. Contributions 8/8

    D. Deductions 8/11

    E. Ongoing Administration 8/15

    F. Distributions 8/16

    G. Penalties 8/22

    H. Multiple IRAs and Qualified Plans 8/28

    I. Terminating Your IRA 8/29

9 Roth IRAs

    A. What Is a Roth IRA? 9/3

    B. How to Establish a Roth IRA 9/5

    C. Contributions 9/8

    D. Ongoing Administration 9/16

    E. Distributions 9/17

    F. Penalties 9/24

    G. Multiple IRAs and Qualified Plans 9/37

    H. Terminating Your Roth IRA 9/37

Glossary

Appendix

Index

Introduction

Retirement plans are arguably the biggest bargain in the U.S. Tax Code. Think about it. Congress lets you take money that you earn, put it into a retirement account for yourself and claim a tax deduction on your tax return. While the money is in this retirement account, you don't have to pay tax on any interest or capital gains that the money earns over the years. When you retire, you have this huge pile of money you can use to pay your living expenses, to travel, to play bocce ball, to buy a villa, to pay for your granddaughter's college or to do whatever else your heart desires.

For example, suppose you work for 30 years and put $5,000 per year into a retirement plan. Over the years, your contributions earn an average of 8% a year. At the end of that 30 years, you will have accumulated $566,416 inside the plan—even though you only contributed $150,000 of your hard-earned money. If you contribute $10,000 per year for 30 years instead of $5,000, you will have accumulated $1,132,832 (assuming 8% interest) by the time you retire—even though you only contributed $300,000.

Keep in mind that those big numbers are before taxes. You must pay tax on the money as you draw it out of the plan, but you might be in a lower tax bracket than you are in now. Even if you aren't, you'll still have a large chunk of change left after taxes.

What this means for most people is that if you have the opportunity to participate in a retirement plan, you should. As a self-employed individual, you can create that opportunity for yourself. Unlike people who work for someone else, you don't have to wait for your employer to establish a plan. You can do it yourself.

Indeed, self-employed individuals have virtually the same retirement plan options available to them that corporations do. So don't assume that because you are in business for yourself, you will miss out on the retirement savings bonanza. Furthermore, don't assume that setting up a retirement plan is too complicated for you to handle yourself. It's easier than you think, as you will discover while reading this book.

A. Who Should Read This Book

1. Self-Employed People

This book is for people who are self-employed in the eyes of the IRS. Self-employed people include people who are in business by themselves (sole proprietors) or who are in business with others (partners). They also include people who operate their businesses as limited liability companies or limited liability partnerships. They do not include people who operate their businesses as either S corporations or C corporations.

People who work for a corporation or other employer can also be self-employed if they have a side business of their own. Such people often include writers, musicians, artists and consultants of various types.

2. People Without Employees

This book is for people who have only owner employees in their business. Owner employees are yourself, your partners if you have any, and your spouse and your partners' spouses if they work in your business. When we use the term "employee" in this book, we do not mean owner employees; we mean everyone else—that is, non-owner employees. If you have non-owner employees in your business, then this book is not for you.

Bear in mind that if you have no employees right now, but plan to add them in the near future, you will need to consider that fact now, because you might want to select a plan that works well both with and without employees. Chapters 1 and 2 will help you identify which plans work well when you have employees, but the individual plan chapters (chapters 3 through 9) do not discuss the issues or rules that apply after you hire employees.

B. Who Should Not Read This Book

Let us emphasize this point: If you have any non-owner employees in your business, this book is not for you. Self-employed people who also have employees generally need to hire a plan administrator to put a retirement plan together and maintain it for them because employees make retirement plans too complex for most people to handle on their own.

If your business is a corporation (either an S corporation or a C corporation), you are not self-employed in the eyes of the IRS (even if you are your own boss) and this book is not for you.

C. How to Use This Book

Chapters 1 and 2 of this book are designed to help you select one or more retirement plans that you can set up for your business or for yourself as an individual taxpayer. Chapter 1 contains information on the following topics:

- reasons for establishing a plan
- an overview of the different types of plans
- features to consider when selecting a plan, and
- the ongoing tasks that are required to administer and maintain a plan.

Chapter 2 matches employers to types of retirement plans. If you fit a certain profile, this chapter will point you in the direction of a particular plan. If you don't fit any of the profiles, you can still use the comparison charts in the chapter to find the plan or plans that are the best for you.

Once you identify the plans that interest you, chapters 3 through 9 provide the details for each type of plan. You do not need to read all of the plan chapters (indeed, this might get a little dry since information is repeated in each chapter)—you can simply review the ones relating to the plans that are most appealing to you. Each chapter is devoted to one type of plan. For example, Chapter 3 is all about SIMPLE IRAs. Each of the plan chapters contains the following information about a particular plan:

- description of the plan
- advantages and disadvantages of the plan

- who qualifies to set up the plan
- step-by-step instructions for completing the forms to establish the plan
- instructions on how to calculate contributions to the plan
- deadlines and reporting requirements
- pitfalls and penalties
- information on how to add a second plan, and
- information on how to terminate the plan.

The Glossary in the back of the book will help you with unfamiliar terms. And, finally, the Appendix contains sample forms and important IRS notices that you might find useful.

D. What This Book Does Not Do

This book is not about investing. It does not explain how to invest your retirement money to maximize returns and minimize risk.

This book does not describe how to prepare for retirement in non-financial ways. If you are looking for that kind of information, you might want to pick up a copy of *Get a Life* by Ralph Warner (Nolo).

This book does not explain the fine points of taking money out of a retirement plan. If that's the information that you seek, you can find it in *IRAs, 401(k)s & Other Retirement Plans: Taking Your Money Out*, by Twila Slesnick and John Suttle (Nolo).

E. Icons Used in This Book

 Alerts you to potential problems or pitfalls.

 Provides ideas and strategies for dealing with certain situations.

 Books, websites or other resources that you might find helpful.

 Alerts you to issues that might arise if you ever choose to add employees to your plan.

■

Chapter 1

Retirement Plans for the Self-Employed: An Overview

A. **Why Establish a Retirement Plan?** 1/2

   1. Current Tax Deduction 1/2

   2. Forced Savings While You Have Money 1/3

   3. Retirement Security Through Tax Deferral 1/3

   3. Creditor Protection 1/6

B. **Choosing a Plan** 1/6

   1. Keogh Plans 1/7

   2. Types of Keogh Plans 1/16

   3. Individual Retirement Accounts (IRAs) 1/19

   4. Types of IRAs 1/20

   5. Combining Plans 1/22

   6. Features to Consider in Choosing a Plan 1/23

C. **Putting the Plan in Place** 1/26

   1. Selecting a Financial Institution 1/26

   2. Completing the Paperwork 1/26

D. **Maintaining the Plan** 1/28

   1. Contributions 1/28

   2. Tax Returns 1/29

   3. Ongoing Administration and Compliance 1/30

   4. Managing Investments 1/30

*S*etting up a retirement plan as a self-employed person does not have to be difficult. Here in Chapter 1, we summarize for you the different types of plans, the businesses (or individuals) that qualify to set up each type of plan, features to consider when selecting a plan and administrative procedures for establishing and maintaining the plan. As part of this discussion, we answer key questions:

- Why should I set up a plan?
- What kinds of plans are there?
- How do I decide which plan is right for me?
- Can I set up more than one plan?
- How will my traditional or Roth IRA affect my options?
- What kind of tax break will I get?
- Can I do it on my own?

In Chapter 2, we'll help you figure out how to choose a plan that fits your situation. In subsequent chapters, we describe each plan in great detail—one plan per chapter—to help you make your final decision. In each of those plan chapters, you will find detailed instructions for completing the initial paperwork, making contributions and even terminating the plan when the time is right.

A. Why Establish a Retirement Plan?

Let's say you've made the break—jumped off the corporate treadmill and headed out on your own. Or perhaps you're still working for someone else, but your side business has started making some real money. For a while you were so busy trying to get your business going that you didn't have time to think about a retirement plan. Maybe there was no money before, but now there is. Should you set up a plan? Of course you should. In the following sections, we discuss some of the most compelling reasons to do so.

1. Current Tax Deduction

You might be financially savvy and meticulous yet still be disinclined to save a good portion of your money for your retirement. You want to live now. In that case, the prime attraction of a retirement plan contribution will be to reduce your current tax bill rather than to build a nest egg. Current tax savings come to you in the form of a tax deduction for the contribution you make to your retirement plan. For example, if you are in the top federal tax bracket (39.6%) and you are permitted to contribute $30,000 to a retirement plan, you will save $11,880 in taxes for the year you make the contribution. Of course, one day you will have to pay tax on the money—when you take it out. But having a retirement plan sure saves you a lot of money now. And when you eventually take the money out, chances are good that you will be in a lower tax bracket, meaning you would owe something less than $11,880 of tax on the $30,000 by the time you withdraw it from your retirement plan.

Although most retirement plan contributions are tax deductible (after all, that's one of the carrots Congress uses to get you to contribute in the first place), some are not—or some circumstance might prevent you from claiming a deduction on your tax return. We explain this issue more fully in the individual plan chapters.

Of course, if your retirement contribution is not deductible, you have lost one incentive for making the contribution, but there are others, as you will see in the following sections.

2. Forced Savings While You Have Money

Many of those who recognize that money burns holes in their pockets will grab at the chance to stash some cash where they can't get to it easily. When you put money into a retirement plan, there are strict rules about taking the money out. With some exceptions, if you take it out before you reach age 59½, you will be subject to penalties. Those penalties serve as a strong incentive to leave the money alone.

3. Retirement Security Through Tax Deferral

Perhaps the best reason to contribute to a retirement plan is … to save for retirement! And let's face it, that's what Congress in-

tended in the first place. Recognizing that Social Security will not meet all the income needs of most retirees, Congress provided an incentive for businesses and individuals to set up their own retirement plans. If you take advantage of these opportunities, you will surely increase your financial security during retirement.

Here's why: Making a retirement plan contribution allows you to delay or defer the payment of income tax on the amount of the contribution. And when you have a choice, it is usually best to defer income tax for as long as possible. During the deferral period, you have the use of money that would otherwise have gone to taxes. If you invest that money, it will help generate more tax-deferred income. As the tables below show, even a one-year delay can be beneficial. So imagine what happens if you put money into a retirement plan while you are working and let it grow for many years until you retire.

Many people vastly underestimate the benefits of tax-deferred compounding of investment returns inside of a retirement plan account. Take a look at Tables I and II below. Both cases assume a simple 8% return on your investment and a flat 28% tax rate. Table I shows what happens if you take $10,000 of your hard-earned money, pay tax on it and then invest the remainder for 15 years. Because the investment is outside your retirement plan, each year you will pay tax on your interest, dividends and capital gains.

Table I:
Taxed Growth Outside a Retirement Plan

Assumptions:
Income: $10,000
Current income tax: $2,800
Amount to invest (income after tax): $7,200
Investment return: 8%
Tax rate: 28%

Year	Starting account balance	Interest earned	Tax on interest	Ending account balance
1	$7,200	$576	$161	$7,615
2	7,615	609	171	8,053
3	8,053	644	180	8,517
4	8,517	681	191	9,008
5	9,008	721	202	9,527
6	9,527	762	213	10,075
7	10,075	806	226	10,656
8	10,656	852	239	11,269
9	11,269	902	252	11,919
10	11,919	953	267	12,605
11	12,605	1,008	282	13,331
12	13,331	1,066	299	14,099
13	14,099	1,128	316	14,911
14	14,911	1,193	334	15,770
15	15,770	1,262	353	16,678

Total account balance after 15 years of taxed growth: $16,678

Now compare Table I with Table II (below), which shows what happens if you contribute the $10,000 to a retirement plan. Table II projects the value of your investment after one year, two years, or more. After 15 years, the total value of your retirement plan will be $31,722. But to compare apples and apples, you must subtract the income tax you must eventually pay. Still, when you compare the after-tax balance in both accounts, the retirement account comes out way ahead ($22,840 compared with $16,678). This is true even though in both situations, you start with the same amount of income, earn the same investment return and are subject to the same tax rate.

Table II: Tax-Deferred Growth Inside a Retirement Plan					

Assumptions:
Income: $10,000
Contribution to retirement plan: $10,000
Current income tax: $0
Investment return: 8%
Tax rate: 28%

Year	Starting retirement plan balance	Interest earned	Current year tax interest	Total investment at year end	Deferred tax	Ending retirement plan balance
1	$10,000	$800	$0	$10,800	$3,024	$7,776
2	10,800	864	0	11,664	3,266	8,398
3	11,664	933	0	12,597	3,527	9,070
4	12,597	1,008	0	13,605	3,809	9,796
5	13,605	1,088	0	14,693	4,114	10,579
6	14,693	1,175	0	15,869	4,443	11,425
7	15,869	1,269	0	17,138	4,799	12,340
8	17,138	1,371	0	18,509	5,183	13,327
9	18,509	1,481	0	19,990	5,597	14,393
10	19,990	1,599	0	21,589	6,045	15,544
11	21,589	1,727	0	23,316	6,529	16,788
12	23,316	1,865	0	25,182	7,051	18,131
13	25,182	2,015	0	27,196	7,615	19,581
14	27,196	2,176	0	29,372	8,224	21,148
15	29,372	2,350	0	31,722	8,882	22,840

Total account balance after 15 years of tax-deferred growth: $22,840

3. Creditor Protection

Corporate retirement plans are generally safe from creditors, thanks to the Employee Retirement Income Security Act of 1974, commonly known as ERISA. But retirement plans for self-employed individuals are not considered ERISA plans and therefore are not protected from creditors under the terms of ERISA. In addition, ERISA does not protect IRAs of any kind.

But ERISA is a federal law. And although IRAs and self-employed plans are not automatically protected under federal law, they may well be protected under state law. Many states have put safeguards in place that specifically protect IRAs from creditors' claims, whether or not you are in bankruptcy. And often the language of those state laws is broad enough to protect self-employed plans as well.

B. Choosing a Plan

Once you have persuaded yourself to establish a retirement plan, your next task is to pick one. In choosing a plan, you should consider various issues:

- **What are the tax benefits?** Some plans allow you to make larger contributions than other plans do. Generally, the larger the contribution, the bigger the tax break.
- **What are the costs of the plan?** Some plans require a lot of administrative work. Some plans require the use of an actuary (a number-crunching specialist) to figure contributions. Some plans require you to make reports to the government. All of these things cost money, and you will have to calculate whether the benefits of the plan outweigh those administrative costs.
- **Does the plan require you to make contributions every year?** This is an important consideration if the income from your business varies from year to year. In lean years, you may want the option of making a small contribution or no contribution at all. Not all plans will give you this option, however, so it's something to watch for when picking a plan.
- **What is the deadline for establishing the plan?** It almost goes without saying that if you pass the deadline for establishing one sort of plan, you'll have to pick a different plan.
- **How difficult does the plan become if you decide to hire employees?** As we will stress over and over in this book, employees make all retirement plans more expensive and more complicated. Some plans become prohibitively expensive once you add employees. Others become difficult to administer. Still others might unexpectedly limit your own contribution once you add employees. If you anticipate hiring employees, you need to know if the plan you choose will still work for you—

and if not, how easy it will be to terminate the plan and establish another.

The two broad categories of retirement plans that you, as a self-employed individual, have to choose from are Keoghs and IRAs. Within each category are a number of different types of plans, all with different benefits and drawbacks.

In this section, we give you an overview of the different types of Keoghs and IRAs with an eye toward the issues described above. In the next chapter, we make a side-by-side comparison of the plans to help you find the ones that are most suitable for you. Each of the subsequent plan chapters explains a particular plan in detail. There's no need to read each and every plan chapter—just read the ones that describe the plan or plans that you think might meet your needs. In the plan chapters, you will find information that will fine-tune your understanding of the pros and cons of the plan. You will also find information about establishing the plan, calculating contributions to the plan, taking distributions (money) from the plan and terminating the plan.

1. Keogh Plans

A Keogh is a retirement plan that can be established by a business that is owned by a self-employed individual. All of the rules for Keoghs are in the Tax Code, as you would expect. However, you won't find the term Keogh in the Code anymore. All of the Keogh rules, which once occupied a unique section of the Tax Code, have been subsumed under the "qualified plan" section of the Code. Qualified plans are retirement plans that satisfy certain requirements and, as a result, produce tax benefits, such as tax deductible contributions, for employers who establish them. When people use the term Keogh these days (as we do in this book), they simply mean a qualified plan to which some special rules apply because the employer is self-employed.

a. Plan Requirements

Qualified plans, and therefore Keoghs, are described in Section 401(a) of the Tax Code. Types of Keoghs include profit sharing plans, money purchase pension plans and defined benefit plans. (See Section 2, below, for more information about each type of plan.) All Keoghs must satisfy the following requirements if employers are to enjoy the available tax benefits:

- The plan must be written.
- The plan cannot have a predetermined expiration date. You must establish it with the intention of maintaining it more or less permanently. You can subsequently terminate the plan for business reasons—if you go out of business or if you can no longer afford to make contributions, for example—but you cannot establish a plan with the intention of terminating it at a particular time.

- The plan assets must be held either by a custodian or in trust by a trustee. (See Section C.2, below, for more about trustees and custodians.)
- The plan must be established by an employer, such as a sole proprietor, a partnership or a limited liability company (LLC), and not by an individual, such as an employee, an LLC member or a partner in a partnership.
- If the employer setting up the plan has employees, the plan cannot discriminate in favor of the officers, shareholders or highly compensated employees. If, however, the plan is a one-participant plan—meaning that the only employees are you, your partners and any of your spouses who work in the business—you do not need to worry about this requirement.
- The plan must provide a specific period over which participants vest in their retirement accounts or benefits. A participant is vested if she can take her retirement benefits with her when she terminates employment. For example, if an employee is 50% vested, she can take 50% of her benefits. The Tax Code provides several vesting schedules from which you must choose. You cannot simply make up a schedule that is to your liking.

If the plan satisfies all of the requirements of Section 401(a) and related code sections, the plan is deemed qualified and receives special tax treatment. Generally, contributions to the plan are deductible on the tax return of the employer (in this case, your business). The employee (in this case, you) pays no tax on either the contribution or the earnings until the money comes out of the plan, presumably during retirement.

Thank You, Mr. Keogh

For years, the tax benefits of Section 401(a) went only to corporations. If you had your own business, but you were not incorporated, you were out of luck.

But in 1962, self-employed people found a friend in Eugene Keogh. His bill, known officially as the Self-Employed Individual Tax Retirement Act, paved the way for unincorporated businesses to establish retirement plans. Today those plans are known as Keogh plans or self-employed plans.

Over the years, an entire body of law for Keogh plans developed separately from the corporate qualified plan rules. Although Keoghs were always considered qualified plans, a host of restrictions, most notably lower contribution limits, made them less attractive than the corporate variety. Consequently, many business owners formed corporations simply to increase their retirement plan contributions and deductions.

Then in 1982, Tax Code changes brought Keogh plans closer to parity with corporate plans. Now, your Keogh can take the form of a profit sharing plan, money purchase pension plan or defined benefit plan with benefits that are almost identical to those of corresponding corporate plans. (See Section 2, below, for detailed information about the different types of plans.)

Although Mr. Keogh's name endures, there really is no such thing as a Keogh plan any more. Qualified plans for self-employed individuals are now governed by the qualified plan rules in Section 401(a) and are no longer considered separate creatures, even though some special rules apply. But it's a lot easier to say "Keogh plan" than it is to say "qualified plan for self-employed individuals," when referring to those special rules. So Keogh has become part of the lexicon of retirement planning professionals. Even the IRS continues to use the term in its publications, and you'll find vestigial references in the income tax regulations. But you won't find Keogh in the Tax Code.

Thus, we too use the term Keogh throughout this book to mean a qualified plan for self-employed individuals—hoping to save some ink and some trees.

b. Who Qualifies to Establish a Keogh?

Keogh plan rules apply only to the self-employed. (See the Introduction for an explanation of who is self-employed.) If your business is organized as a corporation, whether an S corporation or a C corporation, your business does not qualify to establish a Keogh.

i. Sole Proprietors

If you are a sole proprietor, you own 100% of the interest in an unincorporated trade or business. In other words, you have gone into business by yourself—you have not formed a partnership, an S corporation or a C corporation. Although you might hire employees, you have no co-owner, no partner and no shareholders.

If you are a sole proprietor, you are considered both an employer and an employee for retirement plan contribution purposes. This dual status is key, because the Tax Code allows employers to make contributions on behalf of their employees. If a sole proprietor wasn't considered an employee, he or she would not be able to make contributions to his or her own retirement plan account. And because only employers can set up Keoghs, a sole proprietor must also be considered an employer.

 Working for a corporation doesn't preclude you from establishing a business on the side that is a sole proprietorship. Perhaps you are an Amway distributor or you have a band with regular weekend gigs for which you actually get paid. You can use the money you earn in those side jobs to establish a Keogh to save for retirement (not to mention the nice little tax deduction you'll get for your Keogh contribution!).

You do not need formal documents to form a sole proprietorship. All you need to do is earn income from self-employment. It's not always as easy as it seems, however, to figure out what the IRS considers self-employment income. Here are some situations that cause confusion:

- **Director fees:** If you serve on the board of directors of a company and are paid a fee, that fee is self-employment income (making you eligible to establish a Keogh), as long as you are not an employee of the company.

- **Trustee or executor or guardian fees:** If you serve as trustee of a trust, executor of an estate or guardian of a minor child and receive payment for your services, the income is self-employment income only if you provide those services as a profession. If you are simply providing the services for a deceased friend or relative, the income is generally not self-employment income (and therefore you would not be eligible to establish a Keogh) unless you are managing a business owned by the trust or the estate.

- **Royalties:** If you receive royalties from an invention, from writing a book or from other items that you have created, the income is generally self-employment income.

 IRS Publication 533 offers some additional guidance for determining which items of income constitute self-employment income. You can obtain a copy of this publication from the regional office of the IRS or by calling 800-TAX-FORM. You can also download this publication from the agency's website at http://www.irs.gov.

ii. Partnerships

If you and one or more others are co-owners of a business and if you do not form a corporation, you are generally considered to have a partnership, whether or not you have a formal written agreement. You can have any number of partners in a partnership, and you can share ownership and profits any way you like.

As a partner in a partnership, you are both an owner and an employee. But unlike a sole proprietor, you are not an employer. The partnership is the employer, even if you have no employees other than

the partners. And because Keoghs must be established by an employer, the partnership, not the individual partners (not even you!), must establish the Keogh.

⚠️ **A limited liability partnership (LLP) is a form of partnership and is treated as such for tax purposes.** That means an LLP qualifies to establish a Keogh. To form an LLP, however, you must generally file registration papers with the state in which you reside. If your business is an LLP, the rules described in this book that apply to partnerships also apply to your LLP.

iii. Limited Liability Companies

A limited liability company (LLC) has some of the characteristics of a corporation and some of the characteristics of a partnership. For federal income tax purposes, however, it is usually treated as a partnership. To form an LLC, you must generally file a document called "articles of organization" with the state in which you reside. Then, if you have net earnings from self-employment through your LLC and if the earnings are from services you perform for the LLC, you are considered self-employed. You are also considered both an owner and an employee, but you are not the employer. The LLC is the employer. That means the LLC must establish the Keogh.

c. Restrictions on Keoghs

As we explained earlier, Keogh plans have a few rules that apply only to them. Some of those rules come in the form of restrictions. Even though the different types of Keoghs have the same names as corporate qualified plans—names like profit sharing plan, money purchase pension plan and defined benefit plan—you shouldn't assume that you can always do the same things with Keoghs that you can do with corporate plans. Keoghs are just slightly different. In this section, we alert you to these differences.

i. Compensation vs. Net Earnings From Self-Employment

Contributions to many corporate retirement plans are based on the plan participant's compensation. For example, a corporate employer might set up a qualified plan and contribute 15% of each employee's compensation to the plan. If an employee receives annual compensation of $50,000, the employer would deposit $7,500 (15% x $50,000) into the retirement plan account of that employee.

Now let's assume you are self-employed and you made $50,000 after expenses. You also have a Keogh that allows you to contribute 15% of your compensation for the year. Logically, you might assume the contribution would be 15% of $50,000, which is $7,500. You would be wrong. That's because the definition of compensation for a self-employed individual isn't the same as

it is for a corporate employee. For self-employed people, compensation is "net earnings from self-employment," which, according to the Tax Code, is your income reduced by all business expenses. Your business expenses include the deductible portion—50%—of your self-employment tax (more about this deduction in the individual plan chapters), as well as the deduction for your Keogh plan contribution. That means you must reduce your net profit from the business by your Keogh contribution to arrive at your net earnings from self-employment. Then you multiply the result by the plan contribution percentage (15% in the above example) to arrive at the Keogh contribution. Sound circular? Sound impossible? Sound nonsensical?

The calculation is hard, but not impossible. It just requires a little algebra. For the mathematically minded among you, the calculation is laid out in the box below. For the rest of you, just know that for any plan contribution percentage you choose, there is a corresponding multiplier that you can use to figure out how much money you must contribute for yourself. (See the chart below for plan percentages and their corresponding multipliers.) Just multiply the multiplier by your net profit from your business after subtracting you self-employment deduction but before subtracting the Keogh deduction. The resulting number is your plan contribution.

Multipliers for Calculating Your Plan Contribution	
Percentage of Compensation You Choose for the Plan	Multiplier
1%	.9901%
2%	1.9608%
3%	2.9126%
4%	3.8462%
5%	4.7619%
6%	5.6604%
7%	6.5421%
8%	7.4074%
9%	8.2569%
10%	9.0909%
11%	9.9099%
12%	10.7143%
13%	11.5044%
14%	12.2807%
15%	13.0435%
16%	13.7931%
17%	14.5299%
18%	15.2542%
19%	15.9664%
20%	16.6667%
21%	17.3554%
22%	18.0328%
23%	18.6992%
24%	19.3548%
25%	20.0000%

EXAMPLE: You collected $20,000 from your letter-writing business last year. Your expenses, including supplies, advertising, equipment maintenance and the deductible portion of your self-employment taxes, totaled $6,000. Thus, your net profit was $14,000. You have a qualified plan with a contribution rate of 15%. Looking at the chart, you see that the multiplier for a plan rate of 15% is 13.0435%. Therefore, to arrive at the dollar amount of your plan contribution, you multiply 13.0435% by $14,000 (your net profit), which is $1,826.

Want the Algebra?

If math is your forte, keep reading and you'll see why 15% of net earnings from self-employment is equivalent to 13.0435% of the profit from your business.

The Assumptions:

P = profit (income less expenses and less your self-employment tax deduction, which is 50% of your self-employment tax, but not including your Keogh contribution)

N = net earnings from self-employment (profit minus your Keogh contribution)

.15N = the contribution percentage that you have chosen for your plan (15% of compensation).

The Formula:

N = P – .15N (in other words, net earnings equals profit reduced by Keogh contribution)

The Algebra:

Step 1:

N + .15N = P

Step 2:

1.15N = P

Step 3:

N = P/1.15

Step 4:

Multiply the equation in Step 3 by .15 to obtain the Keogh contribution:

(.15)(N) = (.15)(P/1.15)

.15N = (.15 P)/1.15

Keogh contribution = (.15 P)/1.15

Step 5:

Keogh contribution = .130435 P

Now that you have seen the mathematical detail, you might have spotted a shortcut. For Keogh plans with a 15% contribution rate, you can find the self-employed contribution percentage by dividing .15 by 1.15. Similarly, if the plan contribution rate is 25%, the self-employed contribution limit would be .25 divided by 1.25 or 20%. Keogh plan contribution rates can vary from 0% to 25%.

ii. Insurance

Contributions to some corporate plans (C corporations, but not S corporations) can be used to purchase various types of insurance, such as life, health or accident insurance, without affecting the deductibility of the contributions. Not so with Keoghs. Any portion of your Keogh contribution that you use to purchase and hold life or other insurance protection inside the Keogh plan account is not deductible.

iii. Loans

In an effort to protect retirement plans and ensure that they are used as intended, Congress prepared a list of things you cannot do with your plan assets. These are called prohibited transactions. In subsequent chapters, we examine all the prohibited transactions that apply to each type of plan. For now, we want to mention just one key transaction that is permitted to corporate employees but forbidden to you as a self-employed individual with a Keogh plan: **You cannot borrow from your Keogh.** (Got it?)

Many employees borrow from their 401(k) plans or tax deferred annuities. However, the provisions of the Tax Code that permit borrowing from plans were enacted to benefit employees, not owners. As the owner of your business and the sponsor of your Keogh, you may not borrow from the plan.

 For purposes of this prohibition against borrowing, you are considered an owner if you are a sole proprietor, because you own 100% of the business. If your business is a partnership, you are considered an owner if you own more than a 10% interest in either the capital or the profits of the partnership. If your interest is 10% or less, you would be able to borrow from the plan if the plan permits loans and you satisfy the loan requirements established by the plan.

d. Employees Complicate Keoghs

When you have no employees, Keogh plans are easy to establish and maintain. You just set up a one-participant plan (recall that a one-participant plan is one in which the only participants are you, your partners and any spouses of you or your partners who work in the business) and make your annual contributions.

Once you add employees, however, the rules become vastly more complex due primarily to what are called nondiscrimination rules—rules that are designed to ensure that your retirement plan benefits all employees, not just you or other highly paid employees. Nondiscrimination rules govern contributions, plan participation and vesting. In general, the laws prohibit you from doing the following:

- making disproportionately large contributions for some plan participants (like yourself) and not for others

- unfairly excluding certain employees from participating in the plan, and
- unfairly withholding benefits from former employees or their beneficiaries.

If the IRS finds the plan to be discriminatory at any time (usually during an audit), the plan could be disqualified. As a result, you and your employees would owe income tax and probably penalties, as well.

Having employees also increases the plan's reporting requirements. You must provide employees with a summary of the terms of the plan, notification of any changes you make and an annual report of contributions. And you must file an annual tax return for your Keogh.

Because of this complexity, most employers turn to professional consultants for help in administering a Keogh plan that includes employees. The consultant handles all the reporting requirements, computes contributions, makes nondiscrimination calculations and takes responsibility for keeping the plan up to date when laws change. Consequently, Keogh plans that include employees are beyond the scope of this book.

2. Types of Keogh Plans

There are many different types of Keogh plans in the Tax Code, some of which are moribund, and some of which are appropriate only in the rarest of business situations. In this book we discuss only those plans that you are most likely to use in your business.

Generally, Keogh plans fall into one of two broad categories: Defined contribution plans (which include profit sharing plans and money purchase pension plans) and defined benefit plans. The type of Keogh you choose—indeed, whether you choose one at all—will depend on many things. You will need to consider the amount of profit your business makes, the amount of money you are permitted to contribute to the plan and the flexibility of those contributions. Your age and the number of years you have before retirement will also be factors. In this section, we offer an overview of the various types of Keoghs with an eye toward these and other issues.

a. Defined Contribution Plans

One of the distinguishing characteristics of a defined contribution plan, as its moniker suggests, is that contributions are typically based on a specific, or defined, percentage of compensation. In the case of a self-employed person, the contribution is a percentage of net earnings from self-employment as described in Section B.1.c.i, above. And when you retire, your retirement benefit—your nest egg—is whatever happens to be in your account at the time.

Defined contribution plans themselves generally can be divided into two types— profit sharing plans and money purchase pension plans.

i. Profit Sharing Plans

A profit sharing plan allows you, as a self-employed individual, to choose to make or forgo a contribution to your own retirement account whenever your business makes a profit. In other words, the contribution is discretionary. However, your business must make a profit before you can contribute to your own account, because your contribution is a percentage of that profit. If you are losing money, your contribution must be zero.

The maximum contribution you can make to a profit sharing plan is the lesser of 15% of compensation or $25,500. But don't forget the algebra that we did earlier. Fifteen percent of your compensation means 15% of your net earnings from self-employment, which is actually only 13.0435% of your business income reduced by business expenditures ("net profit") and reduced further by your self-employment tax deduction. (See Section B.1.c, above, for more information about computing plan contributions.)

A Maximum That Isn't

If you take a gander at the Tax Code, you will find that divining the maximum possible contribution to your profit sharing plan is not exactly straightforward.

Although you can compute your maximum contribution to be the lesser of 15% of compensation or $25,500, the Tax Code lays it out less simply. It says you can contribute the lesser of 15% of compensation (or net earnings from self-employment) or $30,000. However, when computing the dollar limit, you cannot take into account more than $170,000 of compensation (or net earnings from self-employment) regardless of how much you actually make, and—of course—15% of $170,000 is $25,500. Confused? Consider the following scenario.

Let's say you run your own company, and you have one employee who earns $60,000. Your net profit from the business reduced by the self-employment tax deduction is $250,000. If your profit sharing plan calls for a 15% contribution, you calculate the contributions as follows:

The contribution you make on behalf of your employee is the lesser of:
15% of $60,000 or $9,000; or $30,000; or 15% of $170,000, which is $25,500

Therefore you would contribute $9,000 to your employee's profit sharing plan account.

Your own contribution is limited to the lesser of: 13.0435% of $250,000, which is $32,613; or $30,000; or 15% of $170,000, which is $25,500

Thus the contribution to your own account would be limited to $25,500, because that is the smallest amount.

Why, you might ask, is there a $30,000 limit if you can never get to it? (15% of $170,000 is only $25,500.) The answer is that the IRS plans to increase the $170,000 for inflation from time to time. Note that when the compensation ceiling reaches $200,000, the second and third limits, above, will coincide (because 15% of $200,000 is $30,000). However, the $30,000 limit is also slated to increase for inflation. In fact, it will increase to $35,000 beginning in the 2001 tax year.

Chapter 5 contains detailed information about establishing and contributing to profit sharing plans.

ii.   401(k) Plans

A 401(k) plan is a special type of profit sharing plan that allows a participant to defer a certain portion of his or her compensation into the plan. By doing so, participants can delay paying income tax on the contributions until the assets come out of the plan.

If you are self-employed and have no employees, you can still set up your own 401(k) plan, although as a practical matter you would never do so. First, you can always find a plan that will allow you to contribute as much or more. Second, 401(k) plans are more complex to administer than other types of plans, even if you don't have employees.

For these reasons, we have not included 401(k) plans in the detailed chapters of this book. However, we have included them among the side-by-side comparisons in Chapter 2 so that you can see how they measure up to other plans if you ever decide to hire employees.

iii.   Money Purchase Pension Plans

A money purchase pension plan is similar to a profit sharing plan (discussed above) in that the amount that you contribute to your account is based on your earnings.

Despite this similarity, one significant difference between the two—a difference that will be important to you in choosing between the plans—is that contributions to money purchase pension plans are mandatory when your business makes a profit, while contributions to profit sharing plans are not. If your money purchase plan contribution percentage is set at 25% of compensation and you make a profit, you must contribute that 25%. You cannot forgo or reduce a contribution one year simply because you would like to use the money for something else.

The good news about money purchase pension plans is that they generally permit larger contributions than do profit sharing plans. Whereas a profit sharing plan limits contributions to 15% of compensation (13.0435% of your net profit reduced by the self-employment tax deduction), a money purchase pension plan permits a contribution percentage of up to 25% of compensation (20% of your net profit reduced by the self-employment tax deduction).

But the contribution limits for money purchase pension plans are quirky. The maximum you can contribute to your own money purchase pension plan account as a self-employed individual is the lesser of:

- 20% of your net profit (after the self-employment tax deduction) or
- $30,000 or
- 25% of $170,000, which is $42,500.

Thus, regardless of how much you make, you can't contribute more than $30,000 to a money purchase pension plan (as compared to $25,000 for a profit sharing plan). However, the $30,000 limit increases to $35,000 beginning in the 2001 tax year.

See Chapter 6 for more information about money purchase pension plans.

b. Defined Benefit Plans

Like money purchase pension plan contributions, defined benefit plan contributions are mandatory. But they are not based on a percentage of compensation. Instead, defined benefit plans promise to pay each participant a specific dollar amount as an annuity (for example, an annual or monthly payment for life) beginning at retirement. The promised payment is usually based on a combination of factors, such as final compensation and number of years of employment. Once the retirement benefit is determined, the annual contribution must be recomputed every year to be sure the plan will have enough assets to meet the benefit goal. The computation is not simple. It requires the services of an actuary (a number-crunching specialist) who uses a projection of salary increases and investment returns and other factors to determine each year's contribution.

Furthermore, there is no specific dollar limit on annual defined benefit plan contributions. Instead, it is the projected retirement benefit that is limited. Currently, the annual retirement benefit is limited to the lesser of $135,000 or 100% of the participant's average compensation for his or her three consecutive highest-paid years. (The $135,000 limit will increase to $140,000 beginning in the 2001 tax year.)

Frequently, older participants are able to contribute significantly more to a defined benefit plan than to either a profit sharing plan or a money purchase pension plan because they have a shorter time before retirement—and less time for the funds to earn interest and grow. In order to ensure that the promised benefit can be paid, more money must be contributed each year. Current interest rates also play a big role in the size of the annual contribution. Potentially large contributions and hefty administrative costs can make defined benefit plans quite expensive. But if you are the only participant—that is, you have no employees—you may be able to put more money away with a defined benefit plan than you could with any other type of plan.

See Chapter 7 for more information about defined benefit plans.

3. Individual Retirement Accounts

Individual retirement accounts, or IRAs, have enormous appeal for these reasons: Like Keoghs, they offer tax benefits and attractive retirement savings opportunities, and yet they are much simpler to establish and maintain than are Keoghs.

IRAs, including SEPs and SIMPLE IRAs, are not governed by Section 401(a) of the Tax Code, which means they are not qualified plans or Keoghs. Instead they have their own code sections—408 and 408A.

Within the broad category of IRAs, you will find plans that don't seem to resemble each other at all. At one end of the spectrum, you have SEPs and SIMPLE IRAs, which are IRAs that can be established by businesses. But unlike Keogh plans, which are specifically for the self-employed, SEPs and SIMPLE IRAs can be established by corporations as well as by sole proprietors and partnerships. (See Sections 4.a and b, below, for more about SEPs and SIMPLE IRAs, respectively.)

At the other end of the spectrum, you have traditional IRAs and Roth IRAs. They are not for businesses, but for individuals, and they can be established by people who have income from employment or self-employment. That means you might be able to set up a qualified plan or SEP or SIMPLE IRA for your business and also set up a traditional IRA or Roth IRA for yourself as an individual. (See Sections 4.c and d, below, for more information about traditional IRAs and Roth IRAs, respectively.)

4. Types of IRAs

Species of IRAs are proliferating and taking on so many different forms that it's hard to keep them straight. Some look like the old traditional contributory IRA. Others have some of the characteristics of a Keogh. Nonetheless, as you read this book, it will be important to remember they are all IRAs because the IRA rules—not the Keogh plan rules—govern these creatures.

a. SEP

A SEP is a retirement plan that must be established by a business entity. If you are self-employed, this simply means your SEP must be established by you as a sole proprietor, or by your partnership if you are doing business as a partnership. Although technically an IRA, a SEP has the same contribution limit as a profit sharing Keogh plan: 15% of compensation (or 13.0435% of your net profit from self-employment, reduced by the self-employment tax deduction) up to a maximum of $25,500.

As with a profit sharing plan, you are not permitted to make a contribution to a SEP for those years in which you don't make a profit, and you are not required to contribute when you do make a profit.

SEPs are attractive because they have no tax reporting requirements. Also, a SEP is the only employer plan that can be set up after the end of your tax year. (Keogh plans and SIMPLE IRAs must be established before the end of the year.)

See Chapter 4 for more information about SEPs.

b. SIMPLE IRA

SIMPLE IRAs, like SEPs, are employer plans and must be established by your business entity, not by you as an individual. Fortunately, the name SIMPLE IRA is not an oxymoron. This is indeed the simplest type of employer plan that you can establish. However, simplicity comes at a price. Although you can establish multiple Keoghs—or a SEP and a Keogh—to boost your contribution limits (see Section 5, below), you cannot maintain a SIMPLE IRA and also maintain a SEP or a Keogh. The SIMPLE IRA must be your only employer plan.

 This restriction does not preclude you from establishing a traditional IRA or a Roth IRA to supplement your SIMPLE. As mentioned above, you may establish either or both even if you have a SIMPLE IRA, because traditional and Roth IRAs are retirement plans for individuals and are not considered employer plans.

If you have a SIMPLE IRA, you may contribute as much as $6,000 plus a matching contribution that cannot exceed 3% of your net profit reduced by your self-employment tax deduction. The total combined contribution is limited to $12,000. (The $6,000 limit increases to $6,500 for the 2001 tax year, bringing the total combined contribution limit to $13,000.)

Like a SEP, a SIMPLE IRA typically has no tax reporting requirements. However, the plan generally must be set up by October 1 of the year for which you want to make a contribution.

See Chapter 3 for more information about SIMPLE IRAs.

c. Traditional IRA

A traditional IRA is established by an individual, not a business. You may establish a traditional IRA no matter how high your income is or what other type of plan you have in place, whether a Keogh, a SEP, a SIMPLE IRA or a Roth IRA. (The contribution might not be deductible, however, as described below.)

In general, you may contribute a maximum of $2,000 (whether or not it is deductible) as long as your income from employment is at least that amount. However, if you have a Roth IRA as well as a traditional IRA, the maximum contribution you can make to both combined is $2,000. Thus, any amount you contribute to a Roth IRA will reduce the amount that you can contribute to a traditional IRA. Contributing to Keoghs, SEPs and SIMPLE IRAs generally will not reduce the amount you can contribute to a traditional IRA.

Although you can always set up a traditional IRA and contribute to it if you have earned income (meaning, income from employment), you might not always be able to deduct your contribution. The deductibility of your contribution is determined by how high your income is and what other retirement plans you have in place.

If you establish a traditional IRA, you are not required to make a contribution every year, nor are you required to contribute the maximum. You may contribute any amount up to the limit.

See Chapter 8 for more information about traditional IRAs.

d. Roth IRA

Like traditional IRAs, Roth IRAs are individual plans, not employer plans. But they are more restrictive than traditional IRAs. For one thing, no contribution you make to a Roth is ever deductible. For another thing, there is a ceiling on how much you can earn and still contribute to a Roth IRA. If you are married and filing a joint return with your spouse, and if the adjusted gross income on your tax return is $170,000 or more, you cannot make any contribution to a Roth IRA. If your adjusted gross income is between $160,000 and $170,000, you can make only a partial contribution. If you are married and filing a separate return from your spouse, the income limit is a measly $10,000. If you are single, your ability to make a contribution starts to phase out at $95,000 and you are totally out of luck when your income reaches $110,000.

If you can't deduct any contributions to your Roth, then why bother contributing at all? Because the big attraction of the Roth lies in the tax benefits you receive as your money grows and as you take distributions. Once your money finds its way into a Roth IRA, the interest and capital gains you earn inside the Roth and all future distributions are potentially tax free.

If you do qualify to make a contribution, the most you can contribute is $2,000 or your earned income, whichever is less. If you contribute to a traditional IRA in the same year you contribute to a Roth IRA, the total contribution to both the Roth and the traditional IRA combined cannot exceed $2,000.

Contributions to SEPs, SIMPLE IRAs or Keoghs are completely irrelevant for determining the amount you can contribute to a Roth IRA.

See Chapter 9 for more information about Roth IRAs.

5. Combining Plans

After reading the basic overview of retirement plans in this chapter and in the next, and after reading the more detailed plan chapters, you might find that there is no single type of plan that offers just what you want. For example, in profitable years you might not want to be restricted by the profit sharing plan contribution limit of 15%. You would rather be able to contribute 25% as permitted under the terms of a money purchase pension plan. But what if you establish a money purchase plan, with its mandatory contributions, and then you have a bad year?

The solution might be to use a combination of plans. For example, you might establish a profit sharing plan that has a contribution limit of 15% and tack on a money purchase pension plan with a contribution limit of 10% or less. The advantage of this approach is that the mandatory contribution to the money purchase pension plan can be much lower than the maximum 25%, which could be burdensome in some years. And because contributions to a profit sharing plan are discretionary, not mandatory, you can contribute the maximum 15% in good years, and contribute a smaller amount or even skip the contribution altogether in lean years. You would still have to make the mandatory money purchase pension plan contribution, but any additional contribution (which would be to the profit sharing plan) would be optional.

The law does put limits on the total amount you can contribute to each category of plan. For example, the maximum contribution you can make to all defined contribution plans you establish is 25% of compensation or $30,000 (or $35,000 beginning in the 2001 tax year), whichever amount is less. (Remember, when the plan percentage is 25%, the maximum contribution you can make is actually 20% of your net self-employment income after the self-employment tax deduction.) Because a profit sharing plan and a money purchase pension plan are both defined contribution plans, your combined plan contribution percentage (if you establish one of each type of plan for your business) cannot exceed 25%.

If business is booming, you might want to add a defined benefit plan. Just remember that the defined benefit plan, like a money purchase pension plan, has mandatory contributions that could be quite large. You should talk to a defined benefit plan consultant and get an estimate of what that contribution might be before you put the plan in place.

See the "Multiple Plans" section of the individual plan chapters for more information about establishing combinations of plans.

6. Features to Consider in Choosing a Plan

When deciding which plan or combination of plans to adopt, your first inclination will be to choose a plan that allows you to make the largest contribution. But other factors will weigh in eventually, so it is best to consider them in advance.

a. Contribution Limits

If you are making a lot of money, plans that offer the largest deductible contribution will have magnetic appeal. If your primary concern is to stow as much as possible in one or more retirement plans, your best bet might be to establish a defined benefit plan (depending on your age and prevailing interest rates).

If that's a little more than you can afford, or if the other characteristics of a defined benefit plan are unattractive—mandatory contributions, complexity and high administrative costs—you might consider a combined profit sharing and money purchase plan, as described in Section 5, above. The flexibility of such a combination along with a fairly generous contribution limit of $30,000 ($35,000 beginning in the 2001 tax year) makes it the retirement plan strategy

of choice for many self-employed individuals.

If you are not making huge amounts of
money, but enough that you want to establish a retirement plan and contribute as
much as possible, a SIMPLE IRA might
give you the best result. It allows you to
contribute $6,000 (which goes up to
$6,500 beginning in the 2001 tax year)
plus 3% of your net profit (after taking into
account the self-employment tax deduction), as long as your earnings are at least
as large as the total contribution. So if your
net profit is $20,000, you can contribute
$6,600 to a SIMPLE IRA ($6,000 + 3% x
$20,000). In contrast, your money pur-
chase pension plan contribution would be
limited to $4,000 (20% of $20,000).

b. Plan Cost

Some people are surprised to learn that
there are often fees and administrative expenses associated with maintaining a retirement plan. Furthermore, those costs
can vary dramatically depending on the
type of plan you choose.

If you set up a SEP or a SIMPLE IRA,
you will almost certainly use the prototype
(pre-approved) plan documents available
at most financial institutions. You will pay
a small set-up fee, usually between $10
and $100, although the fee is sometimes
waived when you make a minimum deposit. Often, there is an annual administrative fee, as well, which can also range
from $10 to $100. But there are no reporting requirements, so you would have no
other costs associated with establishing
and maintaining the plan.

Similarly, if you set up a defined contribution plan at a financial institution, you
can usually use the institution's plan documents. As with the employer IRAs, you
will have start up fees and an ongoing annual fee, which might be a little higher
than IRA fees because the documents are
more complex. You will also have tax reporting requirements if the assets of the
plan reach $100,000 or more or if you ter-
minate the plan. If the financial institution
will not handle those reporting requirements for you, you must either do it yourself or hire someone else to take care of it.

A defined benefit plan is altogether different. Generally, financial institutions do
not provide boilerplate plans. You'll have
to hire someone to draft a plan just for
you, and you can expect to pay between
$750 and several thousand dollars just for
the plan. Furthermore, because your contribution must be actuarially determined,
you will have to pay an actuary to compute it for you each year. That service isn't
free either. Most individuals hire a pension
plan consultant to draft the plan document, compute the contribution each year
and handle all reporting requirements including the tax return if and when it is required. It's impossible to do all of this
work yourself, which is why these plans
are so expensive.

You will find more information on the
costs and administrative requirements for

each type of plan in the individual plan chapters.

 Once you add employees, your costs will go up, even if you have only a SEP or SIMPLE IRA and even if you are using the prototype plan of a financial institution. Aside from the contributions themselves, the increased cost is due to the administrative expense of tracking contributions for employees, making timely and accurate deposits, providing reports to employees and filing whatever reports may be required by the IRS. Most self-employed individuals who have employees hire a consultant, no matter what kind of plan they adopt. Consequently, the complications and costs associated with adding employees are beyond the scope of this book.

c. Deadlines

Suppose you buy this book in May because your business has taken off. You've decided it's time to set up a retirement plan. You spend weeks or even months poring over each chapter. You confer with other entrepreneurs, watch pension plan talk shows, meditate and agonize. Finally you decide to establish a SIMPLE IRA. Whew.

On November 3, long before the end of the year, you call your favorite mutual fund and ask for a SIMPLE IRA application. You receive it one week later and while browsing through the instructions you discover that the deadline for establishing a SIMPLE IRA was October 1.

Argh! Back to the drawing board. If you still want to establish a plan for this year, you'll have to pick a different one—one that has a later deadline.

The point is this: Different plans have different deadlines for putting the plan in place. And sometimes there's yet another deadline for making contributions to the plan. If you aren't on your toes, you might be forced to establish a retirement plan that is your second choice because you missed the deadline for your first choice.

A Keogh plan, whether a defined contribution plan or defined benefit plan, must be established by the end of the tax year for which you want to make a contribution (usually December 31). You are permitted to make the contribution as late as the due date for filing your tax return (including extensions), but if you don't set up the plan in time, the extended due date for contributions will do you no good.

It's even worse for a SIMPLE IRA. Generally it must be set up by October 1. Once you've established the SIMPLE IRA, contributions for employees must be deposited into the plan at the time the salary is paid, and no later than 30 days after the end of the pay period. For the self-employed owner who has no fixed pay period, the contribution must be made within 30 days of the end of the year for which you want to make a contribution (usually by January 30). The matching portion can be made as late as the due date of the tax return (including extensions).

Because of these restrictions, many self-employed individuals end up with a SEP by default. SEP deadlines are the most liberal. You can set up a SEP and make a contribution as late as the due date of the tax return (including extensions).

For traditional and Roth IRAs, accounts can be set up and contributions can be made after the end of the year, but no later than April 15. In other words, even if you request and receive an extension of time for filing your tax return, you must still make your contribution by April 15.

C. Putting the Plan in Place

Once you have settled on the type of plan you want, you must sign documents to establish the plan. Then you must open an account with the institution that will hold the plan assets. This process is a little different for each type of plan, so check the individual plan chapters for the fine points of the process. Here's an overview.

1. Selecting a Financial Institution

Before you sign anything, you should think about what you want to do with the money you contribute to your plan. Will it sit in cash? Do you want to put it all into Treasury notes? All in stock? Mutual funds? Corporate bonds? Are you going to have someone else manage the investments for you?

Deciding how you will invest your funds will help you decide which financial institution should hold the assets. If you want the flexibility to purchase individual stocks, bonds, Treasuries, certificates of deposit and even some mutual funds, you will probably want your plan assets at a brokerage firm like Vanguard, Merrill Lynch, Charles Schwab or an online-only broker like E*Trade.

If you are starting small, you might want to select a mutual fund that will provide a diversified portfolio with a minimum investment. In that case, you would most likely contact the fund directly.

If you have no intention of ever investing in anything but cash and certificates of deposit, you can simply go to your local bank.

And finally, if you decide to have somebody else manage the investments for you, your money manager is likely to want some input into the selection of a financial institution.

See Section D.4, below, for more information about choosing investments.

2. Completing the Paperwork

Once you have selected a financial institution, you will need to complete the necessary paperwork to put the plan in place. You have two choices: You can use a plan that has been pre-approved by the IRS and adopted by the financial institution you have chosen, or you can hire someone to design a plan from scratch. Let's assume for the moment that you will use an institution's pre-approved plan.

Your next step will be to call the financial institution and request plan documents. Some financial institutions do not have plan documents for every type of plan, so you will need to check.

When you receive the documents, you will complete them according to the instructions found in the appropriate chapter of this book, then return them with enough money to open the account.

As mentioned above, if you are setting up a Keogh, the plan assets may be held in a trust or in a custodial account. If you decide to use a trust, the plan documents you sign are essentially a trust document. In fact, when you complete the documents, you will be asked to name a trustee. Generally, you will want to serve as trustee of your own plan so that you have immediate authority to sign plan documents and amendments, to make investment decisions and so on. The trustee is ultimately responsible for all aspects of the plan, including administration, investment management and compliance. That's not to say you cannot hire others to take care of some or all of those tasks for you, but as trustee, the buck stops with you.

The alternative to a trust—a custodial account—is usually simpler, because the cus-todian takes care of much of the paperwork for you. A custodian (most often the financial institution itself), is an institution approved by the IRS that you designate to hold the plan assets, carry out transactions and protect the assets for you. There is very little practical difference between a trust and a custodial account. The purpose behind the law that allows both is to permit institutions other than trust companies to hold such assets—spreading the wealth, if you will.

IRAs, including SEPs and SIMPLE IRAs, are almost always set up as custodial accounts. You are not permitted to serve as custodian or trustee of your own IRA.

If You Want a Custom Fit

If you hire a consultant to design a customized plan for you, you or the consultant must take some additional steps.

- Craft all the features of the plan, such as how contributions will be computed, when distributions will be permitted, what vesting schedule you will use, and so on.

- Submit the document to the IRS for approval. Specifically, you will request a "letter of determination" from the IRS, confirming that the plan is a qualified plan. (Remember, prototype plans are pre-approved. If you decide to design your own, it is not automatically approved.) Although this step is not required, many individuals want the IRS to bless the plan to ensure that the plan is qualified and the contributions will be deductible.

- Confirm with the financial institution that it is willing to hold your assets under the terms of your plan. Most will, but they will want a copy of the plan documents for their files.

As a practical matter, it is rare that you would need or want a customized plan if you have no employees (unless you want a defined benefit plan and therefore have no choice). If you, or you and your partners, are the only participants, you can generally maximize your benefits under the simplest prototype plan.

D. Maintaining the Plan

Unfortunately, your work isn't over after you set up a plan and make your first contribution. For as long as you maintain the plan, you will have ongoing responsibilities to make appropriate and timely contributions, to file tax returns for the plan (if necessary), to keep the documents up to date, to comply with distribution rules and, of course, to manage your ever-growing investments.

If you have no employees, it is a relatively simple matter to handle all aspects of the plan yourself. If you take on employees, however, a complex body of nondiscrimination rules kicks in to protect the interests of rank-and-file employees. Also, once you have employees, tax returns become mandatory for Keogh plans. Depending on the type of plan and how you set it up, you might even be responsible for investing and safeguarding the plan assets for the accounts of your employees. Because keeping up with the law and the paperwork can be overwhelming, you will want help from a consultant if you have employees.

1. Contributions

Unless your business is foundering, you will probably want to make a contribution to your retirement plan every year. Contributions must be timely and accurate. If you contribute too much or deposit the funds too late, you will not be able to deduct the contribution and you will owe income tax and, most likely, penalties.

It is your responsibility to compute the correct contribution to your plan. Financial institutions generally will not do it for you. You can hire a plan consultant or an accountant to compute the proper contribution for you, but the responsibility ultimately sits on your shoulders. If your advisors err, you still pay the penalty.

See the individual plan chapters for more information about contribution requirements for each type of plan.

2. Tax Returns

A number of factors will determine whether you have to file a tax return for your plan. These factors include the type of plan you have, the value of the assets in the plan and whether you have employees who are participating in the plan. The individual plan chapters explain this in more detail.

Although you might have to file a tax return for the plan, you generally won't have to pay income tax. Qualified plans and IRAs are tax-exempt. In general, neither the plan nor the participants will owe income tax as long as the assets remain in the plan and the plan complies with the law.

Plans can be subject to income tax if they engage in a business or if the assets are invested in a business. See the tax returns section in the individual plan chapters for more information.

The tax return you might have to file is a special type of return, called an information return. These returns help the IRS monitor the operation of the plan to ensure that the plan remains qualified and that employees' rights (if you have employees) are not being violated.

Different plans have different tax reporting requirements. You are rarely required to file a tax return for a SEP or SIMPLE IRA. A Keogh is a trust, however, and trustees are generally required to file a tax return for the trust. A special relief provision in the law exempts the trustee from annual tax filings if the trust is a one-participant Keogh plan and if the plan assets total less than $100,000. Unfortunately, the exemption doesn't extend to the final year of the plan. You must always file a tax return for a Keogh for the year it is terminated.

 If you add employees, you generally won't have to file a tax return if your plan is a SEP or a SIMPLE IRA. But you must always file an annual tax return for a Keogh when you have employees.

For details about the reporting requirements of each type of plan, see the individual plan chapters.

CREATING YOUR OWN RETIREMENT PLAN

3. Ongoing Administration and Compliance

In addition to making timely and accurate contributions to your plan, you will have administrative responsibilities, including keeping your plan documents up to date, avoiding prohibited transactions and complying with strict distribution rules.

a. Updating Documents

When you use a financial institution's prototype plan, the institution generally takes responsibility for keeping the plan up to date and qualified. If you decide to design your own plan, most financial institutions will still hold the assets of the plan, but they are unlikely to take responsibility for making sure the plan documents are always in compliance with the law. That will be your responsibility (or your consultant's).

b. Prohibited Transactions

The prohibited transaction rules exist to keep you (or anyone else with access to the plan) from using the plan assets for personal purposes and frittering them away. Lest you find that insulting, remember: Congress bestowed tax benefits on retirement plans in exchange for your promise to use them for one purpose—retirement. Frittering is your privilege, of course, but if you fritter, you'll have to return the tax benefits.

When you engage in a prohibited transaction, the least punitive repercussion will be a penalty on the amount of the transaction. But in the worst case, the Keogh or IRA will be disqualified. Disqualification is disastrous, because it results in a total distribution of the plan assets, disallowance of deductions and, of course, current income tax and penalties.

Prohibited transactions vary with the type of plan you have. See the individual plan chapters for details.

c. Distributions

Because of those tax benefits we keep mentioning, you are not permitted to take money out of your retirement plan whenever the temptation arises. If you do, you might have to pay penalties along with the regular income tax you will owe. Fortunately, the Tax Code provides many exceptions to the distribution restrictions. Those exceptions can give you access to your plan assets, even before retirement.

See the individual plan chapters for more information about distribution rules.

4. Managing Investments

If your business does well and you conscientiously contribute as much as you can to your retirement plan each year, the account balance is likely to reach a critical mass. That critical mass is the point at which you must decide what to do with the money. You have essentially three choices:

- You can let it sit in cash.
- You can invest it in stocks, bonds, mutual funds or other securities, actively monitoring and managing the assets yourself.
- You can hire someone to manage the account for you.

Leaving the money in cash would certainly be easy, but it doesn't make a lot of sense. The biggest advantage of a retirement plan is the tax-deferred compounded growth of the assets in the plan. If the assets sit in cash, there will be no growth, except for the additional contributions you make each year.

So, as a practical matter, you have only two sound choices: You can actively manage your own account or you can hire someone to do it for you.

Many individuals elect to manage their own account to save fees, especially in the early days of the plan when the account is relatively small. Often the plan assets are invested in mutual funds, which offer diversification (a mix of investments to reduce the impact of any single security's performance) and a built-in portfolio manager.

 A mutual fund is an investment company that raises money from shareholders and invests the money in a portfolio of stocks and bonds or other securities. Shareholders can invest relatively small amounts of money and still own part of a diversified portfolio. Diversification is hard to accomplish when you have limited

funds and must purchase your stocks and bonds individually. For example, if all your favorite stocks sell for more than $100 a share and your plan contribution for the year is $8,000, you won't even be able to buy a round lot (100 shares) of a single company among your favorites.

Most mutual funds will serve as custodian of your plan assets, just as any other financial institution might. To establish a mutual fund account, you simply contact the retirement services department of the mutual fund of your choice and request the documents for the type of plan that you've chosen.

You might choose to hire a money manager if your plan assets grow large or you find you are too busy to handle the investments yourself. Most money managers charge a percentage (often 1%) of the plan assets to construct a portfolio and manage it for you.

Although some individuals are comfortable letting a broker or financial planner manage their investments, it is wise to take some precautions. If a financial planner or broker tells you there is no fee, ask how he or she is compensated. If compensation is through commissions from the sale of securities or other products, you must do some soul-searching to determine how confident you feel that assets will not be purchased and sold for your account simply to generate income for the person who is managing it. ■

Chapter 2

Comparing Plans

A. Employer Plans 2/3

   1. If You Have No Non-Owner Employees 2/3

   2. If You Have Non-Owner Employees 2/6

   3. How to Use the Charts 2/9

B. Individual Plans: Traditional IRAs and Roth IRAs 2/10

*E*veryone has different needs and desires when it comes to choosing a suitable retirement plan. In this chapter, we provide you with some guidelines to follow in selecting one or more plans for your business and for yourself. Before reading this chapter, be sure to read Chapter 1, which provides an overview of all of the retirement plans that we compare in this chapter.

Take a moment to think about your situation. Maybe even jot down on a sheet of paper answers to the following questions:

- What do I think my net earnings from self-employment will be for this year?
- What were my net earnings from self-employment last year?
- Are those net earnings pretty steady from year to year, or do they fluctuate significantly?
- How much of those net earnings can I afford to contribute to a retirement plan?
- How do I feel about a plan that will require me to contribute each year, regardless of how well my business is doing?
- Do I want the flexibility of a plan that will allow me to forgo contributions in lean years?
- Do I want to contribute as much as the law will allow?
- How big of a tax benefit do I want to receive from contributing to my retirement plan?

- How many years do I have until retirement?
- Do I want to establish a plan for this year? If so, can I establish it before October 1 of this year? Before December 31?

Answering these questions will give you the information you need to identify the plan or plans that suit you best. Once you have a list of possible plans, skip forward in the book to specific plan chapters for details. In those chapters you will find a thorough discussion that will help you finalize your decision about whether the plan is right for you. That discussion will include instructions for establishing the plan, administering the plan, making contributions to the plan and terminating the plan.

In this chapter, we place retirement plans into two broad categories: employer plans and individual plans. Then we compare each plan to the other plans in its category. After considering the differences among the plans, you should be able to identify which ones appeal to you.

Employer plans are those that can only be established by you as an employer on behalf of yourself as an employee. Those plans allow you to take a tax deduction for contributions to the plan. Depending on which employer plan you choose, you can sometimes add another employer plan to it. Not all employer plans can be combined, however. We discuss multiple plans in more detail in each of the plan chapters.

Individual plans are those that you can establish for yourself as an individual. You can always add an individual plan to any employer plan that you might have.

Remember: The guidelines in this chapter are just that—guidelines. To come to a firm conclusion about whether a particular plan is right for you, you will have to read the chapter devoted to that plan.

A. Employer Plans

The employer plans we discuss in this book include:

- SIMPLE IRA
- SEP
- profit sharing plan
- money purchase pension plan, and
- defined benefit plan.

We do not discuss 401(k) plans in depth in this book because they are not suitable for people who do not have employees. Nonetheless, we have included them in this comparison chapter so that you can see how they measure up if you ever do hire employees.

As we have undoubtedly made clear by now, choosing a retirement plan is not as cut-and-dried as you might like it to be. The guidelines in this chapter might point you in the direction of a particular type of plan, but your own peculiar circumstances might warrant another choice.

With that warning, here are some simplified business situations, or profiles, that fit a particular type of plan. Try to keep your own extenuating circumstances in mind as you browse through the examples.

1. If You Have No Non-Owner Employees

In this section, we assume that you have only yourself and other owner employees in your business. Remember: Owner employees include you; your spouse, if he or she works in the business; your partners, and your partners' spouses, if they work in the business.

Profile 1: SIMPLE IRA

You have net earnings from self-employment of $30,000 or less. Also, you have been watching the calendar and you are prepared to establish your plan by October 1, if necessary. You want to contribute as much as possible to a retirement plan.

If this describes your situation, a SIMPLE IRA is likely to be your best choice. It will give you the largest possible contribution for your salary range. For example, if your net earnings are $30,000 in tax year 2000, a SIMPLE IRA will allow you to contribute $6,600, whereas a money purchase pension plan contribution will be limited to $6,000 and a profit sharing plan contribution to $3,913. Once your net earnings exceed $30,000, another plan is likely to allow you to contribute more than a SIMPLE IRA will.

Contributions to SIMPLE IRAs are not mandatory. You can skip the contribution in years when money is tight or when you want to use the money for something else. This feature might be attractive if your income fluctuates from year to year.

Profile 2: SEP

It's January and you never did get around to establishing a retirement plan before the end of the previous year. If you still want to make a contribution for the prior year—and deduct it on your tax return—a SEP is your only option. It is the only employer plan that can be established after the end of the tax year.

In almost all other respects a SEP accomplishes exactly what a traditional profit sharing plan does. (See Profile 3, below.) However, the paperwork for establishing a SEP is simpler than the paperwork for setting up a profit sharing plan—and so is the ongoing administration. If simplicity is more important to you than contributing as much as possible to a retirement plan, a SEP is superior to either a profit sharing plan or a money purchase pension plan.

If maximizing your contribution to a plan is your top priority, a SEP is not your best choice. (It might be your only choice, though, if the end of the year has come and gone.)

Profile 3: Profit Sharing Plan

December 31 looms, but you still have time to set up a retirement plan before the end of the year. You will have net earnings of more than $30,000 in the current year, but you have no idea how business will be in the future. Your income fluctuates significantly from year to year. You would like the flexibility to contribute more in banner years while reserving the option to cut back or even eliminate contributions in other years.

A profit sharing plan will give you that flexibility; a money purchase pension plan or a defined benefit plan will not.

If you want a plan that will allow high contributions in good years, a profit sharing plan alone will not give you this. For flexibility combined with high contributions, combine a profit sharing plan (flexibility) with a money purchase pension plan (high contributions). Many financial institutions have streamlined the process of adding a money purchase plan to a profit sharing plan or of setting up both at the same time.

If you have no intention of ever adding a money purchase pension plan to your profit sharing plan, a SIMPLE IRA will allow you to make a larger contribution than a stand-alone profit sharing plan when your income is less than $50,000. Once your income exceeds $50,000, you can do better with a stand-alone profit sharing plan.

 The difference between the $30,000 and $50,000 thresholds can be confusing. In brief, a SIMPLE IRA will almost always allow the largest contribution when net earnings are less than $30,000. When they exceed $30,000, a money purchase pension plan alone or in combination with a profit sharing plan will be better than a SIMPLE IRA. But if you compare a stand-alone profit sharing plan to a SIMPLE IRA, the SIMPLE IRA will be better as long as your net earnings are less than about $50,000.

Profile 4: Money Purchase Pension Plan

You are looking ahead. You are prepared to set up a plan before December 31. If you are younger than 50 and you make substantial amounts of money year after year, then a money purchase pension plan is likely to be the best plan for you. The age guideline is a rough one. The older you are, the more likely it is that a defined benefit plan will allow you to make a larger contribution than will a money purchase pension plan.

Unlike contributions to profit sharing plans or SEPs or SIMPLE IRAs, contributions to money purchase pension plans are mandatory when you have net earnings from self-employment. (You are not required to make a contribution in years you have no net earnings from self-employment.) So, if your income fluctuates dramatically from year to year or if you would rather not make a retirement plan contribution every year, you might not want to establish a money purchase pension plan. Without one, however, you would not be able to contribute the maximum the law allows in the years you are cash-rich.

You can solve this problem by establishing both a money purchase pension plan and a profit sharing plan. You can set the mandatory money purchase pension plan contribution rate relatively low (say 5%) and then make or forgo the discretionary profit sharing plan contribution each year, depending on how you want to use your extra cash.

Profile 5: Defined Benefit Plan

You can meet a December 31 set-up deadline. Your net earnings from self-employment are a steady $135,000 or more, and you are older than 50. Chances are good that a defined benefit plan will allow you to contribute (and deduct) the largest amount of money. If your net earnings are less or if you are younger, it is possible that another type of plan will allow you to make a larger contribution.

It's true that a defined benefit plan is the most expensive plan to establish and maintain. But even if the plan costs you $2,000 to establish and $1,000 annually to maintain, you can easily recover those costs in tax benefits each year, provided your business continues to produce significant income. That's because the large contributions carry with them large tax deductions.

Beware, though. If your income is unpredictable, a defined benefit plan can become a burden. Contributions are mandatory, and you might have to make them in years in which you have no net earnings from self-employment. If you have no resources you can tap when this situation occurs, a defined benefit plan might not be your best choice.

Profile 6: 401(k) Plan

As a self-employed individual without non-owner employees, there is no reason for you to establish a 401(k) plan. There are no circumstances under which you would be able to contribute more to a

401(k) plan than to a traditional profit sharing plan or a money purchase pension plan. And because 401(k) plans are governed by some peculiar rules that make them fairly complex to administer, there are real disadvantages to choosing this type of plan.

2. If You Have Non-Owner Employees

As you know by now, employees make retirement plans more complicated and more expensive. If you have employees, you must think not only about what you personally want from your retirement plan, but also about how much your choices are going to cost you when applied, not just to yourself, but to your employees as well.

Let's say, for example, that you want to establish a plan that allows you to make the largest possible contribution to your own retirement account. You will have to balance that desire against the fact that such a choice might force you to make the largest possible contribution to the accounts of your employees as well. This could boost the total cost of contributions to an unaffordable level. Not only that, but the nondiscrimination rules might require you to reduce your own contribution in some cases.

Still, if you are like most self-employed individuals, you want to provide good retirement benefits to your employees as well as yourself, but not at a cost that cripples your business.

The following profiles take into account that you would like to contribute as much as you can to a retirement plan while keeping costs under control.

Profile 1: SIMPLE IRA

If your net earnings from self-employment are $30,000 or less, you will almost certainly want to consider a SIMPLE IRA first. It generally allows you to contribute more to your own account than other plans do when your net earnings are less than $30,000. In addition, it allows you to keep the cost of contributions for your employees fairly low. Most contributions for employees are in the form of salary reduction contributions—amounts that you would ordinarily pay to them as salary, but that you can direct into their retirement accounts instead.

Although you must also make a contribution on behalf of employees in addition to the salary reduction contribution, that additional contribution would never exceed the lesser of 3% of the employee's compensation or $6,000. (The $6,000 limit will increase to $6,500 beginning in tax year 2001.)

Another attractive feature of a SIMPLE IRA is its low administrative cost. You don't have to file a tax return for the plan, and there are no complex nondiscrimination calculations to perform because SIMPLE IRAs are automatically nondiscriminatory. (See Chapter 1, Section B.1.d, for more information about nondiscrimination rules.)

When you establish a SIMPLE IRA, you must generally allow all employees to participate who have worked for you for two years and who earn at least $5,000. But that also means you can exclude employees who do not satisfy those requirements. If you have high turnover, you might find the cost of the SIMPLE IRA is even lower than you expected. On the other hand, if your employees are all long term, you will find it more difficult to exclude them from a SIMPLE IRA than from other types of plans.

Three additional restrictions to remember:

- You must generally establish the plan by October 1 in order to contribute for that same tax year.
- You can have no more than 100 employees.
- You cannot establish and contribute to any other retirement plan for your business as long as you are contributing to a SIMPLE IRA.

Profile 2: SEP

A SEP is the only employer plan that you can set up after the end of the year. For this reason, you might be stuck with this plan by default.

But in general, if your intention is to establish only one plan for your business, and if you want the flexibility to reduce or discontinue contributions in some years, a SEP or a SIMPLE IRA are your likely choices. A SEP will produce larger contributions than a SIMPLE IRA only if your net earnings exceed $50,000.

SEPs have some special features that make them particularly attractive to small, cost-conscious employers who have high turnover among their employees:

- Like a SIMPLE IRA, a SEP is relatively inexpensive to establish.
- You don't have to make complex nondiscrimination calculations.
- You don't have to file a tax return.
- You can exclude employees from participating for up to three years, which will make the cost of the plan quite low if you have high turnover.

Bear in mind that, with a SEP, you must contribute to the accounts of virtually all employees who have worked for you for three years—whether full time or part time—if they earn more than $450 for the year. In contrast, a profit sharing plan would allow you to exclude many part-time workers and apply a vesting schedule to the employees' benefits, if your goal is to reward long-time employees.

Profile 3: Profit Sharing Plan

Your net earnings from self-employment exceed $50,000. Your income fluctuates from year to year, so you want to be able to make discretionary contributions to your retirement plan. You also want flexibility in allocating contributions among employee accounts—perhaps shifting disproportionately more of the contribution share to you and other highly compensated employees. Perhaps you want to reward long-term employees and exclude as many short-timers as you can.

A profit sharing plan can do those things more effectively than can either a SEP or a SIMPLE IRA. You can exclude employees who aren't employed on the last day of the year, for example, or who didn't work at least 1,000 hours. And you can apply a vesting schedule to their benefits, which means they would have to work for you for a certain period of time before they could take their benefits when they leave.

Unfortunately, the cost of that flexibility is additional administrative complexity. You will need a consultant to help both with making contribution calculations and nondiscrimination calculations and with preparing a tax return—all of which are required for profit sharing plans that cover employees.

⚠ **Once your income exceeds $30,000,** you might want to consider combining a profit sharing with a money purchase pension plan. See Profile 4, below.

Profile 4: Money Purchase Pension Plan

If you are younger than 50, and if you always have net earnings in excess of $30,000 per year, a money purchase pension plan is likely to allow you to make the largest contribution.

But if you have employees, a money purchase pension plan with a maximum contribution rate can be expensive. That's because, unlike a SEP or a profit sharing plan, contributions to a money purchase pension plan for employees are mandatory. If you have no net earnings from self-employment one year, you are not required to make a contribution to your own account—in fact, you are not permitted to do so—but you must continue to make contributions to employees' accounts.

For example, suppose you were raking in the dough for a number of years and you established a money purchase pension plan with the maximum contribution rate—25% of compensation. You must contribute at that rate for yourself and for your employees. Now, assume business stalls and you lose money one year. Although you aren't permitted to contribute to your own account for that year, you must still contribute 25% of compensation to the accounts of all employees who are participating in the plan.

For this reason, it generally makes sense to establish a profit sharing plan along with the money purchase pension plan when you have employees. You can set the mandatory money purchase pension plan contribution rate relatively low (say 5%) and then make or forgo the discretionary profit sharing plan contribution depending on the fortunes of your business.

The administrative costs and requirements of a money purchase pension plan are otherwise similar to those of a profit sharing plan:

- You might have complex contribution calculations if you decide to use an unconventional contribution formula.

- You will have to make nondiscrimination calculations.
- You must file a tax return each year.

Profile 5: Defined Benefit Plan

If you steadily take home $135,000 or more per year and if you are older than 50, you might be able to contribute dramatically more to a defined benefit plan than to any other type of plan—maybe twice as much or more. But if you have employees who have been with you for quite a while and who are older than 50, you will have to make larger contributions on their behalf as well. Defined benefit plan contribution amounts tend to increase with age, length of service and income. And because contributions are mandatory, you will have to make them whether your business is profitable or not.

Consequently, defined benefit plans prove to be prohibitively expensive for many businesses with employees. Such a plan works best if you are earning lots of money, you are older than 50 and if you have a new young staff—or no staff at all. In that case, the cost of contributions on behalf of employees is likely to be low relative to the contribution you can make on your own behalf.

Defined benefit plans are also administratively complex, making them more costly to maintain than most plans. And you must file a tax return for the plan every year.

Profile 6: 401(k) Plan

401(k) plans are popular among mid-sized and large business owners with many employees. That's because 401(k) plans serve as a compromise between plans that offer big benefits but are expensive for employers and plans that are less expensive but don't allow employers to contribute much on their own behalf.

A 401(k) plan, like a SIMPLE IRA, allows employers to shift much of the contribution costs to employees through salary reduction contributions. And the ceiling on contributions to a 401(k) plan is higher than the ceiling on contributions to a SIMPLE IRA.

Like other profit sharing plans, a 401(k) plan can impose a variety of restrictions on participation and vesting. In this way, employers can reward long-term employees without being forced to make significant contributions on behalf of part-time or short-term employees.

The advantages of a 401(k) plan are offset to a certain extent by the complex nondiscrimination rules that tend to add to the administrative cost of the plan. These costs can be quite burdensome to small business owners with few employees. Also, 401(k) plans require a tax return every year.

3. How to Use the Charts

At the end of this chapter, you will find a number of charts that summarize the key differences and similarities among plans.

They should help you sort out which plan or combination of plans is best for you. The charts cover the following information:

- Chart 1 compares employer eligibility restrictions among plans
- Chart 2 compares deadlines for establishing the plan and for making contributions
- Chart 3 compares contribution limits and requirements
- Chart 4 compares the administrative tasks and costs of the plans
- Chart 5 compares the types of distributions that are permissible under each plan, and
- Chart 6 summarizes the optimum employer profile for each type of plan.

The first step in your quest for the right plan should be to eliminate those plans you are not even eligible to establish. For example, if you already have a profit sharing plan, you are not eligible to establish a SIMPLE IRA. Even if you don't have another employer plan, you might not be eligible to establish a SIMPLE IRA because you have passed the October 1 deadline for setting it up. Charts 1 and 2 will help you with this elimination process.

Next, you will want to determine which plan will allow you to contribute and deduct the largest amount of money. Chart 3 will help with that.

Even though a plan might look great in almost every respect, you might have to rule it out simply because the ongoing costs associated with maintaining the plan are too high. Chart 4 summarizes the relative cost of the plans.

Occasionally, your choice of plan might be a function of how easy it is to get money out when you need or want it. Chart 5 helps with that.

Chart 6 summarizes—for easy review—the employer profiles described in Section 1, above.

B. Individual Plans: Traditional IRAs and Roth IRAs

Traditional IRAs and Roth IRAs are not employer plans. They are established by individuals rather than by businesses. That means you can have an employer plan for your business and also set up a traditional IRA or a Roth IRA for yourself as an individual.

Although you might be able to establish both a Roth IRA and a traditional IRA, generally you will choose one or the other, because the most you can contribute to both combined is $2,000 per year.

The most dramatic difference between a traditional IRA and a Roth IRA is in the tax treatment of investment returns inside the IRA. In the case of a traditional IRA, those returns are tax-deferred, which means you don't pay taxes on them until you take money out of the account. In contrast, the investment returns that accumulate inside a Roth IRA are tax-free (provided you satisfy certain requirements), which means you will not owe any tax on money you take out of the account.

There is another marked difference between these two types of IRAs: Contributions to Roth IRAs are never deductible, but contributions to traditional IRAs are deductible if they satisfy certain requirements.

Also, as long as you have earnings from employment, you can contribute to a traditional IRA—no matter how high your income is. In order to make a Roth IRA contribution, you also must have earnings from employment, but if your total income reported on your tax return—from all sources, including investments—exceeds a certain threshold, you will not be able to make any contribution at all to a Roth IRA.

At the end of this chapter, you will find two charts comparing traditional IRAs to Roth IRAs.

Chart 1
Employer Plans: Restrictions on Eligibility

Plan type:	Eligibility restrictions:
SIMPLE IRA	No more than 100 non-owner employees; No other retirement plan for the business
SEP	None
Profit sharing plan	None
Money purchase pension plan	None
Defined benefit plan	None
401(k) plan	None

Chart 2
Employer Plans: Deadlines

Plan type:	Deadline for establishing the plan:	Deadline for making matching or nonelective contributions:*
SIMPLE IRA	October 1	Due date of tax return (plus extensions)
SEP	Due date of tax return (plus extensions)	Due date of tax return (plus extensions)
Profit sharing plan	End of year	Due date of tax return (plus extensions)
Money purchase pension plan	End of year	Due date of tax return (plus extensions)
Defined benefit plan	End of year	Due date of tax return (plus extensions)
401(k) plan	End of year	Due date of tax return (plus extensions)

* If you do not meet this deadline, your contribution might not be deductible.

** If you do not meet this deadline, your plan could be penalized or disqualified.

Deadline for making salary reduction contributions:*	Deadline for making employer contribution (the minimum funding deadline):**
30 days after pay period	N/A
N/A	N/A
N/A	N/A
N/A	8½ months after year end
N/A	8½ months after year end
15 days after pay period	N/A

Chart 3
Employer Plans: Contribution Rules

Plan Type	Employer contribution limit (not including the salary reduction portion)	Salary reduction limit per participant
SIMPLE IRA	Lesser of 3% of compensation or $6,000* (per participant)	$6,000* (per participant)
SEP	Lesser of 15% of compensation or $25,500 (per participant)	N/A
Profit sharing plan	**15% of compensation (for all participants combined) where compensation is capped at $170,000 per participant	N/A
Money purchase pension plan	Lesser of 25% of compensation or $30,000*** (per participant)	N/A
Defined benefit plan	Annual retirement benefit limited to the lesser of 100% of final average compensation or $135,000**** (per participant)	N/A
401(k) plan	**Combined employer contribution and salary reduction limit is 15% of compensation (for all participants combined) where compensation is capped at $170,000 per participant	$10,500

* This number increases to $6,500 beginning in tax year 2001.
** If you have non-owner employees, once the contribution is made to the plan, the contribution can be allocated to the employees' accounts in various ways. It is possible to use a formula that allocates more than 15% to some accounts.
*** This number increases to $35,000 beginning in tax year 2001.
**** This number increases to $140,000 beginning in tax year 2001

Discretionary or mandatory contributions?

Discretionary for the salary reduction portion;
mandatory for the matching or nonelective portion

Discretionary

Discretionary

Mandatory

Mandatory

Discretionary

Chart 4
Employer Plans: Administrative Duties

Plan type	Tax return required? (IRS Form 5500)
SIMPLE IRA	No
SEP	No
Profit sharing plan	Yes, if: • plan assets ever exceed $100,000, • non-owner employees participate in the plan, or • it is the final year of the plan
Money purchase pension plan	Yes, if: • plan assets ever exceed $100,000, • non-owner employees participate in the plan, or • it is the final year of the plan
Defined benefit plan	Yes, if: • plan assets ever exceed $100,000, • non-owner employees participate in the plan, or • it is the final year of the plan
401(k) plan	Yes, if: • plan assets ever exceed $100,000, • non-owner employees participate in the plan, or • it is the final year of the plan

COMPARING PLANS 2/17

Administrative cost	Cost of contributions if you add non-owner employees
Low	Low
Low	Moderate
Low without non-owner employees; moderate with non-owner employees	Moderate
Low without non-owner employees; moderate with non-owner employees	Moderate to high
High	Moderate if non-owner employees are young; high if non-owner employees are older
Moderate to high	Low

Chart 5
Employer Plans: Rules Governing Distributions

Plan type	Are loans permitted?	Are distributions allowed for hardship?
SIMPLE IRA	No	No
SEP	No	No
Profit sharing plan	Yes, to non-owner employees only	Yes
Money purchase pension plan	Yes, to non-owner employees only	No
Defined benefit plan	Yes, to non-owner employees only	No
401(k) plan	Yes, to non-owner employees only	Yes

* An inservice distribution occurs when a participant takes money out of the plan while he or she is still working for the employer who sponsors the plan.

** Although inservice distributions might be permitted, the participant might have to pay a penalty if he or she is younger than 59½ and if an exception to the early distribution penalty does not apply.

*** QDRO stands for qualified domestic relations order. The QDRO rules spell out the circumstances under which your qualified plan benefits can go to someone else—an "alternate payee"—such as your soon-to-be former spouse. These rules also provide liability protection to the trustee who distributes the assets under the terms of the QDRO.

Are distributions allowed in the event of divorce?	Are other inservice* distributions allowed?
Yes, with a written agreement	Yes**
Yes, with a written agreement	Yes**
Yes, with a QDRO***	Yes, after a specified number of years (usually two)
Yes, with a QDRO***	No
Yes, with a QDRO***	No
Yes, with a QDRO***	No

Chart 6
Employer Plans: Which Plan Will Work for You?

Plan type	If you don't have non-owner employees, this plan will work for you if:
SIMPLE IRA	Your business has net income less than $30,000, and you can establish the plan by October 1
SEP	You intend to establish the plan after the end of the year (which would be December 31 if you operate on a calendar year), and/or simplicity and flexibility are more important to you than maximizing contributions
Profit sharing plan	Your business income exceeds $30,000; your business income is variable, so you need the flexibility of discretionary contributions, and you intend to add a money purchase pension plan to this plan to maximize contributions
Money purchase pension plan	Your business income exceeds $30,000; your future business income will be steady or increasing, and you have no need for flexibility and can handle mandatory contributions
Defined benefit plan	Your business income exceeds $135,000; your future business income will be steady or increasing, and you are age 50 or older
401(k) plan	This plan is never appropriate for a business without non-owner employees

If you do have non-owner employees, this plan will work for you if:

Your business generates a modest amount of income;
you want to keep administrative costs and burdens low, and
you want to keep the cost of contributions low

You want to keep administrative costs and burdens low, and
your business income is variable, so you need the flexibility
of discretionary contributions

You need a plan that allows discretionary contributions, and
you want provisions in the plan that will allow you to
restrict employee participation more effectively than a SEP will

You want to maximize your own contribution;
you are comfortable making sizable contributions for non-owner employees;
you don't want a defined benefit plan either because you are young relative to your
non-owner employees or because you don't want the administrative burden and expense;
your future business income will be steady or increasing, and
you have no need for flexibility and can handle mandatory contributions

You business income exceeds $135,000;
your future business income will be steady or increasing;
your age is older relative to the ages of your employees, and
you want to fund your retirement nest egg as quickly as possible

Your business income exceeds $30,000;
you want to keep the cost of contributions low;
you don't mind the high administrative expense because the cost of contributions is low, and
you have more than a handful of non-owner employees

Chart 7
Comparing Traditional IRAs to Roth IRAs: If You Are Single

Traditional IRA

	If you participate in an employer plan	If you do not participate in an employer plan
Contribution eligibility	You must be younger than 70½	Same
Contribution limit*	$2,000	Same
Deduction eligibility	If your modified AGI** is less than $32,000, your contribution is fully deductible; if your modified AGI** is between $32,000 and $42,000, the deduction slowly phases out, and if your modified AGI** is more than $42,000, no deduction	Fully deductible
When are distributions required?	When you reach age 70½ or die	Same
Are distributions taxable?	Distributions of deductible contributions and earnings are taxed at ordinary rates; distributions of nondeductible contributions are not taxable	Same

* These limits reflect the limit to traditional IRAs and Roth IRAs combined. If you contribute $2,000 to a traditional IRA, you cannot contribute anything to a Roth IRA and vice versa. If you contribute $500 to a traditional IRA, the most you can contribute to a Roth IRA (provided you earn more than $2,000 in the year), is $1,500 and vice versa.
** AGI stands for adjusted gross income. (See Glossary for a definition of AGI.)
*** See Chapter 9, Section E, for an explanation of qualified distributions.

Roth IRA

	If you participate in an employer plan	If you do not participate in an employer plan
Contribution eligibility	You can only contribute if your modified AGI** is less than $110,000 (note that the amount of the contribution will start to phase out when your modified AGI** reaches $95,000)	Same
Contribution limit*	The lesser of $2,000 or your earned income	Same
Deduction eligibility	No deduction allowed	Same
When are distributions required?	Upon your death	Same
Are distributions taxable?	All distributions of your contributions are tax free; all distributions of other money will be tax free only if they are "qualified"***	Same

Chart 8
Traditional IRA vs. Roth IRA, Married Filing Joint Return

Traditional IRA

	Contribution for Yourself	
	If you are a participant in an employer plan	**If you are not a participant in an employer plan**
Contribution eligibility	You must be younger than age 70½	Same
Contribution limit*	$2,000 or earned income, whichever is less*	Same
Deduction eligibility	Contributions are fully deductible if modified AGI is less than $52,000. Deductions begin to phase out when modified AGI is between $52,000 and $62,000. No deduction when modified AGI exceeds $62,000.	Fully deductible
Age When Distributions are Required	When you reach age 70½ or die	Same
Taxation of Distributions	Distributions of deductible contributions and all earnings are taxed at ordinary rates. Distributions of nondeductible contributions are not taxable (but nondeductible contributions come out pro rata, not all at once)	Same

*Combined contributions of husband and wife cannot exceed the lesser of $4,000 or the earned income reported on their tax return

**A nonparticipant spouse is a spouse who is not a participant in an employer plan. A spouse who is a participant in an employer plan will be subject to the same rules as you if you are covered by an employer plan.

Contribution for Your Nonparticipant Spouse**

	If you are a participant in an employer plan	If you are not a participant in an employer plan
Contribution eligibility	Your spouse must be younger than age 70½	Same
Contribution limit*	$2,000 or earned income, whichever is less*	Same
Deduction eligibility	Contributions are fully deductible if modified AGI is less than $150,000. Deductions begin to phase out when modified AGI is between $150,000 and $160,000. No deduction when modified AGI exceeds $160,000.	Fully deductible
Age When Distributions are Required	When you reach age 70½ or die	Same
Taxation of Distributions	Distributions of deductible contributions and all earnings are taxed at ordinary rates. Distributions of nondeductible contributions are not taxable (but nondeductible contributions come out pro rata, not all at once)	Same

Chart 8
Traditional IRA vs. Roth IRA, Married Filing Joint Return, Cont'd
Roth IRA

	Contribution for Yourself	
	If you are a participant in an employer plan	**If you are not a participant in an employer plan**
Contribution eligibility	Your modified AGI must be less than $160,000. Your eligibility phases out when your modified AGI is between $150,000 and $160,000	Same
Contribution limit*	$2,000 or earned income, whichever is less*	Same
Deduction eligibility	No deductions allowed	Fully deductible
Age When Distributions are Required	Beginning at the death of the surviving spouse-beneficiary	Same
Taxation of Distributions	All qualified distributions are tax free. If the distribution is not qualified the earnings are taxable.	Same

*Combined contributions of husband and wife cannot exceed the lesser of $4,000 or the earned income reported on their tax return

**A nonparticipant spouse is a spouse who is not a participant in an employer plan. A spouse who is a participant in an employer plan will be subject to the same rules as you if you are covered by an employer plan.

Contribution for Your Nonparticipant Spouse**

	If you are a participant in an employer plan	If you are not a participant in an employer plan
Contribution eligibility	Your modified AGI must be less than $160,000. Your eligibility phases out when your modified AGI is between $150,000 and $160,000	Same
Contribution limit*	$2,000 or earned income, whichever is less*	Same
Deduction eligibility	No deductions allowed	Same
Age When Distributions are Required	Beginning at the death of the surviving spouse-beneficiary	Same
Taxation of Distributions	All qualified distributions are tax free. If the distribution is not qualified the earnings are taxable.	Same

Chapter 3

SIMPLE IRAs

A. What Is a SIMPLE IRA? 3/3

   1. Who May Establish a SIMPLE IRA? 3/4

   2. Advantages 3/5

   3. Disadvantages 3/5

B. How to Establish a SIMPLE IRA 3/6

   1. Trustee or Custodian 3/6

   2. Plan Documents 3/6

   3. Deadlines 3/7

   4. Plan Year 3/7

C. Contributions 3/8

   1. Maximum Contribution 3/8

   2. Salary Reduction Plan Limitation 3/13

   3. No Minimum Contribution 3/14

   4. Cash Only 3/15

   5. Deadlines 3/15

   6. How to Claim the Tax Deduction 3/15

D. Ongoing Administration 3/15

   1. Tax Returns 3/15

   2. Plan Administration 3/16

   3. Updating Plan Documents 3/16

E. **Distributions** **3/16**

  1. Inservice Distributions 3/17

  2. Divorce Payments 3/18

  3. Early Distributions and Exceptions to the Early Distribution Penalty 3/19

  4. Mandatory Distributions 3/23

F. **Penalties** **3/23**

  1. Excess Contributions 3/24

  2. Early Distributions 3/27

  3. Prohibited Transactions 3/27

  4. Life Insurance 3/29

  5. Collectibles 3/29

  6. Pledging the Account As Security 3/30

  7. Mandatory Distribution Penalty 3/30

G. **Terminating Your SIMPLE IRA** **3/30**

H. **Multiple Employer Plans** **3/31**

  1. If You Are Self-Employed With a Day Job on the Side
     (or Vice Versa) 3/32

  2. If You Are Self-Employed and Own Only One Business 3/32

  3. If You Are Self-Employed and Own Two or More Businesses 3/33

I. **Adding a Traditional or Roth IRA to Your SIMPLE IRA** **3/34**

J. **Filling Out the Forms** **3/34**

*N*o one would blame you for scoffing at the name SIMPLE when it is attached to any part of the Internal Revenue Code (also known as the Tax Code). You're no fool. You know that legislators believe that if they mention simple and tax in the same sentence, you'll vote for them. You may vote for them, but you know better than to believe you'll get what's promised.

Well, it may be time to become a believer—of sorts. Although SIMPLE IRAs may not be as simple as you'd like them to be, they do come pretty close. True, when Congress gave us the Savings Incentive Match Plan for Employees (SIMPLE) in 1996, Congress didn't package it with a Dick-and-Jane instruction booklet. (Instead, the new type of retirement plan came with a 19-page primer in IRS-ese.) Nonetheless, if you list all retirement plans an employer might set up, and then arrange the plans in order from simplest to most complex, you'll find the SIMPLE IRA at the bottom of the list. As plans go, it is indeed simple.

⚠️ **The Small Business Jobs Protection Act of 1996 created two types of SIMPLE plans,** SIMPLE IRAs and SIMPLE 401(k)s. In this chapter, we discuss only SIMPLE IRAs. SIMPLE 401(k) plans are a variation of standard 401(k) plans and are not discussed in this book.

The Ideal Candidate for This Plan

A SIMPLE IRA works best for people with modest net income from self-employment—$30,000 per year or less—including people who actually work for someone else but earn small amounts of money on the side.

A. What Is a SIMPLE IRA?

SIMPLE IRAs belong in the broad category of Individual Retirement Accounts (IRAs). Because a SIMPLE IRA is a type of IRA, the rules that apply to traditional IRAs generally apply to SIMPLE IRAs, with a few exceptions. For example:

- Traditional IRAs may be established by individuals. SIMPLE IRAs, however, must be established by an employer, not by an individual. In other words, you must have a business to set up a SIMPLE IRA.

- Traditional IRAs prohibit you from contributing and deducting more than $2,000 a year. The maximum deductible contribution to a SIMPLE IRA is $12,000 per year ($13,000 per year beginning in 2001).

See Chapter 8 for more information about traditional IRAs.

This Plan in a Nutshell

✓ A SIMPLE IRA is indeed simple, and that's a big draw. It's easier to set up and administer than a Keogh.

✓ Most retirement plans restrict your contribution to a small percentage of your earnings, but with a SIMPLE IRA you can contribute 100% of your earnings—up to $6,000—and then contribute an additional amount that is a small percentage of earnings. (The $6,000 limit goes up to $6,500 beginning in the 2001 tax year.)

✓ You don't have to contribute to the SIMPLE IRA if you don't want to, which means you can forego contributions in years when money is tight. This makes the SIMPLE IRA particularly attractive to people whose self-employment income varies from year to year.

✓ You will have few administrative responsibilities for this plan. You won't even have to file a tax return for it!

✓ No matter how good or how poor your accounting skills are, you can set up and maintain the SIMPLE IRA yourself. You won't need the assistance of an expert.

✓ A big drawback of the plan is that you cannot maintain it along with another employer plan, such as a Keogh or a SEP, at the same business. You can, however, combine it with a Roth IRA or a traditional IRA. You can also have another employer plan at a separate company.

✓ The deadline to establish a SIMPLE IRA is usually October 1 of the year for which you want to make a contribution.

1. Who May Establish a SIMPLE IRA?

If you have no employees, you can establish a SIMPLE IRA as long as you have no other retirement plan in place for your business. Generally, you are deemed to have no other plan if you make no contribution to another plan. Other retirement plans include Keoghs and SEPs.

 If you eventually hire employees, you can still keep your SIMPLE IRA as long as you don't employee more than 100 people who each earn $5,000 or more during the year.

 Having a traditional IRA or Roth IRA does not preclude you from establishing a SIMPLE IRA, because traditional IRAs and Roth IRAs are individual plans, not employer plans.

If you own more than one business, you can establish a SIMPLE IRA as long as you have no other plan in place for either business. If one of the businesses already has a plan, determining whether or not you can establish a SIMPLE IRA for the second business is more complex. It depends on the form of each business (sole proprietorship or partnership) and whether or not you own a majority interest in each business. (For more information about multiple plan rules, see Section H, below.)

2. Advantages

Chapter 2 contains a detailed comparison of the different types of retirement plans you can establish—both for your business and for yourself as an individual. In the next two sections, we summarize some of the advantages and disadvantages of SIMPLE IRAs when compared to other employer plans.

First, the advantages:

- Setting up a SIMPLE IRA is straightforward—far easier than setting up a Keogh.
- You generally don't have to file tax returns for your SIMPLE IRA.
- If you are just getting started in your business and are making modest amounts of money, a SIMPLE IRA might allow you to contribute more than either a SEP or a Keogh will.
- You can forgo making a contribution in any given year—or simply reduce

the contribution to a level that is more palatable.

 If you someday hire employees, a SIMPLE IRA will cover them at relatively low additional cost to you and with only modest administrative requirements.

3. Disadvantages

Some of the disadvantages of a SIMPLE IRA include the following:

- Once the net income from your business exceeds approximately $30,000, other types of employer plans will allow you to make larger contributions.

 For purposes of this approximation, net income is your business income reduced by your deductible business expenses, which include half of your self-employment tax. (For more information about computing contributions, see Section C, below.)

- As your business grows, you cannot add another retirement plan to your SIMPLE IRA to increase the contribution limit, as you can with other types of employer plans. You would have to terminate the SIMPLE IRA before establishing and contributing to another type of plan. (For more information about terminating your SIMPLE IRA, see Section G, below.)

- A SIMPLE IRA generally must be set up by October 1 of the year for which you want to make a contribution. This deadline is earlier than the deadline for other types of plans.

 If you ever decide to add employees, you might find that you will spend more on contributions to this plan than to some other plans. That's because you can place few restrictions on employee participation in a SIMPLE IRA, and therefore more employees will be eligible to participate—even part-time workers. When you are forced to cover part-time employees as well as full-time employees, the total cost of contributions can become a burden, even though the cost per employee might be fairly low.

B. How to Establish a SIMPLE IRA

A SIMPLE IRA must be established by an employer, not by an individual. If you are doing business as a sole proprietorship, you can set up the SIMPLE IRA in your name as the employer (or the name you are using for your business). If you are doing business as a partnership, the partnership, and not the individual partners, must establish the SIMPLE IRA, because the partnership is the employer.

1. Trustee or Custodian

Your SIMPLE IRA must be funded through a trust or custodial account, which means the money you contribute must be held by a trustee or custodian. Most likely your SIMPLE IRA will be held as a custodial account by a bank, credit union, brokerage firm or mutual fund. You can also establish a SIMPLE IRA with an insurance company. But you cannot serve as trustee or custodian of your own SIMPLE IRA. (See Chapter 1, Section C.2, for more information about trustees and custodians.)

2. Plan Documents

As a self-employed individual with no employees, you have two options for establishing your SIMPLE IRA. Your first option is to use the SIMPLE IRA form provided for free by your financial institution. In many cases this will be the IRS's model document—Form 5305-SIMPLE—or something quite similar.

Your second option is to hire someone to create a customized SIMPLE IRA for you. As a practical matter, there is rarely a reason to choose this option. It's quite expensive to pay for a customized plan, and the IRS model document allows you to add provisions to the plan, as long as you do not violate any SIMPLE IRA laws. It's possible that some financial institutions might not permit the added provisions you request, in which case you would need to commission a customized SIMPLE IRA or find another institution. But just what those unacceptable provisions might be is hard to fathom, because the provisions you can add to a SIMPLE IRA are narrowly defined in the Tax Code and most are available as options on Form 5305-SIMPLE.

Section J, below, contains instructions for completing the forms necessary to establish a SIMPLE IRA. You can find sample forms at the end of the chapter.

3. Deadlines

If you have never before maintained a SIMPLE IRA, you can establish one and make it effective on any date between January 1 and October 1 of the tax year for which you want to begin making contributions. If you previously maintained a SIMPLE IRA that you have since terminated, your new SIMPLE IRA must have an effective date of January 1. And in all cases, the effective date of the plan can never be earlier than the date you sign the plan documents.

There is one exception that will extend the October 1 deadline. If you start your business after October 1, you may still establish a SIMPLE IRA before the end of the year, as long as you do so as soon as is "administratively feasible." Those are the IRS's words. Just what those words mean is left to your best judgment—and the

IRS's concurrence, if you are audited. Thirty days is often considered reasonable by reasonable people and by the IRS.

Start at the Beginning

When you are self-employed, the date you start your business might seem a little mushy to you. Is it when you first receive income? Make your first business purchase? Obtain a business license? Print up business cards? You know best, but bear in mind that you'll have to convince the IRS if you are audited. The IRS is likely to use start-up expenses described in Section 195 of the Tax Code as a benchmark. Although Section 195 purports to define start-up expenses, you won't find a concrete list there, either. Instead you'll find broad categories of expenses, such as:

- expenses of investigating the creation or acquisition of a business
- expenses of creating a business, and
- any activity engaged in for profit in anticipation of its becoming a business.

---

4. Plan Year

A SIMPLE IRA must be maintained on a calendar year basis. That means the plan year must be January 1 to December 31, and you must use the compensation you receive during that period to compute your SIMPLE IRA contribution—even if you use a fiscal year for your business. (But see Section C.5, below, for information about when the contribution must be made.)

A fiscal year is generally any 12-month period that ends on the last day of any month except December. If your business is maintained on a fiscal year, you must take your SIMPLE IRA deduction for the business tax year in which the plan year ends. Note that this has the effect of delaying the deduction—generally a disadvantage. It is usually best if your business tax year and plan year coincide.

> EXAMPLE: Your business tax year runs from July through June. Your compensation for calendar year 2001 will allow you to contribute $12,000 to your SIMPLE IRA. However, because your business tax year doesn't end until June 30, 2002, you cannot claim your deduction until you file your tax return after the close of your fiscal year—in the second half of 2002. If the plan year and the business year both ended December 31, 2001, you could file your tax return and claim a tax deduction early in 2002—assuming you were able to gather all your financial information by then.

C. Contributions

As with other IRAs, you may contribute any amount to your SIMPLE IRA, as long as you don't exceed the maximum. The maximum varies depending on your net income from self-employment. Just keep in mind that you cannot make a contribution to your SIMPLE IRA unless you make a profit. If you have a loss from your business, your contribution must be zero.

1. Maximum Contribution

The maximum contribution you can make to your SIMPLE IRA is based on the net income from your business. For this purpose, your net income is your income from the business, reduced by all of your business deductions. Your business deductions include half of your self-employment tax, but they do not include your SIMPLE IRA contribution.

 SIMPLE IRAs differ from Keogh plans and SEPs in this way. Keoghs and SEPs treat the retirement plan contribution as a business expense for purposes of computing the maximum contribution.

Although your maximum contribution is based on how much money you make, there is a cap. The most you can contribute to a SIMPLE IRA for the 2000 tax year is $12,000. (This will increase to $13,000 for the 2001 tax year.) And the truth is, you must make a lot of money to reach the limit.

All SIMPLE IRA contributions are made up of two parts: a salary reduction part and either a matching or a nonelective part. For the first part—the salary reduction part—the employer contributes a portion of the employee's salary to the SIMPLE IRA instead of paying it to the employee in cash. For the second part of the contribution, the employer must either match the salary reduction contribution or contribute a flat percentage of the employee's compensation.

But what about you? As a self-employed person, you don't have a salary, so how do you make a salary reduction contribution for yourself—let alone a matching contribution? Here's how it works.

a.   Part One: Salary Reduction Contribution

You may contribute up to 100% of your net income from your business as the salary reduction part of your contribution—but no more than $6,000 ($6,500 beginning with the 2001 tax year). These are the steps in the computation:

Step 1:
Calculate your net profit from the business. Your net profit is your business income reduced by all of your business expenses except your self-employment tax deduction.

Step 2:
Compute your self-employment tax deduction. Your self-employment tax deduction is always half of your self-employment tax. IRS Schedule SE (see Example 1, below) walks you through the calculation.

 If you have no other employer during the year, you should be able to use the short form of Schedule SE. If you worked for another employer and your wages were subject to FICA (Social Security tax), you might have to use the long version of Schedule SE. You can find sample copies of both the long and short Schedule SE in the Appendix.

Step 3:
Subtract Step 2 from Step 1.

Step 4:
If the result in Step 3 is $6,000 or more, your maximum salary reduction contribution is $6,000. If the result in Step 3 is less than $6,000, then the Step 3 amount is your maximum salary reduction contribution.

b. Part Two: Matching or Nonelective Contribution:

You have two options for computing the second part of the contribution.

i. Option One: Matching Contribution

You can make a matching contribution equal to your salary reduction contribution (see Part 1, above), as long as the matching contribution does not exceed 3% of your net profit reduced by your self-employment tax deduction. (This is the same number you came up with in Step 3 of Part 1, above.) Note that to reach $6,000 in matching contributions, your net income would have to be $200,000 (3% x $200,000 = $6,000) after all business deductions, including the self-employment tax deduction.

To compute the matching portion, multiply the result from Step 3 in Part 1, above, by 3%. This is the maximum matching contribution you can make to your SIMPLE IRA. However, it cannot exceed your salary reduction contribution, which you calculated in Part 1, above. In other words, the matching portion is the lesser of 3% of net income (after the self-employment tax deduction) or your salary reduction contribution.

ii. Option Two: Nonelective Contribution

As an alternative to matching, you can contribute a flat 2% of your net income. For purposes of this computation, your net income is deemed to be no more than $170,000. Although the $170,000 is to be increased for inflation from time to time, this option would currently limit the second part of your contribution to $3,400 or less. Consequently, you would not use this option if your goal is to contribute the maximum amount you can to your SIMPLE IRA. Instead, you would choose a matching contribution.

 Generally, the maximum you can contribute to your SIMPLE IRA each year is the sum of Part 1 and Part 2, above. But Section 2, below, describes a limitation that could reduce the amount you can contribute.

c. Examples of Calculations

EXAMPLE 1: Prakash has his own accounting business and works for no other employer. His business grossed $30,000 in the year 2000. His business expenses (as reported on his Schedule C) totaled $5,180. He wants to contribute as much as he can to his SIMPLE IRA.

Salary Reduction Contribution:

Step 1: Prakash's income after expenses is $24,820, which is $30,000 – $5,180.

Step 2: Prakash completes the short Schedule SE (see below) to arrive at his self-employment tax deduction of $1,753.

Step 3: Prakash determines his net income (after the self-employment tax deduction) by subtracting Step 2 from Step 1:

$24,820 – $1,753 = $23,067.

Step 4: Because Prakash's net income is greater than $6,000, his maximum salary reduction contribution is $6,000.

Matching Contribution:

Step 1: Prakash's matching contribution is the lesser of his salary reduction contribution or 3% of Step 3. Because .03 x $23,067 = $692 and is less than $6,000, his matching contribution is $692.

The maximum contribution Prakash can make to his SIMPLE IRA is the sum of the salary reduction and matching contributions, or:

$6,000 + $692 = $6,692.

SCHEDULE SE (Form 1040) Department of the Treasury Internal Revenue Service (99)	**Self-Employment Tax** ▶ See Instructions for Schedule SE (Form 1040). ▶ Attach to Form 1040.	OMB No. 1545-0074 **2000** Attachment Sequence No. **17**
Name of person with **self-employment** income (as shown on Form 1040) Prakash Jones	Social security number of person with **self-employment** income ▶	555 : 55 : 5555

Who Must File Schedule SE

You must file Schedule SE if:

- You had net earnings from self-employment from **other than** church employee income (line 4 of Short Schedule SE or line 4c of Long Schedule SE) of $400 or more **or**
- You had church employee income of $108.28 or more. Income from services you performed as a minister or a member of a religious order **is not** church employee income. See page SE-1.

Note. Even if you had a loss or a small amount of income from self-employment, it may be to your benefit to file Schedule SE and use either "optional method" in Part II of Long Schedule SE. See page SE-3.

Exception. If your only self-employment income was from earnings as a minister, member of a religious order, or Christian Science practitioner **and** you filed Form 4361 and received IRS approval not to be taxed on those earnings, **do not** file Schedule SE. Instead, write "Exempt–Form 4361" on Form 1040, line 52.

May I Use Short Schedule SE or Must I Use Long Schedule SE?

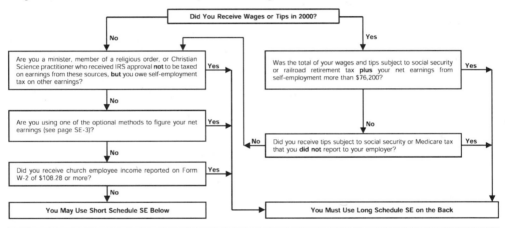

Section A—Short Schedule SE. Caution: *Read above to see if you can use Short Schedule SE.*

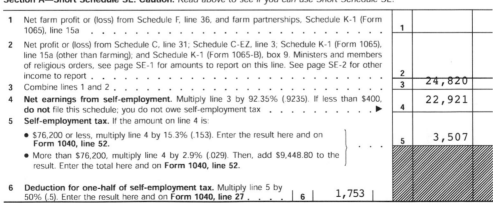

1	Net farm profit or (loss) from Schedule F, line 36, and farm partnerships, Schedule K-1 (Form 1065), line 15a	**1**	
2	Net profit or (loss) from Schedule C, line 31; Schedule C-EZ, line 3; Schedule K-1 (Form 1065), line 15a (other than farming); and Schedule K-1 (Form 1065-B), box 9. Ministers and members of religious orders, see page SE-1 for amounts to report on this line. See page SE-2 for other income to report	**2**	
3	Combine lines 1 and 2	**3**	24,820
4	**Net earnings from self-employment.** Multiply line 3 by 92.35% (.9235). If less than $400, **do not** file this schedule; you do not owe self-employment tax . . . . ▶	**4**	22,921
5	**Self-employment tax.** If the amount on line 4 is: • $76,200 or less, multiply line 4 by 15.3% (.153). Enter the result here and on **Form 1040, line 52.** • More than $76,200, multiply line 4 by 2.9% (.029). Then, add $9,448.80 to the result. Enter the total here and on **Form 1040, line 52.**	**5**	3,507
6	**Deduction for one-half of self-employment tax.** Multiply line 5 by 50% (.5). Enter the result here and on **Form 1040, line 27**	**6**	1,753

For Paperwork Reduction Act Notice, see Form 1040 instructions.   Cat. No. 11358Z   **Schedule SE (Form 1040) 2000**

EXAMPLE 2: In 2001, Prakash went to India for a six-month vacation. Consequently, he only made $5,900 from his business, and his expenses were only $350. Prakash still wants to contribute as much as possible to his SIMPLE IRA.

Salary Reduction Contribution:

Step 1: Prakash's income after expenses is $5,450, which is $5,900 – $350.

Step 2: Prakash completes another short Schedule SE to arrive at his self-employment tax deduction of $385.

Step 3: Prakash determines his net income by subtracting Step 2 from Step 1.
$5,450 – $385 = $5,065.

Step 4: Because Prakash's net income (after the self-employment tax deduction) is less than $6,000, his salary reduction contribution is limited to his net income, which is $5,065.

Matching Contribution:

Prakash's matching contribution is the lesser of his salary reduction contribution or 3% of Step 3. Because .03 x $5,065 = $152 and is less than $5,065, his matching contribution is $152.

Therefore, the maximum contribution Prakash can make to his SIMPLE IRA is the sum of the salary reduction and matching contributions:
$5,065 + $152 = $5,217.

d. Choosing an Option

As a self-employed person with no employees, there would be no reason for you to choose a nonelective contribution (Option 2) over a matching contribution (Option 1). Because you may deposit into your SIMPLE IRA any amount from zero to your maximum, there is no reason to impose a lower limit by selecting the nonelective method for computing Part 2. It will always produce a lower contribution than would Option 1 (matching).

EXAMPLE: Your net income after all business deductions and the self-employment tax deduction is $20,000. If you elect Option 1 with a 3% match, the maximum contribution you can make to your SIMPLE IRA is $6,600, which is a $6,000 salary reduction contribution plus a matching contribution of .03 x $20,000 or $600. If, instead, you choose Option 2 with a 2% nonelective contribution, your maximum contribution is $6,400 ($6,000 plus .20 x $20,000). No matter which option you choose, you can contribute less, but you cannot contribute more.

2. Salary Reduction Plan Limitation

In the vast world of retirement plans, a handful—including SIMPLE IRAs—fall into the category of salary reduction plans.

These plans allow participants to contribute some of their salary to a retirement plan instead of receiving the salary in cash. In addition to SIMPLE IRAs, salary reduction plans include 401(k) plans, tax-deferred annuity or 403(b) plans (which generally cover employees of public schools and universities and other charitable organizations), and 457 plans (sponsored by state and local governments and other tax exempt organizations).

As you might expect, the amount of salary or compensation you can defer into any one of these plans is limited (currently $10,500 for 401(k) and 403(b) plans, $8,000 for 457 plans and $6,000 for SIMPLE IRAs). But the law also puts a limit on the total amount you can defer into all such plans combined, if you happen to be covered by more than one. The overall limit cannot exceed the largest limit among the plans in which you are participating.

EXAMPLE: You work for a corporation and contribute to its 401(k) plan. You also have your own business, and you decide to set up a SIMPLE IRA. You have calculated your maximum salary reduction contribution to the SIMPLE IRA to be $6,000. Your maximum 401(k) contribution is $10,500. Because the 401(k) maximum is the greater of the two, and because both plans are salary reduction plans, you can contribute only $10,500 to both plans combined. Therefore, if you contribute $10,500 to your corporate 401(k), you are not permitted to make a salary reduction contribution to your SIMPLE IRA. On the other hand, if you contribute $6,000, to your SIMPLE IRA first, the maximum salary you could defer into your employer's 401(k) plan would be $4,500.

In all cases, it is your responsibility, not your employer's, to make sure you do not exceed the limit.

It is important to note that this overall limit applies only to the salary reduction portion of plan contributions. The limit does not include matching or nonelective employer contributions. Those are additional contributions to which you are entitled—with limits that apply on a per-employer basis instead of an individual basis.

3. No Minimum Contribution

As is the case with a traditional IRA, you are not required to make a contribution to your SIMPLE IRA every year, even if you make a profit. You can skip the contribution for the year, or just contribute less than the maximum.

 If you ever add employees to your SIMPLE IRA, you may be required to contribute to their accounts even if you don't make a profit.

4. Cash Only

All contributions to your SIMPLE IRA must be in cash. You may not contribute jewelry, art or shares of stock, for example. If you do, it will be treated as an excess contribution (see Section F.1, below, for a discussion of excess contributions)—even if the value of the property is below your contribution limit—and you could be subject to penalties. But your gaffe won't disqualify the SIMPLE IRA, as long as you remove the property on a timely basis.

5. Deadlines

You are required to make the salary reduction portion of a SIMPLE IRA contribution within 30 days after the end of the month for which the salary is earned. If you are self-employed, your income is considered earned on the last day of the year. Therefore, this portion of your contribution should be deposited by January 30 after the end of the year.

The matching portion of the contribution is not due until the due date of your tax return. And if you requested and received an extension of time for filing your tax return, you have until the extended due date. As a practical matter, most self-employed individuals make the salary reduction and matching contributions at the same time because it is convenient. However, there is no reason you cannot make the contribution in pieces, if you prefer.

6. How to Claim the Tax Deduction

Once you have computed your SIMPLE IRA contribution, you claim your deduction on page 1, line 29, of your individual income tax return (Form 1040). This will be true whether you are doing business as a partnership or as a sole proprietor. (See the Appendix for a sample copy of IRS Form 1040.)

 If you ever add employees to your plan, you will claim the deduction for contributions to your employees' SIMPLE IRA accounts—the combined salary reduction and matching or non-elective portions—on Schedule C (if you are a sole proprietor) or on IRS Form 1065 (if your business is a partnership).

D. Ongoing Administration

No other retirement plan for your business is as easy to maintain as a SIMPLE IRA.

1. Tax Returns

Your SIMPLE IRA is a tax exempt entity, which is why it generally doesn't have to pay tax each year on the income it produces. As a result, you will generally not have to file a tax return for your SIMPLE IRA.

But if your SIMPLE IRA engages in a business that produces more than $1,000 of income during the year, you must file a special tax return—IRS Form 990-T—for the SIMPLE IRA. (You can find a sample copy of Form 990-T in the Appendix.) Income from a business inside a SIMPLE IRA is called unrelated business taxable income, or UBTI. Once UBTI exceeds $1,000 in a year, it is subject to tax and the tax must be paid out of the SIMPLE IRA assets.

Most people invest their SIMPLE IRA assets in stocks, bonds and other standard investments, none of which generate UBTI. But suppose you invest some of the assets in a limited partnership. Many limited partnerships are in fact businesses. And when the business (the limited partnership) starts throwing off income, it will be taxable, even though it is inside your SIMPLE IRA.

2. Plan Administration

Not only do you escape tax returns (for the most part) with a SIMPLE IRA, but you escape all other administrative requirements as well (so long as you don't have employees). The custodian of your SIMPLE IRA, on the other hand, has some chores to do. The custodian must report your contributions to the IRS each year on Form 5498 and must also provide you with a statement of your account by January 31 after the end of the year.

3. Updating Plan Documents

Changes in the law might require your SIMPLE IRA plan documents to be updated from time to time. Your financial institution should take responsibility for this.

 If you want to change your SIMPLE IRA beneficiary, you don't have to complete a new set of plan documents. Generally, you can simply request a "Change of Beneficiary Designation" form from your financial institution, drop in the name of the new beneficiary, sign and date the form and return it to the financial institution. (See Section J, below, for information about completing plan documents.)

E. Distributions

It's your money in that SIMPLE IRA, so you might think you should be able to get at it when you want, for whatever reason you want. You can, but not without penalty. The government may require you to pay back those tax benefits you've been enjoying all those years. In exchange for tax breaks, the government requires you to follow certain rules related to your retirement plan. At their most simplistic, the rules are:

- With certain exceptions, you are not permitted to take money out of a qualified plan while you still work for the business that sponsors the plan. Such distributions while you are still working are called inservice distributions, and they are particularly tricky creatures when you're dealing with a qualified plan. When you're dealing with a SIMPLE, they are a little more manageable, but some restrictions still apply.

- Prior to reaching age 59½, money you take out of your SIMPLE IRA will be considered an early distribution, and you'll face a penalty unless that distribution qualifies for an exception.

- You may begin taking money out of your SIMPLE IRA without penalty once you reach age 59½.

- You are required to begin taking money out of your SIMPLE IRA in the year you turn age 70½.

In this section, we explain those rules in more detail—and we take a look at the exceptions to the early distribution penalty.

First, we examine inservice distributions, paying particular attention those that are permitted under the terms of some qualified plans but never under the terms of SIMPLE IRAs.

Second, we examine what can happen to your SIMPLE IRA in the event of a divorce.

Third, we explain both the penalty that you must pay if you take money out of your SIMPLE IRA prior to reaching age 59½ (the so-called early distribution penalty) and the exceptions to that penalty.

Fourth, we briefly describe the mandatory distribution requirement that kicks in when you reach age 70½.

 This is not a book about retirement plan distributions. Although we provide an overview of the distribution rules for each type of plan, you must look elsewhere for the details. One source is *IRAs, 401(k)s & Other Retirement Plans: Taking Your Money Out*, by Twila Slesnick and John C. Suttle (Nolo).

1. Inservice Distributions

It is generally much more difficult to get money out of a qualified plan while you are still working for the company that sponsors the plan (in other words, while you are inservice), than it is to get money out of a SIMPLE IRA. But over the years, Congress has carved out some distribution exceptions for qualified plans—to accommodate special situations—which Congress did not extend to SIMPLE IRAs. If you are accustomed to corporate qualified plan rules, be aware that the following types of distributions are not permitted from a SIMPLE IRA.

a. Loans

You are not permitted to borrow from your SIMPLE IRA. Doing so is considered a prohibited transaction, and you will be penalized accordingly. (See Section F.3, below, for more about prohibited transactions.)

Loans for 60 Days or Less

A special IRA rule called the 60-day rule essentially allows you to borrow from your SIMPLE IRA for up to 60 days. The rule provides that you can take money out of an IRA and, as long as it goes into another IRA or back into the same one within 60 days, there will be no income tax and no penalties. This strategy works for SIMPLE IRAs, too, but with these restrictions:

- If you remove money from your SIMPLE IRA within two years of the date you first contributed to a SIMPLE IRA, you must return the money to the same SIMPLE IRA or to a new SIMPLE IRA within 60 days to avoid income tax and penalties. You cannot deposit the money into any other type of IRA. If you do, you might incur penalties, such as an early distribution penalty (from the SIMPLE IRA) and possibly an excess contribution penalty (to the other IRA). But after two years you can withdraw money from your SIMPLE IRA and deposit it within 60 days to either a SIMPLE IRA or a traditional IRA without penalty or income tax.

- You are permitted to use this short-term loan strategy with your SIMPLE IRA only once during any 12-month period.

- When you put the money back into the SIMPLE IRA or a traditional IRA within 60 days, you must return exactly the amount you took out. Furthermore, if you removed cash you must return cash. You may not deposit stock of equal value, for example.

b. Hardship

Although some types of qualified plans, such as 401(k) plans, allow participants to take money out of the plan in the case of hardship, there is no such thing as a hardship distribution from a SIMPLE IRA (or any other type of IRA, for that matter).

2. Divorce Payments

If you and your spouse divorce and your divorce agreement states that you must give some or all of your SIMPLE IRA assets to your former spouse, don't simply withdraw the SIMPLE IRA funds and hand them over. If you do, you (and not your spouse) will have to pay the income tax on the distribution. And if you are younger than 59½, you'll owe penalties, as well, even though the money is going to your former spouse.

To avoid tax liability for your former spouse's share of the SIMPLE IRA, you must transfer the funds according to IRS procedures. As long as the distribution is required by a divorce or maintenance decree, or a written separation agreement, you may instruct the custodian of your SIMPLE IRA to transfer some or all of the assets directly into a SIMPLE IRA in your former spouse's name.

If the distribution to your former spouse occurs within two years of your first SIMPLE IRA contribution and you are younger than age 59½, your spouse's portion must be transferred to another SIMPLE IRA or you could incur an early distribution penalty. If more than two years have passed, your spouse's share can be transferred to either a SIMPLE IRA or a traditional IRA.

Alternatively, you can roll over or transfer your former spouse's share into a new SIMPLE IRA in your name (or a traditional IRA, if two years have passed since your first SIMPLE IRA contribution) and then change the name on the new SIMPLE IRA to your former spouse's name. The critical point in every case is to be sure your former spouse does not take possession of the funds before they are deposited into a SIMPLE IRA in his or her name.

3. Early Distributions and Exceptions to the Early Distribution Penalty

Once you reach age 59½, you are permitted to take money out of your SIMPLE IRA without penalty. That means that distributions you take on or after the day you turn 59½ will be subject to income tax but no additional penalties. SIMPLE IRA distributions that you take before you reach age 59½, however, are considered early distributions and are subject to both regular income tax and an early distribution penalty unless an exception applies. (For more information about computing the penalty, see Section F.2, below.)

The following are the exceptions to the early distribution penalty. If your distributions fits in one of the exceptions, that means only that you will escape paying a penalty. You will still have to pay income tax on the money.

a. Death

Distributions from your SIMPLE IRA after you die are not subject to an early distribution penalty, no matter how old you are when you die or how old your beneficiaries are when they withdraw the money. Escaping the penalty when you die won't do you much good, but your heirs will benefit. They will still have to pay income tax on the distributions, though.

b. Disability

If you become disabled, you can take money from your SIMPLE IRA without penalty, as long as you satisfy the IRS's definition of disabled, which is hardly a model of clarity. Here's how it reads: You must be unable to "engage in any substantial gainful activity by reason of any medically determinable physical or mental impairment which can be expected to result in death or to be of long-continued and indefinite duration." The IRS's own regulations state that the gainful activity refers specifically to the type of work you were doing before becoming disabled. Thus it would seem that you need not be unfit for all work—just the work you customarily do. Even if you do qualify for this exception to the penalty, your distributions will be subject to income tax.

c. Periodic Payments

You can begin taking distributions from your Keogh plan regardless of your age as long as you take them in equal annual installments over your life expectancy. These distributions are called "substantially equal periodic payments." Be warned, however, that this is not quite the gaping loophole it appears to be. In order to use this exception, you must terminate your employment with the employer who sponsored the plan. Thus, when you are self-employed, presumably you must terminate or otherwise dispose of your business.

To compute substantially equal periodic payments, you must use one of the IRS-approved methods for computing the payments—you cannot simply choose a monthly or annual payment that suits you. (See IRS Notice 89-25 in the Appendix for more information about how to calculate substantially equal payments.)

You must continue the payments for at least five years or until you are at least age 59½, whichever comes later. For example, if you begin at age 58, you must continue the payments for at least five years even though you pass age 59½ in the meantime.

Or if you begin at age 52, you must continue until at least age 59½, even though more than five years have passed.

d. Medical Expenses

Although you can take money out of your SIMPLE IRA prior to age 59½ to pay for medical expenses, you won't escape the penalty entirely. The exemption applies only to the portion of your medical expenses that would be deductible on Schedule A of your tax return if you were to itemize deductions (whether or not you actually do itemize deductions). The remainder is subject to the penalty. All of it will be subject to income tax.

> EXAMPLE: Your adjusted gross income is $50,000. You had medical bills of $6,000 during the year, which you paid with funds you withdrew from your SIMPLE IRA. (The $6,000 distribution is included in the $50,000 of income.) For income tax purposes, you are permitted to deduct medical expenses that exceed 7.5% of your adjusted gross income. Thus:
>
> Adjusted gross income (AGI), including the SIMPLE IRA distribution = $50,000;
>
> 7.5% of AGI (.075 x $50,000) = $3,750 in nondeductible expenses;
>
> Excess ($6,000 − $3,750) = $2,250 in deductible expenses.
>
> Although you took $6,000 from your SIMPLE IRA to pay medical expenses,

only $2,250 will escape the early distribution penalty. The remaining $3,750 will be subject to the penalty (unless you qualify for another exception). And don't forget that the entire $6,000 is subject to regular income tax, as well.

e.   Health Insurance Premiums

People who are unemployed, or were recently unemployed, may draw money from a SIMPLE IRA to pay health insurance premiums. They will owe income tax on the distribution but no penalty, as long as they satisfy all of the following conditions:

- They received unemployment compensation for at least 12 consecutive weeks.
- They received the funds from the SIMPLE IRA during a year in which they received unemployment compensation or during the following year.
- They received the SIMPLE IRA distribution no more than 60 days after they returned to work.

It might sound as though this won't work for you if you are self-employed. However, the rules specifically permit this exception if you were self-employed before you stopped working, as long as you would have qualified for unemployment compensation under state law except for the fact that you were self-employed.

f.   Higher Education Expenses

If you use distributions to pay higher education expenses, you will not be subject to the early distribution penalty, as long as you satisfy all of the following requirements:

- You must use the money to pay the higher education expenses for you, your spouse, your child or your grandchild.
- You must use the money to pay for tuition, fees, books, supplies and equipment. You may also use the money for room and board if the student is carrying at least half of a normal study load (or is considered at least a half-time student).
- The distributions cannot exceed the amount of the higher education expenses. Furthermore, when computing the amount of the distribution that is exempt from the penalty, you must reduce the total expenses (tuition, fees and so on) by any tax-free scholarships or other tax-free assistance the student receives, not including loans, gifts or inheritances.

g.   Purchasing a First Home

You may take an early distribution without penalty if the money is used to buy a first home. Although the purpose of this exception is to make it easier for people to buy a home, there is a lifetime distribution limit of only $10,000. Other restrictions include the following:

- You must use the SIMPLE IRA money for the acquisition, construction or reconstruction of a home.
- You must use the funds within 120 days of receiving them. If the home purchase is canceled or delayed, you may roll the funds back into the same SIMPLE IRA or into another SIMPLE IRA (or a traditional IRA, if two years have passed since your first SIMPLE IRA contribution), as long as you complete the rollover within 120 days of the initial distribution.
- You must use the funds for the benefit of a first-time home buyer. A first-time home buyer is someone who has had no interest in a principal residence during the two years ending on the date of purchase of the new home. If the individual happens to be married, then neither the individual nor the spouse may have owned any part of a principal residence during the preceding two-year period.
- The first-time home buyer can be you or your spouse. The buyer can also be an ancestor (for example, a parent, grandparent, great grandparent and so on), a child or a grandchild of either you or your spouse.
- The lifetime limit of $10,000 applies regardless of whose home is purchased or improved. If you withdraw $10,000 and give it to your child, the lifetime limit is used up and you may not use the exception for any future distribution (from any IRA, no matter what type), even if it is to buy a house for a different relative or for yourself. The $10,000 does not have to be distributed all at once or even in a single year. For example, you could withdraw $5,000 one year, giving it to a qualified person for a home purchase, and then withdraw another $5,000 in a later year.

h. Federal Tax Levy

If you owe back taxes, you can be reasonably certain the government will try to collect them. If you have assets in a SIMPLE IRA, the government can take those assets (in other words, the IRS can levy on your SIMPLE IRA) to pay your debt. If it does, those amounts taken for taxes will not be subject to the early distribution penalty even if you happen to be younger than 59½, but you will still pay income tax on the distribution. Whew. Thanks, Uncle Sam.

Keep in mind that even though you will not owe an early distribution penalty on the above distributions, you will still owe regular income tax. And taking money out of a retirement plan before you really have to is not usually the best financial strategy.

4. Mandatory Distributions

Beginning in the year you turn 70½, you are required to start taking money out of your SIMPLE IRA, even if you are still working. The income tax regulations provide a formula for calculating the minimum required distribution. You may take more than the minimum, but you may not take less. If you do take less, you will be fined 50% of the amount that you should have taken out of the SIMPLE IRA but didn't.

If you are still working when you reach 70½, you may continue to make contributions to a SIMPLE IRA and deduct those contributions. It could very well make sense for you to do so even though you are also required to take some money out each year. Not only can you claim a deduction and reduce your tax liability, but you can also add to the assets that will grow tax-deferred.

F. Penalties

Because the SIMPLE IRA rules are relatively few and blessedly simple, it's easy to stay out of trouble. Slip-ups are still possible, though. Perhaps you contribute too much one year, take a distribution too early or do something with the money that the IRS frowns on. Here are the consequences.

Infractions and Their Consequences	
Problem	**Penalty**
Excess contributions	6% of the excess
Early distributions: • Within two years of contribution: • Two or more years after the contributions:	 25% of the distribution 10% of the distribution
Prohibited transactions • If owner of SIMPLE IRA engages in the transaction: • If another disqualified person engages in the transaction:	 Disqualification 15% of transaction
Failure to take a required distribution	50% of the amount that should have been distributed but was not

1. Excess Contributions

If you contribute too much to your SIMPLE IRA, you will be fined 6% of the excess over what you were permitted to contribute. A new 6% penalty will be assessed on any of the excess that remains in the account at the beginning of each year. So if the error is not corrected, you could really pile up some penalties. It would be like leaving your car in a no parking zone for a week hoping the meter person won't give you multiple tickets.

If you keep meticulous records, you might wonder how an error could go uncorrected. But let's suppose your business has had a string of good years and you are expecting another banner year. So in February, you contribute $12,000 to your SIMPLE IRA. December comes and goes. In April, as you are preparing your tax return, you discover that you made less than you thought. In fact, you contributed too much to your SIMPLE IRA. Now what?

Here are your options:

a. Option One: Remove Excess Before Due Date

One way you can correct the error is to remove the excess contribution plus any earnings attributable to the excess by the due date of your tax return (plus extensions, if you applied for and received an extension for filing your tax return).

When you remove the contribution and earnings, you must report the earnings, but not the contribution, as income on your tax return. Report the earnings in the year you made the excess contribution. (The year you remove the funds might be different from the year you made the excess contribution.) If you are not yet 59½, you will have to pay an early distribution penalty on the earnings, but not on the excess contribution.

EXAMPLE: You contributed $8,000 to your SIMPLE IRA in January 2001. You contributed to no other IRAs or retirement plans during the year. At the end of the year, you discovered that the maximum you were permitted to contribute to your SIMPLE IRA was $7,000. The excess SIMPLE IRA contribution is $1,000. If you remove the $1,000 plus any investment returns attributable to the $1,000 before you file your tax return on April 15, you will avoid the 6% excess contribution penalty.

If you earned $960 on the $8,000 SIMPLE IRA contribution, then $120 of it would be attributable to the $1,000 excess. ($1,000/$8,000 x $ 960 = $120). Therefore, you must remove earnings of $120, in addition to the $1,000. If you remove the money by April 15, you won't owe any excess contribution penalty at all. If you are younger than age 59½, however, you might owe an early distribution penalty on the earnings ($120), unless you can find an exception that applies. (See Section E.3, above, for information about exceptions.)

On your tax return you will report only the $120 of earnings that you withdrew, and you will claim a SIMPLE IRA deduction for $7,000 on page 1 of Form 1040.

If you filed your return early and claimed a SIMPLE IRA deduction for too much, you can still prepare an amended return before the actual due date of your tax return and avoid the 6% penalty.

EXAMPLE: As in the previous example, you contributed $8,000 to your SIMPLE IRA in January 2001. The end of the year comes and goes. You file your tax return in February 2002 claiming a deduction of $8,000. In March, you were at a party when you ran into an accountant. During the conversation, you learned you made an error when computing your SIMPLE IRA contribution. The amount should have been 7,000. To avoid an excess contribution penalty, you must do all of the following before April 15:

Remove the $1,000 excess contribution.

Remove the $120 of earnings attributable to the $1,000.

File an amended tax return claiming only a $7,000 SIMPLE IRA deduction and reporting the $120 of earnings.

If you follow these procedures, you will not owe a 6% excess contribution penalty. However, you might owe an early distribution penalty on the $120

of earnings if you are younger than 59½.

b. Option Two: Remove Excess After Due Date

Another way to deal with the situation is to remove the excess contribution late— after the due date (or extended due date) of your tax return and leave the earnings in the account.

You must pay a 6% penalty on the excess contribution, but not on the earnings if you leave them in the SIMPLE IRA. In addition, you avoid an early distribution penalty on the earnings—something you would have had to deal with had you taken the earnings out as described in Option 1, above. (Presumably Congress considers the 6% penalty adequate payback for any benefit you might derive from leaving the earnings in the account.)

You will not have to pay any income tax on the corrective distribution as long as you did not take a deduction for the full excess contribution on your tax return. If you did, you will have to submit an amended tax return with the correct deduction (the correct SIMPLE IRA contribution) and pay the additional income tax.

EXAMPLE: In 2001, you contributed $3,000 too much to your SIMPLE IRA. Although you knew about the excess before your filing deadline (and deducted only the correct amount on your tax return), you forgot to remove the excess from the SIMPLE IRA. The earnings on the excess are $250. You remove the $3,000 after your tax filing deadline and leave the $250 of earnings in the account. You will owe a penalty of $180 (6% of $3,000), but no other penalties will apply.

c. Option Three: Leave Excess In, Deduct Next Year

Your third option is to leave the excess in the SIMPLE IRA and deduct it in the next tax year.

You still have to pay the 6% excise tax for the first year (on the excess contribution, but not the earnings), because the excess remained in the account after the due date of your tax return. But as long as the excess does not exceed the deductible SIMPLE IRA amount for the second year, there will be no penalty for that year.

EXAMPLE: In 2001, you contributed $3,000 too much to your SIMPLE IRA. Again you deducted the correct amount but forgot to remove the excess. You decide to leave the excess in the account and deduct it the following year. In 2002 you have enough income to make an $8,000 SIMPLE IRA contribution. You apply the $3,000 excess from the previous year and add an additional $5,000 in cash by the due date of your tax return to complete the $8,000 contribution. You must still pay a $180 penalty for 2001,

but no additional penalty will be assessed for 2002 or beyond.

d. Which Method Is Best?

If the excess is large, the 6% penalty could become painful. In that case, you should work hard to remove the excess by the tax filing deadline (Option 1). Although you might have to pay an early distribution tax on the earnings, that penalty could be significantly less than the 6% penalty on the excess contribution.

If you miss the tax filing deadline, you cannot avoid the 6% penalty. So you must choose between Option 2 and Option 3. If you expect to be able to deduct the excess in the next year, Option 3 is your better choice, because your money can be working for you all year inside the SIMPLE IRA. However, if you don't think you'll be able to use the deduction the second year, you will probably want to use Option 2 and remove the excess until you have enough income from your business to support a SIMPLE IRA deduction.

Excess contributions to your SIMPLE IRA are reported on Form 5329 for the year the excess contribution was made. Do not use the current year's Form 5329. You can find a sample copy of Form 5329 in the Appendix of this book.

EXAMPLE: You made an excess contribution of $1,000 to your SIMPLE IRA in 2001. You discovered your error in June 2002 long after you filed your tax return. You should complete Form 5329 for the year 2001 (not Form 5329 for the year 2002) even though you have already filed the rest of your tax return. Sign and date the form and send it in with your check for $60 (6% of $1,000), which is the amount of the excess contribution penalty.

2. Early Distributions

If you take money out of your SIMPLE IRA before you reach age 59½ and the distribution does not fall into any of the categories described in Section E.3, above, then you will be subject to an early distribution penalty in addition to the income tax you must pay.

If the early distribution occurs within two years of the date you first contribute to a SIMPLE IRA, the penalty is 25% of the distribution. If it occurs after the two-year anniversary of your first contribution, the penalty is only 10%. The financial institution that serves as custodian of your SIMPLE IRA is required to track the two-year period and report to the IRS any early distributions.

The IRS requires you to report the early distribution penalty on Form 5329 for the year of the early distribution.

3. Prohibited Transactions

The Tax Code prohibits certain transactions involving your SIMPLE IRA assets. The prohibited transaction rules are part of Congress's strategy to protect your SIMPLE IRA assets so that they will be available when you retire. The rules are designed to keep you or any other disqualified person (see below) from using the assets for personal gain or engaging in transactions that put the assets at risk.

A disqualified person is someone who might reasonably have access to your SIMPLE IRA assets. In addition to you, such persons include your spouse, your lineal descendants (such as children and grandchildren) and your ancestors (such as parents and grandparents). The list also includes fiduciaries (those responsible for handling the assets of the SIMPLE IRA, such as a custodian or money manager), a person who provides services to the SIMPLE IRA (such as an administrator) and certain co-owners of your business.

The penalties for engaging in a prohibited transaction are severe. If you, as the SIMPLE IRA owner, or your beneficiary engages in a prohibited transaction, the SIMPLE IRA is disqualified and all of the assets are deemed distributed as of the first day of the year in which the prohibited transaction took place. You will have to pay income tax on the entire account, which might be pretty expensive if the distribution throws you into a higher tax bracket. And if you are not yet 59½, you will have to pay a 10% early distribution penalty, as well.

If a disqualified person (other than you or your beneficiary) engages in the prohibited transaction, the penalty is generally 15% of the transaction. If the transaction is not corrected, an additional tax of 100% is imposed. That's a total of 115%! But the tax is assessed on the disqualified person, not on you.

The following are the transactions to avoid. Note that they are all transactions that occur inside your SIMPLE IRA or with the use of SIMPLE IRA assets.

- The sale, exchange or lease of any property between a disqualified person and the SIMPLE IRA. For example, you cannot sell your house to your SIMPLE IRA.

- The furnishing of goods or services or facilities between a disqualified person and the SIMPLE IRA. For example, you cannot hire your spouse to manage the SIMPLE IRA, paying him a big salary out of the SIMPLE IRA assets.

- The lending of money or extending of credit between a disqualified person and the SIMPLE IRA. For example, you cannot borrow from the SIMPLE IRA to buy a car, even if you intend to return the money. If you want to use your SIMPLE IRA assets to buy that car, you must withdraw the money permanently and hope you can find an exception to the

early distribution penalty (if you are younger than age 59½).

- The transfer to or use by a disqualified person of any assets or income of the SIMPLE IRA. For example, you cannot use SIMPLE IRA funds to invest in a house (held by the SIMPLE IRA) which you then occupy as your principal residence. Again, if you want to use the funds to buy yourself a house, you must withdraw the funds permanently and pay income tax on the distribution. Hopefully, you'll be able to use the $10,000 first-home exception to reduce any early distribution penalty that might apply. (See Section E.3, above, for an explanation of the first-home exception.)

- Any act of self-dealing, which occurs when a disqualified person uses the assets or income of the SIMPLE IRA for that person's own interest or account while the assets are still in the SIMPLE IRA. For example, if your money manager invests all of your SIMPLE IRA assets in the stock of a company of which she owns 80%, such an investment would clearly benefit her as a majority shareholder and, therefore, might be deemed a prohibited transaction.

- The receipt of payment by a fiduciary in connection with a transaction involving the income or assets of the plan. A kickback, for example.

If you engage in a prohibited transaction, you must file Form 5329 with the IRS. Furthermore, your SIMPLE IRA will be disqualified from the moment of the transgression. All of the assets must be distributed and any income must be reported on your tax return, along with any early distribution penalty that applies.

If another disqualified person engages in the prohibited transaction, he or she must complete IRS Form 5330 and pay the 15% penalty. You can find a sample copy of Form 5330 in the Appendix to this book.

4. Life Insurance

You are not permitted to use assets in your SIMPLE IRA to invest in (purchase) a life insurance policy that you hold inside the SIMPLE IRA. If you do, the SIMPLE IRA becomes disqualified as of the first day of the year during which you made the purchase. That means you must pay income tax and possibly an early distribution penalty on the entire balance in your SIMPLE IRA, not just the portion invested in life insurance. Although purchasing life insurance isn't defined as a prohibited transaction in the Tax Code, it is treated as such if the purchase is made with assets that are currently inside a SIMPLE IRA.

5. Collectibles

You cannot invest your SIMPLE IRA in collectibles. The Tax Code carefully lists all those items that are considered collectibles, followed, of course, by a list of exceptions.

Collectibles include the following:
- works of art
- rugs or antiques
- metals or gems
- stamps or coins, and
- alcoholic beverages.

Exceptions include the following:
- certain U.S. minted gold, silver and platinum coins
- coins issued under the laws of any state, and
- gold silver, platinum or palladium bullion equal to or exceeding the minimum fineness required by a contract market for metals delivered in satisfaction of a regulated futures contract (and only if the bullion is in the physical possession of the IRA custodian). Don't you wonder what this means and who thought it up?

If you invest your SIMPLE IRA assets in unacceptable collectibles, you are deemed to have made a distribution in an amount equal to the cost of the collectible. The transaction does not disqualify the SIMPLE IRA, however. Instead, even if you don't withdraw the collectible from your account, you will owe income tax on the cost of it and you must report an early distribution penalty on Form 5329 as though you did withdraw it—unless you qualify for an exception. Meanwhile you can keep the collectible in your SIMPLE IRA if you like. When it is ultimately distributed, the amount of the deemed distribution—the portion on which you already paid tax and penalties—will not be included in your income.

> EXAMPLE: Last year, you purchased an antique Persian rug with $5,000 of your SIMPLE IRA funds. This year your accountant told you it was a prohibited transaction. You must pay income tax on $5,000, even though the SIMPLE IRA continues to hold title to the rug. You must also pay a 10% early distribution penalty of $500 ($5,000 x 10%) because you are younger than 59½—even though you did not actually take a distribution. Some years later you distribute the rug from the SIMPLE IRA. At the time of the distribution the fair market value of the rug is $20,000. You must pay income tax (and perhaps an early distribution penalty) on $15,000 (which is $20,000 reduced by the $5,000 on which you have already paid taxes).

6. Pledging the Account As Security

If any portion of your SIMPLE IRA is used as security for a loan to you (for example, you borrow money using your SIMPLE IRA as collateral), that portion is treated as a distribution subject to income tax and an early distribution penalty, unless you qualify for an exception. You report the distribution on your tax return and include Form 5329 if you owe an early distribution penalty. However, the rest of the SIMPLE IRA will not be disqualified. This is different from actually borrowing the funds from the SIMPLE IRA. If you do that, the SIMPLE IRA is disqualified. (See Section E.1.a, above.)

7. Mandatory Distribution Penalty

In the year you turn age 70½, you must begin taking money out of your retirement plan. These are called mandatory distributions. If you fail to take them, you will pay a penalty of 50% of the amount that you should have taken out but didn't.

For example, if you were required to take $10,000 out of your SIMPLE IRA for the year you turned 70½ but you forgot, you will owe a penalty of $5,000 ($10,000 x 50%).

Report this penalty on IRS Form 5329. You can find a sample copy of this form in the Appendix.

G. Terminating Your SIMPLE IRA

Recall that you are not required to make a contribution to your SIMPLE IRA each year. Consequently, you don't have to terminate your SIMPLE IRA just because you cannot afford to contribute one year.

But let's say you know you will never make another contribution. Perhaps you have retired or sold your business and you don't plan to maintain the SIMPLE IRA anymore. Termination is easy. You simply stop making contributions. After two years from the date you first established your SIMPLE IRA, you can roll it over to a traditional IRA (if you want to consolidate accounts, for example). If you have maintained the SIMPLE IRA in your business for at least two years already, you can roll it over to a traditional IRA right away. And if you terminate your business and let your SIMPLE IRA assets just sit for two years, after the two-year period, your SIMPLE IRA account is treated as a traditional IRA.

 Although you are permitted to roll over or transfer one SIMPLE IRA to another SIMPLE IRA at any time, you may not roll over or transfer the SIMPLE IRA to a traditional IRA until two years from the date of your first contribution to a SIMPLE IRA. If you transfer or roll over a SIMPLE IRA to a traditional IRA within the two-year period, the transaction is deemed a distribution from the SIMPLE IRA and a contribution to the traditional IRA. You will owe income tax on the SIMPLE IRA distribution. Furthermore, if you were not permitted to make a traditional IRA contribution in the amount rolled over, then you will have made an excess contribution to the traditional IRA.

H. Multiple Employer Plans

SIMPLE IRAs are attractive in many respects, but the prohibition against maintaining another employer plan for yourself at the same time is a big drawback. It means no Keogh and no SEP, and therefore no opportunity to boost your contributions.

There is some relief from this rule, however. First, the rule is applied on a per-employer basis. In other words, if you have your own business and you also work for a corporation, you have two employers (yourself and the corporation), not one. That means you could have a SIMPLE IRA for yourself (as one employer) and also participate in a plan sponsored by the corporation (as a second employer). This rule is known as the separate employer rule.

 If you and members of your family together own more than 50% of the corporation that employs you, then you, as the sole proprietor of your own business (or as a partner in a partnership) might not be considered a separate employer. If not, then you would not be able to establish a SIMPLE IRA for your business if the corporation already has a retirement plan in place.

Second, the rule against establishing another plan while you have a SIMPLE IRA does not preclude you from establishing a traditional or Roth IRA, because those plans are for individuals, not for businesses. (See Section I, below, for more information about adding an individual IRA to your SIMPLE IRA.)

The remainder of this Section H examines various employment scenarios and explains more fully the separate employer rule described above. This discussion should help you determine if you can establish a SIMPLE IRA.

1. If You Are Self-Employed With a Day Job on the Side, or Vice Versa

Because of the separate employer rule described above, if you are covered by an employer's plan (at your day job, for example), you can still establish a SIMPLE IRA for your own business and take a tax deduction to offset some of your self-employment profit.

 As a rule, contribution limits are applied on a per-employer basis. However, salary reduction plans, such as SIMPLE IRAs and 401(k)s, are an exception to that rule. If two or more of your employers (including yourself, if you are self-employed) have salary reduction plans, your contribution to all such plans will be limited, as though you had only one such plan. You and your corporate employer can both still have SIMPLE IRAs. Or you could have a SIMPLE IRA while your employer has a 401(k). However, the total amount that can be contributed to both plans combined will be limited. (See Section C.2, above, for more about salary reduction plan limits.)

2. If You Are Self-Employed and Own Only One Business

If you are self-employed and you have no other employer and no other business, you may establish a SIMPLE IRA only if you have no other retirement plan for your business. Generally, you are deemed to have no other plan if you make no contribution to another plan.

Because of this rule, if your business grows to the point where you would like to make a larger contribution than the SIMPLE IRA allows, you would have to discontinue contributions to the SIMPLE IRA and establish another type of plan.

 If your business is a partnership, a SIMPLE IRA might be your best choice if one partner wants to make contributions and the other does not. Although other retirement plans generally require that all participants contribute the same percentage of compensation, a SIMPLE IRA allows each participant to designate an amount or percentage of compensation deferred into the plan. Thus one partner could designate zero while another could contribute the maximum.

3. If You Are Self-Employed and Own Two or More Businesses

Suppose you have two different businesses. Can you establish a SIMPLE IRA for one and a different plan for the other? Maybe. Maybe not. If your businesses are considered two separate employers, then, yes, you can have a SIMPLE IRA for one and another employer plan (or another SIMPLE IRA) for the other. If, however, the businesses are under something called common control, then the businesses are considered to be the same employer, and if you have a SIMPLE IRA for one, then that's it. The definition of common control can be tricky. The following discussion should help you understand how it works.

a. If You Have Two Sole Proprietorships

The concept of common control is straightforward if you have two sole proprietorships. By definition, you own 100% of both businesses and the businesses are under common control because they have the same employer (you). Consequently, if you establish a Keogh or SEP for one sole proprietorship, you cannot establish a SIMPLE IRA for the other, because you already have a plan in place.

b. If You Have a Sole Proprietorship and Partnership; or Two Partnerships

If you are a sole proprietor and you also have an interest in a partnership, the common control picture changes. You are the employer of your sole proprietorship, but the partnership, not the individual partners, is the employer in a partnership. In general, that means each business must set up its own plan.

But here's where the issue of common control comes in. A sole proprietorship and a partnership are under common control if the sole proprietor has more than a 50% interest in the capital (the assets) or the profits of the partnership. In that case, the businesses are combined for purposes of determining SIMPLE IRA eligibility.

> EXAMPLE: You are the sole proprietor of a Web design business that produced a profit of $40,000 in 2001. You established a money purchase pension plan for that business when you first started in 1998. In 2001, you and a partner started a house painting business. By agreement, you have an 80% interest in the profits of the business. Your share of the profits in 2001 was $35,000. Because your interest in the profits of the partnership exceeds 50% and you also own 100% of the Web design business, your partnership and your sole proprietorship are under common control. And because you al-

ready have a money purchase pension plan for the Web design business, you cannot establish a SIMPLE IRA for the house painting business.

If you have precisely a 50% interest in both the capital and the profits of the partnership, or if your interest in each is less than or equal to 50%, then the partnership and sole proprietorship are different employers for plan sponsorship purposes. Then, in the example above, you could set up a SIMPLE IRA for the house painting business.

If you are involved in two partnerships, the same principles apply. Those partnerships in which your interest in either the capital or the profits is greater than 50% must be combined and treated as one for purposes of determining SIMPLE IRA eligibility.

 If you own interests in several partnerships that provide services to one another, or if you and other individuals have an interest in the same partnerships, the partnerships might be under common control. If you think this situation might apply to you, talk to a plan consultant to help you sort out this complicated common-control issue.

I. Adding a Traditional or Roth IRA to Your SIMPLE IRA

Having a SIMPLE IRA does not preclude you from establishing a traditional or Roth IRA, because traditional IRAs and Roth IRAs are not employer plans.

However, contributing to a SIMPLE IRA might limit the deductibility of your traditional IRA contribution. (Roth IRA contributions are never deductible.)

When you are covered by your own SIMPLE IRA (or SEP or Keogh, for that matter), or when you are covered by a plan of another employer, any traditional IRA contribution you make is fully deductible only if the adjusted gross income (with certain modifications) on your tax return is less than $62,000 (if you are married) or $42,000 (if you are single).

For more information about traditional IRAs, including how to compute deductible and nondeductible contributions, see Chapter 8. For more information about Roth IRAs, see Chapter 9.

J. Filling Out the Forms

Let's assume you have decided that a SIMPLE IRA is the right plan for you. It's time to do the paperwork. These are the steps you will take to establish the plan.

Step 1:

Identify the bank, brokerage firm or other financial institution you want to hold your SIMPLE IRA assets.

Step 2:

Call the financial institution and tell the person who answers the phone that you would like to establish a SIMPLE IRA. Ask him or her to mail the appropriate documents to you.

Step 3:

You will receive a thick package in the mail. Buried in that pile of papers are three documents you will need to complete:

- IRS Form 5305-SIMPLE, which is the document that states the terms of the plan.

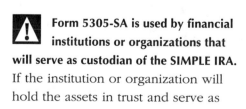 **You might also receive Form 5304-SIMPLE,** but if you have no employees, you will not use this form.

- IRS Form 5305-SA, which is the SIMPLE Individual Retirement Custodial Account Agreement. When you and a representative of the financial institution sign this document, you will have established an account to hold the assets of the plan.

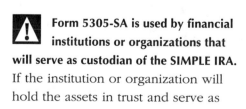 **Form 5305-SA is used by financial institutions or organizations that will serve as custodian of the SIMPLE IRA.** If the institution or organization will hold the assets in trust and serve as

trustee, the proper form is 5305-S. The forms are virtually identical except for the terms custodian and trustee.

- A SIMPLE IRA adoption agreement, in which you provide the financial institution with additional information it needs for its records, such as whom you wish to name as beneficiary of your account when you die.

Step 4:

Complete Form 5305-SIMPLE. Here's an explanation on how to complete the form. You can find a sample of Form 5305-SIMPLE at the end of this chapter.

- *Name:* If you are a sole proprietor, enter your own name (or the name you are using for your business if you are not using your own name). If your business is a partnership, enter the name of the partnership.
- *Article I, Question 1:* If you have no employees and do not anticipate hiring employees, you can check the box next to Full Eligibility, which ensures that you (and any other owner-employees) will be able to make a contribution in the current year.
- *Article I, Question 2:* You can leave this blank because you don't have employees.
- *Article II, Question 2b:* Because you have no employees, you will likely want to give yourself as much flexibility as possible, so you should enter "daily" in the blank. If you leave

it blank, 2a automatically will apply and you will have only a 60-day window each year to make changes.

- *Article II, Question 2d:* Because you do not want to restrict your participation in any way, leave this blank.
- *Article III, Question 2bi:* As described in Section C of this chapter, you must choose either a matching or a nonelective contribution to augment your salary reduction contribution. In order to preserve the option to contribute the maximum allowed by law, you should choose a matching contribution. You do this by leaving Question 2b blank. (See Section C, above, for more information about computing contributions.)
- *Article VII:* Fill in the effective date of the plan. You cannot have an effective date that is before the date you adopt the plan. (See Section B.3, above.)

Step 5:

Complete Form 5305-SA to set up the account with your financial institution as custodian. You can find a sample form at the end of this chapter. When you look at it, you will notice that there are two boxes in the upper right-hand corner of the form, underneath the blanks for your Social Security number. If you are establishing a new SIMPLE IRA, don't worry about those boxes. Leave both of them blank.

However, if you are moving money from another SIMPLE IRA, check the transfer box (which is the top of the two boxes).

If you are using this form to amend a SIMPLE IRA that you have already established, check the amendment box (which is the bottom of the two boxes).

Finally, sign and date the form. Don't worry about having your signature witnessed unless the custodian asks you to.

Step 6:

Complete the Adoption Agreement. Most adoption agreements are fairly straightforward and ask for such things as your name, address and beneficiary. (See below for more information about naming a beneficiary.) Some will also ask how you want to invest your funds.

Step 7:

Send the completed Form 5305-SIMPLE, Form 5305-SA and the Adoption Agreement to the financial institution. You do not need to send anything to the IRS. If you have already computed your contribution for the year (see Section C, above), you can send it in, too, along with any setup fee required by the financial institution. If you don't know how much your contribution will be, you can send in the minimum amount required by the financial institution to open the account and deposit the rest later.

The financial institution will sign Form 5305-SIMPLE and return it to you.

Naming a Beneficiary

When you name a beneficiary of your SIMPLE IRA, you are identifying the person or organization you want to receive your SIMPLE IRA assets when you die. That's important, certainly. But the person or organization you name as beneficiary can be crucial for other reasons, as well. For example, your choice of beneficiary will determine how quickly you must take distributions from the SIMPLE IRA after you reach age 70½ (see Section E.4, above)—and how quickly the SIMPLE IRA must be liquidated after your death.

If you are married and you name your spouse as beneficiary, he or she will have options that other beneficiaries do not have. Your spouse can roll over your SIMPLE IRA into an IRA in his or her own name, pick new beneficiaries and, in most cases, prolong or delay distributions. (Remember, when you delay distributions from an IRA, the assets can continue to grow tax-deferred—a big benefit!)

On the other hand, if you want to make a sizable donation to charity when you die, your SIMPLE IRA assets might well be a good source of that donation, because charities will not have to pay income tax on the distributions. Unfortunately when you name a charity as beneficiary, you generally must distribute assets from the plan more quickly during your lifetime than you would if you named a person as beneficiary.

And it is almost never right to simply name your "estate" as beneficiary. Doing so could present your heirs with income tax problems and perhaps increase probate fees, as well.

For most married individuals, naming a spouse as beneficiary is the best option. But if you are single or if your situation is unusual, choosing a beneficiary can be quite complex and you might want to seek help from a knowledgeable accountant or lawyer.

For more information about the effect of your beneficiary designation on your retirement plan, see *IRAs, 401(k)s & Other Retirement Plans: Taking Your Money Out*, by Twila Slesnick and John Suttle (Nolo).

Form **5305-SIMPLE**	Savings Incentive Match Plan for	OMB No. 1545-1502
(Rev. January 2000)	Employees of Small Employers (SIMPLE)	**DO NOT File with**
Department of the Treasury Internal Revenue Service	(for Use With a Designated Financial Institution)	**the Internal** **Revenue Service**

_____ establishes the following SIMPLE

IRA plan under section 408(p) of the Internal Revenue Code and pursuant to the instructions contained in this form.

Article I—Employee Eligibility Requirements (*Complete appropriate box(es) and blanks- see instructions.*)

1   General Eligibility Requirements. The Employer agrees to permit salary reduction contributions to be made in each calendar year to the SIMPLE individual retirement account or annuity established at the designated financial institution (SIMPLE IRA) for each employee who meets the following requirements *(select either **1a** or **1b**)*:

a   ☐ **Full Eligibility.** All employees are eligible.

b   ☐ **Limited Eligibility.** Eligibility is limited to employees who are described in both **(i)** and **(ii)** below:

    (i) Current compensation. Employees who are reasonably expected to receive at least $ _____ in compensation *(not to exceed $5,000)* for the calendar year.

    (ii) Prior compensation. Employees who have received at least $ _____ in compensation *(not to exceed $5,000)* during any _____ calendar year(s) *(insert 0, 1, or 2)* preceding the calendar year.

2   Excludable Employees

    ☐ The Employer elects to exclude employees covered under a collective bargaining agreement for which retirement benefits were the subject of good faith bargaining. **Note:** *This box is deemed checked if the Employer maintains a qualified plan covering only such employees.*

Article II—Salary Reduction Agreements (*Complete the box and blank, if appropriate- see instructions.*)

1   Salary Reduction Election. An eligible employee may make a salary reduction election to have his or her compensation for each pay period reduced by a percentage. The total amount of the reduction in the employee's compensation cannot exceed $6,000* for any calendar year.

2   Timing of Salary Reduction Elections

a   For a calendar year, an eligible employee may make or modify a salary reduction election during the 60-day period immediately preceding January 1 of that year. However, for the year in which the employee becomes eligible to make salary reduction contributions, the period during which the employee may make or modify the election is a 60-day period that includes either the date the employee becomes eligible or the day before.

b   In addition to the election periods in **2a,** eligible employees may make salary reduction elections or modify prior elections _____
_____ . *(If the Employer chooses this option, insert a period or periods (e.g. semi-annually, quarterly, monthly, or daily) that will apply uniformly to all eligible employees.)*

c   No salary reduction election may apply to compensation that an employee received, or had a right to immediately receive, before execution of the salary reduction election.

d   An employee may terminate a salary reduction election at any time during the calendar year. ☐ If this box is checked, an employee who terminates a salary reduction election not in accordance with **2b** may not resume salary reduction contributions during the calendar year.

Article III—Contributions (*Complete the blank, if appropriate- see instructions.*)

1   Salary Reduction Contributions. The amount by which the employee agrees to reduce his or her compensation will be contributed by the Employer to the employee's SIMPLE IRA.

2   Other Contributions

a   Matching Contributions

    (i) For each calendar year, the Employer will contribute a matching contribution to each eligible employee's SIMPLE IRA equal to the employee's salary reduction contributions up to a limit of 3% of the employee's compensation for the calendar year.

    (ii) The Employer may reduce the 3% limit for the calendar year in **(i)** only if:

        (1) The limit is not reduced below 1%; **(2)** The limit is not reduced for more than 2 calendar years during the 5-year period ending with the calendar year the reduction is effective; and **(3)** Each employee is notified of the reduced limit within a reasonable period of time before the employees' 60-day election period for the calendar year *(described in **Article II, item 2a**).*

b   Nonelective Contributions

    (i) For any calendar year, instead of making matching contributions, the Employer may make nonelective contributions equal to 2% of compensation for the calendar year to the SIMPLE IRA of each eligible employee who has at least $ _____ *(not more than $5,000)* in compensation for the calendar year. No more than $170,000* in compensation can be taken into account in determining the nonelective contribution for each eligible employee.

    (ii) For any calendar year, the Employer may make 2% nonelective contributions instead of matching contributions only if:

        (1) Each eligible employee is notified that a 2% nonelective contribution will be made instead of a matching contribution; and

        (2) This notification is provided within a reasonable period of time before the employees' 60-day election period for the calendar year *(described in **Article II, item 2a**).*

3   Time and Manner of Contributions

a   The Employer will make the salary reduction contributions (described in **1** above) to the designated financial institution for the IRAs established under this SIMPLE IRA plan no later than 30 days after the end of the month in which the money is withheld from the employee's pay. See instructions.

b   The Employer will make the matching or nonelective contributions (described in **2a** and **2b** above) to the designated financial institution for the IRAs established under this SIMPLE IRA plan no later than the due date for filing the Employer's tax return, including extensions, for the taxable year that includes the last day of the calendar year for which the contributions are made.

*This amount reflects the cost-of-living increase effective January 1, 2000. The amount is adjusted annually. The IRS announces the increase, if any, in a news release, in the Internal Revenue Bulletin, and on the IRS's Internet Web Site at **www.irs.gov**.*

For Paperwork Reduction Act Notice, see page 6.   Cat. No. 23063F   Form **5305-SIMPLE** (Rev. 1-2000)

Form 5305-SIMPLE (Rev. 1-2000)   Page **2**

Article IV—Other Requirements and Provisions

1 **Contributions in General.** The Employer will make no contributions to the SIMPLE IRAs other than salary reduction contributions (described in **Article III, item 1**) and matching or nonelective contributions (described in **Article III, items 2a and 2b**).

2 **Vesting Requirements.** All contributions made under this SIMPLE IRA plan are fully vested and nonforfeitable.

3 **No Withdrawal Restrictions.** The Employer may not require the employee to retain any portion of the contributions in his or her SIMPLE IRA or otherwise impose any withdrawal restrictions.

4 **No Cost Or Penalty For Transfers.** The Employer will not impose any cost or penalty on a participant for the transfer of the participant's SIMPLE IRA balance to another IRA.

5 **Amendments To This SIMPLE IRA Plan.** This SIMPLE IRA plan may not be amended except to modify the entries inserted in the blanks or boxes provided in **Articles I, II, III, VI, and VII.**

6 **Effects Of Withdrawals and Rollovers**

a An amount withdrawn from the SIMPLE IRA is generally includible in gross income. However, a SIMPLE IRA balance may be rolled over or transferred on a tax-free basis to another IRA designed solely to hold funds under a SIMPLE IRA plan. In addition, an individual may roll over or transfer his or her SIMPLE IRA balance to any IRA after a 2-year period has expired since the individual first participated in any SIMPLE IRA plan of the Employer. Any rollover or transfer must comply with the requirements under section 408.

b If an individual withdraws an amount from a SIMPLE IRA during the 2-year period beginning when the individual first participated in any SIMPLE IRA plan of the Employer and the amount is subject to the additional tax on early distributions under section 72(t), this additional tax is increased from 10% to 25%.

Article V—Definitions

1 **Compensation**

a **General Definition of Compensation.** Compensation means the sum of the wages, tips, and other compensation from the Employer subject to federal income tax withholding (as described in section 6051(a)(3)) and the employee's salary reduction contributions made under this plan, and, if applicable, elective deferrals under a section 401(k) plan, a SARSEP, or a section 403(b) annuity contract and compensation deferred under a section 457 plan required to be reported by the Employer on Form W-2 (as described in section 6058(a)(8)).

b **Compensation for Self-Employed Individuals.** For self-employed individuals, compensation means the net earnings from self-employment determined under section 1402(a) prior to subtracting any contributions made pursuant to this plan on behalf of the individual.

2 **Employee.** Employee means a common-law employee of the Employer. The term employee also includes a self-employed individual and a leased employee described in section 414(n) but does not include a nonresident alien who received no earned income from the Employer that constitutes income from sources within the United States.

3 **Eligible Employee.** An eligible employee means an employee who satisfies the conditions in **Article I, item 1** and is not excluded under **Article I, item 2.**

4 **Designated Financial Institution.** A designated financial institution is a trustee, custodian, or insurance company (that issues annuity contracts) for the SIMPLE IRA plan that receives all contributions made pursuant to the SIMPLE IRA plan and deposits those contributions to the SIMPLE IRA of each eligible employee.

Article VI—Procedures for Withdrawal (*The designated financial institution will provide the instructions (to be attached or inserted in the space below) on the procedures for withdrawals of contributions by employees.*)

Article VII—Effective Date

This SIMPLE IRA plan is effective _____ .(See instructions.)

*   *   *   *   *

Name of Employer   By: Signature   Date

Address of Employer   Name and title

The undersigned agrees to serve as designated financial institution, receiving all contributions made pursuant to this SIMPLE IRA plan and depositing those contributions to the SIMPLE IRA of each eligible employee as soon as practicable. Upon the request of any participant, the undersigned also agrees to transfer the participant's balance in a SIMPLE IRA established under this SIMPLE IRA plan to another IRA without cost or penalty to the participant.

Name of designated financial institution   By: Signature   Date

Address   Name and title

Form **5305-SIMPLE** (Rev. 1-2000)

Form **5305-SA**
(Rev. January 2000)
Department of the Treasury
Internal Revenue Service

SIMPLE Individual Retirement Custodial Account
(Under section 408(p) of the Internal Revenue Code)

DO NOT File
With the
Internal
Revenue Service

Name of participant	Date of birth of participant	Social security number

Address of participant	Check if transfer SIMPLE IRA . ▶ ☐ Check if amendment . . . . . ▶ ☐

Name of custodian	Address or principal place of business of custodian

The participant whose name appears above is establishing a savings incentive match plan for employees of small employers individual retirement account (SIMPLE IRA) under sections 408(a) and 408(p) to provide for his or her retirement and for the support of his or her beneficiaries after death.

The custodian named above has given the participant the disclosure statement required under Regulations section 1.408-6.

The participant and the custodian make the following agreement:

Article I

The custodian will accept cash contributions made on behalf of the participant by the participant's employer under the terms of a SIMPLE IRA plan described in section 408(p). In addition, the custodian will accept transfers or rollovers from other SIMPLE IRAs of the participant. No other contributions will be accepted by the custodian.

Article II

The participant's interest in the balance in the custodial account is nonforfeitable.

Article III

1. No part of the custodial funds may be invested in life insurance contracts, nor may the assets of the custodial account be commingled with other property except in a common trust fund or common investment fund (within the meaning of section 408(a)(5)).

2. No part of the custodial funds may be invested in collectibles (within the meaning of section 408(m)) except as otherwise permitted by section 408(m)(3), which provides an exception for certain gold, silver, and platinum coins, coins issued under the laws of any state, and certain bullion.

Article IV

1. Notwithstanding any provision of this agreement to the contrary, the distribution of the participant's interest in the custodial account shall be made in accordance with the following requirements and shall otherwise comply with section 408(a)(6) and Proposed Regulations section 1.408-8, including the incidental death benefit provisions of Proposed Regulations section 1.401(a)(9)-2, the provisions of which are incorporated by reference.

2. Unless otherwise elected by the time distributions are required to begin to the participant under paragraph 3, or to the surviving spouse under paragraph 4, other than in the case of a life annuity, life expectancies shall be recalculated annually. Such election shall be irrevocable as to the participant and the surviving spouse and shall apply to all subsequent years. The life expectancy of a nonspouse beneficiary may not be recalculated.

3. The participant's entire interest in the custodial account must be, or begin to be, distributed by the participant's required beginning date (April 1 following the calendar year end in which the participant reaches age 70½). By that date, the participant may elect, in a manner acceptable to the custodian, to have the balance in the custodial account distributed in:

(a) A single sum payment.

(b) An annuity contract that provides equal or substantially equal monthly, quarterly, or annual payments over the life of the participant.

(c) An annuity contract that provides equal or substantially equal monthly, quarterly, or annual payments over the joint and last survivor lives of the participant and his or her designated beneficiary.

(d) Equal or substantially equal annual payments over a specified period that may not be longer than the participant's life expectancy.

(e) Equal or substantially equal annual payments over a specified period that may not be longer than the joint life and last survivor expectancy of the participant and his or her designated beneficiary.

4. If the participant dies before his or her entire interest is distributed to him or her, the entire remaining interest will be distributed as follows:

(a) If the participant dies on or after distribution of his or her interest has begun, distribution must continue to be made in accordance with paragraph 3.

(b) If the participant dies before distribution of his or her interest has begun, the entire remaining interest will, at the election of the participant or, if the participant has not so elected, at the election of the beneficiary or beneficiaries, either

(i) Be distributed by the December 31 of the year containing the fifth anniversary of the participant's death, or

(ii) Be distributed in equal or substantially equal payments over the life or life expectancy of the designated beneficiary or beneficiaries starting by December 31 of the year following the year of the participant's death. If, however, the beneficiary is the participant's surviving spouse, then this distribution is not required to begin before December 31 of the year in which the participant would have reached age 70½.

(c) Except where distribution in the form of an annuity meeting the requirements of section 408(b)(3) and its related regulations has irrevocably commenced, distributions are treated as having begun on the participant's required beginning date, even though payments may actually have been made before that date.

(d) If the participant dies before his or her entire interest has been distributed and if the beneficiary is other than the surviving spouse, no additional cash contributions or rollover contributions may be accepted in the account.

Cat. No. 23698C   Form **5305-SA** (Rev. 1-2000)

Form 5305-SA (Rev. 1-2000)   Page **2**

5. In the case of a distribution over life expectancy in equal or substantially equal annual payments, to determine the minimum annual payment for each year, divide the participant's entire interest in the custodial account as of the close of business on December 31 of the preceding year by the life expectancy of the participant (or the joint life and last survivor expectancy of the participant and the participant's designated beneficiary, or the life expectancy of the designated beneficiary, whichever applies). In the case of distributions under paragraph 3, determine the initial life expectancy (or joint life and last survivor expectancy) using the attained ages of the participant and designated beneficiary as of their birthdays in the year the participant reaches age 70½. In the case of a distribution in accordance with paragraph 4(b)(ii), determine life expectancy using the attained age of the designated beneficiary as of the beneficiary's birthday in the year distributions are required to commence.

6. The owner of two or more individual retirement accounts may use the "alternative method" described in Notice 88-38, 1988-1 C.B. 524, to satisfy the minimum distribution requirements described above. This method permits an individual to satisfy these requirements by taking from one individual retirement account the amount required to satisfy the requirement for another.

Article V

1. The participant agrees to provide the custodian with information necessary for the custodian to prepare any reports required under sections 408(i) and 408(l)(2) and Regulations sections 1.408-5 and 1.408-6.

2. The custodian agrees to submit reports to the Internal Revenue Service and the participant as prescribed by the Internal Revenue Service.

3. The custodian also agrees to provide the participant's employer the summary description described in section 408(l)(2) unless this SIMPLE IRA is a transfer SIMPLE IRA.

Article VI

Notwithstanding any other articles which may be added or incorporated, the provisions of Articles I through III and this sentence will be controlling. Any additional articles that are not consistent with sections 408(a) and 408(p) and the related regulations will be invalid.

Article VII

This agreement will be amended from time to time to comply with the provisions of the Code and related regulations. Other amendments may be made with the consent of the persons whose signatures appear below.

Note: *The following space (Article VIII) may be used for any other provisions the participant and custodian want to add. If no other provisions will be added, draw a line through this space. If provisions are added, they must comply with applicable requirements of state law and the Internal Revenue Code.*

Article VIII

Participant's signature .... Date ....

(If an individual other than the participant signs this form for the participant, indicate the individual's relationship to the participant.)

Custodian's signature .... Date ....

Witness' signature ....

(Use only if signature of the participant or the custodian is required to be witnessed.)

General Instructions

Section references are to the Internal Revenue Code unless otherwise noted.

Purpose of Form

Note: *Users of the December 1996 version of Form 5305-SA or of subsequent revisions are not required to use the January 2000 revision of this form.*

Form 5305-SA is a model custodial account agreement that meets the requirements of sections 408(a) and 408(p) and has been automatically approved by the IRS. A SIMPLE individual retirement account (SIMPLE IRA) is established after the form is fully executed by both the individual (participant) and the custodian. This account must be created in the United States for the exclusive benefit of the participant or his or her beneficiaries.

Do not file Form 5305-SA with the IRS. Instead, keep it for record purposes.

For more information on Simple IRAs, including the required disclosures the custodian must give the participant, see **Pub. 590,** Individual Retirement Arrangements (IRAs) (including Roth IRAs and Education IRAs).

Definitions

Participant. The participant is the person who establishes the custodial account.

Custodian. The custodian must be a bank or savings and loan association, as defined in section 408(n), or any person who has the approval of the IRS to act as custodian.

Transfer SIMPLE IRA

This SIMPLE IRA is a "transfer SIMPLE IRA" if it is not the original recipient of contributions under any SIMPLE IRA plan. The summary description requirements of section 408(l)(2) do not apply to transfer SIMPLE IRAs.

Specific Instructions

Article IV. Distributions made under this article may be made in a single sum, periodic payment, or a combination of both. The distribution option should be reviewed in the year the participant reaches age 70½ to ensure that the requirements of section 408(a)(6) have been met.

Article VIII. Article VIII and any that follow it may incorporate additional provisions that are agreed to by the participant and custodian to complete the agreement. They may include, for example, definitions, investment powers, voting rights, exculpatory provisions, amendment and termination, removal of the custodian, custodian's fees, state law requirements, beginning date of distributions, accepting only cash, treatment of excess contributions, prohibited transactions with the participant, etc. Use additional pages if necessary and attach them to this form.

Note: *Form 5305-SA may be reproduced and reduced in size.*

Chapter 4

SEPs

A. **What Is a SEP?** **4/3**

   1. Who May Establish a SEP? 4/4

   2. Advantages 4/5

   3. Disadvantages 4/6

B. **How to Establish a SEP** **4/6**

   1. Trustee or Custodian 4/6

   2. Plan Documents 4/6

   3. Deadlines 4/7

   4. Plan Year 4/7

C. **Contributions** **4/8**

   1. Maximum Contribution 4/8

   2. No Minimum Contribution 4/10

   3. Cash Only 4/10

   4. Deadlines 4/10

   5. How to Claim the Tax Deduction 4/12

D. **Ongoing Administration** **4/12**

   1. Tax Returns 4/12

   2. Plan Administration 4/12

   3. Updating Plan Documents 4/12

E. **Distributions** **4/13**

　　1. Inservice Distributions: Comparing SEPs and Qualified Plans 4/13

　　2. Divorce Payments 4/14

　　3. Early Distributions and Exceptions to the Early Distribution Penalty 4/15

　　4. Mandatory Distributions 4/18

F. **Penalties** **4/18**

　　1. Excess Contributions 4/19

　　2. Early Distributions 4/23

　　3. Prohibited Transactions 4/23

　　4. Life Insurance 4/25

　　5. Collectibles 4/25

　　6. Pledging the Account As Security 4/26

　　7. Mandatory Distribution Penalty 4/26

G. **Terminating Your SEP** **4/27**

H. **Multiple Employer Plans** **4/27**

　　1. If You Are Self-Employed
　　　 With a Day Job on the Side,
　　　 or Vice Versa 4/28

　　2. If You Are Self-Employed With Only One Business 4/28

　　3. If You Are Self-Employed With Two or More Businesses 4/30

I. **Adding a Traditional or Roth IRA to Your SEP** **4/32**

J. **Filling Out the Forms** **4/33**

　　1. Prototype SEP 4/33

　　2. IRS Form 5305-SEP 4/34

　　3. Beneficiary Designation 4/35

*S*implified employee pensions, or SEPs, are to Keoghs as TV dinners are to home-cooked meals: They are more convenient and simple than Keoghs, but they don't offer quite the same amount of substance. Still, they might be just what you are looking for.

Before SEPs were introduced in 1978, a self-employed individual could choose only a traditional IRA or Keogh. An IRA was convenient but had a deductible contribution limit of only $1,500. (That limit has since increased to $2,000.) A Keogh provided more tax benefits and greater savings, but the reporting requirements and ongoing administrative burdens were intimidating. SEPs offered something in between.

To this day, SEPs are the plan of choice for many who are self-employed. If you are a sole proprietor or a partner in a partnership and have no employees, the rules for establishing and maintaining a SEP are almost as simple as those for a traditional IRA.

Employees muddy the waters, as employees are wont to do. If you ever decide to add employees to your SEP, your employees will be protected by a set of rules meant to keep you from discriminating against them in the amount of contributions you make to a retirement plan. (Not that you ever would, of course.) But a SEP accommodates the addition of employees with less fuss than does a Keogh.

The Ideal Candidate for This Plan

A SEP works well for anyone who didn't manage to meet the deadline for establishing either a SIMPLE IRA or a Keogh. A SEP is the only employer plan you can establish after the end of your tax year. A SEP is also a good choice for you if the simplicity of establishing and maintaining the plan is more important to you than the size of the contributions you can make.

★ ★ ★ ★ ★ ★ ★ ★ ★ ★ ★ ★ ★ ★ ★

A. What Is a SEP?

Although a SEP is technically an IRA, it doesn't look much like one. Here's why:

- Only individuals can establish traditional IRAs; only employers can establish SEPs. In other words, you must have a business to set up a SEP.
- You are prohibited from contributing and deducting more than $2,000 a year to a traditional IRA. The maximum deductible contribution you can make to a SEP is currently $25,500.
- If you contribute to both a traditional IRA and a SEP, the law treats a SEP like a qualified plan for determining whether your traditional IRA contribution is deductible. When you are covered by a qualified plan, your

This Plan in a Nutshell

✓ You must make a profit to contribute to a SEP.

✓ If you make a profit, contributions to a SEP are completely discretionary. You can contribute the maximum the law allows, or you can contribute less (whatever amount you choose) or you can contribute nothing at all.

✓ If the net income from your business exceeds $50,000, you will be able to contribute more to a SEP than to a SIMPLE IRA. If your income is less than $50,000, then a SIMPLE will allow for higher contributions.

✓ You can always contribute more to a money purchase pension plan than to a SEP, but money purchase pension plans are less flexible.

✓ Once your net income exceeds $30,000 you might consider establishing a SEP along with a money purchase pension plan to combine flexibility (SEP) with higher contribution limits (money purchase pension plan).

✓ You can set up a SEP and make your contribution after the end of the year for which you want to make a contribution.

✓ Generally, you have no ongoing filing requirements for a SEP—no tax returns to file and no approval letters to seek from the IRS.

---

contribution to a traditional IRA is not deductible if your income exceeds a certain threshold. (See Section I, below, for more information about combining a traditional IRA with a SEP. See Chapter 8 for a discussion of traditional IRAs.)

• If you have established or are considering establishing more than one type of plan for your business, the law will treat a SEP like a profit sharing plan when applying contribution limits for multiple plans. (See Section H, below, for more about the multiple plan rules. See Chapter 5 for information about profit sharing plans.)

1. Who May Establish a SEP?

Generally, if you own your own business and are making a profit, you may establish a SEP. You must have net earnings from the business, because your SEP contribution is based on a percentage of those earnings.

If you slave under the thumb of a big corporate employer by day, but by night you run your own business—perhaps painting (and selling) portraits of the rich and soon-to-be famous—you can set up a SEP for your painting business regardless of what plan your employer provides. That's because the Tax Code applies contribution limits separately to each employer. This is called the separate employer rule.

But if you already own one business and then start a second, you might not be able to contribute to a separate plan for each business. (See Section H, below, for more information about the separate employer rule and about multiple plans.)

2. Advantages

In Chapter 2 you can find a detailed comparison of the different types of retirement plans you can establish—both for your business and for yourself as an individual. In the next two sections, we summarize some of the advantages and disadvantages of SEPs when compared to other employer plans.

First, the advantages:

- You can set up a SEP and make your contribution after the end of the year for which you want to make a contribution. In fact, you have until the due date for filing your tax return. And if you apply for and receive an extension of time for filing your tax return, the deadline for setting up the SEP is the extended due date of the tax return. In contrast, Keogh plans must be set up before the end of the year.
- You can forgo making a contribution to a SEP in any year for any reason. Or you can simply reduce the contribution to a manageable level.
- Setting up a SEP is generally much less complicated than setting up a Keogh plan.
- Generally, you have no ongoing filing requirements for a SEP—no tax returns to file and no approval letters to seek from the IRS.
- If the net income from your business exceeds about $50,000, you will be able to contribute more to a SEP than to a SIMPLE IRA. (See Section C, below, for more information about computing contributions.)

 If you eventually add employees to your SEP, you will be able to delay making SEP contributions on their behalf until they have worked for you for three years, which is a longer delay than would be permitted under the terms of a Keogh. This feature might be attractive if money is tight.

3. Disadvantages

SEPs have many attractive features, but they also have some drawbacks:

- You can always contribute more to a money purchase pension plan than to a SEP.
- You can often contribute more to a defined benefit plan than to a SEP.
- If your net income is less than about $50,000, a SIMPLE IRA will permit a larger contribution. (See Section C, below, for more information about contributions.)

 If you ever decide to add employees to your SEP, you'll encounter some additional disadvantages. For example, employees who are participating in your SEP must be immediately 100% vested in the contributions you make to the SEP on their behalf. That means employees can withdraw their funds at any time (although penalties might apply) and take their accounts with them when they leave. This is an important consideration if you want to use a retirement plan as an incentive to keep good employees around.

Also, it is more difficult to exclude employees from a SEP than from other types of plans. For example, if you employ many part-time employees you might have to make contributions on their behalf under the terms of a SEP (which could be costly), whereas you might be able to exclude them under the terms of a Keogh.

B. How to Establish a SEP

A SEP must be established by an employer. So, if you have a sole proprietorship, you would set up the SEP in your name as the employer (or in the name you are using for your business). If you are doing business as a partnership, however, the partnership—and not you—must establish the SEP, because the partnership is the employer.

1. Trustee or Custodian

Your SEP must be funded through a trust or custodial account, which means the money you contribute must be held by a trustee or custodian. You will usually use a custodian because it's most convenient to do so. Most banks, credit unions, brokerage firms and mutual funds will serve as custodian of a SEP. You can also establish a SEP with an insurance company. You cannot serve as trustee or custodian of your own SEP, however.

2. Plan Documents

As a self-employed individual with no employees, you have two practical options for establishing your SEP. You can use the SEP documents provided by the financial institution of your choice (prototype SEPs). That's the easiest. Or you can use the IRS's model SEP, Form 5305-SEP. That's also easy. Your third option is to hire a consultant to craft a customized SEP document just for you. That's less practical, and it's certainly more expensive. But most important, it's generally not necessary unless you plan to hire employees—and rarely necessary then, either.

See Section J, below, for instructions on completing the necessary forms. You can find sample copies of the forms in the Appendix.

3. Deadlines

No other retirement plan is as liberal as a SEP when it comes to deadlines. A SEP doesn't have to be established by the end of the year. You can set it up just before you file your tax return if that suits you. If your tax return is on extension, you have until the extended due date of your return to establish and contribute to the SEP.

4. Plan Year

Although most self-employed individuals maintain their SEPs (and their businesses) on a calendar year, you can maintain your SEP on either a calendar year or a fiscal year basis. The plan year determines what compensation is used for computing contributions. If you maintain your SEP on a calendar year, you would use the compensation you receive between January 1 and December 31 to compute your SEP contri-

bution. (See Section C.4, below, for information about when the contribution must be made.)

A fiscal year is generally any 12-month period that ends on the last day of any month except December. You can use a fiscal year for your SEP only if the tax year for your business is a fiscal year. But oddly enough, you can run your business on a fiscal year and maintain your SEP on a calendar year. That option is not necessarily a benefit, though. If you maintain your SEP on a calendar year while the business is on a fiscal year, your SEP deduction must be taken for the tax year in which the plan year ends. This has the effect of delaying your deduction.

> **EXAMPLE:** You maintain your SEP on a calendar year basis, but your business tax year runs from July through June. Your compensation for calendar year 2001 will allow you to contribute $20,000 to your SEP. However, because your business tax year doesn't end until June 30, 2002, you cannot claim your deduction until you file your tax return after the close of your fiscal year—in the second half of 2002. If the plan year and the business year both ended June 30, 2002, you would use the compensation you received between July 1, 2001, and June 30, 2002 to compute your SEP contribution. Then you could file your tax return and claim a tax deduction immediately after the close of the tax year.

C. Contributions

When you first establish a retirement plan, it is often because your business is generating income and you are looking for a tax shelter. But businesses have good years and bad. Not only do you need to know how to compute the maximum contribution, you also need to know what your options are in lean years. What if you feel you cannot afford to contribute to your SEP one year? Can you skip the SEP contribution and use the money elsewhere? Can you contribute property instead of cash? In addition, there's more to contributions than just dollars. You need to know about the timing of your contributions, as well.

 You can only make a contribution to your SEP in years when you make a profit. That's the rule for self-employed individuals. If you have a loss from the business, you cannot contribute to your own SEP account.

 If you ever add employees to your SEP, you will have the option to contribute to their SEP accounts even if you don't make a profit, although you won't have to and you might be disinclined to do so.

1. Maximum Contribution

Generally speaking, your contribution to a SEP is limited to the lesser of 15% of your compensation or $30,000. (The $30,000 limit increases to $35,000 beginning with the 2001 tax year.) But there are two additional limits that will affect the maximum amount you are allowed to contribute.

a. Additional Limit One: Limit on Compensation

For purposes of computing the maximum contribution, your compensation is deemed to be no more than $170,000 for the year 2000. (This number might increase in future years.) That means the maximum contribution you can make to a SEP is $25,500 (15% of $170,000), even if you earn much more than $170,000 from your business.

b. Additional Limit Two: Definition of Compensation

The Tax Code defines compensation differently for self-employed individuals than for others. It is not simply your net profit, which is your business income reduced by expenditures directly related to the business. It is your net earnings from self-employment, which is your business income reduced by *all* deductible business expenses. And for a self-employed individual, deductible business expenses include your self-employment tax deduction (which is always half of your self-employment tax) and your SEP deduction itself. So, before you multiply your net profit by 15%, you must first reduce it by half of your self-employment tax and reduce it further by your SEP contribution. But the SEP contribution is what you are trying to compute! We show you how to get around this conundrum in the paragraphs that follow. The point is, if you simply multiply your profit by 15% and contribute that amount to your SEP, you will almost certainly come up with the wrong number.

 If you mistakenly use 15%, you will make an excess contribution to your SEP, and the excess will be subject to penalties unless corrected. (See Section F.1, below, for more information about excess contributions.)

c.   The Calculation

Calculating your maximum SEP contribution is a five-step process.

Step 1:
Calculate your net profit, which is your business income reduced by your business expenses (but not including your SEP contribution or your self-employment tax deduction).

Step 2:
Compute your self-employment tax deduction. The deductible portion is half of your total self-employment tax. IRS Form 1040 Schedule SE (see Example One, below) walks you through the calculation. You can find a sample copy of Schedule SE in the Appendix to this book.

Step 3:
Subtract the amount in Step 2 from the amount in Step 1.

Step 4:
Multiply the result from Step 3 by 13.0435%. (See Chapter 1, Section B.1.c.i for an explanation of why you use 13.0435% instead of 15%.)

Step 5:
Compare the result from Step 4 with the contribution limit of $25,500. Your maximum contribution is the lesser of $25,500 or Step 4.

EXAMPLE ONE: Roxie raked in $98,450 from her Web design business in the year 2000. Her expenses amounted to $26,780. She wants to contribute as much as she can to her SEP.

Step 1: Roxie's net profit is $71,670, which is $98,450 – $26,780.

Step 2: Roxie completes Schedule SE to arrive at her self-employment tax deduction of $5,064. (See Line 6 of Schedule SE in the Appendix).

Step 3: Roxie reduces her net profit by her self-employment tax deduction. $71,670 – $5,064 = $66,606 (Step 1 – Step 2).

Step 4: Finally to compute her maximum SEP contribution, she multiplies Step 3 by 13.0435%. $66,606 x 13.0435% = $8,688.

Step 5: Because that amount does not exceed $25,500, Roxie can contribute $8,688 to her SEP and take a deduction on her tax return.

EXAMPLE TWO: In 2001, Roxie's business really took off. She was paid $320,000 for her services and had expenses of $50,820.

Step 1: Roxie's net profit is $269,180, which is $320,000 – $50,820.

Step 2: Roxie completes Schedule SE and determines that her self-employment tax deduction is $7,846.

Step 3: Roxie reduces her net profit by her self-employment tax deduction. $269,180 – $7,846 = $261,334 (which is Step 1 – Step 2).

Step 4: Finally, to compute her maximum SEP contribution, she multiplies Step 3 by 13.0435%. $261,334 x 13.0435% = $34,087.

Step 5: Roxie wishes she could contribute and deduct $34,087, but her maximum SEP contribution is $25,500 (15% of $170,000). So Roxie can contribute only $25,500 and claim a $25,500 deduction on her tax return.

2. No Minimum Contribution

One of the most attractive features of a SEP is that you are not required to make a contribution every year. When you establish your SEP, you can choose to make contributions discretionary. In fact, most plan documents assume that you want contributions to be discretionary. So, if you want to use extra cash to buy new computers for your business one year instead of making a SEP contribution, you are free to do so. Or you can contribute less than the maximum—only as much as you feel you can afford.

3. Cash Only

All contributions to your SEP must be in cash. You cannot deposit that old savings bond you found at the bottom of your desk drawer last year and treat it as this year's SEP contribution. If you do contribute property other than cash, it is treated as an excess contribution—even if the value is below your contribution limit— and you could be subject to penalties. Fortunately, that little mistake won't completely disqualify the SEP, as long as you correct it by removing the property from your SEP on a timely basis. (See Section F.l, below, for a discussion of excess contributions.)

4. Deadlines

You may make your SEP contribution any time during the year. Generally, the earlier you make it, the better, because the money can be working for you. Unfortunately you don't always know how much money you will make until late in the year, or even after the end of the year. That's why the government gives you until the due date of your tax return to make the precise contribution. And if you request and receive an extension of time for filing your tax return, you have until the extended due date to make your SEP contribution. However, you could make a partial contribution early in the year and contribute the remainder when you have final income numbers.

 It is sufficient that your contribution be postmarked by the due date of your tax return. In other words, you can write a check and take it to the post office on the day your tax return is due. The money doesn't actually have to be in the account by then. Just be sure to obtain proof of mailing.

Using Your Tax Refund

Suppose you are short of cash for making your SEP contribution but you are expecting a big tax refund—enough to cover the SEP contribution. As it happens, you are not required to make your contribution before you file your tax return. But you must make it by the due date of your tax return. That means you can file your return, receive the refund, and then use the refund to make the contribution.

The only problem with this strategy is that you must file your tax return early enough so that you receive the refund before the actual filing deadline of your tax return—which is when the contribution is due. For example, if your tax return is due April 15, you would have to file your return in January, February or March and hope you receive the refund before April 15 when the SEP contribution is due.

But be careful! Suppose April 15 looms and you still have not received your refund. It won't work to request an extension at the last minute, because you have already filed your tax return. Instead you will have to find another source of funds for making the SEP contribution.

As a precaution, you might want to request an extension before you file your tax return in the first place. Then you will have until the extended due date to receive the refund and make the SEP contribution.

5. How to Claim the Tax Deduction

Once you have computed your SEP contribution, you claim your deduction on page 1, line 29, of your individual income tax return (Form 1040). This will be true whether you are doing business as a partnership or as a sole proprietor. (You can find a sample copy of Form 1040 in the Appendix.)

D. Ongoing Administration

Not only is it an easy matter to establish the SEP, but the ongoing administration is a minimalist's dream.

1. Tax Returns

Your SEP is a tax exempt entity, which is why it generally doesn't have to pay tax each year on the income it produces—and usually does not have to file a tax return.

But if your SEP engages in a business that produces more than $1,000 of income during the year, you must file a special tax return—Form 990-T—for the SEP. Income from a business inside a SEP is called unrelated business taxable income, or UBTI. Once UBTI exceeds $1,000 in a year, it is subject to tax and the tax must be paid out of the SEP assets.

Most people invest their SEP assets in stocks, bonds and other standard investments that don't generate UBTI. But suppose you invest some of the assets in a limited partnership. Many limited partnerships are in fact businesses. And when the business (the limited partnership) starts throwing off income, it will be taxable, even though it is inside your SEP.

2. Plan Administration

Because you have no employees, you have no reporting or other administrative responsibilities for your SEP. Your SEP custodian must report your SEP contribution to the IRS each year on Form 5498, but that is the custodian's responsibility, not yours.

3. Updating Plan Documents

Changes in the law might require your SEP agreement to be updated from time to time. If you are using a prototype plan provided by your financial institution, the institution will take responsibility for updating the plan.

If you want to change your SEP beneficiary, you don't have to complete an entirely new set of plan documents. Generally, you can simply request a "Change of Beneficiary Designation" form, drop in the name of the new beneficiary, sign and date the form and return it to the financial institution. (See Section J, below, for information about completing plan documents.)

E. Distributions

When you put your money somewhere, it's always a good idea to know how to get it out. But before we talk about taking money out of your SEP, let's talk about free lunches. Congress has offered us what appears to be a great deal. You can put piles of money into a retirement plan (such as a SEP), take a big tax deduction, and then forgo paying taxes on either the contribution or the investment returns for years and years. If there's no free lunch, what's the catch?

The catch is that the government wants you to use those funds for your retirement years—after you have quit working. If you tap the money early (generally before age 59½), the government will try to reclaim your tax benefits through penalties. But as you might expect, there are exceptions that will allow you early access to your money. We discuss those exceptions in Section 3, below.

First, however, we take a look in Section 1 at distributions that are permitted from qualified plans but that are not permitted from SEPs. In Section 2, we look at what happens to distributions that are made as a result of divorce. In Section 4, we look at mandatory distributions.

This is not a book about retirement plan distributions. Although we provide an overview of the distribution rules for each type of plan, you must look elsewhere for the details. One source is *IRAs,*
401(k)s & Other Retirement Plans: Taking Your Money Out, by Twila Slesnick and John C. Suttle (Nolo).

1. Inservice Distributions: Comparing SEPs and Qualified Plans

It is generally much more difficult to get money out of a qualified plan while you are still working for the company that sponsors the plan (in other words, while you are inservice), than it is to get money out of a SEP. But over the years, Congress has carved out some distribution exceptions for qualified plans—to accommodate special situations—that Congress did not extend to SEPs. Although the following inservice distributions might be permitted under the terms of some qualified plans, if you take such distributions from a SEP, they could lead to penalties or even disqualification of your SEP.

a. Loans

The Tax Code does not allow you to borrow money from your SEP. Borrowing is prohibited transaction and will be penalized accordingly. (See Section F.3, below, for more information about penalties.)

Loans for 60 Days or Less

Because a SEP is technically an IRA, a special IRA rule called the 60-day rule essentially allows you to borrow from your SEP for up to 60 days. The rule provides that you can take money out of an IRA without paying income tax or penalties as long as you put the money back into an IRA—either the same one or a different one—within 60 days. This strategy works for SEPs in the same way it works for traditional IRAs. However, you should beware of two restrictions:

- You are permitted to use this strategy with your SEP only once during each 12-month period.
- When you put the money back in, you must return exactly the amount you took out. Furthermore, if you removed cash, you must return cash. (You may not deposit stock of equal value, for example.)

b. Hardship

Some types of qualified plans, such as 401(k) plans, allow participants to take money out of the plan in the case of hardship. There is no such thing as a hardship distribution from a SEP or any other type of IRA.

2. Divorce Payments

If you and your spouse divorce and your divorce agreement states that you must give some or all of your SEP assets to your former spouse, don't simply withdraw the SEP funds and hand them over. If you do, you (and not your spouse) will have to pay income tax on the distribution. And if you are younger than 59½, you'll owe penalties as well, even though the money is going to your former spouse.

It might be distressing to inadvertently become liable for your former spouse's taxes. Fortunately, there is a way to transfer the funds without incurring either income tax or penalties. As long as the distribution is required by a divorce or maintenance decree, or by a written separation agreement, you may instruct the custodian of your SEP to transfer some or all of the SEP assets directly into a traditional IRA in your former spouse's name. Alternatively, you can roll over your former spouse's share of the SEP into a new traditional IRA in your name and then change the name on the new IRA to your former spouse's name. The critical point in every case is to be sure your former spouse does not take possession of the funds before they are deposited into an IRA in his or her name.

3. Early Distributions and Exceptions to the Early Distribution Penalty

Once you reach age 59½, you are permitted to take money out of your SEP without penalty. However, SEP distributions that you take before you reach age 59½ are considered early distributions and are subject to both regular income tax and a 10% early distribution penalty—unless an exception applies.

In this section, we explain those exceptions. As you read the paragraphs below, keep in mind that fitting your distribution into an exception only allows you to escape the early distribution penalty. You'll still have to pay income tax on the money.

a. Death

Distributions from your SEP after you die are not subject to the penalty, no matter how old you are when you die or how old your beneficiaries are when they withdraw the money. They will still have to pay income tax on the distributions, though.

b. Disability

If you become disabled, you can take money from your SEP without penalty. But first you must satisfy the IRS's definition of disabled. Here's how it reads: You must be unable to "engage in any substantial gainful activity by reason of any medically determinable physical or mental impairment

which can be expected to result in death or to be of long-continued and indefinite duration." The IRS's own regulations state that the gainful activity refers specifically to the type of work you were doing before becoming disabled. Thus it would seem that you need not be unfit for all work—just the work you customarily do. Even if you do qualify for this exception to the penalty, your distributions will be subject to income tax.

c. Periodic Payments

You can begin taking distributions from your SEP regardless of your age as long as you take them in equal annual installments over your life expectancy. These distributions are called "substantially equal periodic payments." Be warned however, that this is not quite the gaping loophole it appears to be. In order to use this exception, you must terminate your employment with the employer who sponsored the plan. Thus, when you are self-employed, presumably you must terminate or otherwise dispose of your business.

To compute substantially equal periodic payments, you must use one of the IRS-approved methods for computing the payments—you cannot simply choose a monthly or annual payment that suits you. (See IRS Notice 89-25 in the Appendix for more information about how to calculate substantially equal payments.)

You must continue the payments for at least five years or until you are at least age

59½, whichever comes later. For example, if you begin at age 58, you must continue the payments for at least five years even though you pass age 59½ in the meantime. Or if you begin at age 52, you must continue until at least age 59½, even though more than five years have passed.

d. Medical Expenses

Although you can take money out of your SEP prior to age 59½ to pay for medical expenses, you won't escape the penalty entirely. The exemption applies only to the portion of your medical expenses that would be deductible on Schedule A of your tax return if you were to itemize deductions (whether or not you actually do itemize deductions). The remainder is subject to penalty. All of it will be subject to income tax.

> EXAMPLE: Your adjusted gross income is $50,000. You had medical bills of $6,000 during the year, which you paid with funds you withdrew from your SEP. (The $6,000 distribution is included in the $50,000 of income.) For income tax purposes, you are permitted to deduct medical expenses that exceed 7.5% of your adjusted gross income. Thus:
>
> Adjusted gross income (AGI), including the SEP distribution = $50,000;
> 7.5% of AGI (.075 x $50,000) = $3,750 nondeductible expenses;

> Excess ($6,000 − $3,750) = $2,250 deductible expenses.

Although you took $6,000 from your SEP to pay medical expenses, only $2,250 will escape the early distribution penalty. The remaining $3,750 will be subject to the penalty (unless you qualify for another exception). And don't forget that the entire $6,000 is subject to regular income tax, as well.

e. Health Insurance Premiums

People who are unemployed, or were recently unemployed, may draw money from a SEP to pay health insurance premiums without penalty, as long as they satisfy all of the following conditions:

- They received unemployment compensation for at least 12 consecutive weeks.
- They received the funds from the SEP either during a year in which they received unemployment compensation or during the following year.
- They received the SEP distribution no more than 60 days after they returned to work.

It might sound as though this won't work for you if you are self-employed. However, the rules specifically permit this exception if you were self-employed before you stopped working, as long as you would have qualified for unemployment compensation under state law except for the fact that you were self-employed.

f. Higher Education Expenses

If you use SEP distributions to pay higher education expenses, you will not be subject to the early distribution penalty, as long as you satisfy all of the following requirements:

- You must use the money to pay the higher education expenses of you, your spouse, your child or your grandchild.
- You must use the money to pay for tuition, fees, books, supplies and equipment. You may also use the money for room and board if the student is carrying at least half of a normal study load (or is considered at least a half-time student).
- The distributions cannot exceed the amount of the higher education expenses. Furthermore, when computing the amount of the distribution that is exempt from the penalty, you must reduce the total expenses (tuition, fees and so on) by any tax-free scholarships or other tax-free assistance the student receives, not including loans, gifts or inheritances.

g. Purchasing a First Home

You may take an early distribution without penalty if the money is used to buy a first home. Although the purpose of this exception is to make it easier for people to buy a home, there is a lifetime distribution limit

of only $10,000. Other restrictions include the following:

- You must use the SEP money for the acquisition, construction or reconstruction of a home.
- You must use the funds within 120 days of receiving them. If the home purchase is canceled or delayed, you may roll the funds back into the same SEP or into another SEP or a traditional IRA, as long as you complete the rollover within 120 days of the initial distribution.
- You must use the funds for the benefit of a first-time home buyer. A first-time home buyer is someone who has had no interest in a principal residence during the two years ending on the date of purchase of the new home. If the individual happens to be married, then neither the individual nor the spouse may have owned any part of a principal residence during the preceding two-year period.
- The first-time home buyer can be you or your spouse. The buyer can also be an ancestor (for example, a parent, grandparent, great grandparent and so on), a child or a grandchild of either you or your spouse.
- The lifetime limit of $10,000 applies regardless of whose home is purchased or improved. If you withdraw $10,000 and give it to your child, the lifetime limit is used up and you may not use the exception for any future

distribution (from any IRA, no matter what type), even if it is to buy a house for a different relative or for yourself. The $10,000 does not have to be distributed all at once or even in a single year. For example, you could withdraw $5,000 one year, giving it to a qualified person for a home purchase, and then withdraw another $5,000 in a later year.

h. Federal Tax Levy

If you owe back taxes, you can be reasonably certain the government will try to collect them. If you have assets in a SEP, the government can take those assets (in other words, the IRS can levy on your SEP) to pay your debt. If it does, those amounts taken for taxes will not be subject to the early distribution penalty even if you happen to be younger than 59½.

Although you will not owe penalty taxes on the above distributions, you will still owe regular income tax in each case. And taking money out of a retirement plan before it's had time to work its magic is not usually the best strategy (from a strictly financial perspective).

4. Mandatory Distributions

Beginning in the year you turn 70½, you are required to start taking money out of your SEP, even if you are still working. The income tax regulations provide a formula for calculating the minimum required distribution. You may take more than the minimum, but you may not take less. If you do take less, you will be fined 50% of the amount that you should have taken out of the SEP but didn't.

 If you are still working when you reach 70½, you may continue to make contributions to a SEP and deduct those contributions. It could very well make sense for you to do so even though you are also required to take some money out each year. Not only can you claim a deduction and reduce your tax liability but you can also add to the assets that will grow tax-deferred.

F. Penalties

Because the SEP rules are relatively simple, you have few opportunities to get into trouble. But it's still possible. Perhaps you contribute too much one year, take a distribution too early or do something with the money that the IRS considers creative but inappropriate. Here are the consequences.

Infractions and Their Consequences	
Problem	**Penalty**
Excess contributions	6% of the excess
Early distributions	10% of the distribution
Prohibited transactions: • If owner of SEP engages in the transaction: • If another disqualified person engages in the transaction:	Disqualification of the plan 15% of transaction
Failure to take a required distribution	50% of the amount that should have been distributed but was not

1. Excess Contributions

If you contribute too much to your SEP, you will be fined 6% of the excess over what you were permitted to contribute. A new 6% penalty will be assessed on any of that same excess that remains in the account at the beginning of each year.

It's probably easier than you think to make such a mistake. Let's suppose your business has had a string of good years and you are expecting another banner year. So in February, you contribute the maximum $25,500 to your SEP. December comes and goes. In April, you begin to prepare your tax return. As you slave over your records, you discover that you made less than you thought. In fact, you contributed $1,800 too much to your SEP. Now what?

Fortunately there is a safety net. Any excess contribution you make to your SEP is deemed to be a contribution to a traditional IRA. In fact, you can just leave the excess in the SEP, because a SEP can receive traditional IRA contributions, as well as SEP contributions.

However, you cannot deduct the excess as a SEP contribution. Rather, the excess is treated as a traditional IRA contribution. As such, it will be deductible only if you qualify to make a deductible contribution to a traditional IRA (as described in Section I, below). If you do not qualify, you must treat the excess as a nondeductible contribution to a traditional IRA.

EXAMPLE: You contributed $25,500 to your SEP in January 2001. At the end of the year, you discover that the maximum you were permitted to contribute was $23,700. You can only deduct $23,700 as a SEP contribution on your tax return. The extra $1,800 will be treated as a contribution to a traditional IRA.

If the excess SEP contribution exceeds even the amount you are permitted to contribute to a traditional IRA, you will have to take some corrective action or pay a penalty. In the following sections, we discuss your options for corrective action.

You are generally permitted to contribute up to $2,000 to a traditional IRA, so your excess SEP contribution cannot exceed that amount. However, if you have already contributed to a traditional IRA or a Roth IRA for the year of the excess SEP contribution, the amount of the excess that can be treated as a traditional IRA contribution and escape penalties must be reduced by the amount of the IRA contributions you have already made.

a. Option One: Remove Excess Before Due Date

One way you can correct the error is to remove the excess contribution plus any earnings attributable to the excess by the due date of your tax return (plus extensions, if you requested and received an extension for filing your tax return).

When you remove the contribution and earnings, you must report the earnings,

but not the contribution, as income on your tax return. Report the earnings in the year you made the excess contribution. (The year you remove the funds might be different from the year you made the excess contribution.) If you are not yet 59½, you will have to pay an early distribution penalty on the earnings, but not on the excess contribution.

EXAMPLE: You contributed $24,000 to your SEP in January 2001. You contributed to no other IRAs or retirement plans during the year. At the end of the year, you discovered that the maximum you were permitted to contribute to your SEP was $21,000. The excess SEP contribution is $3,000. You elect to treat $2,000 of the excess as a traditional IRA contribution. But you still have an excess contribution of $1,000. If you remove the $1,000 plus any investment returns attributable to the $1,000 before you file your tax return on April 15, you will avoid the 6% excess contribution penalty.

If you earned $2,400 on the $24,000 SEP contribution, then $100 of it would be attributable to the $1,000 excess ($1,000/$24,000 x $2,400 = $100). Therefore you must remove earnings of $100 in addition to the excess contribution of $1,000.

If you remove the money by April 15, you won't owe an excess contribution penalty on the $1,100. If you are younger than age 59½, however, you might owe an early distribution penalty on the earnings (the $100), unless you can find an exception that applies. (See Section E.3, above, for information about exceptions to the early distribution penalty.)

On your tax return you will report only the $100 of earnings that you withdrew, and you will claim a SEP deduction for $21,000 on line 29 of Form 1040. Because your income is greater than $60,000, the $2,000 traditional IRA contribution is nondeductible and must be reported on Form 8606. (See Chapter 8, Section D, for more information about deductible and nondeductible IRA contributions.)

If you filed your return early and claimed a SEP deduction for too much, you can still prepare an amended return before the actual due date of your tax return and avoid the 6% penalty.

EXAMPLE: As in the previous example, you contributed $24,000 to your SEP in January 2001. The end of the year comes and goes. You file your tax return in February 2002 claiming a deduction of $24,000. In March, you were at a party when you ran into an accountant. During the conversation, you learned you made an error when computing your SEP contribution. The amount should have been $21,000, so you have contributed $3,000 too much. You decide to treat $2,000 of

the excess as a nondeductible traditional IRA contribution. To avoid an excess contribution penalty, you must do all of the following before April 15:

Remove the $1,000 excess contribution that cannot be treated as a traditional IRA contribution.

Remove the $100 of earnings attributable to the $1,000.

File an amended tax return claiming only a $21,000 SEP deduction and reporting the $100 of earnings.

Include with your tax return Form 8606 showing the nondeductible IRA contribution.

If you follow these procedures, you will not owe a 6% excess contribution penalty. However, you might owe a 10% early distribution penalty on the $100 of earnings if you are younger than 59½.

b. Option Two: Remove Excess After Due Date

Another way of dealing with the mistake is to remove the excess contribution late—after the due date (or extended due date) of your tax return—and leave the earnings in the account.

You must pay a 6% penalty on the excess contribution, but not on the earnings if you leave them in the SEP. In addition, you avoid an early distribution penalty on the earnings—something you would have had to deal with had you taken the earnings out as described in Option 1, above.

(Presumably, Congress considers the 6% penalty adequate payback for any benefit you might derive from leaving the earnings in the account.)

You will not have to pay any income tax on the corrective distribution as long as you did not take a deduction for the full excess contribution on your tax return. If you did, you will have to submit an amended tax return with the correct deduction (the correct SEP contribution) and pay the additional income tax.

> **EXAMPLE:** In 2001, you contributed $5,000 too much to your SEP. You designated $2,000 as a traditional IRA contribution, leaving an excess of $3,000. Although you knew about the excess before your filing deadline (and deducted only the correct amount on your tax return), you forgot to remove the excess from the SEP account. The earnings on the excess are $250. You remove the $3,000 after your tax filing deadline and leave the $250 of earnings in the account. You will owe a penalty of $180 (6% of $3,000), but no other penalties will apply.

c. Option Three: Leave Excess In, Deduct Next Year

Your third option is to leave the excess in the SEP and deduct it in the next tax year.

You still have to pay the 6% excise tax for the first year (on the excess contribution, but not the earnings), because the ex-

cess remained in the account after the due date of your tax return. But as long as the excess does not exceed the deductible SEP amount for the second year, there will be no penalty for that year.

> **EXAMPLE:** In 2001, you contributed $3,000 too much to your SEP. You deducted the correct amount but forgot to remove the excess. You already contributed $2,000 to a traditional IRA for the year 2001, so you cannot treat any of the $3,000 as a traditional IRA contribution. You decide to leave the excess in the account and deduct it the following year. In 2002 you have enough income to make an $8,000 SEP contribution. You apply the $3,000 excess from the previous year and add an additional $5,000 in cash by the due date of your tax return to complete the $8,000 contribution. You must still pay a $180 penalty for 2001, but no additional penalty will be assessed for 2002 or beyond.

d. Which Method Is Best?

If the excess is large, the 6% penalty could become painful. In that case, you should work hard to remove the excess by the tax filing deadline (Option One). Although you might have to pay an early distribution tax on the earnings, that penalty could be significantly less than the 6% penalty on the excess contribution.

If you miss the tax filing deadline, you cannot avoid the 6% penalty. So you must choose between Option Two and Option Three. If you expect to be able to deduct the excess in the second year, Option Three is your better choice because your money can be working for you all year inside the SEP. However, if you don't think you'll be able to use the deduction the second year, you will probably want to use Option Two and remove the excess until you have enough income from your business to support a SEP deduction.

⚠️ **The 6% penalty for excess contributions to a SEP is an IRA rule.** There is a companion rule for qualified plans, including defined contribution plans, that imposes a 10% penalty on the employer for nondeductible contributions to a defined contribution plan. A strict reading of the code suggests that a SEP could be subject to both penalties. This is because the Code treats a SEP like a defined contribution plan in some instances. Most practitioners believe Congress did not intend this double penalty, however, and that only the 6% IRA penalty would apply. Despite what practitioners think, nobody can be sure that the IRS will not enforce a double tax, so it behooves all SEP owners to take whatever precautions are necessary to avoid making excess contributions.

Report excess contributions to your SEP on IRS Form 5329 for the year you made the excess contribution. Do not use the current year's Form 5329.

EXAMPLE: You made an excess contribution of $1,000 to your SEP in 2001. You discovered your error in June 2002 long after you filed your tax return. You should complete Form 5329 for the year 2001 (not Form 5329 for the year 2002) even though you have already filed the rest of your tax return. Sign and date the form and send it in with your check for $60 (6% of $1,000), which is the amount of the excess contribution penalty.

2. Early Distributions

If you take money out of your SEP before you reach age 59½ and if the distribution does not fall into any of the exceptions to the early distribution penalty described in Section E.3, above, then the distribution will be subject to a 10% early distribution penalty. That penalty is in addition to the income tax you must pay.

The IRS requires you to report the early distribution penalty on Form 5329 for the year of the early distribution.

3. Prohibited Transactions

The Tax Code prohibits certain transactions involving your SEP assets. The prohibited transaction rules are part of Congress's strategy to protect your SEP assets so that they will be available when you retire. The rules are designed to keep you or any other disqualified person (see immediately below) from using the assets for personal gain or engaging in transactions that put the assets at risk.

A disqualified person is someone who might reasonably have access to your SEP assets. In addition to you, such persons include your spouse, your lineal descendants (such as children and grandchildren) and your ancestors (such as parents and grandparents). The list also includes fiduciaries (those responsible for handling the assets of the SEP, such as a custodian, trustee or money manager), a person who provides services to the SEP (such as an administrator) and certain co-owners of your business.

The penalties for engaging in a prohibited transaction are severe. If you, as the SEP owner, or your beneficiary engages in a prohibited transaction, the SEP is disqualified and all of the assets are deemed distributed as of the first day of the year in which the prohibited transaction took place. You will have to pay income tax on the entire account, which might be pretty expensive if the distribution throws you into a higher tax bracket. And if you are not yet 59½, you will have to pay a 10% early distribution penalty, as well.

If a disqualified person (other than you or your beneficiary) engages in the prohibited transaction, the penalty is generally 15% of the transaction. If the transaction is not corrected, an additional tax of 100% is imposed. That's a total of 115%. But the tax is assessed on the disqualified person, not on you.

The following are the transactions to avoid. Note that they are all transactions that occur inside your SEP or with the use of SEP assets.

- The sale, exchange or lease of any property between a disqualified person and the SEP. For example, you cannot sell your house to your SEP.

- The furnishing of goods or services or facilities between a disqualified person and the SEP. For example, you cannot hire your spouse to manage the SEP and pay him a big salary out of the SEP assets.

- The lending of money or extending of credit between a disqualified person and the SEP. For example, you cannot borrow from the SEP to buy a car, even if you intend to return the money. If you want to use your SEP assets to buy that car, you must withdraw the money permanently and hope you can find an exception to the early distribution penalty (if you are younger than age 59½).

- The transfer to or use by a disqualified person of any assets or income of the SEP. For example, you cannot use SEP funds to invest in a house (held by the SEP) that you then occupy as your principal residence. Again, if you want to use the funds to buy yourself a house, you must withdraw the funds permanently and pay income tax on the distribution. Hopefully, you'll be able to use the $10,000 first-home exception to reduce any early distribution penalty that might apply. (See Section E.3, above, for an explanation of the first-home exception to the early distribution penalty.)

- Any act of self dealing, which occurs when a disqualified person uses the assets or income of the SEP for that person's own interest or account while the assets are still in the SEP. For example, if your money manager invests all of your SEP assets in the stock of a company of which she owns 80%, such an investment would clearly benefit her as a majority shareholder and, therefore, might be deemed a prohibited transaction.
- The receipt of payment by a fiduciary in connection with a transaction involving the income or assets of the plan. A kickback, for example.

If you engage in a prohibited transaction, you must file Form 5329 with the IRS. Furthermore, your SEP will be disqualified from the moment of the transgression. All of the assets must be distributed and any income must be reported on your tax return, along with any early distribution penalty that applies.

If another disqualified person engages in the prohibited transaction, he or she must complete IRS Form 5330 and pay the 15% penalty.

4. Life Insurance

You are not permitted to use assets in your SEP to purchase life insurance that you hold inside your SEP. If you do, the SEP becomes disqualified as of the first day of the year during which you made the purchase. That means you must pay income tax and possibly an early distribution penalty on the entire amount in your SEP. Although purchasing life insurance isn't defined as a prohibited transaction in the Tax Code, it is treated as such if the purchase is made with assets that are currently inside a SEP.

5. Collectibles

You cannot invest your SEP in collectibles. The Tax Code carefully lists all those items that are considered collectibles, followed, of course, by a list of exceptions.

Collectibles include the following:
- works of art
- rugs or antiques
- metals or gems
- stamps or coins, and
- alcoholic beverages.

Exceptions include the following:
- certain U.S. minted gold, silver and platinum coins
- coins issued under the laws of any state, and

- gold, silver, platinum or palladium bullion equal to or exceeding the minimum fineness required by a contract market for metals delivered in satisfaction of a regulated futures contract (and only if the bullion is in the physical possession of the IRA custodian).

If you invest your SEP assets in unacceptable collectibles, you are deemed to have made a distribution in an amount equal to the cost of the collectible. The transaction does not disqualify the SEP, however. Instead, even if you don't withdraw the collectible from your account, you will owe income tax on the cost of it, and you must report an early distribution penalty on Form 5329 as though you did take a distribution—unless you qualify for an exception. Meanwhile, you can keep the collectible in your SEP if you like. When it is ultimately distributed, the amount of the deemed distribution—the portion on which you already paid tax and penalties—will not be included in your income.

> **EXAMPLE:** Last year, you purchased an antique Persian rug with $5,000 of your SEP funds. This year your accountant told you it was a prohibited transaction. You must pay income tax on $5,000, even though the SEP continues to hold title to the rug. You must also pay a 10% early distribution penalty of $500 ($5,000 x 10%) because you are younger than 59½—

even though you did not actually take a distribution. Some years later you distribute the rug from the SEP. At the time of the distribution the fair market value of the rug is $20,000. You must pay income tax (and perhaps an early distribution penalty) on $15,000 (which is $20,000 reduced by the $5,000 on which you have already paid taxes).

6. Pledging the Account As Security

If any portion of your SEP is used as security for a loan to you (for example, you borrow money using your SEP as collateral), that portion is treated as a distribution subject to income tax. You will also have to pay an early distribution penalty, unless you qualify for an exception. You report the distribution on your tax return and include Form 5329 if you owe an early distribution penalty. The rest of the SEP will not be disqualified. This is different from actually borrowing the funds from the SEP. If you do that, the SEP is disqualified. (See Section E.1.a, above.)

7. Mandatory Distribution Penalty

If you fail to take required distributions from your SEP beginning at age 70½, you will pay a penalty of 50% of the amount that you should have taken out but didn't.

For example, if you were required to distribute $10,000 from your SEP for the year you turned 70½ but you forgot, you will owe a penalty of $5,000 ($10,000 x 50%).

Report this penalty on IRS Form 5329.

G. Terminating Your SEP

Recall that you are not required to make a contribution to your SEP each year, as long as your plan documents allow you to make discretionary contributions. So you don't have to terminate your SEP just because you cannot afford to contribute one year.

But let's say you know you will never make another contribution. Perhaps you have retired or you sold your business and you don't plan to maintain a SEP. You can simply stop making contributions and treat the SEP as a traditional IRA, or you can roll over the entire SEP into another traditional IRA. The SEP is terminated when you take all your money out.

H. Multiple Employer Plans

Because retirement plans are one of the last great bargains in the Tax Code, taxpayers search hard for ways to contribute more. How about setting up two SEPs? Can you double your contribution? What if you have two businesses? Can you have one plan for each? Or suppose you work for another employer and run a business of your own on the side. Can you set up a plan for your own business even if you are covered by your employer's plan?

The key to understanding what you can and cannot do is this fundamental rule: Retirement plan limits are applied on a per-employer basis. This is known as the separate employer rule.

For example, suppose you work for Conglomerate Corp. from 8 a.m. to 5 p.m. every day and you work for Monopoly Corp. from 7 p.m. to 4 a.m. Suppose also that each company contributes to a SEP on your behalf. Recall that the limit on contributions to a SEP is the lesser of 15% of your compensation or $25,500. But because the two companies are separate employers, they can each contribute the maximum on your behalf. That means it's possible to garner $51,000 in SEP contributions in one year—$25,500 from each employer. The same principle applies if you are one of the separate employers.

 There are some important exceptions to the separate employer rule. Perhaps most important, the law puts a cap on the total amount you can contribute to all salary reduction plans (such as SIMPLE IRAs) in which you participate. (See Chapter 3 for more information about multiple plan limits for SIMPLE IRAs.) However, these restrictions do not apply to SEPs. No matter what type of plan you have with a separate employer, you can establish a SEP for your own business and contribute the maximum the law and your income allow.

The remainder of this Section H examines various employment scenarios and explains whether or not you can contribute to more than one employer plan in the same year. (For information about adding a traditional IRA or a Roth IRA to your SEP, see Section I, below.)

1. If You Are Self-Employed With a Day Job on the Side, or Vice Versa

Let's say you own your own business, but you also work for someone else. Can you be covered by more than one plan? Because of the separate employer rule described in the preceding paragraphs, if you are covered by your employer's plan, you can still establish a SEP for your own business and take a deduction to offset some of your self-employment profit.

⚠ **If you and members of your family together own more than 50% of the corporation that employs you**, then you, as the sole proprietor of your own business (or as a partner in your partnership), might not be considered a separate employer. If not, then your contribution to the SEP you established for your unincorporated business might be limited or eliminated altogether. If this describes your situation or if you are uncertain, you should confer with the plan administrator of the corporate retirement plan. (Also see Section 3, below.)

2. If You Are Self-Employed With Only One Business

Suppose you are self-employed and you have no other employer. If you have a SEP in place, can you set up another plan, as well? This question isn't as odd as it might seem. Perhaps you established the SEP in your first year of business when you wanted the flexibility to discontinue contributions if necessary. But now the business is doing so well you want to contribute more to a retirement plan than the SEP allows. Should you terminate the SEP and replace it with another type of plan? Can you simply add another plan? Or are you stuck with what you have?

You can have as many retirement plans for your business as you choose. However there is a limit on the total amount you can contribute to each type of plan. A SEP is considered a profit sharing plan for purposes of this rule. (See Chapter 5 for more about profit sharing plans.) The maximum a single employer can contribute to all profit sharing plans combined is 15% of compensation (where compensation is currently limited to $170,000). That means you can establish three SEPs if you want, or a SEP and a different type of profit sharing plan, but the total of all contributions to all profit sharing plans and SEPs of the same employer (in this scenario, you) cannot exceed the above limit. (Recall that compensation for a self-employed individual is actually net earnings from self-employment. So 15% of compensation is

13.0435% of net income after the self-employment tax deduction.)

As a practical matter, you are unlikely to establish two separate SEPs for your business when you can contribute the maximum to one. Maintaining two plans of the same type adds administrative time and costs without providing additional benefits. If you want to increase your contribution limit, you must add a different type of plan to your SEP, such as a money purchase pension plan or a defined benefit plan.

If you add a money purchase pension plan, you can increase your contribution limit to the lesser of $30,000 ($35,000 beginning with the 2001 tax year) or 25% of compensation (which works out to 20% of your net income—after the self-employment tax deduction—when you are self-employed). The contribution to your SEP still cannot exceed 15% of your compensation, but the money purchase pension plan can fill in the gap. (See Chapter 6 for more about money purchase pension plans.)

EXAMPLE: You established a SEP when you started your business in 1998. In 2000 you had net income of $60,000 (after subtracting your self-employment tax deduction). Because your SEP limits your contribution to 15% of compensation, you decide to establish a money purchase pension plan with a 10% annual contribution limit. The combination of plans brings your contribution limit to the maximum 25% (20% of your net income af-

ter the self-employment tax deduction).

Therefore, your maximum contribution to both plans is the lesser of $30,000 or 20% of $60,000, which is $12,000.

Your net earnings from self-employment (your business receipts, less expenses, less the self-employment tax deduction, less the retirement plan contribution) is $48,000.

Thus, your contribution to your money purchase pension plan is $4,800 (10% x $48,000) and it is mandatory, so you must make it first. (See Chapter 6 for information about computing contributions to money purchase pension plans.)

You can contribute $7,200 to your SEP (which is $12,000 – $4,800) if you want. (Remember: The SEP contribution is discretionary.)

Note that the maximum contribution you could make to your SEP without a money purchase pension plan contribution is $7,826 (13.0435% of $60,000). But because your total contribution to both plans is limited to $12,000 and the money purchase pension plan contribution is made first, you can only put $7,200 into the SEP.

You can also add a defined benefit plan to your SEP and your money purchase pension plan. But there is a limit on the total combined amount you can contribute to all defined benefit and defined contribution plans (including SEPs) of one employer. That limit is the greater of:

- 25% of your compensation (net earnings from self-employment) up to a maximum of $170,000 of compensation. Thus 25% of 170,000 or $42,500; or
- the amount you are required to contribute to your defined benefit plan. (See Chapter 7 for information about defined benefit plan contributions.)

⚠️ **If you have a SEP, you cannot add a SIMPLE IRA.** If you want to establish a SIMPLE IRA, you cannot contribute to any other employer plan in the same year. (See Chapter 3 for more information about SIMPLE IRAs.)

3. If You Are Self-Employed With Two or More Businesses

An exception to the rule that allows you to participate in a retirement plan with each separate employer (including yourself if you own your own business) occurs when the employers are not separate in the eyes of the law—even though they might look separate to you. Businesses that are under common control are deemed to be one employer and are combined for purposes of determining the ceiling on retirement plan contributions. The definition of common control can be tricky, though.

a. If You Have Two Sole Proprietorships

The concept of common control is straightforward if you have two sole proprietorships. By definition, you own 100% of both businesses, and, therefore, the businesses are under common control because they have the same employer (you). Consequently, they must be combined for determining contribution limits. If you establish a SEP for each business, the maximum contribution you can make to both plans combined is $25,500 or 15% of the combined compensation from both businesses. It's the same limit that would apply if you had only one business or one plan.

EXAMPLE: You have a Web design business that produced net income of $40,000 in 2001 (after taking into account your self-employment tax deduction). You also have a house-painting business that generated $35,000 in net income for 2001. The maximum you can contribute to a SEP is the lesser of $25,500 or 13.0435% of $75,000 ($40,000 + $35,000), which is $9,783. You can contribute the entire amount to one SEP, or you can establish multiple SEPs and contribute whatever you like to each (assuming each allows discretionary contributions), as long as the total contribution to all SEPs does not exceed $9,783.

b. If You Have a Sole Proprietorship and a Partnership; or Two Partnerships

If you are a sole proprietor and you also have an interest in a partnership, the picture changes. You are the employer of your sole proprietorship, but the partnership, not the individual partners, is the employer in a partnership. In general, that means each business must set up its own plan.

But here's where the issue of common control rears its head. If the businesses are under common control, the total contribution to both plans is determined as though there were only one employer and one plan.

A sole proprietorship and a partnership are under common control if the sole proprietor has more than a 50% interest in the capital (the assets) or the profits of the partnership (as defined in your partnership agreement). In that case, the businesses are combined for purposes of the SEP contribution limits. Your contribution to the two SEPs is limited to a total of $25,500 or 15% of your compensation from both businesses combined. However, the amount you deposit into each SEP is determined by the amount of income you receive from each business.

EXAMPLE: You are the sole proprietor of a Web design business that produced net income of $40,000 in 2001. You established a SEP for that business when you first started in 1998. In 2001, you and a partner started a house-painting business. You decided to establish a SEP for that business, as well. By agreement, you have an 80% interest in the profits of the business. Your partnership agreement defines "profits" to be net income from the business. Thus, your share of the profits in 2001 was $35,000. Because your interest in the profits of the partnership exceeds 50% and you also own 100% of the Web design business, your partnership and your sole proprietorship are under common control. Consequently, the maximum you can contribute to all SEPs is the lesser of $25,500 or 13.0435% of $75,000 ($40,000 + $35,000), which is $9,783. However, the most you can contribute to the partnership SEP is $4,565 (.130435 x $35,000). And the most you can contribute to the SEP for your web design business is $5,217 (.130435 x $40,000).

If you establish a SEP for your partnership and if the SEP agreement permits discretionary contributions, you may reduce or eliminate the contribution in any given year. However, all partners must participate in the same way. The term "discretionary" simply means you can vary the percentage each year; it doesn't mean some partners can choose to participate while others do not.

If you have precisely a 50% interest in both the capital and the profits of the partnership, or if your interest in each is less than or equal to 50%, then the partnership and sole proprietorship are different employers for plan sponsorship purposes and also for purposes of determining contribution limits. If you choose a SEP for both, you would set up two separate plans, and the 15% limit would apply separately to your earnings from each business.

If you are involved in two partnerships, the same principles apply. Those partnerships in which your interest in either the capital or the profits is greater than 50% must be combined and treated as one for purposes of determining the contribution limits, even though you must set up a separate plan for each partnership.

 It is possible for two employers (such as your partnership and your sole proprietorship, or perhaps two partnerships) to sponsor the same plan, which might save administrative time and costs. If you elect this option, be sure to confirm with the financial institution providing the plan, or with the IRS, that the plan will pass muster.

 If you own interests in several businesses that provide services to one another, or if you and other individuals own interests in the same business, the businesses might be under common control. Confer with a plan consultant for assistance in sorting out the common control issue.

I. Adding a Traditional or Roth IRA to Your SEP

Having a SEP does not preclude you from establishing a traditional or Roth IRA, because traditional IRAs and Roth IRAs are not employer plans. However, contributing to a SEP might limit the deductibility of your traditional IRA contribution. (Roth IRA contributions are never deductible.)

When you are covered by your own SEP, SIMPLE IRA or Keogh, or when you are covered by a plan of another employer, any traditional IRA contribution you make is fully deductible only if the adjusted gross income (with certain modifications) on your tax return is less than $62,000 (if you are married) or $42,000 (if you are single).

For more information about traditional IRAs including how to compute deductible and nondeductible contributions, see Chapter 8.

 You are always permitted to make a traditional IRA contribution to your SEP. In other words, if you want to contribute to a SEP and a traditional IRA in the same year, you may simply make the $2,000 traditional IRA contribution to the same account to which you make your SEP contribution. However, you might not be able to do the reverse—that is, make a SEP contribution to your traditional IRA. The primary difference between a SEP account and a traditional IRA is that a SEP permits contributions in excess of $2,000.

If your traditional IRA permits such contributions, you can make SEP contributions to it (assuming you have a written SEP agreement in place and filed away in your office somewhere). Before you make a SEP contribution to your traditional IRA, you should confirm with the custodian that the IRA can receive contributions in excess of $2,000.

J. Filling Out the Forms

The vast majority of self-employed individuals use either a financial institution's prototype SEP or they use the IRS's own form.

1. Prototype SEP

Let's assume you plan to establish a SEP using a financial institution's prototype. A prototype SEP is one that has already been approved by the IRS, so all you have to do is fill in the blanks. These are the steps you will take:

Step 1:
Identify the bank, brokerage firm or other financial institution that will hold your SEP assets. This institution will serve as custodian of your SEP in the same way an institution serves as custodian of a traditional IRA.

Step 2:
Call the financial institution you have chosen and ask for the Retirement Services department. Explain that you want to set up a SEP and for the appropriate documents to be mailed to you.

Step 3:
Soon (hopefully) you will receive in the mail the financial institution's prototype SEP agreement. You can find a sample prototype form at the end of this chapter. In the following paragraphs, we explain that sample. Although each financial institution has its own prototype plan, the following discussion should help you no matter which institution you contact because all prototype plans tend to be very similar.

In the first blank space, enter your own name (or the name of your business, if you are not using your own name), if you are a sole proprietor. Enter the name of the partnership if your business is a partnership.

- *Article I, eligibility requirements:*
  ✓ In the first blank space, you must enter the age that employees must be in order to be covered by your SEP. In this context, employees include you. You cannot exclude anyone who is age 21 or older. You may exclude anyone who is younger than 21, but if you do, take note: If you are younger than 21, you will be excluding yourself, as well. Generally, if you are at least 21, you should enter 21 in this space.

✓ Similarly, the second blank allows you to exclude employees (including yourself) who have not worked (in other words, provided service) for you in at least three of the last five years. If this is your first year of business, you won't want to require three years of service, because you, yourself, won't meet the requirement. If you have no employees, you can safely enter zero here.

✓ The next three clauses of this Article I require that you check an appropriate box. Because you have no employees, the box you choose will have little relevance. We recommend that you check the boxes next to "does not include employees covered under a collective bargaining agreement" and "does not include certain nonresident aliens" and "does not include employees whose total compensation during the year is less than $450."

- *Article II, SEP requirements:* Sign and date the form in the blank space under Article II. Then print your name and business title.

Step 4:
Next, complete the Adoption Agreement, which allows you to open the SEP account and name a beneficiary. (See Section 3, below, for more information about naming a beneficiary.) On this form you also indi-cate the amount of your contribution (under "Employer Contribution") and how you want the funds invested. At the end of this chapter, you can find a sample form.

Step 5:
File the completed prototype form in your office with other business documents. You do not have to send it to the financial institution or to the IRS. Make sure you also keep a copy of the terms of the plan and the descriptive information that comes with it.

Step 6:
Send the completed Adoption Agreement to the financial institution. If you have already computed your contribution for the year (see Section C, below), you can send it in with your completed Adoption Agreement and any fee required by the institution. If you do not know how much your contribution will be, you can send enough money to open the account and deposit the rest later.

2. IRS Form 5305-SEP

If your financial institution does not have a prototype SEP or if you do not like the one it does have, you can use the IRS's pre-approved SEP agreement, Form 5305-SEP. You can find a sample of Form 5305-SEP at the end of this chapter. Most financial institutions will allow you to open a SEP account if you notify them that you have adopted the IRS model SEP agreement.

If you decide to use the IRS form, you cannot add any features. Furthermore, you cannot use the form at all if any of the following are true:

- You currently have a qualified plan in place for your business.
- You have eligible employees who have not yet established IRAs into which SEP contributions can be made.
- You use the services of leased employees (leased employees are those who perform services for you but are actually employed by an outside leasing organization).
- You are under common control with other employers or a member of an affiliated service group, unless all eligible employees of all employers are covered. (See Section H, above, for more information about common control.)

! **You might find that the prototype form used by your financial institution** is simply the IRS Form 5305-SEP with the financial institution's logo on it. Many financial institutions elect to use the IRS form so that the institution doesn't have to create its own form and have it approved by the IRS.

3. Beneficiary Designation

When you name a beneficiary of your SEP IRA, you are identifying the person or organization you want to receive your SEP IRA assets when you die. That's important, certainly. But the person or organization you name as beneficiary can be crucial for other reasons, as well. For example, your choice of beneficiary will determine how quickly you must take distributions from the SEP IRA after you reach age 70½ (see Section E.4, below)—and how quickly the SEP IRA must be liquidated after your death.

If you are married and you name your spouse as beneficiary, he or she will have options that other beneficiaries do not have. Your spouse can roll over your SEP IRA into an IRA in his or her own name, pick new beneficiaries and, in most cases, prolong or delay distributions. (Remember, when you delay distributions from an IRA, the assets can continue to grow tax-deferred—a big benefit!)

On the other hand, if you want to make a sizable donation to charity when you die, SEP IRA assets might well be the best source of that donation, because charities will not have to pay income tax on the SEP IRA distributions. Unfortunately when you name a charity as beneficiary, you generally must distribute assets from the plan more quickly during your lifetime than you would if you named a person as beneficiary.

And it is almost never right to simply name your "estate" as beneficiary. Doing so could present your heirs with income tax problems and perhaps increase probate fees, as well.

For most married individuals, naming a spouse as beneficiary is the best option. But if you are single or if your situation is unusual, choosing a beneficiary can be quite complex and you might want to seek help from a knowledgeable accountant or lawyer.

 For more information about the effect of your beneficiary designation on your retirement plan, see *IRAs, 401(k)s & Other Retirement Plans: Taking Your Money Out*, by Twila Slesnick and John Suttle (Nolo).

SEP-IRA
Simplified Employee Pension–Individual Retirement Accounts Contribution Agreement

THE**Vanguard**GROUP.

(Under Section 408(k) of the Internal Revenue Code)   *Derived from IRS Form 5305-SEP*
Do **Not** file with Internal Revenue Service or with Vanguard

_____ makes the following agreement under section 408(k) of the
(Name of employer)
Internal Revenue Code and the instructions to this form.

Article I—Eligibility Requirements (Check appropriate boxes—see **Instructions**.)
The employer agrees to provide for discretionary contributions in each calendar year to the individual retirement account
or individual retirement annuity (IRA) of all employees who are at least _____ years old (not to exceed 21 years old) and
have performed services for the employer in at least _____ years (not to exceed 3 years) of the immediately preceding 5
years. This simplified employee pension (SEP) ☐ includes ☐ does not include employees covered under a collective
bargaining agreement, ☐ includes ☐ does not include certain nonresident aliens, and ☐ includes ☐ does not include
employees whose total compensation during the year is less than $400*.

Article II—SEP Requirements (See **Instructions.**)
The employer agrees that contributions made on behalf of each eligible employee will be:
• Based only on the first $160,000* of compensation.
• Made in an amount that is the same percentage of compensation for every employee.
• Limited annually to the smaller of $30,000* **or** 15% of compensation.
• Paid to the employee's IRA trustee, custodian, or insurance company (for an annuity contract).

_____   _____
Employer's signature and date   Name and title

Paperwork Reduction Act Notice
You are not required to provide the information requested on a
form that is subject to the Paperwork Reduction Act unless the form
displays a valid OMB control number. Books or records relating to a
form or its instructions must be retained as long as their contents
may become material in the administration of any Internal Revenue
law. Generally, tax returns and return information are confidential,
as required by Code section 6103.

The time needed to complete this form will vary depending on indi-
vidual circumstances. The estimated average time is:
Recordkeeping..................................1 hr., 40 min.
Learning about the law or the form.......1 hr., 35 min.
Preparing the form..........................1 hr., 41 min.
If you have comments concerning the accuracy of these time estimates
or suggestions for making this form simpler, we would be happy to
hear from you. You can write to the Tax Forms Committee, Western
Area Distribution Center, Rancho Cordova, CA 95743-0001. **Do not**
send this form to this address. Instead, keep it for your records.

Instructions
Section references are to the Internal Revenue Code unless otherwise noted.
Purpose of Form.—Form 5305-SEP (Model SEP) is used by an employer to make an agreement to provide benefits to all eligible employees
under a SEP described in section 408(k). **Do not** file this form with the
IRS. See **Pub. 560**, Retirement Plans for the Self-Employed, and **Pub.
590**, Individual Retirement Arrangements (IRAs).

Specific Instructions
Instructions to the Employer
Simplified Employee Pension.—A SEP is a written arrangement (a
plan) that provides you with a simplified way to make contributions
toward your employees' retirement income. Under a SEP, you can
contribute to an employee's individual retirement account or annuity
(IRA). You make contributions directly to an IRA set up by or for each
employee with a bank, insurance company, or other qualified financial
institution. When using Form 5305-SEP to establish a SEP, the IRA must
be a Model IRA established on an IRS form or a master or prototype
IRA for which the IRS has issued a favorable opinion letter. Making
the agreement on Form 5305-SEP does not establish an employer IRA
described in section 408(c).

When Not to Use Form 5305-SEP.—Do not use this form if you:
• Currently maintain any other qualified retirement plan. This
does not prevent you from also maintaining another SEP.
• Previously maintained a defined benefit plan that is now terminated.

• Have any eligible employees for whom IRAs have not been established.
• Use the services of leased employees (described in section 414(n)).
• Are a member of an affiliated service group (described in section
414(m)), a controlled group of corporations (described in section
414(b)), or trades or businesses under common control (described in
sections 414(c) and 414(o)), unless all eligible employees of all the
members of such groups, trades, or businesses, participate in the SEP.
• Will not pay the cost of the SEP contributions. Do not use Form
5305-SEP for a SEP that provides for elective employee contributions
even if the contributions are made under a salary reduction agreement. Use Form 5305A-SEP, or a nonmodel SEP if you permit elective
deferrals to a SEP.

Note: SEPs permitting elective deferrals cannot be established after 1996.
Eligible Employees.—All eligible employees must be allowed to
participate in the SEP. An eligible employee is any employee who:
(1) is at least 21 years old, and (2) has performed "service" for you in
at least 3 of the immediately preceding 5 years. *Note: You can establish
less restrictive eligibility requirements, but not more restrictive ones.*
Service is any work performed for you for any period of time, however
short. If you are a member of an affiliated service group, a controlled
group of corporations, or trades or businesses under common control,
service includes any work performed for any other member of any
other member of such group, trades, or businesses.
Excludable Employees.—The following employees do not have to be
covered by the SEP: (1) employees covered by a collective bargaining
agreement whose retirement benefits were bargained for in good faith
by you and their union, (2) nonresident alien employees who did not
earn U.S. source income from you, and (3) employees who received
less than $400* in compensation during the year.
Contribution Limits.—The SEP rules permit you to make an annual
contribution of up to 15% of the employee's compensation or
$30,000,* whichever is less. Compensation, for this purpose, does
not include employer contributions to the SEP or the employee's
compensation in excess of $160,000.* If you also maintain a Model
Elective SEP or any other SEP that permits employees to make elective
deferrals, contributions to the two SEPs together may not exceed the
smaller of $30,000* or 15% of compensation for any employee.
Contributions cannot discriminate in favor of highly compensated
employees. You are not required to make contributions every year.
But you must contribute to the SEP-IRAs of all of the eligible employees who actually performed services during the year of the contribution. This includes eligible employees who die or quit working before
the contribution is made.

_____
* *This amount reflects the cost-of-living increase under section 408(k)(8), effective January 1, 1997. The amount is adjusted annually. The IRS announces the increase, if any, in a news release or*
in the Internal Revenue Bulletin.

You may also not integrate your SEP contributions with, or offset them by, contributions made under the Federal Insurance Contributions Act (FICA).

If this SEP is intended to meet the top-heavy minimum contribution rules of section 416, but it does not cover all your employees who participate in your elective SEP, then you must make minimum contributions to IRAs established on behalf of those employees.

Deducting Contributions.—You may deduct contributions to a SEP subject to the limits of section 404(h). This SEP is maintained on a calendar year basis and contributions to the SEP are deductible for your tax year within or within which the calendar year ends.

Contributions made for a particular tax year must be made by the due date of your income tax return (including extensions) for that tax year.

Completing the Agreement.—This agreement is considered adopted when:

• IRAs have been established for all your eligible employees,
• You have completed all blanks on the agreement form without modification, and
• You have given all your eligible employees the following information:
  (a) A copy of Form 5305-SEP.
  (b) A statement that IRAs other than the IRAs into which employer SEP contributions will be made may provide different rates of return and different terms concerning, among other things, transfers and withdrawals of funds from the IRAs.
  (c) A statement that, in addition to the information provided to an employee at the time the employee becomes eligible to participate, the administrator of the SEP must furnish each participant within 30 days of the effective date of any amendment to the SEP, a copy of the amendment and a written explanation of its effects.
  (d) A statement that the administrator will give written notification to each participant of any employer contributions made under the SEP to that participant's IRA by the later of January 31 of the year following the year for which a contribution is made or 30 days after the contribution is made.

Employers who have established a SEP using Form 5305-SEP and has furnished each eligible employee with a copy of the completed Form 5305-SEP and provided the other documents and disclosures described in *Instructions to the Employer* and *Information for the Employee* are not required to file the annual information returns, Forms 5500, 5500-C/R, or 5500-EZ for the SEP. However, under Title I of ERISA, relief from the annual reporting requirements may not be available to an employer who selects, recommends, or influences its employees to choose IRAs into which employer contributions will be made under the SEP, if those IRAs are subject to provisions that impose any limits on a participant's ability to withdraw funds (other than restrictions imposed by the Code that apply to all IRAs). For additional information on Title I requirements, see the Department of Labor regulation 29 CFR 2520.104-48.

Information for the Employee

The information below explains what a SEP is, how contributions are made, and how to treat your employer's contributions for tax purposes. For more information, see page 1. Also, see Pub. 590.

Questions and Answers

1. Q. What is a simplified employee pension, or SEP?
  A. A SEP is a written arrangement (a plan) that allows an employer to make contributions toward your retirement. Contributions are made to an individual retirement account/annuity (IRA).

Your employer will provide you with a copy of the agreement containing participation rules and a description of how employer contributions may be made to your IRA.

All amounts contributed to your IRA by your employer belong to you even after you stop working for that employer.

2. Q. Must my employer contribute to my IRA under the SEP?
  A. No. An employer is not required to make SEP contributions. If a contribution is made, it must be allocated to all the eligible employees according to the SEP agreement. The Model SEP (Form 5305-SEP) specifies that the contribution for each eligible employee will be the same percentage of compensation (excluding compensation higher than $160,000) for all employees.

3. Q. How much may my employer contribute to my SEP-IRA in any year?
  A. Your employer will determine the amount to be contributed to your IRA each year. However, the amount for any year is limited to the smaller of $30,000* or 15% of your compensation for that year. Compensation does not include any amount that is contributed by your employer to your IRA under the SEP. Your employer is not required to make contributions every year or to maintain a particular level of contributions. (See Question 5.)

4. Q. How do I treat my employer's SEP contributions for my taxes?
  A. Employer contributions to your SEP-IRA are excluded from your income unless there are contributions in excess of the applicable limit. (See Question 3.) Employer contributions within these limits will not be included on your Form W-2.

5. Q. May I also contribute to my IRA if I am a participant in a SEP?
  A. Yes. You may contribute the smaller of $2,000 or 100% of your compensation to an IRA. However, the amount you can deduct may be reduced or eliminated because, as a participant in a SEP, you are covered by an employer retirement plan. (See Question 11.)

6. Q. Are there any restrictions on the IRA I select to have my SEP contributions deposited in?
  A. Contributions must be made to either a Model IRA executed on an IRS form or a master or prototype IRA for which the IRS has issued a favorable opinion letter.

7. Q. What if I do not want to participate in a SEP?
  A. If your employer does not require you to participate in a SEP as a condition of employment, and you elect not to participate, all other employees of your employer may be prohibited from participating. If one or more eligible employees do not participate and the employer tries to establish a SEP for the remaining employees, it could cause adverse tax consequences for the participating employees.

8. Q. Can I move funds from my SEP-IRA to another tax-sheltered IRA?
  A. Yes. You can withdraw or receive funds from your SEP-IRA if within 60 days of receipt, you place those funds in another IRA or SEP-IRA. This is called a "rollover" and can be done without penalty only once in any 1-year period. However, there are no restrictions on the number of times you may make "transfers" if you arrange to have these funds transferred between the trustee or the custodians so that you never have possession of the funds.

9. Q. What happens if I withdraw my employer's contribution from my IRA?
  A. You may withdraw your employer's contribution at any time, but any amount withdrawn is includible in your income unless rolled over. Also, if withdrawals occur before you reach age 59½, you may be subject to a tax on early withdrawal.

10. Q. May I participate in a SEP even though I am covered by another

An employer may not adopt this IRS Model SEP if the employer maintains another qualified retirement plan or has ever maintained a qualified defined benefit plan. This does not prevent your employer from adopting this IRS Model SEP and also participating in an IRS Elective SEP or other SEP. However, if you work for several employers, you may be covered by a SEP of one employer and a different SEP or pension or profit-sharing plan of another employer.

11. Q. What happens if too much is contributed to my SEP-IRA in 1 year?
  A. Contributions exceeding the yearly limitations may be withdrawn without penalty by the due date (plus extensions) for filing your tax return (normally April 15), but is includible in your gross income. Excess contributions left in your SEP-IRA account after that time may have adverse tax consequences. Withdrawals of those contributions may be taxed as premature withdrawals. (See Question 9.)

12. Q. Is my employer required to provide me with information about SEP-IRAs and the SEP agreement?
  A. Yes. Your employer must provide you with a copy of the completed Form 5305-SEP and a yearly statement showing any contributions to your IRA.

13. Q. Is the financial institution where my IRA is established required to provide me with information?
  A. Yes. It must provide you with a disclosure statement that contains the following information in plain, nontechnical language:
  (1) The law that relates to your IRA.
  (2) The tax consequences of various options concerning your IRA.
  (3) Participation eligibility rules, and rules on the deductibility of retirement savings.
  (4) Situations and procedures for revoking your IRA, including the name, address, and telephone number of the person designated to receive notice of revocation. (This information must be clearly displayed at the beginning of the disclosure statement.)
  (5) A discussion of the penalties that may be assessed because of prohibited activities concerning your IRA.
  (6) Financial disclosure that provides the following information:
     (a) Projects value growth rates of your IRA under various contribution and retirement schedules, or describes the method of determining annual earnings and charges that may be assessed.
     (b) Describes whether, and for when, the growth projections are guaranteed, or a statement of the earnings rate and the terms on which the projections are based.
     (c) States the sales commission for each year expressed as a percentage of $1,000.

In addition, the financial institution must provide you with a financial statement each year. You may want to keep these statements to evaluate your IRA's investment performance.

R209 031998

VANGUARD IRA
ADOPTION AGREEMENT

(to be used in conjunction with an employer SEP-IRA plan)

Welcome. Our goal is to provide you with the finest and most flexible retirement program available anywhere. If you have any questions, please call us toll-free at 1-800-662-2003. We'll be glad to help. Please be sure to sign your Adoption Agreement and IRA Asset Transfer Authorization (if applicable).

1. IRA REGISTRATION (Please Print)

Name: ___ First ___ Initial ___ Last ___

Social Security Number _____ Birth Date _____

Mailing Address _____

City _____ State ___ Zip ___

Telephone: Day _____ Evening _____

Employer's Name _____

Employer's Address _____

☐ I already have a Vanguard IRA and would like my employer's SEP contribution to go to my portfolio account(s).

Portfolio Name(s)   Account Number(s)   Percentage(s)

_____ | _____ | _____ %
_____ | _____ | _____ %
_____ | _____ | _____ %
_____ | _____ | _____ %

(Percentages must equal 100%)

2. INVESTMENT AMOUNTS

Type of IRA Investment	Amount
☐ a. SEP-IRA (Employer Contribution)*	
☐ for tax year 199___	$_____
☐ for tax year 199___	$_____
☐ b. Rollover Contribution	
☐ from a corporate plan	$_____
☐ from another IRA	$_____
☐ c. IRA Asset Transfer	

Please complete the attached IRA Asset Transfer Authorization form if you wish to transfer money tax-free directly to Vanguard from an existing IRA.

☐ d. Annual IRA participant contribution
   ☐ for tax year 199___ $_____
   ☐ for tax year 199___ $_____
Maximum IRA contribution (not including SEP) is $2,000 per tax year.

☐ e. Annual Custodial fee of $10 for each Vanguard portfolio account selected.** (See Section 3) $_____

☐ f. Total amount remitted $_____
(Payable to Vanguard Fiduciary Trust Company)

3. INVESTMENT INSTRUCTIONS (to Vanguard)

Please indicate the **full portfolio name(s) and number(s)** (as listed on the back of this form) and the desired allocation by percentage below. If you wish to put your assets into an existing Vanguard IRA, please indicate the account number as well.

Vanguard Portfolio Name(s)/Number(s)	Account Number(s)	Percentage(s)
1. _____	_____	_____ %
2. _____	_____	_____ %
3. _____	_____	_____ %
4. _____	_____	_____ %

(Percentages must equal 100%)

4. BENEFICIARY DESIGNATION (Please print and provide at least one Primary Beneficiary. If you wish to name additional primary or secondary beneficiaries, please list on a separate sheet of paper and attach to this form.)

(a) Primary Beneficiaries

Name _____
Social Security Number _____ Birth Date _____
Relationship _____ Percentage _____

Name _____
Social Security Number _____ Birth Date _____
Relationship _____ Percentage _____

(Percentages must equal 100%)

(b) Secondary Beneficiaries
(in the event your Primary Beneficiaries predecease you)

Name _____
Social Security Number _____ Birth Date _____
Relationship _____ Percentage _____

Name _____
Social Security Number _____ Birth Date _____
Relationship _____ Percentage _____

(Percentages must equal 100%)

*If you do not know the amount of your employer contribution, please check the SEP-IRA box, leave the amount blank, and complete the balance of this form.
**The annual custodial fee is applied to each portfolio account with assets of less than $5,000. For individuals whose total Vanguard assets are $50,000 or greater (excluding Vanguard Brokerage Services assets), all IRA custodial fees are waived regardless of each account's asset value.

(over, please)

5. SIGNATURE AND CUSTODIAN ACCEPTANCE (Your signature must appear in order to establish your IRA.)
The undersigned Depositor and the Custodian hereby adopt the Vanguard Individual Retirement Custodial Account
Agreement that is incorporated herein by reference and that the Depositor acknowledges having received and read. The
Depositor further acknowledges having received and read the Vanguard IRA Disclosure Statement and the prospectus for each
Vanguard fund(s) elected under this Agreement. Under the penalties of perjury, the Depositor certifies that his or her Social
Security number on this form is true, correct, and complete.

VANGUARD FIDUCIARY TRUST COMPANY   DEPOSITOR (Employee)

By: _____   _____
                                                    Your Signature   Date

Title: _____Secretary_____

IMPORTANT: This Adoption Agreement should be returned to your employer, and mailed together with the Contribution
Allocation Form to: Vanguard Fiduciary Trust Company, P.O. Box 2600, Valley Forge, PA 19482. Vanguard will mail each
Depositor a statement confirming the establishment of his or her IRA.

VANGUARD IRA FUNDS / PORTFOLIOS

Name	Number
Money Market Funds	
Vanguard Admiral Funds*	
U.S. Treasury Money Market Portfolio	.0011
Vanguard Money Market Portfolios	
Prime Portfolio	.0030
Federal Portfolio	.0033
Treasury Portfolio	.0050
Bond Funds	
Short-Term	
Vanguard Admiral Funds*	
Short-Term U.S. Treasury Portfolio	.0012
Vanguard Bond Index Fund	
Short-Term Bond Portfolio	.0132
Vanguard Fixed Income Securities Fund	
Short-Term U.S. Treasury Portfolio	.0032
Short-Term Federal Portfolio	.0049
Short-Term Corporate Portfolio	.0039
Intermediate-Term	
Vanguard Admiral Funds*	
Intermediate-Term U.S. Treasury Portfolio	.0019
Vanguard Bond Index Fund	
Intermediate-Term Bond Portfolio	.0314
Total Bond Market Portfolio	.0084
Vanguard Fixed Income Securities Fund	
Intermediate-Term U.S. Treasury Portfolio	.0035
GNMA Portfolio	.0036
Intermediate-Term Corporate Portfolio	.0071
High Yield Corporate Portfolio	.0029
Long-Term	
Vanguard Admiral Funds*	
Long-Term U.S. Treasury Portfolio	.0020
Vanguard Bond Index Fund	
Long-Term Bond Portfolio	.0522
Vanguard Fixed Income Securities Fund	
Long-Term U.S. Treasury Portfolio	.0083
Long-Term Corporate Portfolio	.0028
Balanced Funds	
Domestic	
Vanguard Asset Allocation Fund	.0078
Vanguard Balanced Index Fund	.0002
Vanguard LifeStrategy Portfolios* *	
Income Portfolio	.0723
Conservative Growth Portfolio	.0724
Moderate Growth Portfolio	.0914
Growth Portfolio	.0122
Vanguard STAR Portfolio* *	.0056

Name	Number
Vanguard/Wellesley Income Fund	.0027
Vanguard/Wellington Fund	.0021
International/Global	
Vanguard Horizon Fund	
Global Asset Allocation Portfolio	.0115
Stock Funds	
General	
Vanguard Convertible Securities Fund	.0082
Vanguard Equity Income Fund	.0065
Vanguard Growth and Income Portfolio	.0093
Vanguard Index Trust	
500 Portfolio	.0040
Growth Portfolio	.0009
Total Stock Market Portfolio	.0085
Value Portfolio	.0006
Vanguard/Morgan Growth Fund	.0026
Vanguard/Windsor II	.0073
More Aggressive	
Vanguard Explorer Fund	.0024
Vanguard Horizon Fund	
Aggressive Growth Portfolio	.0114
Capital Opportunity Portfolio	.0111
Vanguard Index Trust	
Extended Market Portfolio	.0098
Mid Capitalization Stock Portfolio	.0859
Small Capitalization Growth Stock Portfolio	.0861
Small Capitalization Stock Portfolio	.0048
Small Capitalization Value Stock Portfolio	.0860
Vanguard Selected Value Portfolio	.0934
Vanguard U.S. Growth Portfolio	.0023
Industry-Specific	
Vanguard Specialized Portfolios	
Energy Portfolio	.0051
Gold & Precious Metals Portfolio	.0053
Health Care Portfolio	.0052
REIT Index Portfolio	.0123
Utilities Income Portfolio	.0057
International/Global	
Vanguard Horizon Fund	
Global Equity Portfolio	.0129
Vanguard International Growth Portfolio	.0081
Vanguard International Index Portfolios	
Emerging Markets Portfolio	.0533
European Portfolio	.0079
Pacific Portfolio	.0072
Total International Portfolio*** *	.0113
Vanguard International Value Portfolio	.0046

*The minimum initial investment for Vanguard Admiral Funds is $50,000.
**Vanguard LifeStrategy Portfolios, Vanguard STAR Portfolio, and Vanguard Total International Portfolio are all part of Vanguard STAR Fund.

| Form **5305-SEP** (Rev. January 2000) Department of the Treasury Internal Revenue Service | **Simplified Employee Pension-Individual Retirement Accounts Contribution Agreement** (Under section 408(k) of the Internal Revenue Code) | OMB No. 1545-0499 **DO NOT File With the Internal Revenue Service** |

_____ makes the following agreement under section 408(k) of the
(Name of employer)
Internal Revenue Code and the instructions to this form.

Article I—Eligibility Requirements (Check appropriate boxes—see **Instructions** below.)

The employer agrees to provide for discretionary contributions in each calendar year to the individual retirement account or individual retirement annuity (IRA) of all employees who are at least _____ years old (not to exceed 21 years old) and have performed services for the employer in at least _____ years (not to exceed 3 years) of the immediately preceding 5 years. This simplified employee pension (SEP) ☐ includes ☐ does not include employees covered under a collective bargaining agreement, ☐ includes ☐ does not include certain nonresident aliens, and ☐ includes ☐ does not include employees whose total compensation during the year is less than $450*.

Article II—SEP Requirements (See **Instructions** below.)

The employer agrees that contributions made on behalf of each eligible employee will be:
A. Based only on the first $170,000* of compensation.
B. Made in an amount that is the same percentage of compensation for every employee.
C. Limited annually to the smaller of $30,000* **or** 15% of compensation.
D. Paid to the employee's IRA trustee, custodian, or insurance company (for an annuity contract).

_____   _____
Employer's signature and date   Name and title

Instructions

Section references are to the Internal Revenue Code unless otherwise noted.

Purpose of Form

Form 5305-SEP (Model SEP) is used by an employer to make an agreement to provide benefits to all eligible employees under a simplified employee pension (SEP) described in section 408(k). **DO NOT** file this form with the IRS. See **Pub. 560,** Retirement Plans for Small Business, and **Pub. 590,** Individual Retirement Arrangements (IRAs) (Including Roth IRAs and Education IRAs).

Note: *Employers that used the January 1997 version of Form 5305-SEP are not required to use the January 2000 revision of the form.*

Instructions to the Employer

Simplified employee pension. A SEP is a written arrangement (a plan) that provides you with a simplified way to make contributions toward your employees' retirement income. Under a SEP, you can contribute to an employee's traditional individual retirement account or annuity (traditional IRA). You make contributions directly to an IRA set up by or for each employee with a bank, insurance company, or other qualified financial institution. When using Form 5305-SEP to establish a SEP, the IRA must be a Model traditional IRA established on an IRS form or a master or prototype traditional IRA for which the IRS has issued a favorable opinion letter. You may **not** make SEP contributions to a Roth IRA or a SIMPLE IRA. Making the agreement on Form 5305-SEP does not establish an employer IRA described in section 408(c).

When not to use Form 5305-SEP. Do not use this form if you:

1. Currently maintain any other qualified retirement plan. This does not prevent you from maintaining another SEP.

2. Have any eligible employees for whom IRAs have not been established.

3. Use the services of leased employees (described in section 414(n)).

4. Are a member of an affiliated service group (described in section 414(m)), a controlled group of corporations (described in section 414(b)), or trades or businesses under common control (described in sections 414(c) and 414(o)), unless all eligible employees of all the members of such groups, trades, or businesses participate in the SEP.

5. Will not pay the cost of the SEP contributions. Do not use Form 5305-SEP for a SEP that provides for elective employee contributions even if the contributions are made under a salary reduction agreement. Use Form 5305A-SEP, or a nonmodel SEP.

Note: *SEPs permitting elective deferrals cannot be established after 1996.*

Eligible employees. All eligible employees must be allowed to participate in the SEP. An eligible employee is any employee who: **(1)** is at least 21 years old, and **(2)** has performed "service" for you in at least 3 of the immediately preceding 5 years.

Note: *You can establish less restrictive eligibility requirements, but not more restrictive ones.*

Service is any work performed for you for any period of time, however short. If you are a member of an affiliated service group, a controlled group of corporations, or trades or businesses under common control, service includes any work performed for any period of time for any other member of such group, trades, or businesses.

Excludable employees. The following employees do not have to be covered by the SEP: **(1)** employees covered by a collective bargaining agreement whose retirement benefits were bargained for in good faith by

you and their union, **(2)** nonresident alien employees who did not earn U.S. source income from you, and **(3)** employees who received less than $450* in compensation during the year.

Contribution limits. The SEP rules permit you to make an annual contribution of up to 15% of the employee's compensation or $30,000*, whichever is less. Compensation, for this purpose, does not include employer contributions to the SEP or the employee's compensation in excess of $170,000*. If you also maintain a Model Elective SEP or any other SEP that permits employees to make elective deferrals, contributions to the two SEPs together may not exceed the smaller of $30,000* or 15% of compensation for any employee.

You are not required to make contributions every year, but when you do, you must contribute to the SEP-IRAs of all of the eligible employees who actually performed services during the year of the contribution. This includes eligible employees who die or quit working before the contribution is made.

Contributions cannot discriminate in favor of highly compensated employees. You may also not integrate your SEP contributions with, or offset them by, contributions made under the Federal Insurance Contributions Act (FICA).

If this SEP is intended to meet the top-heavy minimum contribution rules of section 416, but it does not cover all your employees who participate in your elective SEP, then you must make minimum contributions to IRAs established on behalf of those employees.

Deducting contributions. You may deduct contributions to a SEP subject to the limits of section 404(h). This SEP is maintained on a calendar year basis and contributions to the SEP are deductible for your tax year with or

---

* This amount reflects the cost-of-living increase effective January 1, 2000. The amount is adjusted annually. The IRS announces the increase, if any, in a news release, in the Internal Revenue Bulletin, and on the IRS's Internet Web Site at www.irs.gov.

Cat. No. 11825J   Form **5305-SEP** (Rev. 1-2000)

SEP are deductible for your tax year with or within which the calendar year ends. Contributions made for a particular tax year must be made by the due date of your income tax return (including extensions) for that tax year.

Completing the agreement. This agreement is considered adopted when:

- IRAs have been established for all your eligible employees;

- You have completed all blanks on the agreement form without modification; and

- You have given all your eligible employees the following information:

  1. A copy of Form 5305-SEP.

  2. A statement that traditional IRAs other than the traditional IRAs into which employer SEP contributions will be made may provide different rates of return and different terms concerning, among other things, transfers and withdrawals of funds from the IRAs.

  3. A statement that, in addition to the information provided to an employee at the time the employee becomes eligible to participate, the administrator of the SEP must furnish each participant within 30 days of the effective date of any amendment to the SEP, a copy of the amendment and a written explanation of its effects.

  4. A statement that the administrator will give written notification to each participant of any employer contributions made under the SEP to that participant's IRA by the later of January 31 of the year following the year for which a contribution is made or 30 days after the contribution is made.

  Employers who have established a SEP using Form 5305-SEP and have furnished each eligible employee with a copy of the completed Form 5305-SEP and provided the other documents and disclosures described in **Instructions to the Employer** and **Information for the Employee,** are not required to file the annual information returns, Forms 5500 or 5500-EZ for the SEP. However, under Title I of the Employee Retirement Income Security Act of 1974 (ERISA), this relief from the annual reporting requirements may not be available to an employer who selects, recommends, or influences its employees to choose IRAs into which contributions will be made under the SEP, if those IRAs are subject to provisions that impose any limits on a participant's ability to withdraw funds (other than restrictions imposed by the Code that apply to all IRAs). For additional information on Title I requirements, see the Department of Labor regulation at 29 CFR 2520.104-48.

Information for the Employee

The information below explains what a SEP is, how contributions are made, and how to treat your employer's contributions for tax purposes. For more information, see Pub. 590.

Simplified employee pension. A SEP is a written arrangement (a plan) that allows an employer to make contributions toward your retirement. Contributions are made to a traditional individual retirement account/annuity (traditional IRA). Contributions must be made to either a Model traditional IRA executed on an IRS form or a master or prototype traditional IRA for which the IRS has issued a favorable opinion letter.

An employer is not required to make SEP contributions. If a contribution is made, it

must be allocated to all the eligible employees according to the SEP agreement. The Model SEP (Form 5305-SEP) specifies that the contribution for each eligible employee will be the same percentage of compensation (excluding compensation higher than $170,000*) for all employees.

Your employer will provide you with a copy of the agreement containing participation rules and a description of how employer contributions may be made to your IRA. Your employer must also provide you with a copy of the completed Form 5305-SEP and a yearly statement showing any contributions to your IRA.

All amounts contributed to your IRA by your employer belong to you even after you stop working for that employer.

Contribution limits. Your employer will determine the amount to be contributed to your IRA each year. However, the amount for any year is limited to the smaller of $30,000* or 15% of your compensation for that year. Compensation does not include any amount that is contributed by your employer to your IRA under the SEP. Your employer is not required to make contributions every year or to maintain a particular level of contributions.

Tax treatment of contributions. Employer contributions to your SEP-IRA are excluded from your income unless there are contributions in excess of the applicable limit. Employer contributions within these limits will not be included on your Form W-2.

Employee contributions. You may contribute the smaller of $2,000 or 100% of your compensation to an IRA. However, the amount you can deduct may be reduced or eliminated because, as a participant in a SEP, you are covered by an employer retirement plan.

SEP participation. If your employer does not require you to participate in a SEP as a condition of employment, and you elect not to participate, all other employees of your employer may be prohibited from participating. If one or more eligible employees do not participate and the employer tries to establish a SEP for the remaining employees, it could cause adverse tax consequences for the participating employees.

An employer may not adopt this IRS Model SEP if the employer maintains another qualified retirement plan. This does not prevent your employer from adopting this IRS Model SEP and also maintaining an IRS Model Elective SEP or other SEP. However, if you work for several employers, you may be covered by a SEP of one employer and a different SEP or pension or profit-sharing plan of another employer.

SEP-IRA amounts—rollover or transfer to another IRA. You can withdraw or receive funds from your SEP-IRA if, within 60 days of receipt, you place those funds in another IRA. This is called a "rollover" and can be done without penalty only once in any 1-year period. However, there are no restrictions on the number of times you may make "transfers" if you arrange to have these funds transferred between the trustees or the custodians so that you never have possession of the funds.

Withdrawals. You may withdraw your employer's contribution at any time, but any amount withdrawn is includible in your income unless rolled over. Also, if withdrawals

occur before you reach age 59¹/₂, you may be subject to a tax on early withdrawal.

Excess SEP contributions. Contributions exceeding the yearly limitations may be withdrawn without penalty by the due date (plus extensions) for filing your tax return (normally April 15), but are includible in your gross income. Excess contributions left in your SEP-IRA account after that time may have adverse tax consequences. Withdrawals of those contributions may be taxed as premature withdrawals.

Financial institution requirements. The financial institution where your IRA is maintained must provide you with a disclosure statement that contains the following information in plain, nontechnical language:

  1. The law that relates to your IRA.

  2. The tax consequences of various options concerning your IRA.

  3. Participation eligibility rules, and rules on the deductibility of retirement savings.

  4. Situations and procedures for revoking your IRA, including the name, address, and telephone number of the person designated to receive notice of revocation. (This information must be clearly displayed at the beginning of the disclosure statement.)

  5. A discussion of the penalties that may be assessed because of prohibited activities concerning your IRA.

  6. Financial disclosure that provides the following information:

  a. Projects value growth rates of your IRA under various contribution and retirement schedules, or describes the method of determining annual earnings and charges that may be assessed.

  b. Describes whether, and for when, the growth projections are guaranteed, or a statement of the earnings rate and the terms on which the projections are based.

  c. States the sales commission for each year expressed as a percentage of $1,000.

  In addition, the financial institution must provide you with a financial statement each year. You may want to keep these statements to evaluate your IRA's investment performance.

Paperwork Reduction Act Notice. You are not required to provide the information requested on a form that is subject to the Paperwork Reduction Act unless the form displays a valid OMB control number. Books or records relating to a form or its instructions must be retained as long as their contents may become material in the administration of any Internal Revenue law. Generally, tax returns and return information are confidential, as required by Code section 6103.

The time needed to complete this form will vary depending on individual circumstances. The estimated average time is:

Recordkeeping	1 hr., 40 min.
Learning about the law or the form	1 hr., 35 min.
Preparing the form . . .	1 hr., 41 min.

If you have comments concerning the accuracy of these time estimates or suggestions for making this form simpler, we would be happy to hear from you. You can write to the Tax Forms Committee, Western Area Distribution Center, Rancho Cordova, CA 95743-0001. **DO NOT** send this form to this address. Instead, keep it for your records.

---

* *This amount reflects the cost-of-living increase effective January 1, 2000. The amount is adjusted annually. The IRS announces the increase, if any, in a news release, in the Internal Revenue Bulletin, and on the IRS's Internet Web Site at www.irs.gov.*

Chapter 5

Profit Sharing Plans

A. What Is a Profit Sharing Plan? 5/3

1. Who May Establish a Profit Sharing Plan? 5/5

2. Advantages 5/5

3. Disadvantages 5/6

B. How to Establish a Profit Sharing Plan 5/6

1. Trustee or Custodian 5/7

2. Plan Documents 5/8

3. Deadlines 5/11

4. Plan Year 5/11

C. Contributions 5/11

1. Maximum Contribution 5/12

2. No Minimum Contribution 5/15

3. Cash or Property? 5/15

4. Deadlines 5/16

5. How to Claim the Tax Deduction 5/17

D. Ongoing Administration 5/17

1. Tax Returns 5/17

2. Plan Administration 5/18

3. Updating Plan Documents 5/18

E. Distributions **5/19**

    1. Inservice Distributions 5/19

    2. Loans 5/20

    3. Hardship Distributions 5/20

    4. Divorce Payments 5/21

    5. Early Distributions and Exceptions to the Early Distribution Penalty 5/22

    6. Mandatory Distributions 5/25

F. Penalties **5/26**

    1. Nondeductible Contributions 5/27

    2. Early Distributions 5/28

    3. Prohibited Transactions... 5/29

    4. Life Insurance 5/30

    5. Pledging the Account As Security 5/31

    6. Mandatory Distribution Penalty 5/31

G. Terminating Your Profit Sharing Plan **5/31**

    1. Paperwork 5/32

    2. Distribution of Assets 5/32

H. Multiple Employer Plans **5/33**

    1. If You Are Self-Employed With a Day Job on the Side; or Vice Versa 5/34

    2. If You Are Self-Employed With Only One Business 5/35

    3. If You Are Self-Employed With Two or More Businesses 5/36

I. Adding a Traditional or Roth IRA to Your Profit Sharing Plan **5/39**

J. Filling Out the Forms **5/39**

A profit sharing plan is a Keogh that combines simplicity with flexibility. If you choose this type of plan, you will have little trouble establishing and maintaining it on your own. Although the rules for profit sharing plans can be more complex than those for SEPs and SIMPLE IRAs, most of the complexity doesn't kick in until you hire employees. If you're reading this book, you have no employees (right?), so you've got nothing to worry about. Just consider yourself warned: If you ever do decide to add employees, things will become more complicated.

 If you ever hire employees, we recommend that you seek advice from a plan consultant to learn how you must alter the operation of your profit sharing plan. Although the plan might meet your needs now, you might find that it doesn't suit you once you add employees to the mix.

Although contribution limits aren't as high with this type of plan as with others (such as money purchase pension plans and, often, defined benefit plans), profit sharing plan contributions have the advantage of being discretionary, which means you can reduce or eliminate your contribution in any given year.

The Ideal Candidate for This Plan

A profit sharing plan works best for people who have net business income in excess of $30,000, who have variable income from year to year and who intend to combine the profit sharing plan (with its flexibility and ease) with a money purchase pension plan (with its higher contributions).

A. What Is a Profit Sharing Plan?

Profit sharing plans are part of a category of Keogh plans known as defined contribution plans—as distinguished from defined benefit plans. Contributions to defined contribution plans are typically a specific dollar amount or percentage of compensation—a defined amount, as the name suggests—paid into the separate account of each participant. That account will shrink or grow depending on how the assets in the account are invested and how those investments do. In contrast, defined benefit plans specify an amount—a benefit—the participant will receive at retirement. All assets of the plan are pooled in one large account, and each participant's benefit is paid from that pool.

This Plan in a Nutshell

✓ You must make a profit to contribute to a profit sharing plan.

✓ If you make a profit, contributions to a profit sharing plan are completely discretionary. You can contribute the maximum the law allows. Or you can contribute less (whatever amount you choose). Or you can contribute nothing at all.

✓ If the net income from your business is less than $50,000, you will be able to contribute more to a SIMPLE IRA than to a stand-alone profit sharing plan. However, if your net income exceeds $50,000, then a stand-alone profit sharing plan will allow higher contributions than will a SIMPLE IRA.

✓ You can always contribute more to a money purchase pension plan than to a profit sharing plan, but money purchase pension plans are less flexible.

✓ Once your net income exceeds $30,000, you might consider establishing a profit sharing plan along with a money purchase pension plan to combine flexibility (profit sharing plan) with higher contribution limits (money purchase pension plan).

✓ You must set up your profit sharing plan before the end of the tax year for which you want to make a contribution. Generally, that means you must establish the plan by December 31.

✓ Although not as simple to establish and maintain as a SIMPLE IRA or a SEP, you should have little trouble handling both the setup and the ongoing administration (which is minimal) yourself.

✓ You will have to file an information tax return for the plan once the assets of the plan exceed $100,000, and you must file a final return when you terminate the plan.

Paradoxically, a profit sharing plan isn't literally a plan that allows you and other participants to share in the profits of your business. For one thing, you aren't required to make contributions when you make a profit. For another thing, if you hire employees who eventually participate in the plan, you can contribute to their accounts (but not to your own) even if you don't make a profit. It is this very flexibility that makes profit sharing plans popular. It can be comforting to know you don't have to make a contribution when you feel you can't afford it or when you simply don't feel like it.

Another unique feature of profit sharing plans is that they allow you to take distributions from the plan while you are still working for the business that sponsors the plan (although if you are younger than 59½, you might have to pay an early distribution penalty as explained below). Other Keogh plans typically do not allow these "inservice distributions."

1. Who May Establish a Profit Sharing Plan?

Generally, you may establish a profit sharing plan if you own your own business. However, you must have net earnings from the business in order to make a contribution for yourself, because the profit sharing plan contribution is tied to your earnings.

You can establish a profit sharing plan even if your business is simply a side venture that generates a little extra income for you. For example, if you glue widgets as an employee for a corporation by day, but write novels by night, you can set up a profit sharing plan for your writing royalties regardless of what plan your corporate employer provides for you.

But if you already own one business and then start a second, you might not be able to contribute to a separate plan for each business. (For more information about multiple plan rules, see Section H, below.)

2. Advantages

In Chapter 2, you can find a detailed comparison of the different types of retirement plans that you can establish for your business and for yourself as an individual. That chapter will help you decide which plan or plans are best for you. In the next two sections, however, we summarize some of the advantages and disadvantages of profit sharing plans when compared to other employer plans.

First, the advantages:

- Once your net income exceeds about $50,000, you can contribute more to a profit sharing plan than to a SIMPLE IRA.
- You can tack a money purchase pension plan on to your profit sharing plan to boost the contribution limit even further. If you do so, then the combined profit sharing plan and money purchase pension plan will permit a larger contribution than will a SIMPLE IRA once your income exceeds about $30,000.
- You can forgo making a contribution to your profit sharing plan in any given year—or simply reduce the contribution to a level that is more palatable.
- You can take distributions while you are still working for the employer that sponsors the profit sharing plan (in your case, the employer will be yourself, of course)—called "inservice distributions"—if your plan contains a provision that allows inservice distributions. This option generally is not available with other types of qualified plans, such as money purchase pension plans and defined benefit plans.

 If you ever hire employees, you can restrict their participation in the plan more effectively when you have a profit sharing plan than when you have either a SEP or a SIMPLE IRA. You might want to do this if the

cost of contributions threatens to be pro-
hibitive or if you want to use the plan as a
carrot to keep employees with you.

3. Disadvantages

Disadvantages of profit sharing plans include the following:

- The paperwork required to establish
  a profit sharing plan is more voluminous and complex than for a SEP or
  a SIMPLE IRA.
- Other qualified plans, such as money
  purchase pension plans and (frequently) defined benefit plans permit
  larger contributions and larger tax
  deductions than do profit sharing
  plans. If your net income (business
  income less deductible business expenses, including half of your self-
  employment tax) is less than $50,000,
  even a SIMPLE IRA is likely to permit
  a higher contribution than a profit
  sharing plan. However, this lower
  contribution limit often can be over-
  come by adding a second retirement
  plan to the profit sharing plan. (See
  Section H, below, for more information about multiple plans.)
- Unlike SEPs and SIMPLE IRAs, profit
  sharing plans (like all qualified
  plans) have filing requirements. For
  example, the Tax Code requires you
  to file an information tax return for a
  profit sharing plan if the assets of the
  plan reach $100,000 or if the plan
  covers employees. You must also file

a return in the last year of the plan,
even if you were not required to file
a return in any previous year.

 **If you hire employees, a complex
set of nondiscrimination rules
(rules that apply to all qualified plans)
kicks in,** which will almost certainly
force you to engage a consultant to
help keep the plan in compliance
with the law. (See Chapter 1, Section
B.l.d, for more information about
nondiscrimination rules.)

B. How to Establish a Profit Sharing Plan

A profit sharing plan must be established
by an employer. When you work for yourself and establish a retirement plan, you
wear two hats: You, as the employer, es-

tablish the retirement plan and make contributions on behalf of yourself, as the employee.

If you are a sole proprietor, you would set up the profit sharing plan in your own name as the employer (or in the name you are using for your business). If you are doing business as a partnership, however, the partnership must establish the profit sharing plan, because the partnership is the employer. You and your partner cannot establish two separate plans as individual partners.

1. Trustee or Custodian

Although most qualified plan assets must be held in a trust, a special exception allows Keogh plan assets to be held in a custodial account. If you are self-employed and you plan to establish your profit sharing plan account with a bank, brokerage firm or mutual fund, you generally will have the financial institution serve as custodian. Not only is it simpler, but the custodian will handle administrative details of your plan that would otherwise fall to you if you were serving as trustee. (See Chapter 1, Section C.2, for more information about trustees and custodians.)

Sometimes, You Must Establish a Trust

Occasionally you will be required to use a trust instead of a custodial account. This might happen if you choose an investment vehicle that a bank or other custodian is not willing to hold in the account. For example, you might invest in a limited partnership or an offbeat investment for which the custodian doesn't want responsibility. In that case you would have to establish a trust. The profit sharing plan documents themselves can serve as the trust agreement, but you would need to hire a consultant to create the documents.

Once you establish the trust or plan, you must name a trustee. Although you are not required to serve as trustee (you can hire someone else), you will probably want to do it yourself to save money.

Once the trust is in place, you can open an account with a financial institution, such as a bank, brokerage firm or mutual fund. The account will be in your name as trustee of the profit sharing plan (assuming you are serving as trustee). You cannot simply open an account in your name and deposit contributions. For example, the account title might be "Martha Doles, Trustee of the Martha Doles Profit Sharing Plan." Assets that are not held at the financial institution (those offbeat investments, for example) would be titled in the same way to indicate that they are assets of the profit sharing plan trust.

2. Plan Documents

To establish your profit sharing plan, you can use the profit sharing plan documents provided by the financial institution of your choice—a prototype profit sharing plan. Alternatively, you can hire a consultant to create a customized plan just for you, although there is rarely a reason to do so when you have no employees.

a. Prototype Plan

Most financial institutions have their own pre-approved prototype profit sharing plans. By using such a plan, you save the cost of creating a plan from scratch. In addition, the financial institution generally takes responsibility for keeping its own documents up to date—a task that would fall to you if you created your own plan.

See Section J, below, for instructions on completing sample prototype documents.

The High Price (and Headache) of a Custom Fit

If you decide to hire someone to create a profit sharing plan especially for you, it will cost you—anywhere from several hundred to several thousand dollars.

But cost won't be your only concern. Once the plan is drafted, you will want to make sure it will pass muster with the IRS. You do this by requesting a determination letter from the IRS. Generally, the consultant who crafts the plan for you will seek the determination letter. Although you are not required to seek IRS approval, you might feel more comfortable if you know that all the contributions you are making to your profit sharing plan are deductible. The IRS's stamp of approval is not free. The so-called "user fee" currently ranges from $125 to $1,250.

Next you (or your consultant) must find a financial institution that is willing to serve as custodian of your profit sharing plan assets under the terms of your customized plan. Most institutions will serve as custodian of the funds, but you will be responsible for maintaining the qualified status of the plan. (See Section D, below, for more about plan administration requirements.)

b.   Beneficiary Designation

When you name a beneficiary of your retirement plan, you are identifying the person or organization that you want to receive your plan benefits when you die. That's important, certainly. But the person or organization you name as beneficiary can be crucial for other reasons, as well. For example, your choice of beneficiary will determine how quickly you must take distributions from the plan after you reach age 70½ (see Section E.6, below)—and how quickly the plan must be liquidated after your death.

If you are married and you name your spouse as beneficiary, he or she will have options that other beneficiaries do not have. Your spouse can roll over your retirement plan into an IRA in his or her own name, pick new beneficiaries and, in most cases, prolong or delay distributions from the plan. (Remember, when you delay distributions from a plan, the assets can continue to grow tax-deferred—a big benefit!)

For most married individuals, naming a spouse as beneficiary is the best option. In fact, if you are married, your spouse is automatically presumed to be the beneficiary of your qualified plan.

But suppose you do not want to name your spouse as beneficiary. In that case, you can change the beneficiary to someone else, but your spouse must consent in writing to the change—and to all future changes of beneficiary unless the change reinstates your spouse as beneficiary.

If you want to make a sizable donation to charity when you die, retirement plan assets might well be the best source of that donation, because charities will not have to pay income tax on the distributions. Unfortunately, when you name a charity as beneficiary, you generally must distribute assets from the plan more quickly during your lifetime than you would if you named a person as beneficiary.

And it is almost never right to simply name your "estate" as beneficiary. Doing so could cause income tax problems for your heirs and perhaps increase probate fees as well.

As you can see, choosing a beneficiary can be a complex decision. For more information about the effect of your beneficiary designation on your retirement plan, see *IRAs, 401(k)s & Other Retirement Plans: Taking Your Money Out*, by Twila Slesnick and John Suttle (Nolo).

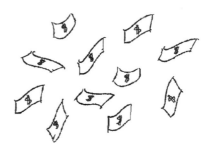

The Joint and Survivor Annuity Requirement

In the old days, it was entirely possible that an employee or her family might never see a dime of her retirement plan benefits, even if she worked for the same company for 40 years. How could this happen? Well, suppose she labored for years and on the day she became fully vested in her retirement plan, she dropped dead of a heart attack. What luck for the company. Now it doesn't have to pay the benefits.

Doesn't sound quite fair, though, does it? After all, the poor woman did own those benefits. Why shouldn't they go to her spouse or to someone else of her choosing? For a long time, nothing in the law prevented those benefits from reverting to the company when a participant died.

Then in 1974 (with modifications in 1984), Congress enacted a new set of laws known as the joint and survivor annuity requirement. These laws provide that a qualified plan must pay out benefits to the plan participant and the participant's spouse as a joint and survivor annuity (as long as the two have been married for at least a year). If the plan participant dies, the surviving spouse will continue to receive the participant's remaining vested retirement benefits.

Despite the law's moniker, the participant and the spouse are not required to take the benefits as an annuity. They can select another form of payment available under the plan, such as a rollover to an IRA, as long as both of them consent to the alternative form of payment. A surviving spouse, too, can generally select another form of payment (besides an annuity) if he or she inherits the plan after the participant's untimely death.

Note that the joint and survivor annuity rule applies in a similar way in cases where the plan participant has designated someone other than his or her spouse to be the beneficiary. However, the participant does not need a non-spouse beneficiary's consent to change the beneficiary designation or the form of payment.

A profit sharing plan can skate out from under this annuity requirement if the plan provides that upon the participant's death, the benefits of the plan are to be paid in full to the surviving spouse (or other designated beneficiary) upon the participant's death.

3. Deadlines

As is the case with all Keogh plans, you must establish your profit sharing plan by the end of the first year for which you want to make a contribution. The Tax Code permits no extensions for establishing the plan. Although you do not need to make the full contribution at that time, some financial institutions require that you open an account with a nominal amount of money. You can send in the rest of your contribution later. (See Section C.4, below, for information on contribution deadlines.)

4. Plan Year

Although most self-employed individuals maintain their plans (and their businesses) on a calendar year, you are permitted to maintain a profit sharing plan on either a calendar year or a fiscal year. A fiscal year is generally any 12-month period that ends on the last day of any month except December. You don't have to use the same year as your business, although it usually makes sense to do so. If you don't, the plan accounting becomes a little more complicated and offers no advantage. For example, to compute the deduction for your tax return, you would use the income you received during your business tax year, not your plan year. Then you would take your deduction for the business tax year in which the plan year ends.

EXAMPLE: You maintain your profit sharing plan on a calendar year, but your business tax year runs from July through June. To compute your deductible contribution to your profit sharing plan you would use the compensation or net earnings you received between July 2001 and June 2002 (fiscal year 2001). You would then claim your deduction on your fiscal year 2001 tax return.

C. Contributions

If you are like most people, you'll only be thinking about maximizing contributions and deductions in the first year of your profit sharing plan. As time goes on, however, your creative juices will start to flow, or your circumstances will change, and you will also want to know answers to other questions, such as: Can you contribute even when your business is losing money? Can you vary the contribution each year? Can you contribute stock? Can you make the contribution at the beginning of the year? After the end of the year? Can you put in a little extra this year while you're flush so you don't have to put in as much next year?

In this section, we answer those questions—and more—by giving you an overview of the rules and regulations governing contributions to profit sharing plans.

If your business operates in the red for a year, you won't have to worry about the finer points of making contributions to your plan. This is because the law won't allow you to contribute to a profit sharing plan in years when you do not make a profit. That's the rule for self-employed individuals.

If you ever add employees, you will be permitted to contribute to their profit sharing plan accounts even if you don't make a profit.

1. Maximum Contribution

Don't listen to that Volvo salesman who tells you it's better to buy an antique off his lot than contribute to your profit sharing plan. It isn't. And once you realize how much potential growth there is in those profit sharing plan contributions, you will make them gleefully, year after year. In fact, you will probably want to put every dollar you can into the plan. Ah, but there's a catch: Congress has put limits on annual contributions and deductions

A quick reading of the rules indicates your contribution to a profit sharing plan is limited to the lesser of 15% of your compensation or $30,000. (The $30,000 limit increases to $35,000 beginning in the 2001 tax year.) That's the general rule. But there are two additional rules that will limit the amount you can contribute. We discuss those additional limits in the following sections.

a. Additional Limit One: Limit on Compensation

For purposes of computing the maximum contribution, your compensation is deemed to be no more than $170,000 (for the year 2000). That means the maximum contribution you can make to a profit sharing plan is $25,500 (15% of $170,000), even if you actually earn $250,000 from your business. Some good news, though. The $170,000 will be increased for inflation occasionally, but not necessarily every year.

b. Additional Limit Two: Definition of Compensation

The Tax Code defines compensation differently for self-employed individuals than for others. It is not simply your net profit, which is your business income reduced by expenditures directly related to the business. Instead, compensation is your net earnings from self-employment, which is your business income reduced by all deductible business expenses. And for a self-employed individual, deductible business expenses include your self-employment tax deduction (which is always half of your self-employment tax) and your profit sharing plan deduction itself. So, before you multiply your net profit by 15%, you must first reduce it by half of your self-employment tax and reduce it further by your profit sharing plan contribution. But the profit sharing plan contribution is what you are trying to compute! We show you how to get around this conundrum in the paragraphs that follow. The point is, if you simply multiply your profit by 15% and contribute that amount to your profit sharing plan, you will come up with the wrong number.

 If you use that wrong number, you will have made an excess contribution to your plan—which will be subject to penalties unless corrected. (See Section F.1, below, for more information about excess contributions.)

c. Calculating the Contribution Amount

Calculating your maximum profit sharing plan contribution is a five-step process:

Step 1:
Calculate your total business income and subtract your expenses (not including your profit sharing plan contribution or your self-employment tax deduction).

Step 2:
Compute your self-employment tax deduction. The deductible portion is half of your total self-employment tax. Schedule SE (see Example 1, below) walks you through the calculation. You can find a sample copy of Schedule SE in the Appendix of this book.

Step 3:
Subtract the amount in Step 2 from the amount in Step 1.

Step 4:
Multiply the result from Step 3 by 13.0435%. (See Chapter 1, Section B.1.c.i, for an explanation of why you use 13.0435% instead of 15%.)

Step 5:
Compare the result from Step 4 with the contribution limit of $25,500. Your maximum contribution is the lesser of $25,500 or Step 4.

> **EXAMPLE 1:** Roxie raked in $98,450 from her Web design business in the year 2000. Her expenses (not including the self-employment tax deduction or the profit sharing plan deduction) amounted to $26,780. She wants to contribute as much as she can to her profit sharing plan.
>
> **Step 1:** Roxie's income less expenses is $71,670, which is $98,450 – $26,780.
>
> **Step 2:** Roxie completes Schedule SE to arrive at her self-employment tax deduction of $5,064. (See Line 6 of Schedule SE below.)
>
> **Step 3:** Roxie reduces the amount from Step 1 by the amount from Step 2.
>
> $71,670 – $5064 = $66,606 (Step 1 – Step 2).
>
> **Step 4:** Finally, to compute her maximum profit sharing plan contribution, she multiplies Step 3 by 13.0435%.
>
> $66,606 x 13.0435% = $8,688.
>
> **Step 5:** Because that amount does not exceed $25,500, Roxie can contribute $8,688 to her profit sharing plan and take a deduction on her tax return.

SCHEDULE SE	Self-Employment Tax	OMB No. 1545-0074
(Form 1040)	▶ See Instructions for Schedule SE (Form 1040).	**2000**
Department of the Treasury Internal Revenue Service (99)	▶ Attach to Form 1040.	Attachment Sequence No. **17**

Name of person with **self-employment** income (as shown on Form 1040) Roxie Woods	Social security number of person with **self-employment** income ▶ 555 ¦55 ¦5555

Who Must File Schedule SE

You must file Schedule SE if:

- You had net earnings from self-employment from **other than** church employee income (line 4 of Short Schedule SE or line 4c of Long Schedule SE) of $400 or more **or**
- You had church employee income of $108.28 or more. Income from services you performed as a minister or a member of a religious order **is not** church employee income. See page SE-1.

Note. Even if you had a loss or a small amount of income from self-employment, it may be to your benefit to file Schedule SE and use either "optional method" in Part II of Long Schedule SE. See page SE-3.

Exception. If your only self-employment income was from earnings as a minister, member of a religious order, or Christian Science practitioner **and** you filed Form 4361 and received IRS approval not to be taxed on those earnings, **do not** file Schedule SE. Instead, write "Exempt–Form 4361" on Form 1040, line 52.

May I Use Short Schedule SE or Must I Use Long Schedule SE?

```
                        ┌─────────────────────────────────────┐
                        │  Did You Receive Wages or Tips in 2000?  │
                        └─────────────────────────────────────┘
              No                                                    Yes

┌────────────────────────────────┐             ┌──────────────────────────────────────┐
│ Are you a minister, member of a │             │ Was the total of your wages and tips   │
│ religious order, or Christian   │  Yes  ▶     │ subject to social security or railroad  │  Yes ▶
│ Science practitioner who        │             │ retirement tax plus your net earnings   │
│ received IRS approval not to be │             │ from self-employment more than          │
│ taxed on earnings from these    │             │ $76,200?                                │
│ sources, but you owe self-      │             └──────────────────────────────────────┘
│ employment tax on other         │                            No
│ earnings?                       │
└────────────────────────────────┘             ┌──────────────────────────────────────┐
              No                                │ Did you receive tips subject to social │  Yes ▶
┌────────────────────────────────┐       No  ◀ │ security or Medicare tax that you did   │
│ Are you using one of the        │  Yes  ▶     │ not report to your employer?            │
│ optional methods to figure your │             └──────────────────────────────────────┘
│ net earnings (see page SE-3)?   │
└────────────────────────────────┘
              No

┌────────────────────────────────┐
│ Did you receive church employee │  Yes ▶
│ income reported on Form W-2 of  │
│ $108.28 or more?                │
└────────────────────────────────┘
              No

┌────────────────────────────────┐             ┌──────────────────────────────────────┐
│ You May Use Short Schedule SE   │             │ You Must Use Long Schedule SE on the   │
│ Below                           │             │ Back                                   │
└────────────────────────────────┘             └──────────────────────────────────────┘
```

Section A—Short Schedule SE. Caution: *Read above to see if you can use Short Schedule SE.*

1	Net farm profit or (loss) from Schedule F, line 36, and farm partnerships, Schedule K-1 (Form 1065), line 15a	**1**	
2	Net profit or (loss) from Schedule C, line 31; Schedule C-EZ, line 3; Schedule K-1 (Form 1065), line 15a (other than farming); and Schedule K-1 (Form 1065-B), box 9. Ministers and members of religious orders, see page SE-1 for amounts to report on this line. See page SE-2 for other income to report	**2**	71,670
3	Combine lines 1 and 2	**3**	71,670
4	**Net earnings from self-employment.** Multiply line 3 by 92.35% (.9235). If less than $400, **do not** file this schedule; you do not owe self-employment tax . . . . ▶	**4**	66,187
5	**Self-employment tax.** If the amount on line 4 is: • $76,200 or less, multiply line 4 by 15.3% (.153). Enter the result here and on **Form 1040, line 52.** • More than $76,200, multiply line 4 by 2.9% (.029). Then, add $9,448.80 to the result. Enter the total here and on **Form 1040, line 52.**	**5**	10,127
6	**Deduction for one-half of self-employment tax.** Multiply line 5 by 50% (.5). Enter the result here and on **Form 1040, line 27**	**6** 5,064	

For Paperwork Reduction Act Notice, see Form 1040 instructions.	Cat. No. 11358Z	Schedule SE (Form 1040) 2000

EXAMPLE 2: In 2001, Roxie's business really took off. She was paid $320,000 for her services and had expenses of $50,820.

Step 1: Roxie's income less expenses is $269,180, which is $320,000 – $50,820.

Step 2: Roxie completes a new Schedule SE and determines that her self-employment tax deduction is $7,846.

Step 3: Roxie reduces the amount from Step 1 by her self-employment tax deduction.

$269,180 – $7,846 = $261,334 (which is Step 1 – Step 2).

Step 4: Finally to compute her maximum profit sharing plan contribution, she multiplies Step 3 by 13.0435%.

$261,334 x 13.0435% = $34,087.

Step 5: Roxie wishes she could contribute and deduct $34,087, but her contribution is limited to $25,500, so Roxie will contribute only $25,500 and claim a $25,500 deduction on her tax return.

 Of course, you do not have to contribute the maximum the law allows. You can contribute any amount you want, as long as the contribution does not exceed the maximum and as long as you made a profit for the year.

2. No Minimum Contribution

One of the most attractive features of a profit sharing plan is that you are not required to make a contribution every year. You can structure your profit sharing plan in such a way that contributions are discretionary. For example, if you want to use extra cash to buy new computers for your business one year instead of making a profit sharing plan contribution, you are free to do so. Or you can contribute less than the maximum—as much as you feel you can afford.

3. Cash or Property?

The law does not specifically prohibit contributions of property to a profit sharing plan. Nonetheless, as a practical matter, contributing property generally does not work. That's because it's almost impossible to contribute property without violating one or more of the prohibited transaction rules. (See Section F.3, below, for more about prohibited transactions.) For example, you cannot contribute property that you plan to use personally (like your house or your car). And you cannot contribute encumbered property—property that has an outstanding loan attached to it. Prohibited transactions can be expensive and, in the worst case, lead to disqualification of your plan. It's best to make your profit sharing contributions in cash.

4. Deadlines

You may make your profit sharing plan contribution any time during the year. Generally, the earlier you make it, the better, because the money can be working for you.

Unfortunately you don't always know how much money you will make until late in the year, or even after the end of the year. That's why the government gives you until the due date of your tax return to make the precise contribution. And if you request and receive an extension of time for filing your return, you have until the extended due date to make your contribution. However, you could make a partial contribution early in the year and contribute the remainder when you have final income numbers.

 If your contribution is postmarked by the due date of your tax return, you will be in compliance with the law. In other words, you can write a check and take it to the post office (or deliver it to yourself, as trustee) on the day your tax return is due. The money doesn't actually have to be in the account by then. Just be sure to obtain proof of mailing.

Using Your Tax Refund to Pay Your Plan Contribution

Suppose you are short of cash for making your profit sharing plan contribution, but you are expecting a big tax refund—enough to cover the profit sharing plan contribution. As it happens, you are not required to make your contribution before you actually file your tax return. But you must make it by the due date of your tax return. That means you can file your return, receive the refund, and then use the refund to make the contribution.

The only problem with this strategy is that you must file your tax return early enough so that you receive the refund before the actual filing deadline of your tax return—which is when the contribution is due. For example, if your tax return is due April 15, you would have to file your return in January, February or March and hope that you receive the refund before April 15 when the profit sharing plan contribution is due.

But be careful! Suppose April 15 looms and you still have not received your refund. It won't work to request an extension at the last minute, because you have already filed your tax return. (After all, you can't get an extension of time for doing something you've already done.) Instead you will have to find another source of funds for making the profit sharing plan contribution.

As a precaution, you might want to request an extension before you file your tax return in the first place. Then you will have until the extended due date to receive the refund and make the profit sharing plan contribution.

5. How to Claim the Tax Deduction

Once you have computed your profit sharing plan contribution, you claim your deduction on page 1, line 29, of your individual income tax return (IRS Form 1040). This will be true whether you are doing business as a partnership or as a sole proprietor. You can find a sample Form 1040 in the Appendix.

D. Ongoing Administration

Although the ongoing administration for a profit sharing plan can be more significant than for a SEP or a SIMPLE IRA, it's quite possible to manage without an expensive plan consultant if you have no employees. Even if you find you must file a tax return for the plan and don't want to tackle it yourself, most accountants can prepare such returns. And accountants typically do not charge exorbitant fees to prepare returns for one-participant plans.

1. Tax Returns

There are two types of tax returns you might have to file for your profit sharing plan: IRS Form 5500-EZ and IRS Form 990-T. You can find sample copies of both forms in the Appendix of this book.

a. IRS Form 5500-EZ

IRS Form 5500-EZ is an information tax return that helps the IRS monitor the operation of your plan. But just because you might be required to file this form does not mean you owe tax. In fact, your profit sharing plan will not owe any income tax while the assets remain in the plan, except in certain rare circumstances when the plan assets generate business income. (See Section b, below.)

You must always file an information tax return (Form 5500-EZ) for your profit sharing plan for its final year. No exceptions. The final year of the plan is the year in which all of the assets are distributed. (See Section G, below, for more information about terminating your plan.)

For other years, including the first, you will not have to file a tax return for the plan if all of the following are true:

- Your plan is a one-participant plan. Recall that a one-participant plan is a plan that covers only you, your partners (if any) and your respective spouses (if they also work in the business).
- The total value of all the assets in the plan is $100,000 or less at the end of the current plan year and all previous plan years since (and including) 1994.
- If you have two or more one-participant Keogh plans for your business, the total value of all assets of all plans is $100,000 or less at the end

of the current plan year and every previous plan year since (and including) 1994.

 If you ever add employees to your plan, you will have to file annual tax returns for your profit sharing plan, regardless of the total value of plan assets. Also you won't be able to use IRS Form 5500-EZ. You will have to use the more complex Form 5500.

Form 5500-EZ must be filed by the last day of the seventh month following the end of the plan year. If your plan year is the calendar year, the tax return for the plan is due July 31. You may apply for an extension of time to file, which will give you an additional 2½ months. If the plan year is the same as your business tax year and you requested and received an extension of time to file your Form 1040, the filing deadline for the Form 5500-EZ is automatically extended, too.

b. IRS Form 990-T

As mentioned above, your profit sharing plan is a tax exempt entity, which is why it generally doesn't have to pay tax each year on the income it produces.

But if your profit sharing plan engages in a business that produces more than $1,000 of income during the year, you must file a special tax return—IRS Form 990-T—for the plan. Income from a business inside a plan is called unrelated business taxable income, or UBTI. Once UBTI exceeds $1,000 in a year, it is subject to tax, and the tax must be paid out of the profit sharing plan assets.

Most people invest their profit sharing plan assets in stocks, bonds and other standard investments which don't generate UBTI. But suppose you invest some of the assets in a limited partnership. Many limited partnerships are in fact businesses. And when the business (the limited partnership) starts throwing off income, it will be taxable, even though it is inside your profit sharing plan.

2. Plan Administration

Your only other filing responsibility, provided you have no employees and you do not run afoul of any laws, is to report distributions from the plan. Distributions are reported to the IRS on Form 1099-R. The reporting is the responsibility of the plan administrator (most likely you, if yours is a one-participant plan) or the employer (also you). Although your financial institution might prepare the 1099-R for you, the IRS will come to you if the reporting is inaccurate.

3. Updating Plan Documents

Changes in the law might require you to update your profit sharing plan agreement from time to time. If you are using a prototype plan provided by your financial institution, the institution generally will take responsibility for updating the plan.

If you want to change your profit sharing plan beneficiary, you don't have to amend the plan. You can simply request a "Change of Beneficiary" form, drop in the name of the new beneficiary, sign and date the form and return it to the financial institution. Don't forget to keep a copy for your own records. (For more information about designating a beneficiary, see Section B.2.b, above.)

E. Distributions

The laws governing distributions from profit sharing plans are a little more relaxed than those for other qualified plans. Generally you cannot take money out of a qualified plan while you are still working in the business that sponsors the plan. If you do, the plan could be disqualified, and you might have to pay back some or all of the tax benefits you have enjoyed over the years—and perhaps pay additional penalties, as well.

But some special rules for profit sharing plans allow a participant to draw on the plan assets while still working for the plan sponsor—or, in the case of a self-employed individual, while the business is still in operation. Be careful, though. Even if the law allows you early access to your profit sharing plan assets without disqualifying the plan, the plan itself might deny you access. And the plan has the final say.

One other warning: If you do gain access to your funds without disqualifying the plan, you will still have to pay income tax. You'll also have to pay an early distribution penalty—for taking the money out early—unless you qualify for an exception. (See Section 5, below, for a discussion of exceptions to the early distribution penalty.)

This is not a book about retirement plan distributions. Although we provide an overview of the distribution rules for each type of plan, you must look elsewhere for the details. One source is *IRAs, 401(k)s & Other Retirement Plans: Taking Your Money Out*, by Twila Slesnick and John C. Suttle (Nolo).

1. Inservice Distributions

The law will allow you to take distributions—in very limited circumstances—from your profit sharing plan while your business is still in operation. The limited circumstances under which you can take these so-called "inservice distributions" are the following:

- A distribution to a participant after he or she has participated in the plan for a fixed number of years, usually at least two.
- A distribution after the participant attains a stated age. (The age is generally set by the plan.)
- A distribution to a participant upon the occurrence of some event, such as layoff, illness, disability, retirement, death or termination of employment.

It is important to keep in mind that even though the law allows these distributions, the plan might not, and the plan's word is the last word. But you, as the employer, can choose whether or not your plan will allow such distributions. If you use a prototype plan that doesn't permit such distributions, you can pay a plan consultant to create a plan for you that does.

 Because you have no employees, you can be as liberal with distributions as the law permits when you create your plan. But once you have employees, your liberal distribution policy might turn into an administrative nightmare. Therefore, we suggest you talk to a plan consultant before adding employees to your profit sharing plan.

 The ease of access to profit sharing plan assets—relative to other types of Keoghs—is an attractive feature. It is virtually impossible to take inservice distributions from a money purchase pension plan or a defined benefit plan without disqualifying the plan—unless the plan is terminated. If inservice distributions are an important escape hatch for you, you might want to consider a profit sharing plan in lieu of (or in addition to) another type of Keogh. Inservice distributions do not generally disqualify an IRA, whether a SEP or a SIMPLE IRA, although premature distributions could be subject to penalties.

2. Loans

Owner-employees may not borrow from their own profit sharing plans. Doing so is considered a prohibited transaction. (See Section F.3, below, for more information about prohibited transactions.) You are deemed to be an owner-employee if you are a sole proprietor or if you are a partner in a partnership and you own more than a 10% interest in either the capital or the profits of the partnership.

3. Hardship Distributions

A special relief provision in the income tax regulations allows participants in profit sharing plans to withdraw money from the plan in the event of hardship. However, it's not sufficient that the law permits such withdrawals, the plan itself must allow them as well.

The Tax Code defines a hardship withdrawal very generally as a distribution because of "immediate and heavy financial need." But the plan must be more specific and establish objective and nondiscriminatory ways of determining whether such a need exists, as well as a method for measuring the amount of money necessary to satisfy that need.

Fortunately, the IRS provides a list of expenditures that qualify for hardship withdrawals. Those expenditures are called safe harbors, because your distribution will almost certainly pass muster if it falls into one of the categories—and if your plan allows hardship distributions. The safe harbor expenditures are:

- medical expenses for you, your spouse or your dependents
- expenses to purchase a principal residence for yourself (but this does not include money to make ongoing mortgage payments)
- expenses (including tuition, room and board) to pay for post-secondary education for a 12-month period for yourself, your spouse, your children or your other dependents, and
- expenditures to prevent eviction from your principal residence or to forestall a foreclosure.

Of course, the plan can make hardship withdrawals more restrictive than the above list of safe harbor expenditures. For example, it might allow hardship distributions only for medical expenses.

But the plan can be more liberal, too. It can permit hardship withdrawals that don't fall into one of the above categories. In that case, however, the plan document must provide some method for determining whether an expenditure constitutes immediate and heavy financial need.

If you ever take a hardship distribution, you must provide a statement declaring that you have exhausted other available resources. For example, if you have a vacation home, you would be required to sell it and use the proceeds before you would qualify to take money out of your profit sharing plan.

Now the coup de grace. Suppose you jump through all the hoops and are eligible for a hardship withdrawal. What you gain is access to your funds without disqualifying the plan. But a hardship withdrawal is still subject to income tax. You will also owe a 10% early distribution penalty unless the withdrawal qualifies for one of the exceptions described in Section 5, below.

4. Divorce Payments

Congress has gone to great lengths to protect your Keogh plan assets. The cornerstone of that protection is a provision known as the "anti-alienation" rule, which attempts to ensure that you (the plan participant) cannot voluntarily or involuntarily transfer your interest in plan assets to another person or entity.

Divorce presents a unique problem, however. What if you want to (or must) use your retirement plan as part of a property settlement? Can you transfer some or all of your interest in plan assets in that situation? And if you can, who should be responsible for the taxes and penalties (if any) on the part you transfer?

Congress addressed these concerns by giving divorcing couples a vehicle for protecting plan assets and minimizing tax and penalties. It's called a Qualified Domestic Relations Order or QDRO (pronounced "Quadro"). The QDRO rules spell out the circumstances under which your qualified plan benefits can go to someone else—an "alternate payee"—such as your soon-to-be former spouse. These rules also provide liability protection to the trustee who distributes the assets under the terms of the QDRO.

A QDRO is a judgment, decree or order (including a court-approved property settlement agreement) that satisfies all of the following requirements:

- It relates to child support, alimony or the marital property rights of your spouse, former spouse, dependent child or some other dependent.

- It gives an alternate payee, such as a spouse, former spouse, dependent child or other dependent, the right to receive all or a portion of your plan benefits.

- It does not alter the form or the amount of the benefit originally intended for you, even though the benefit might now go to an alternate payee. For example, the QDRO cannot require the plan to pay a larger annuity to the alternate payee than it would have paid to you.

- It contains certain language. Specifically:
  - ✓ The alternate payee must be referred to as "the alternate payee" in the QDRO.
  - ✓ The QDRO must identify the plan, as well as the amount of each payment and the number of payments to be made.

- ✓ The QDRO must contain the name and address of both you and the alternate payee.

If you have a QDRO in place, the law will allow the trustee of the plan to distribute to the alternate payee his or her share of your plan assets without disqualifying the plan—as long as the plan also permits the distribution. And generally, if your former spouse is the alternate payee, he or she will be responsible for any income taxes on the distributions he or she receives.

If you and your former spouse simply write up your own agreement, which does not meet the above requirements and is not court-approved, then your agreement is not a QDRO. In that case, you will almost certainly be liable for income tax and penalties on distributions even if they go to your former spouse.

The QDRO rules apply only to qualified plans, not to IRAs (including SEPs and SIMPLE IRAs).

5. Early Distributions and Exceptions to the Early Distribution Penalty

Any distribution you take from your profit sharing plan before you reach age 59½ is considered an early distribution, which means you must pay a 10% penalty in addition to income tax unless an exception applies. The exception will get you out of the penalty, but not out of the income tax.

The law provides for quite a few exceptions to the early distribution penalty. Those exceptions are described below. Bear in mind, however, that the plan documents must also specifically permit such exceptions. For example, if you become disabled, the law says that you can take money out of a Keogh plan without penalty, but if your plan says you can take distributions only after age 59½, or when you terminate employment, or when you die, then you won't be able to take a distribution as a result of a disability. Again, the plan's word is the last word.

If you are using the prototype plan of a financial institution, the plan documents might allow some of these exceptions and not others. In some cases, you might be able to check a box to make an exception apply. But if you find that the prototype plan does not give you all the options you want, you might have to turn to a consultant to craft a plan that does.

These are the exceptions to the early distribution penalty that the laws allows:

 Remember, although these exceptions will give you relief from penalties, you (or your beneficiaries) will still owe income tax on all distributions.

a. Death

Distributions from your profit sharing plan after you die are not subject to the early distribution penalty, no matter how old you are when you die or how old your beneficiaries are when they withdraw the money.

b. Disability

If you become disabled, you can take money from your profit sharing plan without penalty. But first you must satisfy the IRS's definition of disabled, which is hardly a model of clarity. Here's how it reads: You must be unable to "engage in any substantial gainful activity by reason of any medically determinable physical or mental impairment which can be expected to result in death or to be of long-continued and indefinite duration." The IRS's own regulations state that the gainful activity refers specifically to the type of work you were doing before becoming disabled. Thus it would seem that you need not be unfit for all work—just the work you customarily do.

c. Periodic Payments

You can begin taking distributions from your Keogh plan regardless of your age as long as you take them in equal annual installments over your life expectancy. These distributions are called "substantially equal periodic payments." Be warned however, that this is not quite the gaping loophole it appears to be. In order to use this exception, you must terminate your employment with the employer who sponsored the plan. Thus, when you are self-employed, presumably you must terminate or otherwise dispose of your business.

To compute substantially equal periodic payments, you must use one of the IRS-approved methods for computing the payments—you cannot simply choose a monthly or annual payment that suits you. (See IRS Notice 89-25 in the Appendix for more information about how to calculate substantially equal payments.)

You must continue the payments for at least five years or until you are at least age 59½, whichever comes later. For example, if you begin at age 58, you must continue the payments for at least five years even though you pass age 59½ in the meantime. Or if you begin at age 52, you must continue until at least age 59½, even though more than five years have passed.

d. Medical Expenses

Although you can take money out of your profit sharing plan prior to age 59½ to pay for medical expenses, you won't escape the penalty entirely. The exemption applies only to the portion of your medical expenses that would be deductible on Schedule A of your tax return if you were to itemize deductions (whether or not you actually do itemize deductions). The remainder is subject to penalty.

> EXAMPLE: Your adjusted gross income is $50,000. You had medical bills of $6,000 during the year, which you paid with funds you withdrew from your profit sharing plan. (The $6,000 distribution is included in the $50,000 of income.) For income tax purposes, you are permitted to deduct medical expenses that exceed 7.5% of your adjusted gross income. Thus:
>
> Adjusted gross income (AGI), including the profit sharing plan distribution = $50,000;
>
> 7.5% of AGI (.075 x $50,000) = $3,750 nondeductible expenses;
>
> Excess ($6,000 – $3,750) = $2,250 deductible expenses.
>
> Although you took $6,000 from your profit sharing plan to pay medical expenses, only $2,250 will escape the early distribution penalty. The remaining $3,750 will be subject to the penalty (unless you qualify for another exception). And don't forget that the entire $6,000 is subject to regular income tax, as well.

e. Leaving Your Business After Age 55

If you are at least 55 years old when you leave or terminate your business, any distribution you receive from your profit sharing plan will not be subject to an early distribution tax.

To qualify for this exception, you don't have to retire permanently. You can go to work for someone else or start another business some time down the road.

⚠️ **The IRS is aware that it is not always easy to determine when a self-employed individual has terminated his or her business.** If you take a distribution and use the age 55 exception and continue to show self-employment income, be prepared to defend yourself.

To make use of this exception, you need not be age 55 on the day you take the distribution, as long as you turn 55 by December 31 of the same year. However, you must have quit the business before you take the distribution.

f. QDRO Payments

If you are paying child support or alimony from your retirement plan, or if you intend to distribute some or all of the plan to your former spouse as part of a property settlement, none of those payments is subject to the early distribution penalty as long as there is a QDRO in place that orders the payments. (See Section 4, above, for more information about QDROs.)

g. Refunds

If you contributed more to your profit sharing plan than you were permitted to deduct during the year, generally you can remove the excess without penalty if you do so before you file your tax return.

Those "corrective" distributions will not be subject to the early distribution tax, although they might be subject to other taxes and penalties. (See Section F.1, below, for more about excess contributions.)

h. Federal Tax Levy

If you owe back taxes, you can be reasonably certain the government will try to collect them. If you have assets in a profit sharing plan, the government can take those assets (in other words, the IRS can levy on your profit sharing plan) to pay your debt. If it does so, then those amounts taken for taxes will not be subject to the early distribution penalty, even if you happen to be younger than 59½.

6. Mandatory Distributions

If you own your own business, you must start taking money out of your profit sharing plan beginning in the year you turn 70½, even if you are still working. The income tax regulations provide a formula for calculating the minimum amount you must take. You may take more than the minimum, but you may not take less. If you do take less, you will be fined 50% of the amount that you should have taken out of the profit sharing plan but didn't.

If you are still working when you reach 70½, you may continue to make contributions to a profit sharing plan and deduct those contributions. It could very well make sense for you to do so even though you are also required to take some money out each year. Not only can you claim a deduction for new contributions and reduce your tax liability, you can also add to the assets that will grow tax-deferred.

F. Penalties

It would seem that for every misstep you take with your profit sharing plan, there is a penalty lurking in the shadows. To be fair, Congress has provided exceptions and corrective action you can take to avoid or mitigate the penalties in most cases. Here are the traps to watch for, their consequences and, where applicable, steps you can take for damage control.

Infractions and Their Consequences	
Problem	**Penalty**
Nondeductible contributions	10% of the excess
Early distributions	10% of the distribution
Prohibited transactions:	
• If corrected:	15% of the transaction amount
• If not corrected:	100% of the transaction amount
Required distributions	50% of the shortfall

1. Nondeductible Contributions

You cannot contribute more to your profit sharing plan than you are allowed to deduct. If you do, you will have made a nondeductible contribution and you must pay a penalty of 10% on the excess. The IRS will assess a new 10% penalty on any excess that remains in the plan at the beginning of each year.

It's surprisingly easy to contribute too much, especially if you like to plan ahead. Let's suppose your business has had a string of good years and you are expecting another banner year. In February, you contribute $25,500 to your profit sharing plan to get those tax-deferred dollars working for you. December comes and goes. In April, while preparing your tax return, you discover that you made less money than you thought. Consequently, you have contributed $1,800 too much to your profit sharing plan. Now what?

You have two options for correcting nondeductible contributions to your profit sharing plan. We discuss those options in the following sections.

a. Option One: Leave Excess In, Deduct Next Year

Your first option is to leave the excess in the profit sharing plan and deduct it in the next tax year. When computing the amount to contribute in the next year, you will first apply the excess that was carried over and then contribute any additional amounts that might be permitted to bring you up to your deduction limit.

You still have to pay the 10% excise tax for the first year, but as long as the excess does not exceed the deductible amount for the second year, you will not pay a penalty for that year.

EXAMPLE: In 2001, you contributed $3,000 too much to your profit sharing plan. You deducted the correct amount but forgot to remove the excess from the profit sharing plan account. You decide to leave the excess in the account and deduct it the following year. In 2002 you have enough income to make an $8,000 profit sharing plan contribution. You apply the $3,000 excess from the previous year and add an additional $5,000 in cash by the due date of your tax return to complete the $8,000 contribution. You must still pay a $300 (10% of $3,000) penalty for 2001, but you do not have to pay an additional penalty for 2002 or beyond.

If you must pay the nondeductible contribution penalty, you report the offending contribution on IRS Form 5330 for the year for which you made the excess contribution. The form is due by the last day of the seventh month after the end of the year for which you made the nondeductible contribution.

EXAMPLE: You made an excess contribution of $1,000 to your profit sharing plan in 2001. You discovered your error in June 2002, long after you filed your tax return. You should complete Form 5330 for the year 2001. (You can find a sample Form 5330 in the Appendix.) Sign and date the form and send it in by July 31, 2002, along with your check for $100 (10% of $1,000), which is the amount of the nondeductible contribution penalty.

b. Option Two: Remove the Excess

Your second option is more complex, but also more attractive if you qualify, because you can avoid the 10% penalty. The general rule is that the precise amount of the excess (not including any earnings that might have accumulated) can be returned to you without penalty by the due date of your tax return (plus extensions, if you requested and received an extension for filing your tax return), if the excess is returned for one of the following reasons:

- The plan initially failed to qualify. For example, if this is the first year of the plan and you submitted a letter of determination to the IRS and the plan was deemed not to be a qualified plan.
- The contribution is not deductible.
- The contribution was made due to a mistake of fact. For example, an arithmetic error in computing the contribution is a mistake of fact.

The likely problem with your contribution is reason number two—it isn't deductible. But here's the problem. The IRS has ruled that for this exception to apply, the deduction must actually be disallowed by the IRS. Thus, unless you are audited, you would have to request a determination that the deduction is disallowed.

Ah, but wait! There is another exception. You can remove the excess without formal IRS disallowance if you satisfy all of the following conditions:

- The amount of the excess is less than $25,000.
- The terms of your plan specifically provide that nondeductible contributions can be returned if the IRS deems them nondeductible.
- Your plan states that nondeductible contributions must be removed from the plan.

If you qualify to remove the nondeductible contribution from your profit sharing plan and you do so before the due date (including extensions) of your tax return, you will not have to pay any penalty on the excess contribution. You will also avoid an early distribution penalty on the money you took back out of the plan.

2. Early Distributions

If you take money out of your profit sharing plan before you reach age 59½ and the distribution does not fall into any of the categories described in Section E.3, above, then you will have to pay a 10% early distribution penalty. That penalty is in addition to the income tax you must pay.

The IRS requires you to report the early distribution penalty on Form 5329 for the year of the early distribution. (You can find a sample copy of Form 5329 in the Appendix.)

3. Prohibited Transactions

The Tax Code prohibits certain transactions involving your profit sharing plan assets. The prohibited transaction rules are part of Congress's strategy to protect your profit sharing plan assets so that they will be available when you retire. Congress designed the rules to keep you and any other disqualified person (see immediately below) from using the assets for personal gain or from engaging in transactions that put the assets at risk. To put it another way, Congress doesn't want you or anyone else to squander your retirement money—and it has created laws to punish anyone who does.

A disqualified person is someone who might reasonably have access to your plan assets. In addition to you, such persons include your spouse, your lineal descendants (such as children and grandchildren) and your ancestors (such as parents and grandparents). The list also includes fiduciaries (those responsible for handling the assets of the plan, such as a custodian, trustee or money manager), a person who provides services to the plan (such as an administrator) and co-owners of your business.

The penalty for engaging in a prohibited transaction is 15% of the amount of the transaction, and the person who engages in the transaction—not the plan—owes the tax. The penalty is assessed for each year (or part of a year) in the taxable period of the prohibited transaction. The taxable period starts on the date of the transaction and ends on the earliest of the following:

- The day the IRS mails a notice of deficiency for the penalty tax (telling you that you owe the tax).
- The day the IRS assesses the tax (telling you to pay the tax).
- The day the correction of the transaction is complete.

If the transaction is not corrected within the taxable period, an additional tax of 100% of the transaction is imposed. That's a total of 115%.

If you don't manage to correct it within the taxable period, the IRS will usually give you an additional 90 days after the day the IRS mails you a notice of deficiency before requiring you to pay the 100% tax. And the IRS will extend the grace period further if you can convince the IRS you need a little more time—or if you petition the Tax Court. If you are successful, you will not owe the 100% tax, but you will still owe the 15% tax.

The following are all prohibited transactions. Note that these are all transactions that occur inside your profit sharing plan or with the use of your profit sharing plan assets.

- The sale, exchange or lease of any property between a disqualified person and the profit sharing plan. For example, you cannot sell your house to your profit sharing plan.

- The furnishing of goods or services or facilities between a disqualified person and the profit sharing plan. For example, you cannot hire your spouse to manage the profit sharing plan and pay him a big salary out of the plan assets. You also cannot pay yourself for rendering services to the plan.

- The lending of money or extending of credit between a disqualified person and the profit sharing plan. For example, you cannot borrow from the profit sharing plan to buy a car, even if you intend to return the money. If you want to use your profit sharing plan assets to buy that car, you must withdraw the money permanently (if the plan permits) and hope you can find an exception to the early distribution penalty if you are younger than 59½.

- The transfer to or use by a disqualified person of any assets or income of the profit sharing plan. For example, you cannot use profit sharing plan funds to invest in a house (held by the profit sharing plan) which you then occupy as your principal residence. Again, if you want to use the funds to buy yourself a house, you must withdraw the funds permanently and pay income tax (and perhaps penalties) on the distribution.

- Any act of self-dealing, which occurs when a disqualified person uses the assets or income of the profit sharing plan for that person's own interest or account while the assets are still in the profit sharing plan. For example, if your money manager invests all of your profit sharing plan assets in the stock of a company of which she owns 80%, such an investment would clearly benefit her as a majority shareholder and, therefore, might be deemed a prohibited transaction.

- The receipt of payment by a fiduciary in connection with a transaction involving the income or assets of the plan. A kickback, for example.

If you owe tax on a prohibited transaction, you must report it on IRS Form 5330, which is due on the last day of the seventh month after the end of the tax year of the transaction.

4. Life Insurance

If you use part of your profit sharing plan contribution to pay the premium on a life insurance policy for yourself, the portion of your contribution that pays for the life insurance protection itself (known as the "PS 58 cost") is nondeductible. The investment portion of the premium is deductible.

Purchasing life insurance does not necessarily trigger the 10% nondeductible contribution penalty. The penalty applies only when you contribute more than the maximum deductible amount. You can make contributions to your plan that you cannot deduct, as long as the total of all contributions does not exceed the deductible limit. For example, if you compute your maximum deductible contribution—based on your net earnings—to be $20,000 and you contribute that amount but use $1,000 of it to purchase life insurance protection, you may claim a deduction of only $19,000 on your tax return, but no penalty tax would apply.

5. Pledging the Account As Security

If you use any portion of your profit sharing plan as security for a loan (for example, you borrow money using your profit sharing plan as collateral), you will be engaging in a prohibited transaction. The government views this action as equivalent to borrowing from the plan. You will recall from Section 3, above, that borrowing money from your plan is a prohibited transaction.

6. Mandatory Distribution Penalty

If you fail to take required distributions from your profit sharing plan beginning at age 70½, you will pay a penalty of 50% of the amount that should have come out but didn't. (See Section E.6, above, for more information about mandatory distributions.)

Report this penalty on IRS Form 5329. You can find a sample Form 5329 in the Appendix.

G. Terminating Your Profit Sharing Plan

You are permitted to terminate a plan for legitimate business reasons. For example, you can terminate your plan if you dissolve your business or go bankrupt. Or perhaps you simply cannot afford to make contributions any more.

Once you are certain that you won't be making contributions to your profit sharing plan, you should terminate it. If you don't, you will be required to keep the plan documents up to date through all the changes in the law, even though you are not making contributions. If you fail to keep the plan current, you risk disqualifying the plan and, in the worst case, incurring current income tax and penalties, as well as losing prior deductions.

The only impediment to terminating your plan whenever you want is the rule requiring the plan to be permanent. If the IRS, in its wisdom, determines that the plan was never permanent, but was temporary from inception, you face the specter of retroactive disqualification of the plan. The IRS is likely to consider your plan temporary if either of the following is true:

- You do not make substantial and recurring contributions. But in the case of a profit sharing plan, you are not required to make contributions every year, so determining whether or not the plan is permanent and whether you are making substantial and recurring contributions becomes a judgment call—by the IRS.

- You abandon the plan after only a few years (many plan consultants use five years as a guide) for reasons other than business necessity. And here again, you might find yourself at odds with the IRS's view of a business necessity.

But let's say you've had it with your business. Too much stress. Time to go back to that cushy mailroom job you had at Soft Corp. You dissolve your business, and now you want to terminate your profit sharing plan? How do you do it?

1. Paperwork

Once you decide to terminate the plan, you should give written notice, with an effective date of termination, to the trustee and or custodian of the plan, the plan administrator (if other than yourself), the prototype sponsor (which is your financial institution) and all participants.

a. Letter of Determination

Even though you've made the decision to terminate your plan, it is important to keep your plan in compliance with the law until you have distributed all of the assets. For this reason, some plan consultants recommend that you apply for a determination letter from the IRS to preserve the deductibility of contributions for all years that are still open to an IRS audit—and to facilitate corrective actions that might be necessary to ensure that the plan remains qualified

while you are in the process of terminating it. The IRS will also render its opinion of the permanence of the plan.

You are not required to obtain an advance determination letter, and many people do not, especially if the plan is a one-participant plan and the risks of disqualification upon termination are low. When you have a one-participant plan, you are most likely to seek a determination letter when the assets of the plan are large and you want to feel confident that when you roll over the assets of the terminating plan into another plan or into an IRA, you won't trigger income tax or penalties. (See Section 2, below.)

If you decide to seek a determination letter, use IRS Form 5310, Application for Determination Upon Termination. (You can find a sample Form 5310 in the Appendix.) You must also pay a user fee, which is currently about $225.

b. Tax Return

When you decide to terminate your plan, you must file a tax return for the final year (the year all of the assets are distributed from the plan), even if you did not have to file one in the past. (See Section D.l, above, for information about filing a tax return.)

2. Distribution of Assets

Before you can file the final tax return and complete the termination of your plan, you must distribute all of its assets. As you might expect, this task is not as simple as it sounds. You have several distribution options.

a. Option One: Withdraw the Assets and Pay Tax

One rather unattractive option is to take all your money out of the plan and pay income tax on it. You will also have to pay an early distribution tax if you are younger than 59½, unless one of the exceptions in Section E.3, above, applies. If you choose this option, there is a mandatory 20% federal withholding tax at the time of distribution. But if that withholding turns out to be more than you owe at tax time, you can request a refund.

b. Option Two: Transfer the Assets to an IRA

Another option is to have the funds transferred into an IRA in your name. The plan assets should go directly from the financial institution that is now holding the plan assets to the custodian of your IRA. You should not take possession of the funds or temporarily deposit them into a regular (non-IRA) account. If you follow these instructions, you will not have to pay any income tax or penalties. All income tax will be deferred until you take the funds out of the IRA, some time in the future.

⚠ Although you are permitted to take the assets out of your profit sharing plan yourself and then deposit them in an IRA within 60 days, if you move the funds in that way, the profit sharing plan assets will be subject to federal (and possibly state) income tax withholding, and perhaps penalties as well, unless you take remedial measures. For more about the nuances of qualified plan distributions, transfers and withholding, see *IRAs, 401(k)s & Other Retirement Plans: Taking Your Money Out*, by Twila Slesnick and John C. Suttle (Nolo).

c. Option Three: Transfer the Assets to a Qualified Plan

You can have the funds transferred directly into another qualified plan. For example, if your new employer has a plan and the plan permits, you might want to consolidate the two plans. Not all plans permit such commingling, however, so be sure to check first.

H. Multiple Employer Plans

Because retirement plans are one of the last great bargains in the Tax Code, taxpayers search hard for ways to contribute more. How about setting up two profit sharing plans? Can you double your contribution? What if you have two businesses? Can you have one plan for each? Or suppose you work for another employer and run a business of your own on the side. Can you set up a plan for your own business even if you are covered by your employer's plan?

The key to understanding what you can and cannot do is this fundamental rule: Retirement plan limits are applied on a per-employer basis. For example, suppose you work for Conglomerate Corp. from 8 a.m. to 5 p.m. every day and you work for Monopoly Corp. from 7 p.m. to 4 a.m. every night. Suppose also that each company contributes to a standard profit sharing plan on your behalf. Because the two companies are separate employers, they can each contribute the maximum the law allows to separate profit sharing plan accounts for you. The same principle applies if you are one of the separate employers. This is known as the separate employer rule.

⚠ There are some important exceptions to the separate employer rule. Perhaps most important, the law puts a cap on the total amount you can contribute to all salary reduction plans (such as SIMPLE IRAs) in which you participate. (See Chapter 3 for more information about multiple plan limits when you have a SIMPLE IRA.) However, these restrictions do not apply to standard profit sharing plans in which there is no salary reduction component. No matter what type of plan you have with one employer, you can be covered by a standard profit sharing plan of a separate employer and contribute the maximum the law allows.

This section examines various employment scenarios and explains whether or not you can contribute to more than one employer plan in the same year. (For information about adding a traditional IRA or a Roth IRA to your profit sharing plan, see Section I, below.)

1. If You Are Self-Employed With a Day Job on the Side; or Vice Versa

Let's say you own your own business, but you also work for someone else. Can you be covered by more than one plan? Because of the separate employer rule described in the preceding paragraphs, if you are covered by your employer's plan, you can still establish a profit sharing plan for your own business and take a deduction to offset some of your profit. That's because you are a separate employer.

⚠ If you and members of your family together own more than 50% of the corporation that employs you, then you, as sole proprietor of your own business (or of the partnership, if your side business is a partnership), might not be considered a separate employer from the corporation. If not, your contribution to the profit sharing plan you established for your unincorporated business might be limited or eliminated altogether. If this is the case, or if you are uncertain, you should confer with the plan administrator of the corporate retirement plan. (Also see Section 3, below.)

2. If You Are Self-Employed With Only One Business

Suppose you are self-employed and you have no other job. If you have a profit sharing plan in place, can you set up another qualified plan, as well? This question isn't as odd as it might seem. Perhaps you established the profit sharing plan in your first year of business when you wanted the flexibility to discontinue contributions if necessary. But now the business is doing so well you want to contribute more than your profit sharing plan allows. Should you terminate the profit sharing plan and replace it with another type of plan? Can you simply add another plan? Or are you stuck with what you have?

You can have as many qualified plans for your business as you choose. However, there is a limit on the total amount you can contribute to each type of plan and a limit for all plans combined.

The maximum a single employer can contribute to all profit sharing plans combined is 15% of compensation, where compensation is limited to $170,000. (Recall that for a self-employed individual, compensation is actually net earnings from self-employment.) That means you can establish three profit sharing plans if you want, but the total of all contributions to all profit sharing plans of the same employer (in this case, you) cannot exceed the lesser of 15% of your compensation or $25,500 (15% of $170,000). As a practical matter, you are unlikely to establish two separate profit sharing plans for your business when you can contribute the maximum to one. Maintaining two plans of the same type adds administrative time and costs without providing additional benefits.

If you want to increase your contribution limit, you must add a different type of plan to your profit sharing plan, such as a money purchase pension plan or a defined benefit plan. If you add a money purchase pension plan, you can increase your contribution limit to the lesser of $30,000 ($35,000 beginning in tax year 2001) or 25% of compensation (which works out to 20% of your net income—after the self-employment tax deduction—when you are self-employed). The contribution to your profit sharing plan still cannot exceed 15% of compensation, but the money purchase pension plan can fill in the gap.

> EXAMPLE: You established a profit sharing plan when you started your business in 1998. In 2000, you had net income of $60,000 (after subtracting your self-employment tax deduction). Because your profit sharing plan limits you to 15% of net earnings from self-employment, you decide to establish a money purchase pension plan with an annual contribution limit of 10% of net earnings from self-employment.
>
> The combination of plans brings your contribution limit to the maximum 25% (20% of your net income after the self-employment tax deduction). Therefore, your maximum contribution to both plans is the lesser of $30,000 or 20% of $60,000, which is $12,000.

Your net earnings from self-employment (your net income less the self-employment tax deduction, less the retirement plan contribution) is $48,000. Thus, your contribution to your money purchase pension plan is $4,800 (10% x $48,000). It is mandatory, so you must make it first. (See Chapter 6 for information about computing contributions to a money purchase pension plan.) You can also contribute $7,200 to your profit sharing plan (which is $12,000 – $4,800) if you want (recall that contributions to profit sharing plans are discretionary).

Note that the maximum contribution you could make to your profit sharing plan without a money purchase pension plan contribution is $7,826 (13.0435% of $60,000). But because your total contribution to both plans is limited to $12,000 and the money purchase pension plan contribution is made first, that leaves only $7,200 for the profit sharing plan.

You can also add a defined benefit plan to your profit sharing plan and money purchase pension plan to increase your total contributions. But there is a limit on the total combined amount you can contribute to all defined contribution plans (money purchase pension and profit sharing plans) and defined benefit plans of one employer. That limit is the greater of:

- 25% of compensation, up to a maximum of $170,000 of compensation, which is $42,500 (25% of $170,000), or

- the amount you are required to contribute to your defined benefit plan. (See Chapter 7 for information about defined benefit plan contribution limits.)

 For purposes of these multiple plan rules, a SEP is treated as a profit sharing plan.

 If you have a profit sharing plan, you cannot add a SIMPLE IRA. If you want to contribute to a SIMPLE IRA, you cannot contribute to any other employer plan during the same year. (See Chapter 3 for more information about SIMPLE IRAs.)

3. If You Are Self-Employed With Two or More Businesses

There is a wrinkle in the rule that allows you to establish a profit sharing plan with each separate employer (including yourself if you own your own business) and contribute the maximum to each.

The wrinkle is in the definition of separate employer. Two employers might look separate to you but not be separate in the eyes of the law. This can happen when businesses are under common control. Businesses that are under common control are deemed to be one employer and are combined for purposes of determining the ceiling on retirement plan contributions. So it is important to be able to determine if businesses are under common control.

a. If You Have Two Sole Proprietorships

The concept of common control is straightforward if you have two sole proprietorships. By definition, you own 100% of both businesses. The businesses are under common control because they have the same employer (you). Consequently, you must combine them when determining contribution limits. If you establish a profit sharing plan for each business, the maximum contribution you can make to both plans combined is 15% of the combined compensation from both businesses, and the combined compensation cannot exceed $170,000. It's the same limit that would apply if you had only one business or one plan.

> EXAMPLE: You have a Web design business that generated net income of $40,000 in 2001 (after taking into account your self-employment tax deduction). You also have a house-painting business that generated $35,000 net income for 2001. The maximum you can contribute to a profit sharing plan is 13.0435% of $75,000 ($40,000 + $35,000), which is $9,783. You can contribute the entire amount to one profit sharing plan, or you can establish multiple profit sharing plans and contribute whatever you like to each (assuming each allows discretionary contributions), as long as the total contribution to all profit sharing plans does not exceed $9,783.

Recall that if you worked for two separate employers—say, a corporation and yourself—you would be able to contribute 15% of compensation (up to $170,000 of compensation) to the profit sharing plan for your business and also receive the maximum contribution to your corporate employer's plan.

b. If You Have a Sole Proprietorship and a Partnership; or Two Partnerships

If you have both a sole proprietorship and a partnership, the picture changes. You are the employer of your sole proprietorship, but the partnership (not you or the other individual partners) is the employer in a partnership. In general, that means each business must set up its own plan.

But here's where the issue of common control rears its head. If the businesses are under common control, the total contribution to the plans of both employers is determined as though there were only one employer and one plan. This is true despite the fact that each employer will have to set up a separate plan.

A sole proprietorship and a partnership are under common control if the sole proprietor also has more than a 50% interest in the capital (the assets) or the profits of the partnership (as defined in your partnership agreement). In that case, the businesses are combined for purposes of the profit sharing plan contribution limits. Your contribution to the two profit sharing plans is limited to a total of 15% of your combined compensation from both businesses. However, the amount you deposit into each profit sharing plan is determined by the amount of income you receive from each business.

EXAMPLE: You are the sole proprietor of a Web design business. You established a profit sharing plan for that business in its first year—in 1998.

In 2001, you and a partner started a house-painting business. You decided to establish a profit sharing plan for that business, as well. By agreement, you have an 80% interest in the profits of the business. Because your interest in the profits of the partnership exceeds 50% and you also own 100% of your Web design business, your partnership and your sole proprietorship are under common control.

Consequently, the maximum you can contribute to all profit sharing plans is 15% of the combined compensation from both businesses. If your net income (after the self-employment tax deduction) from the partnership is $35,000 and from the Web design business is $40,000, your maximum contribution to both profit sharing plans is 13.0435% of $75,000 ($40,000 + $35,000), which is $9,783. However, the most you can contribute to the partnership profit sharing plan is $4,565 (.130435 x $35,000). And the most you can contribute to the profit sharing plan for your Web design business is $5,217 (.130435 x $40,000).

If you have an interest of 50% or less in both the capital and the profits of the partnership, then the partnership and sole proprietorship are separate employers for plan sponsorship purposes and also for purposes of determining contribution limits. If you choose a profit sharing plan for both, you would set up two separate plans and the contribution limits would apply separately to your earnings from each business.

If you are involved in two partnerships, the same principles apply. Those partnerships for which your interest in either the capital or the profits is greater than 50% must be combined and treated as one for purposes of determining the contribution limits, even though you must set up a separate plan for each partnership.

 It is possible for two employers (such as your partnership and your sole proprietorship, or perhaps two partnerships) to sponsor the same plan, which might save administrative time and costs. If you elect this option, be sure to confirm with the financial institution providing the plan, or with the IRS, that the plan will pass muster.

 If you own interests in several partnerships that provide services to one another, or if you and other individuals own an interest in the same partnerships, the partnerships might be under common control. Confer with a professional plan consultant to ensure that you are not making excess contributions to any plan.

I. Adding a Traditional or Roth IRA to Your Profit Sharing Plan

Contributing to a profit sharing plan for your business does not preclude you from establishing a traditional or Roth IRA. And if you can, you should. Generally, the more you contribute to a retirement plan—any plan—the larger your retirement nest egg is likely to be.

However, participating in the profit sharing plan might limit the deductibility of your traditional IRA contribution. (Roth IRA contributions are never deductible.) When you are covered by your own employer plan (such as a SEP, SIMPLE IRA or Keogh) or when you are covered by a plan of another employer, any traditional IRA contribution you make is fully deductible only if the adjusted gross income (with certain modifications) on your tax return is less than $62,000 (if you are married) or $42,000 (if you are single).

For more information about traditional IRAs including how to compute deductible and nondeductible contributions, see Chapter 8.

J. Filling Out the Forms

Even though you don't have any employees, you will find that all prototype plan documents have questions relating to employees. You must still answer all of the questions, because your plan must contain provisions that would allow it to remain qualified in the event you change your mind and hire help.

Consequently, as you complete the plan documents, you will probably want to make eligibility requirements as restrictive as possible. That way, if you ever do hire employees, you have the option to maintain the restrictive provisions of the plan (usually to keep costs down), or you can relax eligibility requirements. It's more difficult to increase restrictions after you hire employees, because you might run afoul of the nondiscrimination rules. (See Chapter 1, Section B.1.d, for information about nondiscrimination rules.)

Also, even though you initially choose restrictive options, you don't have to worry about excluding yourself. Many prototype profit sharing plans allow you to waive participation restrictions for all employees employed on the effective date of the plan. That means, you can make your plan restrictive from the start, without excluding yourself.

To establish your plan, begin with the following steps.

Step 1:
Identify the bank, brokerage firm or other financial institution that will hold your profit sharing plan assets.

Step 2:
Call the financial institution and explain that you would like to establish a profit

sharing plan. Ask the voice on the other end of the phone to mail the appropriate documents to you. You might also be able to request the forms online through the institution's website, but because the packages tend to be voluminous, most institutions still send the information by regular mail. The institution will mail to you a prototype plan, which is a plan that has already been approved by the IRS.

Step 3:

While you are waiting for the papers to arrive, you can request a taxpayer identification number for your plan. Although you are not required to have a separate taxpayer identification number for the plan, many financial institutions prefer that you do.

Getting a Taxpayer ID Number

To request a taxpayer identification number, complete IRS Form SS-4 (you can find a blank sample form in the Appendix) and mail or fax it to the IRS, as indicated in the instructions. Note that the form is titled "Application for Employer Identification Number." Don't let the title throw you. This particular form has many uses, and one of them is to request an ID number for your plan (which is identified as a trust on the form, even if it's held as a custodial account).

Step 4:

When you receive the prototype plan in the mail, all you have to do is fill in the blanks. Then return the plan to the financial institution.

Because you have no employees, you generally will need to complete only the adoption agreement, a beneficiary designation form and, in the case of a mutual fund, instructions for how you want the funds invested.

At the end of this chapter, you can find a sample profit sharing plan adoption agreement. Bear in mind that prototype plans vary from institution to institution, but the similarities are greater than the differences. The following are explanations for how to fill out the sample form. These explanations should help you complete most prototype plan forms, regardless of which financial institution you choose:

- *Employer name:* Enter your name as the employer (or the name you are using for your business). If you are doing business as a partnership, enter the name of the partnership.
- *Type of organization:* Put a checkmark next to the entity that describes your business.
- *Employer address:* Enter your business address and phone number.
- *Employer tax identification number:* If you are a sole proprietor, your employer tax identification number is generally your own Social Security number. If your business is a part-

nership, enter the tax ID number of the partnership.

- *Company/employer fiscal year:* Enter the month and day of the last day of your business tax year. For example, if your business is on a calendar year, enter December 31.
- *Effective date:* Put a checkmark next to New Plan. You may choose an effective date that is before you sign the plan documents, as long as the effective date is in the current year. As a self-employed individual, your income is deemed received on the last day of the year, so the effective date does not affect the amount of your contribution.
- *Plan year:* You can maintain your plan on a calendar year (ending December 31) or a fiscal year (ending on the last day of any other month). Generally, it is to your advantage to maintain the plan using the same year as your business tax year. (See Section B.4, above, for more information about calendar and fiscal years.) To do so, leave this section blank.
- *Plan administrator:* You are the plan administrator, so enter your name and your business address and phone number. Under Specimen Signatures, print your name and title, then sign your name.
- *Plan trustee:* You will almost certainly want the financial institution to serve as trustee, so check the box next to the name of the financial institution.
- *Frozen plan:* Frozen plans usually result from employer insolvency. Because you are just now establishing your plan, this section does not apply to you.
- *Section 1, participation requirements:* You do not want your contributions curtailed because of your age or the length of time you have been in business, so put a checkmark next to "No minimum age or service conditions."
- *Section 2, employer contributions:* You want your plan contributions to be discretionary, so check Alternative I.
- *Section 5, withdrawals:* A profit sharing plan, unlike other Keogh plans, is permitted to make distributions to participants while they are still working (inservice distributions), provided such permission is written into the plan. If you want to permit such distributions, put a checkmark next to options (a) and (b). Under option (a), you may select an age after which you can take an inservice distribution without disqualifying the plan. Option (b) allows you to take distributions from the plan for certain well-defined hardships. (For more information about inservice distributions, see Section E, above.)
- *Section 6, loans:* You are not permitted to borrow from your profit sharing plan, so leave this section blank.

- *Section 7, limitations on allocations:* The limitation year is the period of time you will use to compute contributions to your plan. For example, if the limitation year is January 1 through December 31, your contribution limits are based on compensation earned during that period. Usually you will want your plan year, limitation year and business tax year to be the same. If so, leave this section blank.
- *Section 8, top-heavy plan provisions:* Assuming this is your only plan, or you are establishing this plan along with a money purchase pension plan, you can leave this section blank.
- *Section 9, execution of plan and trust agreement:* Under "Execution by Employer," print your name and title, then sign and date the form.

Step 5:

Next you complete the Beneficiary Designation form on which you identify those who will receive your plan assets when you die. If you are married and wish to leave those assets to someone other than your spouse, you must obtain your spouse's consent and his or her signature must also appear on this form. (For more information about beneficiary designations, see Section B.2.b, above.)

Step 6:

Your financial institution might also ask you to provide instructions for investing your contribution. For example, a mutual fund company might ask you to select one or more mutual funds from among their family of funds.

Step 7:

Send the completed Adoption Agreement, beneficiary designation and investment instructions to your financial institution. Be sure to keep a copy. If it gets lost, you'd probably rather scrub the bathroom with a toothbrush than fill out the forms again.

The financial institution will sign and return the Adoption Agreement. It will also open an account in the name of the plan.

VANGUARD
PROFIT-SHARING PLAN
SIMPLIFIED ADOPTION AGREEMENT (006)

SAMPLE

Please complete the following:

EMPLOYER NAME _____

TYPE OF ORGANIZATION
____ Corporation
____ Partnership
____ Sole Proprietor/Self-Employed Individual
____ Other (please specify): _____

EMPLOYER ADDRESS
_____
_____
_____

(_____) _____
Telephone Number

EMPLOYER TAX IDENTIFICATION NUMBER _____

Please indicate your company fiscal year. If left blank, we will assume it to be the calendar year.

COMPANY/EMPLOYER FISCAL YEAR _____

The Effective Date establishes when the provisions of this plan become effective. It is also used to determine the dollar amount of compensation for the current plan year which may be taken into account under this plan. For example, if today is November 1, 1994, but you wish the entire calendar year's compensation to be included, enter an Effective Date of January 1, 1994.

EFFECTIVE DATE

____ **New Plan:** if the Employer is adopting the Plan as a new plan for its eligible Employees, the Effective Date of the Plan is _____

____ **Amended Plan:** if the Employer is adopting the Plan as the amended and restated version of an existing plan for its eligible Employees, the Effective Date of the amendment is _____

Note: If you are amending an existing plan with Vanguard, please list your current Vanguard plan accounts below:

Vanguard Fund Name	Vanguard Account Number
_____	_____
_____	_____
_____	_____

PLAN YEAR

The Plan Year shall be the 12-consecutive-month period ending on the last day of the calendar month of _____. (If no designation is made, the Plan Year shall be the Employer's fiscal year.)

Vanguard is not the Plan Administrator. The responsibilities of the Plan Administrator are explained on pages 16 and 17 of the booklet, "The Vanguard Qualified Retirement Program" and in the Plan Document. These responsibilities include: maintaining accurate employee records, submitting required reports to government agencies, determining employee eligibility, and instructing Vanguard as to allocation and disposition of all plan contributions, investments, and payments.

PLAN ADMINISTRATOR

The following individual(s) or committee has been appointed by the Employer to serve as Plan Administrator for the Plan (if no designation is made, the Employer shall be considered the Plan Administrator):

_____
Name

_____
Address

(_____) _____
Telephone Number

Note: Vanguard is *not* the Plan Administrator.

Specimen Signatures

Please provide the name(s), title(s), and specimen signature(s) of the individual(s) authorized to act as, or on behalf of, the Plan Administrator. (Use additional sheets if necessary.)

_____   _____
Name   Title

_____
Signature

_____   _____
Name   Title

_____
Signature

You may select as Plan Trustee:
a) Vanguard,
b) yourself, or
c) any other individual(s) or a qualified corporate fiduciary.
Note: *See the Questions and Answers section of "The Vanguard Qualified Retirement Program" for information on appointing Vanguard Fiduciary Trust Company as Trustee for the Plan.*

PLAN TRUSTEE

The following individual(s) or corporate fiduciary has been appointed by the Employer to serve as Trustee for the Plan in accordance with the terms and conditions of the Trust Agreement. (Check the box if Vanguard Fiduciary Trust Company shall be the Plan Trustee; otherwise provide the Trustee's name(s) and address(es).)

☐ Vanguard Fiduciary Trust Company

_____
Name

_____
Address

(_____) _____
Telephone Number

_____
Name

_____
Address

(_____) _____
Telephone Number

If your Plan is "Frozen," please check here. In many cases you need complete only Section 9 of this adoption agreement.

FROZEN PLAN

☐ The Employer has discontinued all further contributions to the Plan. The Employer and Trustee will, however, continue to maintain the Plan and Trust in accordance with the requirements of the Internal Revenue Code.

SECTION 1
PARTICIPATION REQUIREMENTS

You may require all employees to have attained a minimum age (up to age 21) and/or have completed a minimum period of service (up to two years) in order to be eligible to participate. Of course, you may elect not to impose eligibility requirements, in which case all employees will be immediately eligible. (Owner-Employees must also meet any eligibility requirements specified here.)

Any Employee shall be eligible to participate in the Plan when he or she has satisfied the following eligibility requirements (please complete one of the following):

_____ **No minimum age or service conditions.**

_____ **Minimum age conditions:** Employee shall be required to have attained age _____ (may not exceed age 21).

_____ **Minimum service conditions:** Employees shall be required to have completed _____ (may not exceed two) years of service.

SECTION 2
EMPLOYER CONTRIBUTIONS

Selecting Alternative I will give the employer sole discretion over the amount to be contributed each year, from no contribution up to the Plan's maximum.

ALTERNATIVE I:
Discretionary Profit-Sharing Formula

_____ **If this alternative is selected,** the Employer shall make contributions to the Trust for each Plan Year in an amount determined by the Employer in its sole discretion by resolution duly adopted on or before the last day for filing its Federal income tax return, including extensions, for the taxable year with or within which such Plan Year ends.

ALTERNATIVE II:
Fixed Formula Based On Compensation

_____ **If this alternative is selected,** the Employer shall make contributions to the Trust for each Plan Year in an amount equal to ____% (not to exceed 15%) of the total Compensation of all Participants who are eligible to share in Employer Contributions for the Plan Year, plus such additional amount, if any, as the Employer may determine in its sole discretion by resolution duly adopted on or before the last day for filing the Employer's Federal income tax return, including extensions, for the taxable year with or within which such Plan Year ends.

Important:

Section 404(a)(3) of the Internal Revenue Code generally limits the deduction for employer contributions to a profit-sharing plan for any taxable year to *15% of the total compensation paid to participants during the year.* In light of this limitation, you should ensure that the Employer Contributions for any Plan Year do not exceed 15% of total Participant Compensation for the Plan Year, plus any carryover amount. In addition, in no event may the total Annual Additions (as defined in Article 10.1(a) of the Plan) on behalf of any Participant for any year exceed *the lesser of $30,000 or 25% of the Participant's Compensation.*

SECTION 3
DIRECTED INVESTMENTS BY PARTICIPANTS

Each Participant shall be permitted to direct the investment of all amounts allocated to his or her separate accounts under the Plan. To the extent any Participant does not direct investments, the Plan Administrator shall be responsible for investing and reinvesting amounts contributed to the Plan. See Article 5.7 of the Plan.

SECTION 4
VESTING SCHEDULE

Each Participant shall at all times be fully (100%) vested in all amounts allocated to his/her separate accounts under the Plan.

SECTION 5
WITHDRAWALS

Note:

Each participant (or his/her designated Beneficiaries, in the event of death) shall be entitled to receive the entire amounts credited to his/her separate accounts under the Plan upon termination of employment. In addition, you may select one or both of the "in-service" withdrawal options set forth below.

(a) Withdrawals On Or After Stated Age (Optional)

_____ **If this option is selected,** a Participant shall be permitted to make withdrawals under Article 8.2 of the Plan upon attaining age _____.

(b) Hardship Withdrawals (Optional)

_____ **If this option** selected, articipant shall be permitted to make withdrawals Article 8.3 of Plan upon establishing financial hardship.

SECTION 6
LOANS (Optional)

_____ **If this option is selected,** the Plan Administrator shall be permitted to direct the Trustee to make loans to Participants from their separate accounts in the Plan in accordance with the provisions of Article 9 of the Plan.

Important

The Plan may not permit loans to Owner-Employees (as defined in Article 2.23 of the Plan) if the Employer is a partnership or sole proprietorship, or to Shareholder-Employees if the Employer is a Subchapter S corporation. See Article 9.1 of the Plan for more information.

SECTION 7
LIMITATIONS ON ALLOCATIONS

Note:

You must complete this Section 7 if the Employer maintains or has ever maintained another qualified plan (other than the Vanguard Money Purchase Pension Plan as a Paired Plan) in which any Participant in this Plan is or was a participant or could possibly become a participant. You must also complete this Section 7 if the Employer maintains a welfare benefit fund, as defined in Section 419(e) of the Code, or an individual medical account, as defined in Section 415(1)(2) of the Code, under which amounts are treated as Annual Additions with respect to any Participant in this Plan.

(a) Employers Who Also Maintain a Qualified Defined Contribution Plan Other Than a Master Or Prototype Plan (See Article 10.4 of the Plan)

If a Participant in this Plan is covered under another qualified defined contribution plan maintained by the Employer which is not a Master or Prototype Plan, then the provisions of Article 10.3 of the Plan will automatically apply as if the other plan was a Master or Prototype Plan unless the Employer hereby designates another method of limiting Annual Additions to the Maximum Permissible Amount (in a manner that precludes Employer discretion) by describing such method below:

(b) Employers Who Also Maintain a Qualified Defined Benefit Plan (See Article 10.5 of the Plan)

If a Participant in this Plan is or has been covered under a qualified defined benefit plan maintained by the Employer, then the sum of the Defined Benefit Plan and Defined Contribution Plan Fractions (as defined in Article 10.1 of the Plan) may not exceed 1.0. The method under which the Employer will satisfy this 1.0 limitation is described below:

(c) Limitation Year

For purposes of Article 10 of the Plan, the Limitation Year shall be the Plan Year unless you designate another 12-consecutive-month period as the Limitation Year below:

_____

SECTION 8
TOP-HEAVY PLAN PROVISIONS

Note:

You must complete this Section 8 if the Employer maintains or has maintained an other qualified plan (other than the Vanguard Money Purchase Pension Plan as a Paired Plan).

Minimum Benefits

For any Plan Year in which the Plan is a Top-Heavy Plan (as defined in Article 11.2(b) of the Plan), the minimum benefit requirements of Section 416(c) of the Code shall be satisfied as follows (please select one of the following):

_____ **(i) Minimum allocation under this Plan:** Employer Contributions under this Plan shall be allocated on behalf of every Participant who is not a Key Employee in accordance with Article 11.3(a) of the Plan.

_____ **(ii) Minimum allocation or benefits under another qualified plan(s):** The minimum benefit requirements of Section 416(c) of the Code shall be satisfied through one or more other qualified plans maintained by the Employer that are identified below:

_____

Name of plan(s)

_____

Present Value Determination

This subsection (b) applies if the Employer maintains or has maintained a defined benefit plan which has covered or could cover a Participant in this Plan. If this subsection (b) applies, the following interest rate, mortality table, and valuation date shall apply for purposes of determining the present value of accrued benefits under the defined benefit plan (see Article 11.2(c), (g), and (h) of the Plan):

Interest Rate: _____ %
Mortality Table: _____
Valuation Date: _____ of each year

SECTION 9
EXECUTION OF PLAN AND
TRUST AGREEMENT

IMPORTANT:

(1) Failure to properly complete this Adoption Agreement may result in disqualification of the Plan.

(2) The Sponsor will inform the Employer of any amendments made to the Plan or the discontinuance or abandonment of the Plan.

(3) The name, address, and telephone number of the Sponsor are as follows:

Vanguard Fiduciary Trust Company
P. O. Box 1103
Vanguard Financial Center
Valley Forge, PA 19482
1-800-662-7447

(4) If the Employer maintains or later adopts any plan (including a welfare benefit fund, as defined in Section 419(e) of the Code, which provides post-retirement medical benefits allocated to separate accounts for key employees, as defined in Section 419A(d)(3) of the Code, or an individual medical account, as defined in Section 415(l)(2) of the Code) in addition to this Plan, which is other than the Paired Vanguard Money Purchase Plan, the Employer may not rely on an opinion letter issued by the National Office of the Internal Revenue Service to the Sponsor as evidence that the Plan as adopted by the Employer is qualified under Section 401 of the Internal Revenue Code. If the Employer who adopts or maintains multiple plans wishes to obtain reliance with respect to the qualification of the Plan, the Employer must apply to the appropriate Key District Office of the Internal Revenue Service for a determination letter.

(5) This Adoption Agreement may be used only in conjunction with the Vanguard Prototype Defined Contribution Plan (Basic Plan Document Number 01).

(6) _____ Check here if the Employer is adopting the Paired Vanguard Money Purchase Plan in addition to this Plan.

EXECUTION BY
EMPLOYER

IN WITNESS WHEREOF, and intending to be legally bound, the Employer named above hereby adopts the Vanguard Prototype Defined Contribution Plan in the form of a Profit-Sharing Plan by causing this Adoption Agreement to be executed as of the date set forth below.

EMPLOYER:

By: _____
        Name   Title

Signature: _____

Date: _____

EXECUTION BY
TRUSTEE

IN WITNESS WHEREOF, and intending to be legally bound, the Trustee(s) named above hereby accepts its appointment as Trustee for the Plan, and hereby agrees to the terms and conditions of the Trust Agreement for the Plan.

TRUSTEE:

By: _____
        Name   Title

Signature: _____

Date: _____

TRUSTEE:

By: _____
        Name   Title

Signature: _____

Date: _____

Chapter 6

Money Purchase Pension Plans

A. **What Is a Money Purchase Pension Plan?** 6/3

    1. Who May Establish a Money Purchase Pension Plan? 6/5

    2. Advantages 6/5

    3. Disadvantages 6/5

B. **How to Establish a Money Purchase Pension Plan** 6/6

    1. Trustee or Custodian 6/6

    2. Plan Documents 6/7

    3. Deadlines 6/10

    4. Plan Year 6/10

C. **Contributions** 6/10

    1. Maximum Contribution 6/11

    2. Choosing a Lower Plan Rate 6/15

    4. Minimum Contribution 6/15

    5. Cash or Property? 6/16

    6. Deadlines 6/16

    7. How to Claim the Tax Deduction 6/17

D. **Ongoing Administration** 6/17

    1. Tax Returns 6/17

    2. Plan Administration 6/19

    3. Updating Plan Documents 6/19

E. **Distributions** **6/19**

    1. Inservice Distributions 6/20

    2. Loans 6/21

    3. Hardship 6/21

    4. Divorce Payments 6/21

    5. Early Distributions and Exceptions to the Early Distribution Penalty 6/22

    6. Mandatory Distributions 6/24

F. **Penalties** **6/25**

    1. Nondeductible Contributions 6/25

    2. Early Distributions 6/27

    3. Prohibited Transactions.. 6/27

    4. Life Insurance 6/29

    5. Pledging the Account As Security 6/29

    6. Mandatory Distribution Penalty 6/30

    7. Minimum Funding Deficiency 6/30

G. **Terminating Your Money Purchase Pension Plan** **6/31**

    1. Paperwork 6/31

    2. Distribution of Assets 6/32

H. **Multiple Employer Plans** **6/33**

    1. If You Are Self-Employed With a Day Job on the Side; or Vice Versa 6/34

    2. If You Are Self-Employed With Only One Business 6/34

    3. If You Are Self-Employed With Two or More Businesses 6/36

I. **Adding a Traditional or Roth IRA to Your Money Purchase Pension Plan** **6/38**

J. **Filling Out the Forms** **6/39**

Like profit sharing plans, money purchase pension plans fall into the broad category of defined contribution plans. Although money purchase pension plans are widely used, they are relatively inflexible. Consequently, they are often established along with a profit sharing plan. By establishing both types of plans, you gain flexibility (provided by the profit sharing plan) and higher contribution limits (provided by the money purchase pension plan). You can find more information about this synergy in Section II, below.

Although money purchase pension plans are more complex than profit sharing plans, you should have little trouble handling virtually all aspects of the plan since you have no employees.

If you ever hire employees, your money purchase pension plan will automatically become more complex. Because the government can disqualify the plan if you inadvertently violate a rule designed to protect the benefits of your employees, it is critical to take precautions. Generally, those precautions come in the form of a professional plan consultant who will handle the administrative details of your plan and make sure that the plan operates within the law.

The Ideal Candidate for This Plan

A money purchase pension plan works best for people who have net business income in excess of $30,000 and who want to contribute as much as possible to a retirement plan. Because contributions are mandatory, it is important that you have a steady income so that the contributions don't seem like a burden. This plan generally will allow you to make a higher contribution than will a defined benefit plan if you are younger than 50.

★ ★ ★ ★ ★ ★ ★ ★ ★ ★ ★ ★ ★ ★ ★

A. What Is a Money Purchase Pension Plan?

A money purchase pension plan is a mixed breed. Like a profit sharing plan, it is a defined contribution plan, which means (according to the IRS) that a defined amount is contributed to the separate accounts of the plan participants. The contributions earn investment returns over the years, and the participant eventually is entitled to keep whatever happens to be in the account when he or she retires, leaves the company or quits the business.

The key difference between a money purchase pension plan and a profit sharing plan is that the contributions to the money purchase pension plan are mandatory. That means you must contribute to the plan even in years when you don't want to. The only time you won't make a contribution to a money purchase pension plan

This Plan in a Nutshell

✓ You must make a profit to contribute to a money purchase pension plan.

✓ The contribution limit for a money purchase pension plan is higher than for a profit sharing plan. And once your net income exceeds about $30,000, it beats a SIMPLE IRA, too. This increased contribution limit is the primary advantage of a money purchase pension plan.

✓ Although more complicated than SEPs and SIMPLE IRAs to establish and administer, money purchase pension plans are still easy enough for you to handle on your own.

✓ If you make a profit, contributions to a money purchase pension plan are mandatory. You must contribute the percentage of compensation that is specified in your plan documents and no less. This means that you must make your contribution even in years when money is tight.

✓ If the net income from your business is less than $30,000, you will be able to contribute more to a SIMPLE IRA than to a money purchase pension plan. A SIMPLE IRA has the added bonus of being easier to establish and maintain.

✓ If you are younger than 50 and your net income is less than $135,000, you will usually be able to contribute more to a money purchase pension plan than to any other plan.

✓ Once you pass age 50 and your income exceeds $135,000 you will probably be able to contribute more to a defined benefit plan. A defined benefit plan is more difficult and costly to maintain, however.

✓ Many people whose income fluctuates choose to add a money purchase pension plan to a profit sharing plan to combine flexibility (profit sharing plan) with higher contribution limits (money purchase pension plan).

✓ You must set up your money purchase pension plan before the end of the tax year for which you want to make a contribution. Generally, that means you must establish the plan by December 31.

✓ Although SEPs, SIMPLE IRAs and profit sharing plans might permit you access to your funds while you are still working, money purchase pension plans generally do not.

✓ Unlike SEPs and SIMPLE IRAs, money purchase pension plans (like all Keogh plans) have tax filing requirements.

will be when you do not make a profit. Otherwise, you must contribute. Period.

In contrast, profit sharing plan contributions are discretionary. For example, you can simply choose not to make a contribution to the plan one year, even if you make a profit. (See Chapter 5 for more information about profit sharing plans.)

1. Who May Establish a Money Purchase Pension Plan?

Generally, you may establish a money purchase pension plan if you own your own business. You can establish a money purchase pension plan even if your business is simply a side venture that generates a little extra income for you. For example, if you work for a corporation by day, but sing at weddings on weekends, you can set up a money purchase pension plan for your wedding fees regardless of what plan your corporate employer provides.

But if you already own one business and then start a second, you might not be able to contribute to a separate plan for each business. For more information about multiple plan rules, see Section H, below.

2. Advantages

In Chapter 2 you will find a detailed comparison of the different types of retirement plans you can establish for your business and for yourself as an individual. That chapter will help you decide which plan

or plans are best for you. In the next two sections, however, we summarize some of the advantages and disadvantages of money purchase pension plans when compared to other employer plans.

First, the advantages:

- The contribution limit for a money purchase pension plan is higher than for a profit sharing plan. And once your net income exceeds about $30,000, it beats a SIMPLE IRA, too. This increased contribution limit is the primary advantage of a money purchase pension plan.
- You can use a money purchase pension plan effectively in conjunction with a profit sharing plan to incorporate some flexibility into contributions, allowing you to cut back on contributions in some years and maximize contributions in others. (See Section II, below.)

3. Disadvantages

Money purchase pension plans have some disadvantages, as well:

- Like a profit sharing plan, the paperwork required to establish a money purchase pension plan is more voluminous and complex than for a SEP or SIMPLE IRA.
- If your net income is less than $30,000, a SIMPLE IRA is likely to permit a higher contribution than a money purchase pension plan.

- The older you are and the higher your income, the more likely it is that a defined benefit plan will permit a larger contribution than will a money purchase pension plan.
- Unlike profit sharing plan contributions, money purchase pension plan contributions are mandatory. If you have income from your business, you must make a contribution to the plan, even if you desperately need to use the money elsewhere.

 If you ever add employees who are covered by your plan, the contribution to their accounts (but not yours) is mandatory even if your business does not make a profit.

- Although SEPs, SIMPLE IRAs and profit sharing plans might permit you access to your funds while you are still working, money purchase pension plans generally do not.
- Unlike SEPs and SIMPLE IRAs, money purchase pension plans (like all Keogh plans) have filing requirements. For example, you must always file a tax return for the plan if you have employees or if the assets of the plan reach $100,000 (whether or not you have employees). You must also file a return in the last year of the plan, even if you were not required to file in any previous year.

 If you ever hire employees, a complex set of nondiscrimination rules kicks in, which will almost certainly force you to engage a consultant to help you administer the plan. (See Chapter 1, Section B.1.d, for more information about nondiscrimination rules.)

B. How to Establish a Money Purchase Pension Plan

Only an employer (a business) can establish a money purchase pension plan. When you work for yourself and establish a retirement plan, you wear two hats: You, as the employer, establish the retirement plan and make contributions on behalf of you, the employee. If you are a sole proprietor, you would set up the money purchase pension plan in your own name as the employer (or in the name you are using for your business). If you are doing business as a partnership, however, the partnership must establish the money purchase pension plan, because the partnership is the employer. You and your partner cannot establish two separate plans as individual partners.

1. Trustee or Custodian

Although most qualified plan assets must be held in a trust, a special exception allows Keogh plan assets to be held in a custodial account. (See Chapter 1, Section C.2, for more information about trustees and custodians.) If you are self-employed and you plan to establish your money purchase pension plan account with a bank, brokerage firm or mutual fund, the financial institution generally serves as custodian. The custodian will handle adminis- trative details of your plan that would otherwise fall to you if you were serving as trustee.

2. Plan Documents

To establish your money purchase pension plan, you can use the money purchase pension plan documents provided by the financial institution of your choice—a prototype money purchase pension plan. Alternatively, you can hire a consultant to create a customized plan just for you, although there is rarely a reason to do so when you have no employees.

a. Prototype Plan

Most financial institutions have their own pre-approved prototype money purchase pension plans. By using such a plan, you save the cost of creating a plan from scratch. In addition, the financial institution generally takes responsibility for keeping its own documents up to date—a task that would fall to you if you created your own plan.

See Section J, below, for instructions on completing sample prototype documents.

Sometimes, You Must Create a Trust

Occasionally you will be required to use a trust instead of a custodial account. This might happen if you choose an investment vehicle that a bank (or other) custodian is not willing to hold in the account. For example, you might invest in a limited partnership or an offbeat investment for which the custodian doesn't want responsibility. In that case, you would have to establish a trust. The money purchase pension plan documents themselves can serve as the trust agreement, but you would need to hire a consultant to create the documents.

Once you establish the trust or plan, you must name a trustee. Although you are not required to serve as trustee (you can hire someone else), you will probably want to do it yourself to save money.

Once the trust is in place, you can open an account with a financial institution, such as a bank, brokerage firm or mutual fund. The account will be in your name as trustee of the money purchase pension plan (assuming you are serving as trustee). You cannot simply open an account in your name and deposit contributions. For example, the account title might be "Paul Brown, Trustee of the Paul Brown Money Purchase Pension Plan." Assets that are not held at the financial institution (those offbeat investments, for example) would be titled in the same way to indicate that they are assets of the money purchase pension plan trust.

The High Cost (and Headache) of a Custom Fit

If you decide to hire someone to create a money purchase pension plan especially for you, it will cost you—anywhere from several hundred to several thousand dollars.

And once the plan is drafted, you will want to make sure it will pass muster with the IRS. You do this by requesting a determination letter from the IRS. Generally, the consultant who crafts the plan for you will seek the determination letter. Although you are not required to seek IRS approval, you might feel more comfortable if you know that all the contributions you are making to your money purchase pension plan are deductible. But the IRS's stamp of approval is not free. The so-called "user fee" currently ranges from $125 to $1,250.

Next, you (or your consultant) must find a financial institution that is willing to serve as custodian of your money purchase pension plan assets under the terms of your customized plan. Most institutions will serve as custodian of the funds but will not be responsible for maintaining the qualified status of the plan—they will leave that to you. (See Section D, below, for more about plan administration requirements.)

b. Beneficiary Designation

When you name a beneficiary of your retirement plan, you are identifying the person or organization that you want to receive your plan benefits when you die. That's important, certainly. But the person or organization you name as beneficiary can be crucial for other reasons, as well. For example, your choice of beneficiary will determine how quickly you must take distributions from the plan after you reach age 70½ (see Section E.6, below, for more information about mandatory distributions)—and how quickly the plan must be liquidated after your death.

If you are married and you name your spouse as beneficiary, he or she will have options that other beneficiaries do not have. Your spouse can roll over your retirement plan into an IRA in his or her own name, pick new beneficiaries and, in most cases, prolong or delay distributions from the IRA. (Remember: When you delay distributions from an IRA, the assets can continue to grow tax-deferred—a big benefit!)

For most married individuals, naming a spouse as beneficiary is the best option. In fact, if you are married, your spouse is automatically presumed to be the beneficiary of your qualified plan.

But suppose you do not want to name your spouse as beneficiary. In that case, you can change the beneficiary to someone else, but your spouse must consent in writing to the change—and to all future changes of beneficiary unless the change reinstates your spouse as beneficiary.

The Joint and Survivor Annuity Requirement

In the old days, it was entirely possible that an employee or her family might never see a dime of her retirement plan benefits, even if she worked for the same company for 40 years. How could this happen? Well, suppose she labored for years and on the day she became fully vested in her retirement plan, she dropped dead of a heart attack. What luck for the company. Now it doesn't have to pay the benefits.

Doesn't sound quite fair, though, does it? After all, the poor woman did own those benefits. Why shouldn't they go to her spouse or to someone else of her choosing? For a long time, nothing in the law prevented those benefits from reverting to the company when a participant died.

Then in 1974 (with modifications in 1984), Congress enacted a new set of laws known as the joint and survivor annuity requirement. These laws provide that a qualified plan must pay out benefits to the plan participant and the participant's spouse as a joint and survivor annuity (as long as the two have been married for at least a year). If the plan participant dies, the surviving spouse will continue to receive the participant's remaining vested retirement benefits.

Despite the law's moniker, the participant and the spouse are not required to take the benefits as an annuity. They can select another form of payment available under the plan, such as a rollover to an IRA, as long as both of them consent to the alternative form of payment. A surviving spouse, too, can generally select another form of payment (besides an annuity) if he or she inherits the plan after the participant's untimely death.

Note that the joint and survivor annuity rule applies in a similar way in cases where the plan participant has designated someone other than his or her spouse to be the beneficiary. However, the participant does not need a non-spouse beneficiary's consent to change the beneficiary designation or the form of payment.

If you want to make a sizable donation to charity when you die, retirement plan assets might well be the best source of that donation, because charities do not have to pay income tax on the distributions. Just keep in mind that when you name a charity as beneficiary, you generally must distribute assets from the plan more quickly during your lifetime than you would if you named a person as beneficiary.

And it is almost never right to simply name your "estate" as beneficiary. Doing so could cause income tax problems for your heirs and perhaps increase probate fees as well.

As you can see, choosing a beneficiary can be a complex decision. For more information about the effect of your beneficiary designation on your retirement plan, see *IRAs, 401(k)s & Other Retirement*

Plans: Taking Your Money Out, by Twila Slesnick and John Suttle (Nolo).

3. Deadlines

As is the case with all Keogh plans, you must set up a money purchase pension plan by the end of the first year for which you want to make a contribution. There is absolutely no extension permitted. Although you do not need to make the full contribution at that time, some financial institutions require that you open the account with at least a nominal amount of money. You can send in the rest of your contribution later. (See Section C.6, below, for information on contribution deadlines.)

4. Plan Year

Although most self-employed individuals maintain their plans (and their businesses) on a calendar year, you can maintain a money purchase pension plan on either a calendar year or a fiscal year. A fiscal year is generally any 12-month period that ends on the last day of any month except December. You don't have to use the same year as your business, although it usually makes sense to do so. If you don't, the plan accounting becomes a little more complicated and offers you no advantage. For example, to compute the deduction for your tax return, you would use the income you received during your business tax year, not your plan year. Then you would take your deduction for the business tax year in which the plan year ends.

EXAMPLE: You maintain your money purchase pension plan on a calendar year, but your business tax year runs from July through June. To compute your deductible contribution to your money purchase pension plan you would use the compensation or net earnings you received between July 2001 and June 2002 (fiscal year 2001). You would then claim your deduction on your fiscal year 2001 tax return.

C. Contributions

Two key contribution rules distinguish money purchase pension plans from profit sharing plans, SEPs and SIMPLE IRAs. First, the contribution limit is higher for money purchase pension plans. Second—and just as important—the contributions are mandatory. Thus, choosing this type of plan means that you might be stuck with making contributions to the plan, even if you'd rather use the money for something else, such as upgrading your computer system or expanding your space.

Of course, there's more to contributions than just those two issues. You'll want to know the answers to a variety of questions, such as: Can you contribute even when your business is losing money? Can you vary the contribution each year? Can you contribute stock? Can you make the contribution at the beginning of the year? After the end of the year? Can you put in a little extra this year while you're flush so you don't have to put in as much next year?

In this section, we discuss in detail the contribution rules for money purchase pension plans and, with a little luck, answer all of your questions along the way.

 You cannot make any contribution at all to your money purchase pension plan if you did not make a profit for the year.

If you ever add employees, you will be required to contribute to their money purchase pension plan accounts even if your business doesn't make a profit.

1. Maximum Contribution

When you first establish your money purchase pension plan, you will fix the contribution level to an amount between 0% and 25% of compensation. (Although you are permitted to choose 0% as the contribution rate, one might wonder why you would do so.) In order to contribute the maximum, you must set the plan contribution rate to 25%. Be aware, however, that

you might not be able to contribute the full 25%, because your maximum contribution is actually the lesser of 25% of compensation or $30,000. (The $30,000 limit will increase to $35,000 beginning with the 2001 tax year.)

And that's not the end of it. There are two additional limits on the maximum amount you can contribute, as we explain in the following two sections.

a.   Additional Limit One: Limit on Compensation

For purposes of computing the maximum contribution, your compensation is deemed to be no more than $170,000.

> EXAMPLE 1: Assume you earn $250,000 one year and you have a money purchase pension plan with a contribution rate set at 25%. You cannot calculate your contribution amount using your actual compensation level of $250,000 because it exceeds the cap if $170,000. So, your maximum contribution is the lesser of $30,000 or 25% of $170,000. Because 25% of $170,000 is $42,500, your contribution is limited to $30,000.

Some good news: The $170,000 is the limit for the tax year 2000. That number may be increased for inflation occasionally, but not necessarily every year.

b. Additional Limit Two: Definition of Compensation

The Tax Code defines compensation differently for self-employed individuals than for others. It is not simply your net profit, which is your business income reduced by expenditures directly related to the business. Instead, compensation is your net earnings from self-employment, which is your business income reduced by all deductible business expenses. And for a self-employed individual, deductible business expenses include your self-employment tax deduction (which is always half of your self-employment tax) and your money purchase pension plan deduction itself. So, before you multiply your net profit by the plan contribution rate (for example 25%, if you are contributing the maximum), you must first reduce your net profit by half of your self-employment tax and reduce it further by your money purchase pension plan contribution. But the money purchase pension plan contribution is what you are trying to compute! We show you how to get around this conundrum in the paragraphs that follow. The point is, if you simply multiply your profit by the plan contribution rate and contribute that amount to your money purchase pension plan, you will come up with the wrong number.

 If you use that wrong number, you will have made an excess contribution to your plan—which will be subject to penalties unless corrected. (See Section E.l, below, for more information about excess contributions.)

c. Calculating Your Maximum Contribution

Calculating your maximum money purchase pension plan contribution is a five-step process:

Step 1:
Calculate your total business income and subtract your expenses (not including your money purchase pension plan contribution or your self-employment tax deduction).

Step 2:
Compute your self-employment tax deduction. The deductible portion is half of your total self-employment tax. Schedule SE (see example, below) walks you through the calculation.

Step 3:
Subtract the amount in Step 2 from the amount in Step 1.

Step 4:
Assuming you have set the plan rate to the maximum 25%, multiply the result from Step 3 by 20%. This is the mysterious part. See Chapter 1, Section B.l.c.i, for an explanation of why you use 20% instead of 25%.

Step 5:

Compare the result from Step 4 with $30,000. Your maximum contribution is the lesser of $30,000 or Step 4. (Remember, the $30,000 limit increases to $35,000 beginning with the 2001 tax year.)

> EXAMPLE: Holly has a 25% money purchase pension plan. In the year 2000, she raked in $98,450 from her Web design business. Her expenses (not including the self-employment tax deduction or the money purchase pension plan contribution) amounted to $26,780. She computes her contribution as follows:
>
> **Step 1:** Holly's income less business expenditures is $71,670, which is $98,450 – $26,780.
>
> **Step 2:** Holly completes Schedule SE to arrive at her self-employment tax deduction of $5,064. (See Line 6 of Schedule SE below.)
>
> **Step 3:** Holly reduces the amount from Step 1 by the amount from Step 2.
>
> $71,670 – $5,064 = $66,606 (Step 1 – Step 2).
>
> **Step 4:** Finally, she multiplies Step 3 by 20% to compute her maximum money purchase pension plan contribution.
>
> $66,606 x 20% = $13,321.
>
> **Step 5:** Because the amount from Step 4 does not exceed $30,000, Holly can contribute $13,321 to her money purchase pension plan and deduct that amount on her tax return.

SCHEDULE SE	**Self-Employment Tax**	OMB No. 1545-0074
(Form 1040)	▶ See Instructions for Schedule SE (Form 1040).	**2000**
Department of the Treasury Internal Revenue Service (99)	▶ Attach to Form 1040.	Attachment Sequence No. **17**

Name of person with **self-employment** income (as shown on Form 1040) Holly Jones	Social security number of person with **self-employment** income ▶	555 : 55 : 5555

Who Must File Schedule SE

You must file Schedule SE if:

- You had net earnings from self-employment from **other than** church employee income (line 4 of Short Schedule SE or line 4c of Long Schedule SE) of $400 or more **or**
- You had church employee income of $108.28 or more. Income from services you performed as a minister or a member of a religious order **is not** church employee income. See page SE-1.

Note. Even if you had a loss or a small amount of income from self-employment, it may be to your benefit to file Schedule SE and use either "optional method" in Part II of Long Schedule SE. See page SE-3.

Exception. If your only self-employment income was from earnings as a minister, member of a religious order, or Christian Science practitioner **and** you filed Form 4361 and received IRS approval not to be taxed on those earnings, **do not** file Schedule SE. Instead, write "Exempt–Form 4361" on Form 1040, line 52.

May I Use Short Schedule SE or Must I Use Long Schedule SE?

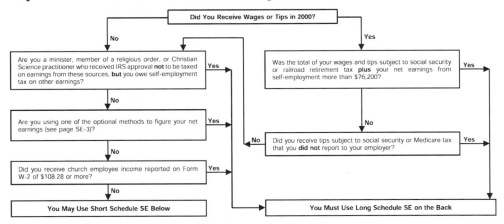

You May Use Short Schedule SE Below	You Must Use Long Schedule SE on the Back

---

Section A—Short Schedule SE. Caution: *Read above to see if you can use Short Schedule SE.*

1	Net farm profit or (loss) from Schedule F, line 36, and farm partnerships, Schedule K-1 (Form 1065), line 15a	**1**	
2	Net profit or (loss) from Schedule C, line 31; Schedule C-EZ, line 3; Schedule K-1 (Form 1065), line 15a (other than farming); and Schedule K-1 (Form 1065-B), box 9. Ministers and members of religious orders, see page SE-1 for amounts to report on this line. See page SE-2 for other income to report	**2**	71,670
3	Combine lines 1 and 2	**3**	71,670
4	**Net earnings from self-employment.** Multiply line 3 by 92.35% (.9235). If less than $400, **do not** file this schedule; you do not owe self-employment tax . . . . ▶	**4**	66,187
5	Self-employment tax. If the amount on line 4 is:		
	• $76,200 or less, multiply line 4 by 15.3% (.153). Enter the result here and on **Form 1040, line 52.** } . . .	**5**	10,127
	• More than $76,200, multiply line 4 by 2.9% (.029). Then, add $9,448.80 to the result. Enter the total here and on **Form 1040, line 52.**		
6	**Deduction for one-half of self-employment tax.** Multiply line 5 by 50% (.5). Enter the result here and on **Form 1040, line 27**	**6**	5,064

For Paperwork Reduction Act Notice, see Form 1040 instructions.   Cat. No. 11358Z   Schedule SE (Form 1040) 2000

Of course, you do not have to set the plan contribution rate to the maximum the law allows. You can choose any percentage between 0% and 25% of compensation. (See Section 2, below).

2. Choosing a Lower Plan Rate

Although you are not required to set your money purchase pension plan rate at the maximum (25%), you must choose a plan rate at the outset and stick to it. This is different from a profit sharing plan, SEP and SIMPLE IRA. With those plans, you don't have to specify a plan rate. You can simply contribute the amount you want, as long as it doesn't exceed the maximum allowed.

 When calculating your money purchase pension plan contribution, don't forget there's a twist that revolves around the word "compensation." As we explained in Section 1, above, your compensation is really your net earnings from self-employment—something that you can't know at the time you are calculating your minimum contribution. (See Chapter 1, Section B.1, for instructions on calculating your net earnings from self-employment.)

4. Minimum Contribution

Unlike profit sharing plans, money purchase pension plans have minimum contribution requirements. The minimum

contribution is precisely the contribution percentage specified in the plan documents. (It also happens to be the maximum you can contribute for the year.) For example, if you set the plan contribution percentage to 10%, the minimum contribution you must make annually is 10% of compensation. You do not have the option to contribute less, like 5%—or zero—as you do when you have a profit sharing plan.

 It is possible to amend the plan before the end of the year to change the plan percentage. If you do, the minimum (and maximum) is determined by the new plan percentage. (If you ever hire employees, however, you should confer with a plan consultant before amending the plan to be sure you are not violating any nondiscrimination rules.)

 The only time you will be allowed to contribute zero to your money purchase pension plan (assuming, of course, that you have chosen a contribution rate of more than 0%) is when your business does not make a profit. Remember: You are not permitted to contribute to your money purchase pension plan if your business does not make a profit.

The law that requires you to honor the promised contribution percentage is known as the minimum funding requirement. If you fail to make the minimum contribution for any year, you will be subject to a 10% penalty on the shortfall. If you do not correct the problem, the penalty could rise to 100%. (For more information about the minimum funding requirement and related penalties, see Section F.7, below.)

5. Cash or Property?

The law does not specifically require that money purchase pension plan contributions be made in cash. Nonetheless, if you contribute property, you are quite likely to run afoul of the prohibited transaction rules.

The prohibited transaction rules (see Section F.3, below) specifically forbid you from selling property to your plan. In a well-known case (*Comr. v. Keystone Consolidated Industries Inc.*, 113 S.Ct. 2006 (1993)), the U.S. Supreme Court ruled that a contribution of property in satisfaction of a minimum funding requirement is, in essence, an imputed sale of the property to the plan. That ruling pretty much brought a halt to contributions of property to money purchase pension and defined benefit plans—both of which have minimum funding requirements.

 If you'd like to look up the *Keystone* decision or any other court decision, you can do so at Nolo's Legal Research Center, which is on Nolo's website at http://www.nolo.com.

6. Deadlines

You may make your money purchase pension plan contribution any time during the year. Generally, the earlier you make it, the better, because the money can be working for you.

Unfortunately, you don't always know how much money you will make until late in the year, or even after the end of the year. That's why the government gives you until the due date of your tax return to make the precise contribution. And if you request and receive an extension of time for filing your return, you have until the extended due date to make your contribution. However, you could make a partial contribution early in the year and contribute the remainder when you have final income numbers.

 In addition to the deadline discussed above, there is another deadline you need to watch out for called the minimum funding deadline, and it could come earlier than the deadline for filing your tax return. (See Section F.7, below, for more about minimum funding requirements.)

 If your contribution is postmarked by the due date of your tax return, you will be in compliance with the law. In other words, you can write a check and take it to the post office (or deliver it to yourself, as trustee) on the day your tax return is due. The money doesn't actually have to be in the account by then. Just be sure to obtain proof of mailing.

Using Your Tax Refund to Cover Your Contribution

Suppose you are short of cash for making your money purchase pension plan contribution but you are expecting a big tax refund—enough to cover the money purchase pension plan contribution. As it happens, you are not required to make your contribution before you file your tax return. But you must make it by the due date of your tax return. That means you can file your return, receive the refund, and then use the refund to make the contribution.

The only problem with this strategy is that you must file your tax return early enough so that you receive the refund before the actual filing deadline of your tax return—which is when the contribution is due. For example, if your tax return is due April 15, you would have to file your return in January, February or March and hope you receive the refund before April 15 when the money purchase pension plan contribution is due.

But be careful! Suppose April 15 looms and you still have not received your refund. It won't work to request an extension at the last minute, because you have already filed your tax return. Instead you will have to find another source of funds for making the money purchase pension plan contribution.

As a precaution, you might want to request an extension before you file your tax return in the first place. Then you will have until the extended due date to receive the refund and make the money purchase pension plan contribution.

7. How to Claim the Tax Deduction

Once you have computed your money purchase pension plan contribution, you claim your deduction on page 1, line 29, of your individual income tax return (Form 1040). This will be true whether you are doing business as a partnership or as a sole proprietor. You can find a sample copy of Form 1040 in the Appendix.

D. Ongoing Administration

Although the ongoing administration for a money purchase pension plan can be more burdensome than for a SEP or a SIMPLE IRA, it's quite possible for you—as someone without employees—to manage without an expensive plan consultant. Even if you find you must file a tax return for the plan and don't want to tackle it yourself, most accountants do not charge exorbitant fees to prepare returns for one-participant plans.

1. Tax Returns

There are two types of tax returns you might have to file for your money purchase pension plan: IRS Form 5500-EZ and IRS Form 990-T.

a. IRS Form 5500-EZ

IRS Form 5500-EZ is an information tax return that helps the IRS monitor the operation of your plan. Being required to file this tax return does not necessarily mean that you will also be required to pay taxes. In fact, your money purchase pension plan will not owe any income tax while the assets remain in the plan, except in certain rare circumstances when the plan assets generate business income. (See Section b, below.)

You must always file an information tax return (Form 5500-EZ) for your money purchase pension plan for its final year. No exceptions. The final year of the plan is the year in which all of the assets have been distributed. (See Section G, below, for more information about terminating your plan.)

For other years, including the first, you will not have to file a tax return for the plan if all of the following are true:

- Your plan is a one-participant plan. Recall that a one-participant plan is a plan that covers only you, your partners (if any) and your respective spouses (if they also work in the business).
- The total value of all the assets in the plan is $100,000 or less at the end of the current plan year and all previous plan years since (and including) 1994.
- If you have two or more one-participant Keogh plans for your business,

the total value of all assets of all plans is $100,000 or less at the end of the current plan year and every previous plan year since 1994.

 If you ever add employees to your plan, you will have to file annual tax returns for your money purchase pension plan, regardless of the total value of plan assets. You won't be able to use Form 5500-EZ. Also, you will have to use the more complex Form 5500.

Form 5500-EZ must be filed by the last day of the seventh month following the end of the plan year. If your plan year is the calendar year, the tax return for the plan is due July 31. You may apply for an extension of time to file, which will give you an additional 2½ months. If the plan year is the same as your business tax year and you requested and received an extension of time to file your Form 1040, the filing deadline for the Form 5500-EZ is automatically extended, too. You can find a sample copy of Form 5500-EZ in the Appendix of this book.

b. IRS Form 990-T

As mentioned above, your money purchase pension plan is a tax exempt entity, which is why it generally doesn't have to pay tax each year on the income it produces.

But if your money purchase pension plan engages in a business that produces more than $1,000 of income during the year, you must file a special tax return—Form 990-T—for the plan. Income from a business inside a plan is called unrelated business taxable income, or UBTI. Once UBTI exceeds $1,000 in a year, it is subject to tax, and the tax must be paid out of the money purchase pension plan assets.

Most people invest their money purchase pension plan assets in stocks, bonds and other standard investments, none of which generates UBTI. But suppose you invest some of the assets in a limited partnership. Many limited partnerships are in fact businesses. And when the business (the limited partnership) starts throwing off income, it will be taxable, even though it is inside your money purchase pension plan.

2. Plan Administration

Because you don't have employees, the only other reporting that will be required of you, provided you do not run afoul of any laws, is to report distributions from the plan—typically when you terminate it. Distributions are reported to the IRS on Form 1099-R. The reporting is the responsibility of the plan administrator (most likely you, if yours is a one-participant plan) or the employer (also you). Your financial institution might prepare the 1099-R for you but you are the person the IRS will come to if the reporting is inaccurate.

3. Updating Plan Documents

Changes in the law might require that you update your money purchase pension plan agreement from time to time. If you are using a prototype plan provided by your financial institution, the institution generally will take responsibility for updating the plan.

 If you want to change your money purchase pension plan beneficiary, you don't have to amend the plan. You can simply request a "Change of Beneficiary" form, drop in the name of the new beneficiary, sign and date the form and return it to the financial institution. Don't forget to keep a copy for yourself.

E. Distributions

Through the qualified plan rules, Congress offers businesses, including self-employed individuals, an incentive to save for retirement and to provide retirement benefits to employees. The incentive is a big tax deduction and tax-deferred growth of the plan's assets. In exchange for those tax benefits, generally you cannot take money out of a qualified plan while you are still working in the business that sponsors the plan. If you do, the plan could be disqualified, and you might have to pay back some or all of the tax benefits—and perhaps pay additional penalties, as well.

The law provides a few exceptions to the general rule that keeps your money purchase plan assets locked up. But even if the law says you qualify for one of those exceptions, your money purchase pension plan documents might still forbid the distribution—especially if you are using a financial institution's prototype plan. (Financial institutions like to keep things simple.) And the plan has the final say.

Finally, even if you do gain access to your funds without disqualifying the plan, you will still have to pay income tax. You'll also have to pay an early distribution penalty—for taking the money out early—unless you qualify for an exception. (See Section 5, below.)

In this section, we explain the money purchase pension plan distribution rules, which are the rules that govern when you can—and cannot (at least not without penalty)—take money out of your retirement plan. They are also the rules that govern when you must—whether you like it or not—take the money out.

This is not a book about retirement plan distributions. Although we provide an overview of the distribution rules for each type of plan, you must look elsewhere for the details. One source is *IRAs, 401(k)s & Other Retirement Plans: Taking Your Money Out*, by Twila Slesnick and John C. Suttle (Nolo).

1. Inservice Distributions

Inservice distributions are distributions you take from a retirement plan while you are still working for the business that sponsors the plan. Generally speaking, these types of distributions are prohibited—which means you may get the plan disqualified if you try to take them.

Inservice distributions do not generally disqualify an IRA, whether a SEP or a SIMPLE IRA, although early distributions could be subject to penalties.

Although inservice distributions are generally prohibited, your money purchase pension plan will not be disqualified if the distribution occurs as a result of any of the following:

- termination of the plan
- death
- disability
- separation from service (which, for a self-employed individual, might mean terminating or selling the business), or
- attainment of normal retirement age (as specified in the plan).

Those are the inservice distributions the law allows. But the plan itself can be more restrictive. If your financial institution's prototype plan does not contain the inservice distribution provisions you want, you can confer with a consultant about establishing a customized plan.

2. Loans

Owner-employees may not borrow from their own money purchase pension plans. Doing so is considered a prohibited transaction. (See Section F.3, below, for more about prohibited transactions.) You are an owner-employee if you are a sole proprietor or if you are a partner in a partnership and you own more than a 10% interest in either the capital or the profits of the partnership.

3. Hardship

Although profit sharing plans can allow hardship distributions, money purchase pension plans cannot.

4. Divorce Payments

Congress has gone to great lengths to protect your Keogh plan assets. The cornerstone of that protection is a provision known as the "anti-alienation" rule, which attempts to ensure that you (the plan participant) cannot voluntarily or involuntarily transfer your interest in plan assets to another person or entity.

Divorce presents a unique problem, however. What if you want to (or must) use your retirement plan as part of a property settlement? Can you transfer some or all of your interest in plan assets in that situation? And if you can, who should be responsible for the taxes and penalties (if any) on the part you transfer?

Congress addressed these concerns by giving divorcing couples a vehicle for protecting plan assets and minimizing taxes and penalties. It's called a Qualified Domestic Relations Order or QDRO (pronounced "Quadro"). The QDRO rules spell out the circumstances under which your qualified plan benefits can go to someone else—an "alternate payee"—such as your soon-to-be ex-spouse. These rules also provide liability protection to the trustee who distributes the assets under the terms of the QDRO.

A QDRO is a judgment, decree or order (including a court-approved property settlement agreement) that satisfies all of the following:

- It relates to child support, alimony or the marital property rights of your spouse, former spouse, dependent child or some other dependent of yours.
- It gives an alternate payee, such as your spouse, former spouse, dependent child or other dependent, the right to receive all or a portion of the participant's plan benefits.
- It does not alter the form or the amount of the benefit originally intended for you even though the benefit might now go to an alternate payee. For example, the QDRO cannot require the plan to pay a larger annuity to the alternate payee than it would have paid to you.

- It contains certain language. Specifically:
  - ✓ The alternate payee must be referred to as "the alternate payee" in the QDRO.
  - ✓ The QDRO must identify the plan, as well as the amount of each payment and the number of payments to be made.
  - ✓ The QDRO must contain the name and address of both you and the alternate payee.

If you have a QDRO in place, the law will allow the trustee of the plan to distribute to the alternate payee his or her share of your plan assets without disqualifying the plan—as long as the plan also permits the distribution. And generally, if your former spouse is the alternate payee, he or she will be responsible for any income taxes on the distributions he or she receives.

 If you and your former spouse simply write up your own agreement, which does not meet the above requirements and is not court-approved, then your agreement is not a QDRO. In that case, you will almost certainly be liable for income tax and penalties on distributions even if they go to your former spouse.

 The QDRO rules apply only to qualified plans, not to IRAs (including SEPs and SIMPLE IRAs).

5. Early Distributions and Exceptions to the Early Distribution Penalty

Any distribution you take from your money purchase pension plan before you reach age 59½ is considered an early distribution, which means you must pay a 10% penalty in addition to income tax unless an exception applies.

The law provides for quite a few exceptions to the early distribution penalty. Those exceptions are described below. Bear in mind, however, that the plan documents must also specifically permit such exceptions. For example, if you become disabled, the law says that you can take money out of a Keogh plan without penalty, but if your plan says you can take distributions only after age 59½, or when you terminate employment, or when you die, then you won't be able to take a distribution as a result of a disability. The plan's word is the last word.

If you are using the prototype plan of a financial institution, the plan documents might allow some of these exceptions and not others. In some cases, you might be able to check a box to make an exception apply. But if you find that the prototype plan does not give you all the options you want, you might have to turn to a consultant to craft a plan that meets your needs.

These are the exceptions to the early distribution penalty that the law allows:

Remember, although these exceptions will give you relief from penalties, you (or your beneficiaries) will still owe income tax on all distributions.

a. Death

Distributions from your money purchase pension plan after you die are not subject to the early distribution penalty, no matter how old you are when you die or how old your beneficiaries are when they withdraw the money.

b. Disability

If you become disabled, you can take money from your money purchase pension plan without penalty. But first you must satisfy the IRS's definition of disabled, which is hardly a model of clarity. Here's how it reads: You must be unable to "engage in any substantial gainful activity by reason of any medically determinable physical or mental impairment which can be expected to result in death or to be of long-continued and indefinite duration." The IRS's own regulations state that the gainful activity refers specifically to the type of work you were doing before becoming disabled. Thus, it would seem that you need not be unfit for all work—just the work you customarily do.

c. Leaving Your Business After Age 55

If you are at least 55 years old when you leave or terminate your business, any distribution you receive from your money purchase pension plan will not be subject to an early distribution tax.

To qualify for this exception, you don't have to retire permanently. You can go to work for someone else or, presumably, start another business sometime down the road.

 The IRS is aware that it is not easy to determine when a self-employed individual has stopped working for herself. If you take a distribution and use the age 55 exception and continue to show self-employment income, be prepared to defend yourself.

To make use of this exception, you need not be age 55 on the day you take the distribution, as long as you turn 55 by December 31 of the same year. However, you must have quit the business before you take the distribution.

d. QDRO Payments

If you are paying child support or alimony from your retirement plan, or if you intend to distribute some or all of the plan to your former spouse as part of a property settlement, none of those payments is subject to the early distribution penalty as long as there is a QDRO in place that orders the payments. (See Section 4, above, for more information about QDROs.)

e. Refunds

If you contributed more to your money purchase pension plan than you were permitted to deduct during the year, generally you can remove the excess without penalty if you do so before you file your tax return. Those "corrective" distributions will not be subject to the early distribution tax, although they might be subject to other taxes and penalties. (See Section F.l, below, for more about excess contributions.)

f. Federal Tax Levy

If you owe back taxes, you can be reasonably certain the government will try to collect them. If you have assets in a money purchase pension plan, the government can take those assets (in other words, the IRS can levy on your money purchase pension plan) to pay your debt. If it does so, then those amounts taken for taxes will not be subject to the early distribution penalty, even if you happen to be younger than 59½.

Although the Tax Code provides some additional exceptions to the early distribution penalty—specifically, for medical expenses and periodic payments—for other types of qualified plans, as a practical matter, those exceptions are not available to you when you have a money

purchase pension plan, because you would not be able to receive the distribution while you are still working without disqualifying the plan. (See Section E.l, above.)

6. Mandatory Distributions

If you own your own business, you must start taking money out of your money purchase pension plan beginning in the year you turn 70½, even if you are still working. The income tax regulations provide a formula for calculating the minimum amount you must take. You may take more than the minimum, but you may not take less. If you do take less, you will be fined 50% of the amount that you should have taken out of the money purchase pension plan but didn't.

 If you are still working when you reach 70½, you may continue to make contributions to a money purchase pension plan and deduct those contributions. It could very well make sense for you to do so even though you are also required to take some money out each year. Not only can you claim a deduction for new contributions and reduce your tax liability, but you can also add to the assets that will grow tax-deferred.

F. Penalties

The Tax Code contains a host of penalties for mishandling a retirement plan, even if the errors are inadvertent. Money purchase pension plans are more complex than profit sharing plans, SEPs and SIMPLE IRAs. Consequently, there are more ways to go wrong and more penalties to avoid. The following paragraphs describe potential missteps, their consequences and, where applicable, opportunities for corrective action.

Infractions and Their Consequences

Problem	Penalty
Nondeductible contributions	10% of the excess
Early distributions	10% of the distribution
Prohibited transactions:	
• If corrected:	15% of the transaction amount
• If not corrected:	100% of the transaction amount
Required distributions	50% of the shortfall
Minimum funding deficiency:	
• If corrected:	10% of the shortfall
• If not corrected:	100% of the shortfall

1. Nondeductible Contributions

The law does not permit you to contribute more to your money purchase pension plan than you are allowed to deduct. If you do, you will have made a nondeductible contribution and you must pay a penalty of 10% of the excess. The IRS will assess a new 10% penalty on any excess that remains in the plan at the beginning of each year.

It's surprisingly easy to contribute too much, especially if you like to plan ahead.

Let's suppose your business has had a string of good years and you are expecting another banner year. In February, you contribute $30,000 to your money purchase pension plan to get those tax-deferred dollars working for you. December comes and goes. In April, while preparing your tax return, you discover that you made less money than you thought. As a result, you contributed too much to your money purchase pension plan. Now what?

You have two options:

a. Option One: Leave the Excess In, Deduct Next Year

Your first option is to leave the excess in the money purchase pension plan and deduct it in the next tax year. When computing the amount to contribute for the next year, you will first apply the excess that was carried over and then contribute any additional amounts that might be permitted to bring you up to your deduction limit.

You still have to pay the 10% excise tax for the first year, but as long as the excess does not exceed the deductible amount for the second year, you will not pay a penalty for that year.

> EXAMPLE: In 2001, you contributed $3,000 too much to your money purchase pension plan. You deducted the correct amount but forgot to remove the excess from the money purchase pension plan account. You decide to leave the excess in the account and deduct it the following year.
>
> In 2002, you have enough income to make an $8,000 money purchase pension plan contribution. You apply the $3,000 excess from the previous year and add an additional $5,000 in cash by the due date of your tax return to complete the $8,000 contribution. You must still pay a $300 (10% of $3,000) penalty for 2001, but you do not have to pay an additional penalty for 2002 or beyond.

If you must pay the nondeductible contribution penalty, you report the offending contribution on Form 5330 for the year for which you made the excess contribution. The form is due by the last day of the seventh month after the end of the year for which you made the nondeductible contribution.

> EXAMPLE: You made an excess contribution of $1,000 to your money purchase pension plan in 2001. You discovered your error in June 2002 long after you filed your tax return. You should complete Form 5330 for the year 2001. (You can find a sample copy of Form 5330 in the Appendix.) Sign and date the form and send it in by July 31, 2002, along with your check for $100 (10% of $1,000), which is the amount of the nondeductible contribution penalty.

b. Option Two: Remove the Excess

Your second option is more complex, but also more attractive if you qualify, because you can avoid the 10% penalty. The general rule is that the precise amount of the excess (not including any earnings that might have accumulated) can be returned to you without penalty by the due date of your tax return (plus extensions, if you requested and received an extension for filing your tax return)—provided the excess is returned for one of the following reasons:

- The plan initially failed to qualify. For example, if this is the first year of the plan and you submitted a letter of determination to the IRS, which found that the plan was not qualified.
- The contribution is not deductible.
- The contribution was made due to a mistake of fact. An arithmetic error in computing the contribution is a mistake of fact.

The likely problem with your contribution is reason number two—because it is not deductible. But the IRS has ruled that for this exception to apply, the deduction must actually be disallowed by the IRS. Thus, unless you are audited, you would have to request a determination that the deduction is disallowed.

Fortunately, there is relief from this rule, too. You can remove the excess without formal IRS disallowance, if you satisfy all of the following conditions:

- The amount of the excess is less than $25,000.
- The terms of your plan specifically provide that nondeductible contributions can be returned if the IRS deems them nondeductible.
- Your plan states that nondeductible contributions must be removed from the plan.

If you qualify to remove the nondeductible contribution from your money purchase pension plan and you do so before the due date (including extensions) of

your tax return, you will not have to pay any penalty on the excess contribution. You will also avoid an early distribution penalty on the money you took back out of the plan.

2. Early Distributions

If you take money out of your money purchase pension plan before you reach age 59½ and if the distribution does not fall under any exception described in Section E.3, above, you will have to pay a 10% early distribution penalty. That penalty is in addition to the income tax you must pay.

The IRS requires you to report the early distribution penalty on Form 5329 for the year of the early distribution. (A sample copy of Form 5329 is in the Appendix.)

3. Prohibited Transactions

The Tax Code prohibits certain transactions involving your money purchase pension plan assets. The prohibited transaction rules are part of Congress's strategy to protect your money purchase pension plan assets so that they will be available when you retire. Congress designed the rules to keep you and any other disqualified person (see below) from using the assets for personal gain or from engaging in transactions that put the assets at risk. In other words, Congress doesn't want you or anyone to misuse or squander your retirement money and the law will penalize the person who does.

A disqualified person is someone who might reasonably have access to your plan assets. In addition to you, such persons include your spouse, your lineal descendants (such as children and grandchildren) and your ancestors (such as parents and grandparents). The list also includes fiduciaries (those responsible for handling the assets of the plan, such as a custodian, trustee or money manager), a person who provides services to the plan (such as an administrator) and co-owners of your business.

The penalty for engaging in a prohibited transaction is 15% of the amount of the transaction, and the person who engages in the transaction owes the tax—not the plan. The penalty is assessed for each year (or part of a year) in the taxable period of the prohibited transaction. The taxable period starts on the date of the transaction and ends on the earliest of the following:

- The day the IRS mails a notice of deficiency for the penalty tax (telling you that you owe the tax).
- The day the IRS assesses the tax (telling you to pay the tax).
- The day the correction of the transaction is complete.

If the transaction is not corrected within the taxable period, an additional tax of 100% of the transaction is imposed. That's a total of 115%!

If you don't manage to correct it within the taxable period, the IRS will usually give you an additional 90 days after the day the IRS mails you a notice of deficiency before requiring you to pay the 100% tax. And the IRS will extend the grace period further if you can convince the IRS you need a little more time—or if you petition the Tax Court. If you are successful, you will not owe the 100% tax, but you will still owe the 15% tax.

The following transactions are prohibited. Note that these are all transactions that occur inside your money purchase pension plan or with the use of your money purchase pension plan assets.

- The sale, exchange or lease of any property between a disqualified person and the money purchase pension plan. For example, you cannot sell your house to your money purchase pension plan.
- The furnishing of goods or services or facilities between a disqualified person and the money purchase pension plan. For example, you cannot hire your spouse to manage the money purchase pension plan, and pay him a big salary out of the plan assets. You also cannot pay yourself for rendering services to the plan.
- The lending of money or extending of credit between a disqualified person and the money purchase pension plan. For example, you cannot borrow from the money purchase pension plan to buy a car, even if you intend to return the money.
- The transfer to or use by a disqualified person of any assets or income

of the money purchase pension plan. For example, you cannot use money purchase pension plan funds to invest in a house (held by the money purchase pension plan) that you then occupy as your principal residence.

- Any act of self-dealing, which occurs when a disqualified person uses the assets or income of the money purchase pension plan for that person's own interest or account while the assets are still in the money purchase pension plan. For example, if your money manager invests all of your money purchase pension plan assets in the stock of a company of which she owns 80%, such an investment would clearly benefit her as a majority shareholder and, therefore, might be deemed a prohibited transaction.

- The receipt of payment by a fiduciary in connection with a transaction involving the income or assets of the plan. A kickback, for example.

If you owe tax on a prohibited transaction, you must report it on IRS Form 5330, which is due on the last day of the seventh month after the end of the tax year of the transaction.

4. Life Insurance

If you use part of your money purchase pension plan contribution to pay the premium on a life insurance policy for your-self, the portion of your contribution that pays for the life insurance protection itself (known as the "PS 58 cost") is nondeductible. The investment portion of the premium is deductible.

Purchasing life insurance does not necessarily trigger the 10% nondeductible contribution penalty. The penalty applies only when you contribute more than the maximum deductible amount. You can make contributions to your plan that you cannot deduct, as long as the total of all contributions does not exceed the deductible limit. For example, if you compute your maximum deductible contribution—based on your net earnings—to be $20,000 and you contribute that amount but use $1,000 of it to purchase life insurance protection, you may claim a deduction of only $19,000 on your tax return, but no penalty tax would apply.

5. Pledging the Account As Security

If you use any portion of your money purchase pension plan as security for a loan (for example, you borrow money using your money purchase pension plan as collateral), you will be engaging in a prohibited transaction. The government views this action as equivalent to borrowing from the plan. As described in Section 3, above, borrowing money from your plan is prohibited.

6. Mandatory Distribution Penalty

If you fail to take required distributions from your money purchase pension plan beginning at age 70½, you will pay a penalty of 50% of the amount that should have come out but didn't. (See Section E.6, above, for more about mandatory distributions.)

Report this penalty on IRS Form 5329. You can find a sample form in the Appendix.

7. Minimum Funding Deficiency

The full amount of your money purchase pension plan contribution must be in the account within 8½ months after the end of the plan year (by September 15, if the plan year is the calendar year). This is called the minimum funding deadline.

If you fail to make a contribution in the amount specified in your money purchase pension plan documents (Remember: You set the contribution rate between 0% and 25% of compensation when you established the plan), your plan won't be disqualified, but you will be subject to a penalty.

⚠️ **The minimum funding deadline is different from the deadline for making a deductible contribution.** To be deductible, your money purchase pension plan contribution must be made by the due date of your tax return. The final due date for

your return (assuming you request and receive all the extensions the law allows) is October 15. But if you wait until October 15 to make your contribution, although the contribution will be deductible, you will be subject to a minimum funding penalty because you made the contribution after September 15—the minimum funding deadline.

The penalty for missing the minimum funding deadline is 10% of the shortfall—the amount that you should have contributed, but didn't. The penalty goes up to 100% if you do not correct the shortfall within the so-called "taxable period" (see below). In other words, you must eventually make the appropriate contribution to the plan. It doesn't work to simply pay the 10% penalty and ignore the contribution obligation.

The taxable period starts at the end of the plan year for which there is a funding deficiency and ends on the earlier of the following:

- the day the IRS mails a notice of deficiency for the 10% tax (telling you that you owe the tax), or
- the day the IRS assesses the 10% tax (telling you to pay the tax).

If you don't manage to correct the shortfall within the taxable period, the IRS will usually give you an additional 90 days after the day the IRS mails you a notice of deficiency before requiring you to pay the 100% tax. Correction forestalls the 100% tax, but you will still have to pay the 10%

penalty and, of course, you'll have to make the contribution to your plan.

You report the funding deficiency penalty on Form 5330. You can find a sample form in the Appendix.

G. Terminating Your Money Purchase Pension Plan

You are permitted to terminate a plan for legitimate business reasons. For example, you can terminate your plan if you dissolve your business or go bankrupt. Or perhaps you simply cannot afford to make contributions any more.

Once you are certain that you won't be making contributions to your money purchase pension plan any more, you should terminate it. If you don't, you will be required to keep the plan documents up-to-date through all the changes in the law, even though you are not making contributions. If you fail to keep the plan current, you risk disqualification of the plan and, in the worst case, incur current income tax and penalties, as well as loss of prior deductions.

The only impediment to terminating your plan whenever you want is the rule requiring the plan to be permanent. If the IRS, in its wisdom, determines that the plan was never permanent, but was temporary from inception, you face the specter of retroactive disqualification of the plan. The IRS is likely to consider your plan temporary if either of the following is true:

- you do not make substantial and recurring contributions, or
- you abandon the plan after only a few years (many plan consultants use five years as a guide) for reasons other than business necessity. And here again, you might find yourself at odds with the IRS's view of a business necessity.

But let's say you've decided to dissolve your business, and now you want to terminate your money purchase pension plan? How do you do it?

1. Paperwork

Once you decide to terminate the plan, you should give written notice—with an effective date of termination—to the trustee and or custodian of the plan, the plan administrator (if other than yourself), the prototype sponsor (which is your financial institution) and all participants.

a. Letter of Determination

Even though you've made the decision to terminate your plan, it is important to keep your plan in compliance with the law until you have distributed all of the assets. For this reason, some plan consultants recommend that you apply for a determination letter from the IRS to preserve the deductibility of contributions for all years that are still open to an IRS audit—and to facilitate corrective actions that might be necessary to ensure that the plan remains qualified while you are in the process of terminating it. The IRS will also render its opinion of the permanence of the plan.

You are not required to obtain an advance determination letter, and many people do not, especially if the plan is a one-participant plan and the risks of disqualification upon termination are low. When you have a one-participant plan, you are most likely to seek a determination letter when the assets of the plan are large and you want to feel confident that you won't trigger income tax or penalties (see Section 2, below) when you roll over the assets of the terminating plan into another plan or into an IRA.

If you decide to seek a determination letter, use Form 5310, Application for Determination Upon Termination. (You can find a sample form in the Appendix.) You must also pay a user fee, which is currently about $225.

b. Tax Return

When you decide to terminate your plan, you must file a tax return for the final year (the year in which all of the plan assets are distributed), even if you did not have to file one in the past. (See Section D.l, above, for information about filing a tax return.)

2. Distribution of Assets

Before you can file the final tax return and complete the termination of your plan, you must distribute all of its assets. As you might expect, this task is not as simple as it sounds. You have several distribution options.

a. Option One: Withdraw the Assets and Pay Tax

One rather unattractive option is to take all your money out of the plan and pay income tax. You will also have to pay an early distribution tax if you are younger than 59½, unless one of the exceptions in Section E.5, above, applies. If you choose this option, there is a mandatory 20% federal withholding tax at the time of distribution. But if that withholding turns out to be more than you owe at tax time, you can request a refund.

b. Option Two: Transfer the Assets to an IRA

Another option is to have the funds transferred into an IRA in your name. The plan assets should go directly from the financial institution that is now holding the plan assets to the custodian of your IRA. You should not take possession of the funds or temporarily deposit them into a regular (non-IRA) account. If you follow these instructions, you will not have to pay any income tax or penalties. All income tax will be deferred until you take the funds out of the IRA, some time in the future.

⚠ **Although you are permitted to take the assets out of your money purchase pension plan yourself and then deposit them in an IRA within 60 days,** it is not a good idea to do so. If you move the funds in that way, the money purchase pension plan assets will be subject to federal (and possibly state) income tax withholding and perhaps penalties unless you take remedial measures. For more about the nuances of qualified plan distributions, transfers, and withholding, see *IRAs, 401(k)s & Other Retirement Plans: Taking Your Money Out*, by Twila Slesnick and John C. Suttle (Nolo).

c. Option Three: Transfer the Assets to a Qualified Plan

You can have the funds transferred directly into another qualified plan. For example, if your new employer has a plan and the plan permits, you might want to consolidate the two plans. Not all plans permit such commingling, however, so be sure to check first.

H. Multiple Employer Plans

When your business is doing well, you will almost certainly find yourself wondering how you can contribute more to your retirement plan. Can you set up two money purchase pension plans and double your contribution? What if you have two businesses? Can you have one plan for each? Or suppose you work for another employer and run a business of your own on the side. Can you set up a plan for your own business even if you are covered by your employer's plan?

The key to understanding what you can and cannot do is this fundamental rule. Retirement plan limits are applied on a per-employer basis. This is called the separate employer rule.

It works like this:

Suppose you work for Company A from 8 a.m. to 5 p.m. every day and you work for Company B from 7 p.m. to 4 a.m. Suppose also that each company contributes to a money purchase pension plan on your behalf. Recall that the limit on contributions to a money purchase pension plan is the lesser of 25% of your compensation or $30,000 ($35,000 beginning in 2001). But because the two companies are separate employers, they can each contribute the maximum on your behalf. That means if is theoretically possible to accumulate $60,000 in money purchase plan contributions in one year—$30,000 from each employer. The same principle applies if you are one of the separate employers.

This section examines various employment scenarios and explains whether or not you can contribute to more than one employer plan in the same year. For information about adding a traditional IRA or a Roth IRA to your money purchase pension plan, see Section I, below.

1. If You Are Self-Employed With a Day Job on the Side; or Vice Versa

Let's say you own your own business, but you also work for someone else. Can you be covered by more than one plan? Because of the separate employer rule described in the preceding paragraphs, if you are covered by your employer's plan, you can still establish a money purchase pension plan for your own business and take a deduction to offset some of your profit. That's because you are a separate employer.

If you and members of your family together own more than 50% of the corporation that employs you, then you, as sole proprietor of your own business, (or the partnership, if your side business is a partnership) might not be considered a separate employer from the corporation. If not, then your contribution to the money purchase pension plan you established for your unincorporated business might be limited or eliminated altogether. If this describes your situation or if you are uncertain, you should confer with the plan administrator of the corporate retirement plan. (Also see Section 3, below.)

2. If You Are Self-Employed With Only One Business

Suppose you are self-employed and you have no other employer. If you have a money purchase pension plan in place, can you set up another plan, as well? This question isn't as odd as it might seem. Perhaps you established the money purchase pension plan the first year your business did well. But now you are feeling the pinch, and you don't want to be locked in to high contributions every year. Should you terminate the money purchase pension plan and replace it with another type of plan? Can you simply add another plan that will give you more flexibility? Or are you stuck with what you have?

You can have as many retirement plans for your business as you choose. However, there is a limit on the total amount you can contribute to each type of plan, and there is a limit for all plans combined.

The maximum a single employer can contribute to all money purchase pension plans combined is the lesser of $30,000 or 25% of compensation—which for a self-employed individual would be 20% of net income after the self-employment tax deduction. (See Section C.1.a, above, for more information about the definition of compensation for a self-employed individual.) That means you can establish three money purchase pension plans if you want, but the total of all contributions to all money purchase pension plans for the same employer (in this case, you) cannot exceed the above limit.

Furthermore, when applying multiple plan limits, all defined contribution plans must be grouped together. Recall from Chapter 1 that profit sharing plans and money purchase pension plans both fall into the general category of defined contribution plans. A single employer may establish both a profit sharing plan and a money purchase plan, but the combined limit for both will be the lesser of $30,000 or 25% of compensation. (Again, recall that the $30,000 amount increases to $35,000 beginning in 2001.)

 If all of your defined contribution plans were profit sharing plans, you would be limited to the lower contribution limit for profit sharing plans, which is the lesser of $25,500 or 15% of compensation. It's the money purchase plan, either alone or along with the profit sharing plan, that boosts the contribution limit for defined contribution plans.

Adding a Dash of Flexibility

As mentioned at the beginning of this chapter, many self-employed individuals are cautious about establishing a money purchase pension plan as a stand-alone plan because it is relatively inflexible. When business is going well, you will want to contribute the maximum to your plan—25% of compensation. However, if you choose to set the plan contribution level at the maximum, you must contribute that much each year, even if in some years you'd rather spend the money elsewhere. On the other hand, if you establish a lower contribution level (for example 5% or 10%) to hedge against the years when you'd rather have the extra cash, you might be chafing against that limit when you are flush.

Happily there's a solution to this problem. You can establish both a profit sharing plan and a money purchase pension plan. You can set the required money purchase pension plan contribution at a modest level and vary your profit sharing plan contribution between 0% and 15% every year, allowing you to contribute the maximum combined plan limit in good years and a lower amount in lean years. This works because profit sharing plan contributions are discretionary.

You can also add a defined benefit plan to your profit sharing plan and money purchase pension plan to increase total contributions. But there is a limit on the total combined amount you can contribute to all defined contribution plans (money purchase pension and profit sharing plans) and defined benefit plans of one employer. That limit is the greater of:

- 25% of compensation, up to a maximum of $170,000 of compensation. Thus, 25% of 170,000 or $42,500; or
- the amount you are required to contribute to your defined benefit plan. (See Chapter 7 for information about defined benefit plan contribution limits.)

 For purposes of these multiple plan rules, a SEP is treated as a profit sharing plan, so if you add a SEP to your money purchase pension plan, it will be subject to the same limits that a profit sharing plan would be.

 If you have a money purchase pension plan, you cannot add a SIMPLE IRA. If you want to contribute to a SIMPLE IRA, you cannot contribute to any other plan during the same year. (See Chapter 3 for more information about SIMPLE IRAs.)

3. If You Are Self-Employed With Two or More Businesses

There is a wrinkle in the rule that allows you to establish a money purchase pension plan with each separate employer and contribute the maximum to each.

The wrinkle is in the definition of separate employer. Two employers might look separate to you but not be separate in the eyes of the law. This can happen when businesses are under common control. Businesses that are under common control are deemed to be one employer and are combined for purposes of determining the ceiling on retirement plan contributions. So it is important to be able to determine if businesses are under common control.

a. If You Have Two Sole Proprietorships

The concept of common control is straightforward if you have two sole proprietorships. By definition, you own 100% of both businesses. The businesses are under common control because they have the same employer (you). Consequently, you must combine them when determining contribution limits. If you establish a money purchase pension plan for each business, the maximum contribution you can make to both plans combined is the lesser of $30,000 ($35,000 in 2001) or 25% of your combined compensation from both businesses (20% of the combined net income from both businesses after the self-employment tax deduction). It's the same limit that would apply if you had only one business or one plan.

> EXAMPLE: You have a Web design business that generated net income of $40,000 in 2000 (after taking into account your self-employment tax deduction). You also have a house-painting business that generated $35,000 of net income for 2000. The maximum you can contribute to a money purchase pension plan is the lesser of $30,000 or 20% of $75,000 ($40,000 + $35,000), which is $15,000. You can establish one money purchase pension plan or you can establish two or more, but the total contribution to all cannot exceed $15,000.

b. If You Have a Sole Proprietorship and a Partnership; or Two Partnerships

If you are a sole proprietor and you also have an interest in a partnership, the picture changes. You are the employer of your sole proprietorship, but the partnership, not you or the other individual partners, is the employer in a partnership. In general, that means each business must set up its own plan.

But here's where the issue of common control rears its head. If the businesses are

under common control, the total contribution to the plans of both employers is determined as though there were only one employer and one plan. This is true despite the fact that each employer will have to set up a separate plan.

A sole proprietorship and a partnership are under common control if the sole proprietor also has more than a 50% interest in the capital (the assets) or the profits of the partnership (as defined in your partnership agreement). In that case, the businesses are combined for purposes of the money purchase pension plan contribution limits. If you have established a money purchase pension plan for each business, your contribution to both plans is limited to a total of $30,000 ($35,000 in 2001) or 25% of your combined compensation from both businesses. However, the amount you deposit into each money purchase pension plan is determined by the amount of income you receive from each business.

> EXAMPLE: You are the sole proprietor of a Web design business. You established a money purchase pension plan for that business in its first year—1998. In 2000, you and a partner started a house-painting business. You decided to establish a money purchase pension plan for that business, as well. By agreement, you have an 80% interest in the profits of the house-painting business. Because your interest in the profits of the partnership exceeds 50% and you also own 100% of your Web

design business, your partnership and your sole proprietorship are under common control. Consequently, the maximum you can contribute to all money purchase pension plans is the lesser of $30,000 or 25% of the combined compensation from both businesses.

If you have an interest of 50% or less in both the capital and the profits of the partnership, then the partnership and sole proprietorship are separate employers for plan sponsorship purposes and also for purposes of determining contribution limits. If you choose a money purchase pension plan for both, you would set up two separate plans, and the contribution limits would apply separately to your earnings from each business.

If you are involved in two partnerships, the same principles apply. Those partnerships for which your interest in either the capital or the profits is greater than 50% must be combined and treated as one for purposes of determining the contribution limits, even though you must set up a separate plan for each partnership.

It is possible for two employers (such as your partnership and your sole proprietorship, or perhaps two partnerships) to sponsor the same plan, which might save administrative time and expense. If you elect this option, be sure to confirm with the financial institution providing the plan, or with the IRS, that the plan will pass muster.

If you own interests in several partnerships that provide services to one another, or if you and other individuals own an interest in the same partnerships, the partnerships might be under common control. Confer with a professional plan consultant to get help with this complicated common-control issue.

I. Adding a Traditional or Roth IRA to Your Money Purchase Pension Plan

Contributing to a money purchase pension plan for your business does not preclude you from establishing a traditional IRA or a Roth IRA. And if you can, you should. Generally, the more you contribute to a retirement plan—any plan—the larger your retirement nest egg is likely to be. However, participating in the money purchase pension plan might limit the deductibility of your traditional IRA contribution. (Roth IRA contributions are never deductible.) When you are covered by your own SEP, SIMPLE IRA or Keogh (including a money purchase pension plan), or when you are covered by a plan of another employer, any traditional IRA contribution you make is fully deductible only if the adjusted gross income (with certain modifications) on your tax return is less than $62,000 (if you are married) or $42,000 (if you are single).

For more information about traditional IRAs including how to compute deductible and nondeductible contributions, see Chapter 8.

J. Filling Out the Forms

All prototype money purchase pension plan documents have questions relating to employees. Even though you don't have employees, you must still answer all of the questions, because your plan must contain provisions that would allow it to remain qualified in the event you change your mind and hire help. Those are the rules.

Consequently, as you complete the plan documents, you will probably want to make eligibility requirements as restrictive as possible. That way, if you ever do hire employees, you have the option to maintain the restrictive provisions of the plan (usually to keep costs down), or you can relax eligibility requirements. It's more difficult to increase restrictions after you hire employees, because you might run afoul of the nondiscrimination rules.

Also, even though you initially choose restrictive options, you don't have to worry about excluding yourself. Many prototype money purchase pension plans allow you to waive participation restrictions for all employees employed on the effective date of the plan. That means, you can make your plan restrictive from the start, without excluding yourself.

To establish your plan, take the following steps:

Step 1:

Identify the bank, brokerage firm or other financial institution that will hold your money purchase pension plan assets.

Step 2:

Call the financial institution and explain that you would like to establish a money purchase pension plan. Ask for the appropriate documents. You might be able to request the forms online through the institution's website, but because the packages tend to be voluminous, most institutions still send the information by mail. You will receive the institution's prototype plan, which is a plan that has already been approved by the IRS.

Step 3:

While you are waiting for the papers to arrive, you can request a taxpayer identification number for your plan. Although you are not required to have a separate taxpayer ID number for the plan, many financial institutions prefer that you do.

Getting an Identification Number

To request an ID number, complete IRS Form SS-4 (you can find a sample form in the Appendix) and mail or fax it to the IRS, as indicated in the instructions. Note that the form is titled "Application for Employer Identification Number." Don't let the title throw you. This particular form has many uses, and one of them is to request an ID number for your plan (which is identified as a trust on the form, even if it's held as a custodial account).

Step 4:

When you receive the prototype plan in the mail, all you have to do is fill in the blanks. Then return the documents to the financial institution.

Because you have no employees, you generally will need to complete only the adoption agreement, a beneficiary designation form and, in the case of a mutual fund, instructions for how you want to invest your money.

At the end of this chapter, you will find a sample form from a financial institution. The accompanying explanations attempt to clarify those questions that are most likely to be confusing. Bear in mind that prototype plans vary from institution to institution, but the similarities are greater than the differences.

- *Employer name:* Enter your name as the employer (or the name you are using for your business). If you are doing business as a partnership, enter the name of the partnership.
- *Type of organization:* Put a checkmark next to the entity that describes your business.
- *Employer address:* Enter your business address and phone number.
- *Employer tax identification number:* If you are a sole proprietor, your employer tax identification number is generally your own Social Security number. If your business is a partnership, enter the tax ID number of the partnership.
- *Company/employer fiscal year:* Enter the month and day of the last day of your business tax year. For example, if your business is on a calendar year, enter December 31.
- *Effective date:* Put a checkmark next to New Plan. You may choose an effective date that is before you sign the plan documents, as long as the effective date is in the current year. As a self-employed individual, your income is deemed received on the last day of the year, so the effective date does not affect the amount of your contribution.
- *Plan year:* You can maintain your plan on a calendar year (ending December 31) or a fiscal year (ending on the last day of any other month). Generally, it is to your advantage to

maintain the plan using the same year as your business tax year. (See Section B.4, above, for more information about calendar and fiscal years.) To do so, leave this section blank.

- *Plan administrator:* You are the plan administrator, so enter your name, and your business address and phone number.
- *Specimen signatures:* Print your name and title, then sign under your name.
- *Plan trustee:* You will almost certainly want the financial institution to serve as trustee, so check the box next to the name of the financial institution.
- *Frozen plan:* Frozen plans usually result from employer insolvency. Because you are just now establishing your plan, this section does not apply to you.
- *Section 1, participation requirements:* You do not want your contributions curtailed because of your age or the length of time you have been in business, so put a checkmark next to "No minimum age or service conditions."
- *Section 2, employer contributions:* Your plan contributions will be based on a percentage of your compensation or net earnings. You may enter any amount between 0% and 25%. To contribute the maximum allowable amount, enter 25%. Just re-

member, the contribution will be mandatory, as long as you are making a profit in your business. (See Section C, above, for more information about contribution limits.)

- *Section 5, loans:* You are not permitted to borrow from your money purchase pension plan, so leave this section blank.
- *Section 6, limitations on allocations:* The limitation year is the period of time you will use to compute contributions to your plan. For example, if the limitation year is January 1 through December 31, your contribution limits are based on compensation earned during that period. Usually you will want your plan year, limitation year and business tax year to be the same. If so, leave this section blank.
- *Section 7, top-heavy plan provisions:* Assuming this is your only plan, or you are establishing this plan along with a money purchase pension plan, you can leave this section blank.
- *Section 8, execution of plan and trust agreement:* Under "Execution by Employer," print your name and title, then sign and date the form.

Step 5:

Next you complete the Beneficiary Designation form on which you identify those who will receive your plan assets when you die. If you are married and wish to leave those assets to someone other than your spouse, you must obtain your spouse's consent and his or her signature must also appear on this form. (For more information about beneficiary designations, see Section B.2.b, above.)

Step 6:

Your financial institution might also ask you to provide instructions for investing your contribution. For example, a mutual fund company might ask you to select one or more mutual funds from among their family of funds.

Step 7:

Send the completed Adoption Agreement, beneficiary designation and investment instructions to your financial institution. Be sure to keep a copy. If it gets lost, you'd probably rather scrub the bathroom with a toothbrush than fill out the forms again.

The financial institution will sign and return the Adoption Agreement. It will also open an account in the name of the plan.

VANGUARD MONEY PURCHASE PENSION PLAN
SIMPLIFIED ADOPTION AGREEMENT (003)

Please complete the following:

EMPLOYER NAME _____

TYPE OF ORGANIZATION
_____ Corporation
_____ Partnership
_____ Sole Proprietor/Self-Employed Individual
_____ Other (please specify): _____

EMPLOYER ADDRESS
_____
_____
_____

(_____) _____
Telephone Number

EMPLOYER TAX IDENTIFICATION NUMBER _____

Please indicate your company fiscal year. If left blank, we will assume it to be the calendar year.

COMPANY/EMPLOYER FISCAL YEAR _____

The Effective Date establishes when the provisions of this Plan become effective. It is also used to determine the dollar amount of compensation for the current Plan Year which may be taken into account under this Plan. For example, if today is November 1, 1997, but you wish the entire calendar year's compensation to be included, enter an Effective Date of January 1, 1997.

EFFECTIVE DATE

_____ **New Plan:** if the Employer is adopting the Plan as a new plan for its eligible Employees, the Effective Date of the Plan is _____

_____ **Amended Plan:** if the Employer is adopting the Plan as the amended and restated version of an existing plan for its eligible Employees, the Effective Date of the amendment is _____

Note: If you are amending an existing plan with Vanguard, please list your current Vanguard plan accounts below:

Vanguard Fund Name	Vanguard Account Number
_____	_____
_____	_____
_____	_____

PLAN YEAR

The Plan Year shall be the 12-consecutive-month period ending on the last day of the calendar month of _____. (If no designation is made, the Plan Year shall be the Employer's fiscal year.)

Vanguard is not the Plan Administrator. The responsibilities of the Plan Administrator are explained in the Questions and Answers Booklet and Plan Document, and include: maintaining accurate employee records, submitting required reports to government agencies, determining employee eligibility, and instructing Vanguard as to allocation and disposition of all plan contributions, investments, and payments.

PLAN ADMINISTRATOR

The following individual(s) or committee has been appointed by the Employer to serve as Plan Administrator for the Plan (if no designation is made, the Employer shall be considered the Plan Administrator):

_____
Name

_____
Address

(_____)_____
Telephone Number

Note: Vanguard is not the Plan Administrator.

Specimen Signatures

Please provide the name(s), title(s), and specimen signature(s) of the individual(s) authorized to act as, or on behalf of, the Plan Administrator. (Use additional sheets if necessary.)

_____   _____
Name   Title

_____
Signature

_____   _____
Name   Title

_____
Signature

You may select as Plan Trustee:
  a) Vanguard,
  b) yourself, or
  c) any other individual(s) or a qualified corporate fiduciary.

Note: *See the Questions and Answers on the Vanguard Retirement Program about appointing Vanguard Fiduciary Trust Company as Trustee for the Plan.*

PLAN TRUSTEE

The following individual(s) or corporate fiduciary has been appointed by the Employer to serve as Trustee for the Plan in accordance with the terms and conditions of the Trust Agreement. (Check the box if Vanguard Fiduciary Trust Company shall be the Plan Trustee; otherwise provide the Trustee's name(s) and address(es).)

☐ Vanguard Fiduciary Trust Company

_____
Name

_____
Address

(_____)_____
Telephone Number

_____
Name

_____
Address

(_____)_____
Telephone Number

If your Plan is "Frozen," please check here. In many cases you need to complete only Section 8 of this Adoption Agreement.

FROZEN PLAN

☐ The Employer has discontinued all further contributions to the Plan. The Employer and Trustee will, however, continue to maintain the Plan and Trust in accordance with the requirements of the Internal Revenue Code.

SECTION 1
PARTICIPATION REQUIREMENTS

You may require all employees to have attained a minimum age (up to age 21) and/or have completed a minimum period of service (up to two years) in order to be eligible to participate. Of course, you may elect not to impose eligibility requirements, in which case all employees will be immediately eligible. (Owner-Employees must also meet any eligibility requirements specified here.)

Any Employee shall be eligible to participate in the Plan when he or she has satisfied the following eligibility requirements (please complete one of the following):

_____ **No minimum age or service conditions.**

_____ **Minimum age conditions:** Employees shall be required to have attained age _____ (may not exceed age 21).

_____ **Minimum service conditions:** Employees shall be required to have completed _____ (may not exceed two) years of service.

SECTION 2
EMPLOYER CONTRIBUTIONS

Under a Money Purchase Pension Plan, the employer is required to contribute a fixed percentage of each participant's compensation, designated by you in this section, each year, regardless of earnings or profits, subject to penalties. (Discretionary contributions are available under a Profit-Sharing Plan.) YOU MUST DECLARE A PERCENTAGE IN THIS SECTION IN ORDER TO ESTABLISH A MONEY PURCHASE PLAN.

The Employer shall contribute to the Trust on behalf of each Participant for a Plan Year an amount equal to _____% (not to exceed 25%) of the Participant's Compensation for the Plan Year.

SECTION 3
DIRECTED INVESTMENTS BY PARTICIPANTS

Each Participant shall be permitted to direct the investment of all amounts allocated to his or her separate accounts under the Plan. To the extent any Participant does not direct investments, the Plan Administrator shall be responsible for investing and reinvesting amounts contributed to the Plan. See Article 5.7 of the Plan.

SECTION 4
VESTING SCHEDULE

Each Participant shall at all times be fully (100%) vested in all amounts allocated to his/her separate accounts under the Plan.

SECTION 5
LOANS (Optional)

_____ **If this option is selected,** the Plan Administrator shall be permitted to direct the Trustee to make loans to Participants from their separate accounts in the Plan in accordance with the provisions of Article 9 of the Plan.

Important:

The Plan may not permit loans to Owner-Employees (as defined in Article 2.23 of the Plan) if the Employer is a partnership or sole proprietorship, or to Shareholder-Employees if the Employer is a Subchapter S corporation. See Article 9.1 of the Plan for more information.

SECTION 6
LIMITATIONS ON ALLOCATIONS

Note: **You must complete this Section 6 if the Employer maintains or has ever maintained another qualified plan (other than a Vanguard Profit-Sharing Plan as a Paired Plan) in which any Participant in this Plan is or was a participant or could possibly become a participant. You must also complete this Section 6 if the Employer maintains a welfare benefit fund, as defined in Section 419(e) of the Code, or an individual medical account, as defined in Section 415(l)(2) of the Code, under which amounts are treated as Annual Additions with respect to any Participant in this Plan.**

Employers Who Also Maintain a Qualified Defined Contribution Plan Other Than a Master Or Prototype Plan (See Article 10.4 of the Plan)

If a Participant in this Plan is covered under another qualified defined contribution plan maintained by the Employer which is not a Master or Prototype Plan, then the provisions of Article 10.3 of the Plan will automatically apply as if the other plan was a Master or Prototype Plan unless the Employer hereby designates another method of limiting Annual Additions to the Maximum Permissible Amount (in a manner that precludes Employer discretion) by describing such method below:

Employers Who Also Maintain a Qualified Defined Benefit Plan (See Article 10.5 of the Plan)

If a Participant in this Plan is or has been covered under a qualified defined benefit plan maintained by the Employer, then the sum of the Defined Benefit Plan and Defined Contribution Plan Fractions (as defined in Article 10.1 of the Plan) may not exceed 1. The method under which the Employer will satisfy this 1.0 limitation is described below:

Limitation Year

For purposes of Article 10 of the Plan, the Limitation Year shall be the Plan Year unless you designate another 12-consecutive-month period as the Limitation Year below:

_____

SECTION 7
TOP-HEAVY PLAN PROVISIONS

Note: **You must complete this Section 7 if the Employer maintains or has maintained another qualified plan (other than the Vanguard Profit-Sharing Plan as a Paired Plan).**

Minimum Benefits

For any Plan Year in which the Plan is a Top-Heavy Plan (as defined in Article 11.2(b) of the Plan), the minimum benefit requirements of Section 416(c) of the Code shall be satisfied as follows (please select one of the following):

_____ **(i) Minimum allocation under this Plan:** Employer Contributions under this Plan shall be allocated on behalf of every Participant who is not a Key Employee in accordance with Article 11.3(a) of the Plan.

_____ **(ii) Minimum allocation or benefits under another qualified plan(s):** The minimum benefit requirements of Section 416(c) of the Code shall be satisfied through one or more other qualified plans maintained by the Employer that are identified below:

_____
Name of plan(s)

Present Value Determination

This subsection (b) applies if the Employer maintains or has maintained a defined benefit plan which has covered or could cover a Participant in the Plan. If this subsection (b) applies, the following interest rate, mortality table, and valuation date shall apply for purposes of determining the present value of accrued benefits under the defined benefit plan (see Article 11.2(c), (g), and (h) of the Plan):

Interest Rate: _____ %
Mortality Table: _____
Valuation Date: _____ of each year

SECTION 8
EXECUTION OF PLAN AND
TRUST AGREEMENT

IMPORTANT:

(1) Failure to properly complete this Adoption Agreement may result in disqualification of the Plan.

(2) The Sponsor will inform the Employer of any amendments made to the Plan or the discontinuance or abandonment of the Plan.

(3) The name, address, and telephone number of the Sponsor are as follows:
Vanguard Fiduciary Trust Company
P. O. Box 1103
Vanguard Financial Center
Valley Forge, PA 19482
1-800-662-2003

(4) If the Employer maintains or later adopts any plan (including a welfare benefit fund, as defined in Section 419(e) of the Code, which provides postretirement medical benefits allocated to separate accounts for key employees, as defined in Section 419A(d)(3) of the Code, or an individual medical account, as defined in Section 415(l)(2) of the Code) in addition to this Plan which is other than the Paired Vanguard Profit-Sharing Plan, the Employer may not rely on an opinion letter issued by the National Office of the Internal Revenue Service to the Sponsor as evidence that the Plan as adopted by the Employer is qualified under Section 401 of the Internal Revenue Code. If the Employer who adopts or maintains multiple plans wishes to obtain reliance with respect to the qualification of this Plan, the Employer must apply to the appropriate Key District Office of the Internal Revenue Service for a determination letter.

(5) This Adoption Agreement may be used only in conjunction with the Vanguard Prototype Defined Contribution Plan (Basic Plan Document Number 001).

(6) _____ Check here if the Employer is adopting the Paired Vanguard Profit Sharing Plan in addition to this Plan.

EXECUTION BY EMPLOYER

IN WITNESS WHEREOF, and intending to be legally bound, the Employer named above hereby adopts the Vanguard Prototype Defined Contribution Plan in the form of a Money Purchase Pension Plan by causing this Adoption Agreement to be executed as of the date set forth below.

EMPLOYER:

By: _____
       Name   Title

Signature: _____

Date: _____

EXECUTION BY TRUSTEE

IN WITNESS WHEREOF, and intending to be legally bound, the Trustee(s) named above hereby accepts its appointment as Trustee for the Plan, and hereby agrees to the terms and conditions of the Trust Agreement for the Plan.

TRUSTEE:

By: _____
       Name   Title

Signature: _____

Date: _____

TRUSTEE:

By: _____
       Name   Title

Signature: _____

Date: _____

Chapter 7

Defined Benefit Plans

A. **What Is a Defined Benefit Plan?** 7/3

    1. Who May Establish a Defined Benefit Plan? 7/5

    2. Advantages 7/5

    3. Disadvantages 7/6

B. **How to Establish a Defined Benefit Plan** 7/6

    1. Trustee or Custodian 7/7

    2. Plan Documents 7/7

    3. Beneficiary Designation 7/8

    4. Deadlines 7/10

    5. Plan Year 7/10

C. **Contributions** 7/10

    1. Maximum Contribution 7/11

    2. Minimum Contribution 7/13

    3. Cash or Property? 7/14

    4. Deadlines 7/14

    5. How to Claim the Tax Deduction 7/15

D. **Ongoing Administration** 7/15

    1. Tax Returns 7/16

    2. Plan Administration 7/17

    3. Updating Plan Documents 7/18

E. **Distributions** **7/18**

    1. Inservice Distributions 7/19

    2. Loans 7/19

    3. Hardship 7/20

    4. Divorce Payments 7/20

    5. Early Distributions and Exceptions to the Early Distribution Penalty 7/21

    6. Mandatory Distributions 7/23

F. **Penalties** **7/23**

    1. Nondeductible Contributions 7/24

    2. Early Distributions 7/26

    3. Prohibited Transactions 7/26

    4. Life Insurance 7/28

    5. Pledging the Plan Benefits As Security 7/28

    6. Mandatory Distribution Penalty 7/28

    7. Minimum Funding Deficiency 7/28

    8. Overstatement Penalty 7/29

G. **Terminating Your Defined Benefit Plan** **7/30**

    1. Paperwork 7/30

    2. Distribution of Assets 7/31

H. **Multiple Employer Plans** **7/32**

    1. If You Are Self-Employed With a Day Job on the Side; or Vice Versa 7/32

    2. If You Are Self-Employed With One Business 7/33

    3. If You Are Self-Employed With Two or More Businesses 7/33

I. **Adding a Traditional or Roth IRA to Your Defined Benefit Plan** **7/35**

One way to bring about tax simplification would be to give all lawmakers pop quizzes on the rules governing defined benefit plans. For every wrong answer, Congress would have to repeal or simplify an existing tax law. We'd have the Tax Code down to ten pages in no time.

In spite of its mind-numbing complexity, a defined benefit plan can be the ideal vehicle for the right person. That person will often be older than 50, self-employed without employees, making a steady income of more than $135,000 a year and searching frantically for a big tax deduction. Of course, a defined benefit plan can be right for other people, as well. Typically, though, defined benefit plans produce the largest contributions and deductions for older participants with high compensation. Contributions can be more than twice the size of contributions to a defined contribution plan. Just why this is so will become clearer as you read through this chapter.

 High contribution limits can be a two-edged sword, especially if you have employees. For example, if you employ a number of individuals who fit the "ideal" defined benefit profile—older workers with big salaries—the contributions you must make on their behalf might be quite large, which is good for them but expensive for you.

The Ideal Candidate for This Plan

A defined benefit plan works best for people who are approximately 50 years old or older and who have a steady business income in excess of $135,000.

★ ★ ★ ★ ★ ★ ★ ★ ★ ★ ★ ★ ★ ★ ★

If you decide to establish a defined benefit plan, you will need help right from the start. Most financial institutions, such as banks, brokerage firms or mutual funds, do not have pre-approved prototype defined benefit plans, so you can't establish one by filling in a few blanks and signing on the dotted line, as you can with other types of retirement plans. Instead, you'll need a consultant to draw up a plan for you and an actuary to tell you how much to contribute each year. The contribution calculation isn't something you can do yourself unless you've been trained as an actuary.

A. What Is a Defined Benefit Plan?

A defined benefit plan is a type of Keogh that promises to pay each participant a specific dollar amount in installments (in other words, as an annuity) for life, beginning at retirement. Those retirement payments are known as the participant's

This Plan in a Nutshell

✓ This is an expensive type of plan to establish and maintain, because you must pay a plan consultant to create the plan and an actuary to calculate your annual contribution.

✓ If you are older than age 50 and making lots of money, you will generally be able to contribute more to a defined benefit plan than to any other type of plan.

✓ Contributions to a defined benefit plan are mandatory.

✓ You might be required to contribute to a defined benefit plan even if you don't make a profit.

✓ You must set up your defined benefit plan before the end of the tax year for which you want to make a contribution. Generally that means you must establish the plan by December 31.

✓ Unlike SEPs and SIMPLE IRAs, defined benefit plans (like all Keoghs) have tax filing requirements.

✓ Although SEPs, SIMPLE IRAs and profit sharing plans might permit you access to your funds while you are still working, defined benefit plans will not.

"benefit." The benefit can ultimately be paid in a form other than an annuity—as a lump sum, for example—but the alternative payment must be equivalent to a lifetime annuity.

The promised payment is defined in the plan documents and typically is based on a combination of factors, such as the participant's final compensation and the length of time the participant worked for the employer. If the participant retires early, the benefit is reduced according to yet another complex formula.

With a defined benefit plan, it is the employer's responsibility to make sure there is enough money in the plan to pay each participant's benefit at retirement. Contributions are not allocated to individual participants' accounts, but are

pooled in one large account and participants are paid from the pool when they retire. Each year the employer must contribute enough to ensure all benefits can be paid at the appropriate time. The computation is not simple. It requires the services of an actuary, who uses projections of compensation, investment returns and other variables to determine the annual contribution amount. The computation must be repeated every year to take into account changes in the assumptions. For example, if the investments don't do as well as expected, the employer must make up the difference with a larger contribution the following year.

Because retirement benefits are guaranteed, contributions to a defined benefit plan are mandatory. The employer must make annual contributions that reasonably assure the benefit target will be reached. This is true for you, too, even though you are self-employed and have no employees. It's even possible that you will have to make a contribution in a year when you have no income from your business.

⚠ **This rule is unique to defined benefit plans.** For example, although contributions to a money purchase pension plan are mandatory, you are not permitted or required to contribute to your own account unless you have net income from your business (in other words, a profit).

⚠ **In this chapter, you will find that the terminology used to discuss defined benefit plans is somewhat different** from the terminology used to discuss other types of qualified plans and IRAs. Much of this difference stems from the fact that participants in defined contribution plans and IRAs accumulate cash or other investment assets in individual accounts. But participants in defined benefit plans don't have individual accounts. Instead, they "accrue a benefit," which means they earn a promised retirement annuity.

1. Who May Establish a Defined Benefit Plan?

Generally, if you own your own business, you may establish a defined benefit plan. This is true even if you work for a corporation, but you own a business on the side. You can set up a defined benefit plan for your side business regardless of what plan your corporate employer provides for you.

But if you already own one business and then start a second, you might not be able to contribute to a separate plan for each business. For more information about multiple plan rules, see Section II, below.

2. Advantages

In Chapter 2 you can find a detailed comparison of the different types of retirement plans you can establish for your business or for yourself as an individual. That chapter will help you decide which plan or plans are best for you. In the next two sections, however, we summarize some of the advantages and disadvantages of defined benefit plans compared to other employer plans. Let's start with the most compelling reason to establish a defined benefit plan.

The primary advantage a defined benefit plan offers over other types of plans is the potential for larger contributions and deductions. That doesn't mean you can always contribute more to a defined benefit plan. But if you are older than the average worker, or nearing retirement, and if you are making mounds of money (say, more than $135,000 per year), you might be able to contribute significantly more to a defined benefit plan than to a defined contribution plan (which will allow a maximum contribution of $30,000 in 2000 or $35,000 beginning in 2001).

To see how high contributions and deductions to a defined benefit plan can be, consider what happens if you are able to contribute $75,000 to your defined benefit plan and deduct that amount on your tax return. The federal tax savings for that year alone (assuming you are in a 39.6% tax bracket) are roughly $29,700. Compare that to tax savings of $11,880 if you contribute the maximum $30,000 to a defined contribution plan.

3. Disadvantages

The many disadvantages of defined benefit plans have caused the plans to lose favor over the last decade. Although recent legislation has revived interest, many disadvantages remain.

- Defined benefit plan contributions are mandatory.
- You might have to make contributions for years in which you have no income.
- Although SEPs, SIMPLE IRAs and profit sharing plans allow you access (under certain circumstances) to your funds while you are still working for the business that sponsors the plan, defined benefit plans generally do not.
- Unlike SEPs and SIMPLE IRAs, defined benefit plans have filing requirements. You must always file a tax return for your defined benefit plan if you have employees or if the assets of the plan reach $100,000 (whether or not you have employees). You must also file a return in the last year of the plan, even if you did not have to file in previous years.
- Defined benefit plans tend to be costly. Even though you have no employees, you must hire a consultant and an actuary to create your plan and compute your annual contributions.

As with all plans, adding employees to your defined benefit plan will make the plan more expensive and more complicated:

- You will have to comply with a complex set of nondiscrimination rules. (See Chapter 1, Section B.1.d, for more information about nondiscrimination rules.)
- You will have to pay increased administrative costs.
- You will have to pay for the cost of contributions on behalf of your employees.
- You will have to pay for insurance to protect employee benefits.

B. How to Establish a Defined Benefit Plan

A defined benefit plan must be established by an employer, not by an individual. When you work for yourself and establish a retirement plan, you wear two hats: You, as the employer, establish the retirement plan and make contributions on behalf of you, the employee. If you are a sole proprietor, you would set up the profit sharing plan in your own name as the employer (or in the name you are using for your business). If you are doing business as a partnership, the partnership would set up the plan, because the partnership is the employer. You and your partner cannot establish two separate plans as individual partners.

1. Trustee or Custodian

Although most qualified plan assets must be held in a trust, a special exception allows Keogh plan assets to be held in a custodial account. But because most financial institutions do not provide IRS pre-approved documents for defined benefit plans, those institutions usually will not serve as custodian of an untrusteed plan. However, they will serve as custodian if you or someone else serves as trustee. (See Chapter 1, Section C.2, for more information about trustees and custodians.)

Consequently, you will probably have to establish a trust and name a trustee. The defined benefit plan documents themselves will serve as the trust agreement. And although you are not required to serve as trustee (you can hire someone else), you will probably want to in order to save money.

2. Plan Documents

To establish your defined benefit plan, you must hire a pension plan consultant to create the plan documents for you. In addition to creating a plan for your immediate needs, the consultant will also have to insert provisions into your plan that would allow it to remain qualified in the event you do hire employees.

After drafting the plan documents, the consultant will submit them to the IRS for approval. Specifically, she will request a "letter of determination" confirming that the plan is a qualified plan. Although this step is not required, it is customary to ask the IRS to bless the plan—to affirm that it is qualified and that the contributions will be deductible.

Once the trust is established—which will happen when you sign the plan documents—you can open an account with a financial institution, such as a bank, brokerage firm or mutual fund. Confirm with the financial institution that it is willing to hold your assets under the terms of your plan. Most will.

You will have to give your financial institution a copy of the plan documents for its files. Keep the original plan documents in your office. The account will be established in your name as trustee of the defined benefit plan (assuming you are serving as trustee). For example, the account title might be "Paul Brown, Trustee of the Paul Brown Company Defined Benefit Plan." You cannot simply open an account in your name and deposit contributions.

In addition, many financial institutions will want you to have a taxpayer identification number for your plan. To request an ID number, complete IRS Form SS-4 and mail or fax it to the IRS as indicated in the instructions. (You can find a sample form with instructions in the Appendix.) Note that the form is titled "Application for Employer Identification Number." Don't let that throw you. This particular form has many uses, and one of them is to request an ID number for a qualified plan. (Remember, your plan is actually a trust.)

3. Beneficiary Designation

When you name a beneficiary of your retirement plan, you are identifying the person or organization that you want to receive your plan benefits when you die. That's important, certainly. But the person or organization you name as beneficiary can be crucial for other reasons, as well. For example, your choice of beneficiary will determine how quickly you must take distributions from the plan after you reach age 70½ (see Section E.6, below, for more information about mandatory distributions)—and how quickly the plan must be liquidated after your death.

If you are married and you name your spouse as beneficiary, he or she will have options that other beneficiaries do not have. Your spouse can roll over your retirement plan into an IRA in his or her own name, pick new beneficiaries and, in most cases, prolong or delay distributions from the IRA. (Remember: When you delay distributions from an IRA, the assets can continue to grow tax-deferred—a big benefit!)

For most married individuals, naming a spouse as beneficiary is the best option. In fact, if you are married, your spouse is automatically presumed to be the beneficiary of your qualified plan.

But suppose you do not want to name your spouse as beneficiary. In that case, you can change the beneficiary to someone else, but your spouse must consent in writing to the change—and to all future changes of beneficiary unless the change reinstates your spouse as beneficiary.

The Joint and Survivor Annuity Requirement

In the old days, it was entirely possible that an employee or her family might never see a dime of her retirement plan benefits, even if she worked for the same company for 40 years. How could this happen? Well, suppose she labored for years and on the day she became fully vested in her retirement plan, she dropped dead of a heart attack. What luck for the company. Now it doesn't have to pay the benefits.

Doesn't sound quite fair, though, does it? After all, the poor woman did own those benefits. Why shouldn't they go to her spouse or to someone else of her choosing? For a long time, nothing in the law prevented those benefits from reverting to the company when a participant died.

Then in 1974 (with modifications in 1984), Congress enacted a new set of laws known as the joint and survivor annuity requirement. These laws provide that a qualified plan must pay out benefits to the plan participant and the participant's spouse as a joint and survivor annuity (as long as the two have been married for at least a year). If the plan participant dies, the surviving spouse will continue to receive the participant's remaining vested retirement benefits.

Despite the law's moniker, the participant and the spouse are not required to take the benefits as an annuity. They can select another form of payment available under the plan, such as a rollover to an IRA, as long as both of them consent to the alternative form of payment. A surviving spouse, too, can generally select another form of payment (besides an annuity) if he or she inherits the plan after the participant's untimely death.

Note that the joint and survivor annuity rule applies in a similar way in cases where the plan participant has designated someone other than his or her spouse to be the beneficiary. However, the participant does not need a non-spouse beneficiary's consent to change the beneficiary designation or the form of payment.

If you want to make a sizable donation to charity when you die, retirement plan assets might well be the best source of that donation, because charities do not have to pay income tax on the distributions. Just keep in mind that when you name a charity as beneficiary, you generally must distribute assets from the plan more quickly during your lifetime than you would if you named a person as beneficiary.

And it is almost never right to simply name your "estate" as beneficiary. Doing so could cause income tax problems for your heirs and perhaps increase probate fees as well.

As you can see, choosing a beneficiary can be a complex decision. For more information about the effect of your beneficiary designation on your retirement plan, see *IRAs, 401(k)s & Other Retirement Plans: Taking Your Money Out*, by Twila Slesnick and John Suttle (Nolo).

4. Deadlines

As is the case with all Keogh plans, a defined benefit plan must be set up by the end of the first year for which you want to make a contribution. There is absolutely no extension permitted. Although the full contribution does not need to be made at that time, some financial institutions require that you open an account with a nominal amount of money. You can send in the rest of your contribution later. (See Section C.4, below, for information about contribution deadlines.)

5. Plan Year

A defined benefit plan can be maintained on either a calendar year or a fiscal year. A fiscal year is generally any 12-month period that ends on the last day of any month except December. You don't have to use the same year for the plan and your business, although it usually makes sense to do so. If you don't, accounting for the plan becomes a little more complicated with no added benefit.

C. Contributions

No matter how mathematically talented you are, you will not be able to compute your own defined benefit plan contribution. You should accept that at the outset. As mentioned earlier, you need an actuary to make the calculation.

When trying to understand how an actuary computes contributions to a defined benefit plan, it helps to look at the retirement benefit the contributions must produce. When you establish the plan, you will work with your plan consultant to find the benefit that is right for you and then draft the documents accordingly. For example, the plan might provide that you (the participant) will receive annually 100% of your average final three years of salary, beginning at age 65 and continuing for the rest of your life. Or maybe you will receive 1% of your final salary multiplied by the number of years you have worked in the business. Or the plan could provide that you will receive annually a flat dollar amount—say $100—per year of service.

Your contribution each year is the amount you must put into the plan to ensure that the plan contains enough money to pay you the guaranteed benefit at retirement. For example, assume your plan calls for a retirement annuity of 30% of your final salary beginning at age 65. You are currently age 60 and your projected final salary is $50,000. That means you are to receive $15,000 per year beginning at age 65 for the rest of your life. Assuming a 6% return on your investments in the plan (before and after retirement), the actuary might estimate that you would have to contribute $30,000 to the plan each year before retirement in order to generate the $15,000 retirement annuity.

But where does that $30,000 number come from? The IRS provides guidelines for calculating these estimates, but they aren't light reading. Actuaries, those venerated number-crunchers of the insurance world, are charged with learning the rules and coming up with a number for each year's contribution. And it seems to be nearly as much an art as a science, because a plan can take into account many different variables, such as your expected income over your working life, how much interest your investments will earn, how likely it is you will die before you reach retirement, how long you might live after retirement and how likely it is you will stay in business.

 As a practical matter, it is often the case that you, as a self-employed individual, will tell your actuary and your plan consultant how much you can afford to contribute and the actuary will design a retirement benefit to fit your needs.

And you dare not fire your actuary after the first year. You'll need her back again every year to determine the required annual contribution. Remember, the projections are based on guesses about the future. So, what if the actuary's crystal ball was cloudy one year. Suppose she assumed your investments would earn 6% but they only earned 2%. Or maybe instead of going up, your compensation (your net earnings from self-employment) went down one year. Unless you adjust the amount of your contribution, you might miss your retirement benefit target. But you're not allowed to miss it. The benefit described in the plan is guaranteed. If there is a shortfall, you are required to make it up. And it's the actuary's job to tell you how the contribution should be adjusted each year to get back on track.

1. Maximum Contribution

Limits for defined benefit plans are different from limits for defined contribution plans, SEPs and SIMPLE IRAs. Instead of restricting the size of contributions, the law limits the amount of the benefit you can receive at retirement. As long as the projected retirement benefit does not exceed the limits, you are permitted—indeed required—to contribute however much is needed to reach the benefit goal.

If you decide to establish a defined benefit plan as a self-employed individual, it is almost certainly because you are making quite a bit of money and you can contribute significantly more to a defined benefit plan than to another type of plan (based on estimates provided by your actuary). Because you have no employees, you will probably establish a defined benefit plan that allows you to contribute the maximum amount.

a. Benefit Limitations

The maximum annual benefit your defined benefit plan can provide at retirement is the lesser of:

- 100% of your average annual compensation for the highest three consecutive calendar years of earnings, or
- $135,000 per year for life. This figure assumes that the payments will begin at age 65 (the Social Security retirement age). If the plan specifies a normal retirement age that is lower than 65, the $135,000 must be actuarially reduced to an equivalent number (within prescribed guidelines). More work for your actuary. Similarly, if the plan specifies a higher retirement age, the $135,000 can be actuarially increased. Also,

the IRS will increase the $135,000 limit for inflation from time to time. (Beginning in tax year 2001, the $135,000 limit will increase to $140,000.)

b. Small Benefits

If your retirement benefit is no more than $10,000 per year, the 100% of average compensation limit is waived. For example, if your plan provides that you are to receive a retirement benefit of $9,000 per year, but your average compensation for your high three years was only $7,000, you are still permitted the retirement benefit of $9,000.

c. Reduction for Less Than Ten Years

If you reach retirement age before completing ten years of participation in the defined benefit plan, the dollar limit ($135,000 for tax year 2000) on retirement benefits must be reduced proportionately.

Similarly if your total years of service (years working for the company) is less than ten when you retire, the average compensation limit is reduced proportionately.

EXAMPLE: You established your business and set up a defined benefit plan at age 59. You retire at age 65, the plan's normal retirement age. Your plan provides that you will receive 100% of your high three years' average compensation. That amount is $15,000.

However because you only worked for six years before retirement, the $15,000 must be reduced proportionately—to $9,000 (6/10 x $15,000).

d. Actuarial Assumptions

Actuarial assumptions, such as the projected rate of return on your plan investments, can make a substantial difference in the amount of your contributions.

EXAMPLE: Assume your plan calls for a retirement annuity of 30% of your final compensation beginning at age 65. You are currently age 60 and your projected final compensation is $50,000. That means you are to receive $15,000 per year beginning at age 65 for the rest of your life. Assuming an 8% return on your investments in the plan (before and after retirement), the actuary might estimate that you would have to contribute $25,000 to the plan each year before retirement in order to generate the $15,000 retirement annuity.

Now, change the interest rate assumption from 8% to 5%. That will increase your contribution to $34,000.

The IRS requires that an actuary use reasonable assumptions. But what is reasonable? Ultimately, it's a judgment call, but if prevailing long-term interest rates are in the 10% range and your actuary uses 5%,

you might have some explaining to do if you are audited.

At this point, you might be able to see why defined benefit plans tend to produce larger contributions for older participants. The older a participant is, the less time there is to accumulate the amount needed to deliver the promised benefit at retirement.

EXAMPLE: As in the example above, assume your plan calls for a retirement annuity of 30% of your final salary beginning at age 65. Your projected final salary is still $50,000 and you are to receive $15,000 per year beginning at age 65 for the rest of your life. But this time, assume that you are only age 30 instead of 60. With an 8% return on your investments in the plan (before and after retirement), your annual contribution would be about $855 (compared with $25,000 if you were 60).

2. Minimum Contribution

Because a defined benefit plan's retirement benefit is guaranteed, you (the employer) must contribute an amount each year that will move your accumulation inexorably toward that benefit. The actuary will compute the amount and you must contribute it. You have no choice. That amount is your minimum contribution. It also happens to be your maximum contribution. Once you have defined your retirement benefit in your plan documents, the minimum and the maximum amounts you can or must contribute to the plan are the same.

The law that requires you to make the contribution each year is called the minimum funding requirement. If for any year, you fail to make the required contribution, you will be subject to a 10% penalty on the shortfall. If you persist in ignoring the contribution requirements, the penalty could rise to 100%. (For more information about the minimum funding requirement and related penalties, see Section F.7, below.)

One other thing. As mentioned above, you might have to make a contribution to your defined benefit plan even if you don't make a profit. But what happens if your business is losing money? If you want to maintain the plan, you will have to come up with the money. But you won't be able to deduct the contribution in the current year. You can only claim a deduction on your tax return to the extent you have net earnings from the business. The excess would be carried over and deducted in a future year.

3. Cash or Property?

The law does not specifically require that defined benefit plan contributions be made in cash. Nonetheless, if you contribute property, you are quite likely to run afoul of the prohibited transaction rules.

The prohibited transaction rules (see Section F.3, below, for more information about prohibited transactions) specifically forbid you from selling property to your plan. In the oft-cited case of *Comr. v. Keystone Consolidated Industries Inc.*, 113 S.Ct. 2006 (1993), the U.S. Supreme Court ruled that a contribution of property in satisfaction of a minimum funding requirement (mandatory contribution) is, in essence, a sale of the property to the plan. That ruling effectively put an end to contributions of property to money purchase pension plans and defined benefit plans— both of which have minimum funding requirements.

If you'd like to read the *Keystone* case—or any other court case or statute—you can do so through Nolo's Legal Research Center at http://www.nolo.com.

4. Deadlines

As is the case with defined contribution plans, you are permitted to claim a deduction for your defined benefit plan contribution (assuming you have net earnings from the business), as long as you make the contribution by the due date of your tax return. And if you request and receive an extension of time for filing your return, you have until the extended due date to make your contribution.

When You Miss a Contribution

If you failed to make the full required contribution to your defined benefit plan in the previous year—because you didn't have the money, you forgot, or for some other reason—you will have to make your current year contribution in quarterly installments. The quarterly contributions are due 15 days after the end of each quarter. For a calendar-year plan, the due dates are April 15, July 15, October 15 and January 15.

The total amount you must pay in installments is the lesser of:

- 90% of the required contribution for the current year, or
- 100% of the contribution you made for the preceding year.

Each installment payment must be 25% of the required total amount.

Because you rarely know the precise amount of the current year's required contribution before the end of the year, you will usually rely on the prior year's contribution to determine quarterly amounts. If the final number is higher, it is sufficient to pay the additional amount within $8\frac{1}{2}$ months after the end of the year. If it is lower, you might have to remove some of the money. (See Section F.I, below, for a discussion on how to remove excess contributions from the plan.)

If you fail to make quarterly contributions, there is no penalty, but you must pay interest to the plan on the amount that should have been paid on a quarterly basis.

That's the deadline for deductibility. But there is also a minimum funding deadline. Because contributions are mandatory, they must be made by a certain date, which is $8\frac{1}{2}$ months after the end of the year. (See Section F.7, below, for more information about minimum funding.)

5. How to Claim the Tax Deduction

You claim the deduction for your defined benefit plan contribution on page 1, line 29, of your individual income tax return (Form 1040). This will be true whether you are doing business as a partnership or as a sole proprietor. You can find a sample form in the Appendix.

D. Ongoing Administration

Most plan consultants will handle virtually all of the administration of your defined benefit plan, except tax return preparation and investment management.

1. Tax Returns

There are two types of tax returns you might have to file for your defined benefit plan: IRS Form 5500-EZ and IRS Form 990-T.

a. IRS Form 5500-EZ

IRS Form 5500-EZ is an information tax return that helps the IRS monitor the operation of your plan. Having to file this tax return does not mean you will have to pay taxes. In fact, your defined benefit plan will not owe any income tax while the assets remain in the plan, except in certain rare circumstances when the plan assets generate business income. (See Section b, below.)

You must always file Form 5500-EZ for your defined benefit plan for its final year. No exceptions. The final year of the plan is the year in which all of the assets have been distributed. (See Section G, below, for more information about terminating your plan.)

For other years, including the first, you will not have to file a tax return for the plan if all of the following are true:

- Your plan is a one-participant plan. Recall that a one-participant plan is a plan that covers only you, your partners (if any) and your respective spouses (if they also work in the business).
- The total value of all the assets in the plan is $100,000 or less at the end of the current plan year and all previous plan years since (and including) 1994.

- If you have two or more one-participant Keogh plans for your business, the total value of all assets of all plans is $100,000 or less at the end of the current plan year and every previous plan year since 1994.

 Even though a tax return might not be required, most defined benefit plan administrators file actuarial information with the IRS every year. The actuarial information is reported on Schedule B and should be attached to a Form 5500-EZ.

If you ever add employees to your plan, you will have to file annual tax returns for your defined benefit plan, regardless of the total value of plan assets. Also, you won't be able to use Form 5500-EZ. You will have to use the more complex Form 5500.

Form 5500-EZ must be filed by the last day of the seventh month following the end of the plan year. If your plan year is the calendar year, the tax return for the plan is due July 31. You may apply for an extension of time to file, which will give you an additional 2½ months. If the plan year is the same as your business tax year and you requested and received an extension of time to file your Form 1040, the filing deadline for the Form 5500-EZ is automatically extended, too.

b. IRS Form 990-T

As mentioned above, your defined benefit plan is a tax exempt entity, which is why it generally doesn't have to pay tax each year on the income it produces.

But if your defined benefit plan engages in a business that produces more than $1,000 of income during the year, you must file a special tax return—Form 990-T—for the plan. Income from a business inside a plan is called unrelated business taxable income, or UBTI. Once UBTI exceeds $1,000 in a year, it is subject to tax and the tax must be paid out of the defined benefit plan assets.

Most people invest their defined benefit plan assets in stocks, bonds and other standard investments which don't generate UBTI. But suppose you invest some of the assets in a limited partnership. Many limited partnerships are in fact businesses. And when the business (the limited partnership) starts throwing off income, it will be taxable, even though it is inside your defined benefit plan.

2. Plan Administration

Although you are technically responsible for making sure the plan operates in compliance with the law, your plan consultant will take care of computing contributions, making sure you satisfy minimum funding requirements and communicating with the IRS.

a. Minimum Funding Standard Account

As a way of tracking compliance with the minimum funding rules, the IRS requires defined benefit plans to maintain a minimum funding standard account. As mentioned above, generally, your plan consultant or actuary will handle this for you.

The account is actually a ledger—an account book—that contains the following information:

- contributions that have been made to the plan
- current year contributions that are owed to the plan
- experience losses owed to the plan (for example, amounts that are owed to the plan because investments performed more poorly than anticipated)
- benefits owed to the plan as the result of a retroactive amendment (for example, if the changes you make to the plan are to take effect on a date before the date you sign the amendment), and
- past service liabilities of the plan (for example, a plan can permit you to count participants' years of service before the plan was established when computing contributions; that portion of the contribution is called a "past service liability").

⚠ **Amounts necessary to fund past service liabilities** cannot be contributed and deducted all at once. They must be spread over several years.

The law requires that an actuary make a precise determination of what is owed to the plan at least once a year.

b. Hardship Waiver

Because contributions are mandatory, you might wonder what would happen if you could not come up with the money to make your defined benefit contribution one year. Unless you receive a hardship waiver from the IRS, you will have to terminate the plan. The IRS will grant hardship waivers for temporary business hardship. A temporary business hardship must satisfy all of these requirements:

- Your business must be operating at a loss.
- The industry in which you work must be experiencing substantial unemployment.
- The industry must be generally depressed.

Even if you meet those requirements, the waiver will only be granted if the IRS, in its wisdom, determines that your business is likely to be revitalized. If you simply aren't making it, you will have to terminate your plan. But terminating your plan doesn't necessarily relieve you of all funding obligations. (See Section G, below, for information about terminating your plan.)

c. Reporting

Whenever cash or other assets come out of your plan, the plan administrator or the employer (you) must report the distributions to the IRS on Form 1099-R. Your financial institution might prepare the 1099-R for you, but you are the person the IRS will contact if the reporting is inaccurate.

3. Updating Plan Documents

Changes in the law might require you to update your defined benefit plan agreement from time to time. Your pension consultant should review your documents annually to verify that they are in compliance with current laws. If there are changes to be made, you must decide whether or not to seek a new determination letter from the IRS that blesses your revised plan. Your consultant should be able to advise you. Just remember: If the IRS ever decides to audit the plan and discovers that it is fatally flawed, the IRS might disqualify the plan, which would cause all of the assets to be subject to income tax and perhaps penalties, as well.

E. Distributions

Through the qualified plan rules, Congress offers businesses, including self-employed individuals, an incentive to save for retirement and to provide retirement benefits to employees. The incentive is a big tax deduction and tax-deferred growth of the plan's assets. In exchange for those tax benefits, generally you cannot take money out of a qualified plan while you are still working in the business that sponsors the plan. If you do, the plan could be disqualified, and you might have to pay back some or all of the tax benefits—and perhaps pay additional penalties, as well.

The law provides a few exceptions to the general rule that keeps your defined benefit plan assets locked up. But even if the law says you qualify for one of those exceptions, your defined benefit plan documents might still forbid the distribution. And the plan has the final say.

Finally, even if you do gain access to your funds without disqualifying the plan, you will still have to pay income tax. You'll also have to pay an early distribution penalty—for taking the money out early—unless you qualify for an exception. (See Section 5, below.)

 This is not a book about retirement plan distributions. Although we provide an overview of the distribution rules for each type of plan, you must look elsewhere for the details. One source is *IRAs, 401(k)s & Other Retirement Plans: Taking Your Money Out*, by Twila Slesnick and John C. Suttle (Nolo).

In this section, we walk you through the rules that govern when you can—and when you cannot (at least, not without penalty)—take money out of your retirement plan. We also discuss the rules that govern when you must take money out.

1. Inservice Distributions

Inservice distributions are distributions you take from a retirement plan while you are still working for the business that sponsors the plan. Generally, this type of distribution is prohibited unless the distribution occurs for one of the following reasons:

- termination of the plan
- death
- disability
- separation from service (which, for a self-employed individual, might mean terminating or selling the business), or
- attainment of normal retirement age (as specified in the plan).

The inservice distributions listed above are the ones that are specifically allowed by law. Your plan documents, however, may be more restrictive than the law and not allow all of the distributions listed above. When you hire a consultant to create your plan, you will be able to choose whether or not you want the plan to allow the inservice distributions listed above.

2. Loans

Owner-employees may not borrow from their own defined benefit plans. Doing so is considered a prohibited transaction. (See Section F.3, below, for more information about prohibited transactions.) You are an owner-employee if you are a sole proprietor or if you are a partner in a partnership and you own more than a 10% interest in either the capital or the profits of the partnership.

3. Hardship

Although profit sharing plans can allow hardship distributions, defined benefit plans cannot.

4. Divorce Payments

Congress has gone to great lengths to protect your Keogh plan assets. The cornerstone of that protection is a provision known as the "anti-alienation" rule, which attempts to ensure that you (the plan participant) cannot voluntarily or involuntarily transfer your interest in plan assets to another person or entity.

Divorce presents a unique problem, however. What if you want to (or must) use your retirement plan as part of a property settlement? Can you transfer some or all of your interest in plan assets in that situation? And if you can, who should be responsible for the taxes and penalties (if any) on the part you transfer?

Congress addressed these concerns by giving divorcing couples a vehicle for pro-

tecting plan assets and minimizing taxes and penalties. It's called a Qualified Domestic Relations Order or QDRO (pronounced "Quadro"). The QDRO rules spell out the circumstances under which your qualified plan benefits can go to someone else—an "alternate payee"—such as your soon-to-be former spouse. These rules also provide liability protection to the trustee who distributes the assets under the terms of the QDRO.

A QDRO is a judgment, decree or order (including a court-approved property settlement agreement) that satisfies all of the following:

- It relates to child support, alimony or the marital property rights of your spouse, former spouse, dependent child or some other dependent of yours.
- It gives an alternate payee, such as your spouse, former spouse, dependent child or other dependent, the right to receive all or a portion of your plan benefits.
- It does not alter the form or the amount of the benefit originally intended for you even though the benefit might now go to an alternate payee. For example, the QDRO cannot require the plan to pay a larger annuity to the alternate payee than it would have paid to you.
- It contains certain language. Specifically:
  ✓ The alternate payee must be referred to as "the alternate payee" in the QDRO.

✓ The QDRO must identify the plan, as well as the amount of each payment and the number of payments to be made.

✓ The QDRO must contain the name and address of both you and the alternate payee.

If you have a QDRO in place, the law will allow the trustee of the plan to distribute to the alternate payee his or her share of your plan assets without disqualifying the plan—as long as the plan also permits the distribution. And generally, if your former spouse is the alternate payee, he or she will be responsible for any income taxes on the distributions he or she receives.

⚠️ **If you and your former spouse simply write up your own agreement,** which does not meet the above requirements and is not court-approved, then your agreement is not a QDRO. In that case, you will almost certainly be liable for income tax and penalties on distributions even if they go to your former spouse.

5. Early Distributions and Exceptions to the Early Distribution Penalty

Any distribution you take from your defined benefit plan before you reach age 59½ is considered an early distribution, which means you must pay a 10% penalty unless an exception applies.

The law provides for quite a few exceptions to the early distribution penalty. (Those exceptions are described below.) Bear in mind, however, that the plan documents must also specifically permit such exceptions. For example, if you become disabled, the law says that you can take money out of a qualified plan without penalty, but if your plan says you can take distributions only after age 59½, or when you terminate employment, or when you die, then you won't be able to take a distribution as a result of a disability. The plan's word is the last word. So when you hire a consultant to craft a plan for you, be sure to have her include the provisions you want.

In the following sections, we discuss the exceptions to the early distribution penalty that the laws allows.

⚠️ **Although these exceptions will give you relief from penalties,** you (or your beneficiaries) will still owe income tax on all distributions.

a. Death

Distributions from your defined benefit plan after you die are not subject to the early distribution penalty, no matter how old you are when you die or how old your beneficiaries are when they withdraw the money.

b. Disability

If you become disabled, you can take money from your defined benefit plan without penalty. But first you must satisfy the IRS's definition of disabled, which is hardly a model of clarity. Here's how it reads: You must be unable to "engage in any substantial gainful activity by reason of any medically determinable physical or mental impairment which can be expected to result in death or to be of long-continued and indefinite duration." The IRS's own regulations state that the gainful activity refers specifically to the type of work you were doing before becoming disabled. Thus it would seem that you need not be unfit for all work—just the work you customarily do.

c. Leaving Your Business After Age 55

If you are at least 55 years old when you leave or terminate your business, any distribution you receive from your defined benefit plan will not be subject to an early distribution tax.

To qualify for this exception, you don't have to retire permanently. You can go to work for someone else or, presumably, start another business sometime down the road.

 The IRS is aware that it is not easy to determine when a self-employed individual has stopped working for the business that sponsors the plan. If you take a distribution and use the age 55 exception and continue to show self-employment income, be prepared to defend yourself.

To make use of this exception, you need not be age 55 on the day you take the distribution, as long as you turn 55 by December 31 of the same year. However, you must have quit the business before you take the distribution.

d. QDRO Payments

If you are paying child support or alimony from your retirement plan, or if you intend to distribute some or all of the plan to your former spouse as part of a property settlement, none of those payments is subject to the early distribution penalty as long as there is a QDRO in place that orders the payments. (See Section 4, above, for more information about QDROs.)

e. Refunds

If you contributed more to your defined benefit plan than you were permitted to deduct during the year, generally you can remove the excess without penalty if you do so before you file your tax return. Those "corrective" distributions will not be subject to the early distribution tax, although they might be subject to other taxes and penalties. (See Section F.l, below, for more about excess contributions.)

f. Federal Tax Levy

If you owe back taxes, you can be reasonably certain the government will try to collect them. If you have assets in a defined benefit plan, the government can take those assets (in other words, the IRS can levy on your defined benefit plan) to pay your debt. If it does so, then those amounts taken for taxes will not be subject to the early distribution penalty, even if you happen to be younger than 59½.

Although the Tax Code provides some additional exceptions to the early distribution penalty—specifically, for medical expenses and periodic payments—for other types of qualified plans, as a practical matter, those exceptions are not available to you when you have a defined benefit plan, because you would not be able to receive the distribution while you are still working without disqualifying the plan. (See Section E.l, above.)

6. Mandatory Distributions

If you own your own business, you are required to start taking money out of your defined benefit plan in the year you turn 70½, even if you are still working. The income tax regulations provide a formula for calculating the minimum amount you must take. You may take more than the minimum, but you may not take less. If you do take less, you will be fined 50% of the amount that should have come out of the defined benefit plan but didn't.

 If you are still working when you reach 70½, you may continue to make contributions to a defined benefit plan and deduct those contributions. It could very well make sense for you to do so even though you are also required to take some money out each year. Not only can you claim a deduction for new contributions and reduce your tax liability, but you can also add to the assets that will grow tax-deferred.

F. Penalties

It might seem distressingly easy to make a mistake with your defined benefit plan, and then get hit with a penalty. Fortunately, Congress has provided exceptions and corrective steps you can take to avoid or mitigate the penalties in most cases. Here are the traps to watch for, their consequences and, where applicable, opportunities for corrective action.

Infractions and Their Consequences

Problem	Penalty
Nondeductible contributions	10% of the excess
Early distributions	10% of the distribution
Prohibited transactions:	
• If corrected:	15% of the transaction amount
• If not corrected:	100% of the transaction amount
Required distributions	50% of shortfall
Minimum funding deficiency:	
• If corrected:	10% of the shortfall
• If not corrected:	100% of the shortfall
Overstatement penalty:	
• Ordinary overstatements:	20% of tax underpayment
• If the overstatements are "gross":	40% of tax underpayment

1. Nondeductible Contributions

The law does not permit you to contribute more to your defined benefit plan than you can deduct. If you do, you will have made a nondeductible contribution and you must pay a 10% penalty on the excess. A new 10% penalty will be assessed on any excess that remains in the plan at the beginning of each year.

There is an important exception to this rule. You might recall that when you must make a contribution to your plan in years for which your business generated no net income, you cannot deduct the contribution. If you find yourself in this situation, you will not have to pay the 10% nondeductible contribution penalty as long as your contribution is the amount you are required to contribute for the year and no more.

But let's suppose you are easily making enough money to make the required contribution. In your eagerness, you poured a bunch of money into your defined benefit plan early in the year. December comes and goes. In January of the next year, your actuary sends you the final contribution number and you discover you contributed too much to your plan. Now what?

You have two options. We discuss those in the sections below.

a. Option One: Leave in the Excess, Then Deduct

Your first option is to leave the excess in the defined benefit plan and deduct it in the next tax year. When computing the amount to contribute in the next year, you will first apply the excess that was carried over and then contribute any additional amounts needed to bring you up to your deduction limit.

You still have to pay the 10% excise tax for the first year, but as long as the excess does not exceed the deductible amount for the second year, there will be no penalty for that year.

EXAMPLE: In 2001, you contributed $3,000 too much to your defined benefit plan. You deducted the correct amount but forgot to remove the excess from the defined benefit plan account. You decide to leave the excess in the account and deduct it the following year. In 2002, you have enough income to make an $8,000 defined benefit plan contribution. You apply the $3,000 excess from the previous year and add an additional $5,000 in cash by the due date of your tax return to complete the $8,000 contribution. You must still pay a $300 (10% of $3,000) penalty for 2001, but no additional penalty will be assessed for 2002 or beyond.

If you use this option and you are subject to the nondeductible contribution penalty, report the offending contribution on Form 5330 for the year you made the excess contribution. The form is due by the last day of the seventh month after the end of the year in which you made the nondeductible contribution.

EXAMPLE: You made an excess contribution of $1,000 to your defined benefit plan in 2001. You discovered your error in June 2002 long after you filed your tax return. You should complete Form 5330 for the year 2001. Sign and date the form and send it in by July 31, 2002, along with your check for $100 (10% of $1,000), which is the amount of the nondeductible contribution penalty.

b. Option Two: Remove the Excess

Your second option is more complex, but also more attractive if you qualify, because you can avoid the 10% penalty. The general rule is that the precise amount of the excess (not including any earnings that might have accumulated) can be returned to you by the due date of your tax return (plus extensions, if you requested and received an extension for filing your tax return), if the excess is returned for one of the following reasons:

- The plan initially failed to qualify. For example, this might happen if this is the first year of the plan and you submitted a letter of determination to the IRS and the plan was deemed not to be a qualified plan.

- The contribution is not deductible.
- The contribution was made due to a mistake of fact. For example, an arithmetic error in computing the contribution is a mistake of fact.

The likely problem with your contribution will be that it is not deductible. But the IRS has ruled that in order for this exception to apply, the deduction must actually be disallowed by the IRS. Thus, unless you are audited, you would have to request a determination that the deduction is disallowed.

Fortunately, there is another exception. You can remove the excess without formal IRS disallowance, if you satisfy all of the following conditions:

- The amount of the excess is less than $25,000.
- The terms of your plan specifically provide that nondeductible contributions can be returned if the IRS deems them nondeductible.
- Your plan states that nondeductible contributions must be removed from the plan.

If you qualify to remove the nondeductible contribution from your defined benefit plan and you do so before the due date (including extensions) of your tax return, you will not have to pay any penalty on the excess contribution. You will also avoid an early distribution penalty on the money you took back out of the plan.

2. Early Distributions

If you take a distribution from your defined benefit plan before you reach age 59½ and the distribution does not fall under any exception described in Section E.5, above, the distribution will be subject to a 10% early distribution penalty. That penalty is in addition to the income tax you must pay.

The IRS requires you to report the early distribution penalty on Form 5329 for the year of the early distribution. You can find a sample copy of the form in the Appendix.

3. Prohibited Transactions

The Tax Code prohibits certain transactions involving your defined benefit plan assets. The prohibited transaction rules are part of Congress's strategy to protect your defined benefit plan assets. Congress designed the rules to keep you and any other disqualified person (see below) from using the assets for personal gain or from engaging in transactions that put the assets at risk.

A disqualified person is someone who might reasonably have access to your plan assets. In addition to you, such persons include your spouse, your lineal descendants (such as children and grandchildren) and your ancestors (such as parents and grandparents). The list also includes fiduciaries (those responsible for handling the assets of the plan, such as a custodian, trustee or money manager), a person who provides services to the plan (such as an administrator) and co-owners of your business.

The penalty for engaging in a prohibited transaction is 15% of the amount of the transaction, and the person who engages in the transaction—not the plan—owes the tax. The penalty is assessed for each year (or part of a year) in the taxable period of the prohibited transaction. The taxable period starts on the date of the transaction and ends on the earliest of the following:

- The day the IRS mails a notice of deficiency for the penalty tax (telling you that you owe the tax).
- The day the IRS assesses the tax (telling you to pay the tax).
- The day the correction of the transaction is complete.

If the transaction is not corrected within the taxable period, an additional tax of 100% of the transaction is imposed. That's a total of 115%.

If you don't manage to correct it within the taxable period, the IRS will usually give you an additional 90 days after the day the IRS mails you a notice of deficiency before requiring you to pay the 100% tax. And the IRS will extend the grace period further if you can convince the IRS you need a little more time—or if you petition the Tax Court. If you are successful, you will not owe the 100% tax, but you will still owe the 15% tax.

The following are all prohibited transactions. Note that these are all transactions that occur inside your defined benefit plan or with the use of your defined benefit plan assets.

- The sale, exchange or lease of any property between a disqualified person and the defined benefit plan. For example, you cannot sell your house to your defined benefit plan.
- The furnishing of goods or services or facilities between a disqualified person and the defined benefit plan. For example, you cannot hire your spouse to manage the defined benefit plan, paying him a big salary out of the plan assets. You also cannot pay yourself for rendering services to the plan.
- The lending of money or extending of credit between a disqualified person and the defined benefit plan. For example, you cannot borrow from the defined benefit plan to buy a car, even if you intend to return the money.
- The transfer to or use by a disqualified person of any assets or income of the defined benefit plan. For example, you cannot use defined benefit plan funds to invest in a house (held by the defined benefit plan) which you then occupy as your principal residence.
- Any act of self-dealing, which occurs when a disqualified person uses the assets or income of the defined benefit plan for that person's own interest or account while the assets are still in the defined benefit plan. For example, if your money manager invests all of your defined benefit plan assets in the stock of a company of

which she owns 80%, such an investment would clearly benefit her as a majority shareholder, and therefore, might be deemed a prohibited transaction.

- The receipt of payment by a fiduciary in connection with a transaction involving the income or assets of the plan. A kickback, for example.

If you owe tax on a prohibited transaction, it is reported on Form 5330, which is due on the last day of the seventh month after the end of the tax year of the transaction.

4. Life Insurance

If you use part of your defined benefit plan contribution to pay the premium on a life insurance policy for yourself, that portion of your contribution that pays for the life insurance protection itself (known as the "PS 58 cost") is nondeductible. The investment portion of the premium is deductible. Purchasing life insurance does not necessarily trigger the 10% nondeductible contribution penalty. That penalty applies only when you contribute more than the maximum deductible amount.

For example: If you compute your maximum deductible contribution—based on your net earnings—to be $20,000 and you contribute that amount but use $1,000 of it to purchase life insurance protection, you may claim a deduction of only $19,000 on your tax return. However, no penalties will apply. You are permitted to make contri-

butions to your plan that you cannot deduct, as long as the total of all contributions do not exceed the deductible limit.

5. Pledging the Plan Benefits As Security

If you use any portion of your defined benefit plan as security for a loan (for example, you borrow money using your defined benefit plan as collateral), you will be engaging in a prohibited transaction. The government views this action as equivalent to borrowing from the plan. You will recall from Section 3, above, that borrowing money from your plan is a prohibited transaction.

6. Mandatory Distribution Penalty

If you fail to take required distributions from your defined benefit plan beginning at age 70½, you will pay a penalty of 50% of the amount that should have come out but didn't. (See Section E.6, above, for more about mandatory distributions.) Report this penalty on Form 5329. You can find a sample form in the Appendix.

7. Minimum Funding Deficiency

The full amount of your defined benefit plan contribution must be in the account within 8½ months after the end of the plan year (by September 15, if the plan year is the calendar year). If you fail to make the contribution specified by your actuary, your plan won't be disqualified, but you will be subject to a penalty.

⚠️ **The minimum funding deadline is different from the deadline for making a deductible contribution.** To be deductible, your defined benefit contribution must be made by the due date of your tax return. The final due date for your return (assuming you request and receive all the extensions the law allows) is October 15. But if you wait until October 15 to make your contribution, although the contribution will be deductible, you will be subject to a minimum funding penalty because you made the contribution after September 15—the minimum funding deadline.

The penalty for missing the minimum funding deadline is 10% of the shortfall—the amount that you should have contributed, but didn't. The penalty goes up to 100% if you do not correct the shortfall within the so-called "taxable period" (see below). In other words, you must eventually make the appropriate contribution to the plan. It doesn't work to simply pay the 10% penalty and ignore the contribution obligation.

The taxable period starts at the end of the plan year for which there is a funding deficiency and ends on the earlier of the following:

- The day the IRS mails a notice of deficiency for the 10% tax (telling you that you owe the tax).

- The day the IRS assesses the 10% tax (telling you to pay the tax).

If you don't manage to correct the shortfall within the taxable period, the IRS will usually give you an additional 90 days after the day the IRS mails you a notice of deficiency before requiring you to pay the 100% tax. Correction forestalls the 100% tax, but you will still have to pay the 10% penalty and, of course, you'll have to make the contribution to your plan.

You report the funding deficiency penalty on Form 5330. You can find a sample form in the Appendix.

8. Overstatement Penalty

Suppose your actuary puts together a set of assumptions that produces an extra-large contribution. One way to do that is to use a low-interest-rate assumption. You, in turn, get to make a big contribution, which produces a big tax deduction and which increases the amount of tax-deferred dollars that can be working for you.

Ah, but the IRS won't be happy. The IRS wants your actuarial assumptions to be reasonable. If, during an audit, the IRS determines that your assumptions are unreasonable, it will assess a 20% penalty on any underpayment of tax that results from your "substantial overstatement" of pension liabilities (meaning the excessively large contribution). The penalty goes up to 40% if the overstatement is "gross."

A substantial overstatement is one that overstates the pension contribution by 200% or more. It's gross if the overstatement is 400% or more.

G. Terminating Your Defined Benefit Plan

You are permitted to terminate a plan for legitimate business reasons. For example, you can terminate your plan if you dissolve your business or go bankrupt. Or perhaps you simply cannot afford to make contributions any more.

Once you are certain that you won't be making contributions to your defined benefit plan any more, you should terminate it. If you don't, you will be required to keep the plan documents up to date through all the changes in the law, even though you are not making contributions. If you fail to keep the plan current, you risk disqualifying the plan and, in the worst case, incurring current income tax and penalties, as well as loss of prior deductions.

The only impediment to terminating your plan whenever you want is the rule requiring the plan to be permanent. If the IRS, in its wisdom, determines that the plan was never permanent, but was temporary from inception, you face the specter of retroactive disqualification of the plan. The IRS is likely to consider your plan temporary if either of the following is true:

- You do not make substantial and recurring contributions.

- You abandon the plan after only a few years (many plan consultants use five years or less as a guide) for reasons other than business necessity. And here again, you might find yourself at odds with the IRS's view of a business necessity.

But let's say you've decided to dissolve your business, and now you want to terminate your defined benefit plan? How do you do it?

1. Paperwork

Once you decide to terminate the plan, you should give written notice, with an effective date of termination, to the trustee or custodian of the plan, the plan administrator (if other than yourself) and any participants.

a. Letter of Determination

Even though you've made the decision to terminate your plan, it is important to keep your plan in compliance with the law until you have distributed all of the assets. For this reason, some plan consultants recommend that you apply for a determination letter from the IRS to preserve the deductibility of contributions for all years that are still open to an IRS audit—and to facilitate corrective actions that might be necessary to ensure that the plan remains qualified while you are in the process of terminating it. The IRS will also render its opinion of the permanence of the plan.

You are not required to obtain an advance determination letter, and many people do not, especially if the plan is a one-participant plan and the risks of disqualification upon termination are low. When you have a one-participant plan, you are most likely to seek a determination letter when the assets of the plan are large and you want to feel confident that when you roll over the assets of the terminating plan into another plan or into an IRA, you won't trigger income tax or penalties. (See Section 2, below.)

If you decide to seek a determination letter, use Form 5310, Application for Determination Upon Termination. (You can find a sample form in the Appendix.) You must also pay a user fee, which is currently about $225.

b. Tax Return

When you terminate your plan, you must file a tax return for the final year (the year all of the assets are distributed from the plan), even if you did not have to file one in the past. (See Section D.l, above, for information about filing a tax return.)

2. Distribution of Assets

Before you can file the final tax return and complete the termination of your plan, you must distribute all of its assets. As you might expect, this task is not as simple as it sounds. You have several distribution options.

a. Option One: Withdraw the Assets and Pay Tax

You can take all of the assets (your entire accrued benefit) out of the plan and pay income tax. You will also have to pay an early distribution tax if you are younger than 59½, unless one of the exceptions in Section E.5, above, applies. If you choose this option, you will pay a mandatory 20% federal withholding tax at the time of distribution. But if that withholding is more than you owe at tax time, you can request a refund.

b. Option Two: Transfer the Assets to an IRA

Another option is to have the funds transferred into an IRA in your name. The distribution should go directly from the financial institution that is now holding the plan assets to the custodian of your IRA. You should not take possession of the funds or deposit them—even temporarily—into a regular (non-IRA) account. If you follow these instructions, you will not have to pay any penalties, and all income tax will be deferred until you take the funds out of the IRA, some time in the future.

 Although you are permitted to take a distribution of your accrued benefit yourself and then deposit it in an IRA within 60 days, it's not a good idea to do so. If you move the funds in that way, the distribution will be subject to federal (and possibly state) income tax withholding and, perhaps, penalties unless you take remedial measures. For more about the nuances of qualified plan distributions, transfers and withholding, see *IRAs, 401(k)s & Other Retirement Plans: Taking Your Money Out*, by Twila Slesnick and John C. Suttle (Nolo).

H. Multiple Employer Plans

When your business is doing well, you will almost certainly find yourself wondering how you can contribute more to your retirement plan. Can you set up two defined benefit plans and double your contribution? What if you have two businesses? Can you have one plan for each? Or suppose you work for another employer and run a business of your own on the side. Can you set up a plan for your own business even if you are covered by your employer's plan?

The key to understanding what you can and cannot do is this fundamental rule: Retirement plan limits are applied on a per-employer basis. This is called the separate employer rule. It works like this: Suppose you work for Company A from 8 a.m. to 5 p.m. every day and you work for Company B from 7 p.m. to 4 a.m. Suppose also that each company contributes to a defined benefit plan on your behalf. Although each plan's retirement benefit limit is $135,000 per year (or 100% of average compensation for your highest three consecutive years, if less), each can contribute the maximum on your behalf. The same principle applies if you are one of the separate employers.

This section examines various employment scenarios and explains whether or not you can contribute to more than one plan in the same year. For information about adding a traditional IRA or a Roth IRA to your defined benefit plan, see Section I, below.

1. If You Are Self-Employed With a Day Job on the Side; or Vice Versa

Let's say you own your own business, but you also work for someone else. Can you contribute to more than one plan? Because of the separate employer rule described in the preceding paragraphs, if you are covered by your employer's plan, you can still establish a defined benefit plan for your own business and take a deduction to offset some of your profit. That's because you are a separate employer.

If you and members of your family together own more than 50% of the corporation that employs you, then you, as sole proprietor of your own business (or the partnership, if your side business is a partnership), might not be considered a separate employer from the corporation. If not, then your contribution to the defined benefit plan you established for your unincorporated business might be limited or eliminated altogether. If this describes your situation or if you are uncertain, you should confer with the plan administrator of the corporate retirement plan. (Also see Section 3, below.)

2. If You Are Self-Employed With One Business

Suppose you are self-employed and you have no other employer. If you have a defined benefit plan in place, can you set up a second defined benefit plan? Or another type of plan, as well?

You can have as many retirement plans for your business as you choose. However, there is a limit on the total amount a single employer can contribute to each type of plan. If you establish multiple defined benefit plans, the limit for all of them combined is the same as the single-plan limit— a retirement benefit of $135,000 or 100% of average annual compensation for your highest-earning three years. (Remember, the $135,000 increases to $140,000 beginning with tax year 2001.)

 This rule applies even if you established a defined benefit plan in the past that you have since terminated. If you now establish a new one, you must take into account the retirement benefit the old plan will provide when computing the contribution limit for the current year. In other words, the two plans combined cannot provide a retirement benefit in excess of $135,000 per year or 100% of your average annual compensation.

You must also be aware of the limit on the total combined amount you can contribute to all of the defined contribution plans (money purchase pension and profit sharing plans) and defined benefit plans of one employer. That limit is the greater of:

- 25% of your net earnings from self-employment, up to a maximum of $170,000 of net earnings. Thus 25% of 170,000 or $42,500; or
- the amount you are required to contribute to your defined benefit plan.

 For purposes of these multiple plan rules, a SEP is treated as a profit sharing plan.

 If you have a defined benefit plan, you cannot add a SIMPLE IRA. If you want to contribute to a SIMPLE IRA, you cannot contribute to any other plan during the same year. (See Chapter 3 for more information about SIMPLE IRAs.)

3. If You Are Self-Employed With Two or More Businesses

There is a wrinkle in the rule that allows you to establish a defined benefit plan with each separate employer (including yourself, when you own your own business) and contribute the maximum to each.

The wrinkle is in the definition of separate employer. Two employers might look separate to you but not be separate in the eyes of the law. This can happen when businesses are under common control. Businesses that are under common control are deemed to be one employer and are combined for purposes of determining the ceiling on retirement plan contributions. So it is important to be able to determine if businesses are under common control.

a. Sole Proprietorships

The concept of common control is straightforward if you have two sole proprietorships. By definition, you own 100% of both businesses. The businesses are under common control because they have the same employer (you). Consequently, they must be combined when determining contribution and benefit limits. If you establish a defined benefit plan for each business, the maximum contribution you can make to both plans combined is the same limit that would apply if you had only one business and one plan.

b. Sole Proprietorship and Partnership; or Two Partnerships

If you are a sole proprietor and you also have an interest in a partnership, the picture changes. You are the employer of your sole proprietorship, but the partnership, not the individual partners, is the employer in a partnership. In general, that means each business must set up its own plan.

But here's where the issue of common control rears its head. If the businesses are under common control, the total contribution to the plans of both employers is determined as though there were only one employer and one plan. This is true despite the fact that each employer will have to set up a separate plan.

A sole proprietorship and a partnership are under common control if the sole pro-

prietor has more than a 50% interest in the capital (the assets) or the profits of the partnership. If in that case, the businesses are combined for purposes of the defined benefit plan contribution limits. Your contribution to the two defined benefit plans is limited to the lesser of 100% of your average annual compensation from the two businesses combined (for the three consecutive highest-earning years), or a retirement benefit of $135,000 per year (or $140,000 beginning in 2001).

> **EXAMPLE:** You are the sole proprietor of a Web design business. You established a defined benefit plan in 1998, the first year of the business. In 2001, you and a partner started a house-painting business. You decided to establish a defined benefit plan for that business, as well. By agreement, you have an 80% interest in the profits of the business. Because your interest in the profits of the partnership exceeds 50% and you also own 100% of the Web design business, your partnership and your sole proprietorship are under common control.

If you have an interest of 50% or less in both the capital and the profits of the partnership, then the partnership and sole proprietorship are separate employers for plan sponsorship purposes and also for purposes of determining contribution limits. If you choose a defined benefit plan for both businesses, you would set up two separate plans and the maximum retirement benefit limit would apply separately to each plan.

If you are involved in two partnerships, the same principles would apply. Those partnerships of which your interest in either the capital or the profits is greater than 50% must be combined and treated as one for purposes of determining the contribution and benefit limits, even though you must set up a separate plan for each partnership.

 It is possible for two employers (such as your partnership and your sole proprietorship, or perhaps two partnerships) to sponsor the same plan, which might save administrative time and costs. If you elect this option, be sure to confirm with your plan consultant, or with the IRS, that the plan will pass muster.

If you own interests in several businesses that provide services to one another, or if you and other individuals own an interest in the same businesses, the businesses might be under common control. Confer with a professional plan consultant to sort out this complicated common-control issue.

I. Adding a Traditional or Roth IRA to Your Defined Benefit Plan

Participating in a defined benefit plan for your business does not preclude you from establishing a traditional IRA or a Roth IRA. And if you can establish one, you should. Generally, the more you contribute to a retirement plan—any plan—the larger your retirement nest egg is likely to be.

Participating in the defined benefit plan might limit the deductibility of your traditional IRA contribution, however. (Roth IRA contributions are never deductible.) When you are covered by your own SEP, SIMPLE IRA or Keogh (including defined benefit plans), or when you are covered by a plan of another employer, any traditional IRA contribution you make is fully deductible only if the adjusted gross income (with certain modifications) on your tax return is less than $62,000 (if you are married) or $42,000 (if you are single).

For more information about traditional IRAs including how to compute deductible and nondeductible contributions, see Chapter 8. ■

Chapter 8

Traditional IRAs

A. What Is a Traditional IRA? 8/3

   1. Who Can Establish an IRA? 8/4

   2. Advantages 8/4

   3. Disadvantages 8/5

B. How to Establish a Traditional IRA 8/5

   1. Trustee or Custodian 8/5

   2. Paperwork 8/6

   3. Beneficiary Designation 8/7

   4. Deadlines 8/8

C. Contributions 8/8

   1. Contribution Limits 8/8

   2. Cash Only 8/10

   3. Deadlines 8/10

D. Deductions 8/11

   1. No Employer Plan 8/11

   2. Employer Plan 8/11

E. Ongoing Administration 8/15

   1. Reporting the Contribution and Deduction 8/15

   2. Filing Tax Returns 8/16

   3. Preparing Statements 8/16

   4. Updating Documents 8/16

F. Distributions **8/16**

   1. Early Distributions and Exceptions to the Early Distribution Penalty 8/17

   2. Loans 8/20

   3. Hardship 8/21

   4. Divorce Payments 8/21

   5. Mandatory Distributions 8/21

G. Penalties **8/22**

   1. Excess Contributions 8/22

   2. Early Distributions 8/25

   3. Prohibited Transactions 8/25

   4. Life Insurance 8/27

   5. Collectibles 8/27

   6. Pledging the Account As Security 8/28

   7. Mandatory Distribution Penalty 8/28

H. Multiple IRAs and Qualified Plans **8/28**

I. Terminating Your IRA **8/29**

*I*n the preceding chapters, we have looked exclusively at employer plans—plans that can be established only by a business. In the next two chapters of this book, however, we depart from our employer-plan theme and shift our focus to plans that you can establish for yourself as an individual—specifically, traditional IRAs and Roth IRAs.

We have included information on traditional IRAs and Roth IRAs in this book because you might well qualify to establish either or both, even though you already have an employer plan for your business. These individual plans can be an important part of your overall retirement strategy.

A. What Is a Traditional IRA?

A traditional IRA is best seen as a special type of savings account that allows you to put away money for retirement and receive some tax breaks in the process.

As you no doubt know, the big draw of a traditional IRA over an ordinary account (a taxable account) is the promise of tax-deferred growth. When you put money into an IRA (potentially as much as $2,000 per year), it can grow unhampered by yearly taxes. In fact, you won't have to pay any taxes on the earnings in the IRA until you take the money out, usually after you reach age 59½. That generally means you will enjoy a much greater return on your IRA contributions than on money you put into a taxable account.

For some lucky people, a traditional IRA contribution will also mean an immediate tax deduction on their individual income tax return. Depending on how much you earn and whether you or your spouse is covered by an employer plan, you might be able to deduct part or all of your annual contribution to your traditional IRA.

⚠ SIMPLE IRAs and SEPs (described in Chapters 3 and 4, respectively) are also IRAs, but in mutant form. They are employer plans that share some of the characteristics of qualified plans and some of the characteristics of traditional IRAs. In this chapter, though, the term IRA refers to the beast in its original form—a retirement account for individuals.

You can set up a traditional IRA with a bank, brokerage firm or other institutional custodian as a special depository account. Or you can set it up as an individual retirement annuity that you purchase from an insurance company. Once you establish the IRA, you can make annual contributions to it, based on your earned income.

Traditional IRAs are often used to receive distributions from qualified plans in what are called rollover contributions. (You roll over money from the qualified plan to the IRA, thereby making a "rollover contribution" to the IRA.) However, in this chapter we focus primarily on the standard type of contribution to a traditional IRA—based on your earned income—rather than on rollover contributions.

1. Who Can Establish an IRA?

Generally, if you own your own business and are making a profit, or if you have earnings from any other type of employment, you may establish an IRA. Any cocktail party chatter that led you to believe you cannot have a traditional IRA if you make too much money came from an ignorant, if well-meaning, person. There are no income restrictions on making a traditional IRA contribution.

 Just because you can establish and contribute to a traditional IRA does not mean you can deduct the contribution, however. A separate set of rules determines deductibility. In Sections C and D, below, we help you sort out the restrictions on contributions and deductions.

You can establish an IRA even if you have an employer plan for your business or if you are covered by a plan of another employer.

If you have a spouse who is not currently working, he or she might be able to establish an IRA and make contributions based on your earnings. See Section C.l.a, below.

2. Advantages

Because you can establish an IRA even if you have an employer plan for your business, you do not have to choose between them. You can have both. Consequently, you won't generally find yourself weighing the advantages of an employer plan against those of a traditional IRA. Instead, you will be trying to decide if contributing to a traditional IRA makes sense in light of your cash flow needs, investment objectives and other factors.

As is the case with any type of retirement plan, whether it is an employer plan or an individual plan, if you qualify to make a contribution to a traditional IRA and you can afford to do so, you should almost certainly do it. The financial benefits of tax-deferred growth are undeniable.

You might find that you qualify to contribute to either a traditional IRA or a Roth IRA. Again, you can have both, but the annual limit on IRA contributions applies to all traditional and Roth IRAs combined. So if you contribute to a Roth IRA one year, that contribution will reduce the contribution you can make to a traditional IRA, and vice versa. Typically, then, you would choose between a traditional IRA and a Roth IRA. In most cases, you should choose a Roth IRA. (For a detailed comparison of these two types of IRAs, see Chapter 2.)

3. Disadvantages

Contributing to an IRA is not likely to get you into financial trouble. The disadvantages are subtle, not catastrophic. But you should be aware of them nonetheless.

As with any type of retirement plan, once you contribute money to an IRA, it's tough to get it out before age 59½ unless you want to pay some extra tax in the form of penalties. So if you foresee needing to use your IRA money in the near future, it's probably better not to make the IRA contribution in the first place.

If you qualify to contribute to either a traditional or a Roth IRA, you will generally do better to contribute to a Roth IRA, as long as you can leave the funds alone to grow for a number of years. The advantage a Roth offers over a traditional IRA is tax-free (as opposed to tax-deferred) growth of the earnings inside the account. Years of tax-free growth will generally beat the tax-deferred growth of the traditional IRA, even if the traditional IRA contribution is deductible. (Roth IRA contributions are never deductible.) (See Chapter 9 for more information about Roth IRAs. See Chapter 2 for a comparison of the different types of retirement plans.)

Throughout other chapters of this book, we have used the term "traditional IRA," to distinguish it from other types of IRAs, including SIMPLE IRAs, SEPs and Roth IRAs. Unfortunately, the IRS occasionally uses the term "traditional IRA" to mean either a standard contributory IRA for an individual (which is the type we describe in this section)—or a SEP. Although SEPs and contributory IRAs share many common traits, there are still enough differences to make the IRS's use of common terminology somewhat perplexing. (See Chapter 4 for more information about SEPs.)

B. How to Establish a Traditional IRA

IRAs are big business. That means you can randomly select just about any bank, brokerage firm or mutual fund company to serve as custodian of your IRA, and it will be happy to accommodate you. You can even establish an IRA with an insurance company by purchasing insurance contracts that will pay your IRA benefits in the form of an annuity.

1. Trustee or Custodian

Your IRA must be funded through a trust or custodial account, which means the money you contribute must be held by a trustee or custodian, usually a custodian. The custodian is typically a bank, credit union, brokerage firm or mutual fund. You cannot serve as trustee or custodian of your own IRA. Nor can you hand the funds to your business partner and ask her to keep them safe for you. (See Chapter 1,

Section C.2, for more information about trustees and custodians.)

2. Paperwork

Establishing an IRA is not much more difficult than opening an ordinary bank account. These are the steps to take:

Step 1:

First identify the bank, brokerage firm or other financial institution that you want to hold your IRA assets.

Step 2:

Call the institution and request the paperwork for establishing an IRA. You can also walk into a bank or brokerage firm and pick up the paperwork yourself. Or you might be able to download the paperwork from the institution's website.

Step 3:

Once you have the papers (commonly referred to as the IRA adoption agreement), you simply fill in a few blanks. The task is not nearly as daunting as completing the paperwork to establish a qualified plan.

At the end of this chapter, you can find a sample form from a mutual fund company. Although the forms will vary from company to company, you will find that they are essentially the same. The following are instructions on how to complete the sample form at the end of the chapter:

- *Section 1, type of IRA:* Check the box next to Traditional IRA.
- *Section 2, IRA registration:* Enter your Social Security number, birth date, name, address and telephone number.
- *Section 3, traditional IRA instructions:* Because this is a new contribution, check the box next to "Annual contribution." (You'll find it under Part B.) (Note: You would check another box—either in Part A or Part B—if you were rolling over or transferring money from another traditional IRA to this new IRA.) When you establish your IRA with a mutual fund, you must generally select one or more funds in which you would like to invest. The literature that accompanies the application will describe the various funds. You can then indicate how much of your IRA contribution should go into each one. Next, total the amount of the contribution and add the custodial fee. In this case the fee is $10 for each fund in which you choose to invest. This low fee is not uncommon for a mutual fund. Brokerage firms generally charge more (from $30 to $100 per year), although the fee is often waived once your account balance reaches a specific threshold.
- *Section 4, Roth IRA instructions:* You can skip this section if you are establishing only a traditional IRA.

• *Section 5, beneficiary designation:* In Part A (Primary Beneficiaries), name the person or organization who should receive your IRA assets when you die. (See Section 3, below, for more information about naming beneficiaries.) You should indicate whether or not the person is your spouse (spouses have special privileges), the percentage of the assets the person should receive and the person's birth date and Social Security number. On this particular form, if you name more than one beneficiary and one dies before you do, his or her share will be divided among the remaining primary beneficiaries. Not all forms treat a deceased beneficiary's share the same way, so be sure to read the fine print. In Part B (Secondary Beneficiaries), name the individuals or organizations who should receive your IRA assets if all of the primary beneficiaries die before you do.

• *Section 6, signature:* Sign and date the form.

Step 4:

Make a copy of the adoption agreement for your files and send the original to the financial institution, along with a check for your contribution plus the custodial fee. If you do not know the precise amount of your contribution yet, you can send in enough money to open the account and then deposit the rest later.

3. Beneficiary Designation

When you name a beneficiary of your IRA, you are identifying the person or organization you want to receive your IRA assets when you die. That's important, certainly. But the person or organization you name as beneficiary can be crucial for other reasons, as well. For example, your choice of beneficiary will determine how quickly you must take distributions from the IRA after you reach age 70½ (see Section F.5, below)—and how quickly the IRA must be liquidated after your death.

If you are married and you name your spouse as beneficiary, he or she will have options that other beneficiaries do not have. Your spouse can roll over your IRA into an IRA in his or her own name, pick new beneficiaries and, in most cases, delay or prolong distributions from the IRA. (Remember, when you delay distributions from an IRA, the assets can continue to grow tax-deferred—a big benefit!)

On the other hand, if you want to make a sizable donation to charity when you die, IRA assets might well be the best source of that donation, because charities will not have to pay income tax on the IRA distributions. You should be aware, however, that there is a drawback to donating to charity in this way. When you name a charity as beneficiary, you generally must distribute assets from the IRA more quickly during your lifetime than you would if you named a person as beneficiary.

And it is almost never right to simply name your "estate" as beneficiary. Doing so could present your heirs with income tax problems and perhaps increase probate fees, as well.

For most married individuals, naming a spouse as beneficiary is the best option. But if you are single, or if your situation is unusual, choosing a beneficiary can be quite complex, and you might want to seek help from a knowledgeable accountant or lawyer.

 For more information about the effect of your beneficiary designation on your retirement plan, see *IRAs, 401(k)s & Other Retirement Plans: Taking Your Money Out,* by Twila Slesnick and John Suttle (Nolo).

4. Deadlines

You must establish your IRA by your original tax filing due date. For most people, that is April 15 after the end of the tax year. No extensions are permitted. If you receive an extension of time for filing your tax return, you must still set up (and contribute to) the IRA by April 15. (See Section C.3, below, for more about contribution deadlines.) Of course, you can establish the IRA earlier if you like—any time between January 1 of the tax year and April 15 after the tax year.

C. Contributions

When it comes to traditional IRAs, it's important to distinguish between deduction limits and contribution limits. Unlike employer plans, traditional IRAs permit you to make contributions even if they are either not deductible or only partially deductible.

1. Contribution Limits

An individual retirement account by definition belongs to only one individual. Consequently, all of the limits are applied on an individual basis.

Also, you are not permitted to contribute to a traditional IRA after you reach age 70½. That means you cannot make a contribution for the year in which you reach age 70½ or any subsequent year. Note that this rule does not apply to employer plans, which generally permit you to contribute as long as you continue to work, regardless of how old you are.

 If you are still working when you reach 70½, you may not continue to make contributions to your own IRA, but if your spouse is younger than 70½, your spouse can contribute to his or her own IRA based on your earnings.

a. Maximum

You can never contribute more than $2,000 to your own traditional IRA in one year. There is no exception to that rule. However, there are other nuances in the law that might limit a contribution to something less than $2,000. Even your marital status can make a difference (see below).

 Recall that we are excluding from this discussion rollovers or transfers from other IRAs or qualified plans. Rollover contributions can exceed $2,000.

The contribution limits described below represent the total amount you can contribute to all traditional IRAs and Roth IRAs combined. For example, suppose your contribution limit is $2,000 and you have two traditional IRAs. If you contribute $2,000 to one, you cannot contribute to the other in the same year. If you contribute $1,500 to one, the most you can contribute to the other in the same year is $500. Similarly, if you have a Roth and a traditional IRA and you contribute $800 to the Roth, the most you could contribute to the traditional IRA is $1,200. (See Chapter 9 for more information about Roth IRAs.)

i. If You Are Single or Married Filing a Separate Return

If you are single or if you are married filing a separate tax return, your IRA contribution is limited to the smaller of:

- your compensation from employment (for example, if you are self-employed and your net earnings were only $1,300 for the year, your maximum IRA deduction is $1,300), or
- $2,000.

When you are self-employed, your compensation is net earnings from self-employment. That is, your business revenue reduced by business expenses, including the self-employment tax deduction and any contributions you made to a retirement plan you set up for your business. (See Chapter 1, Section B.1.c.i, for more information about net earnings from self-employment.)

ii. If You Are Married Filing a Joint Return

If you are married and you file a joint return with your spouse, the combined total you can contribute to your IRA and your spouse's IRA is the smaller of:

- your and your spouse's combined compensation from employment, or
- $4,000.

Bear in mind that the rigid $2,000 limit per individual still applies. For example, if your combined compensation is $40,000, your maximum contribution to both IRAs combined is $4,000, but you can put no more than $2,000 in your account and no more than $2,000 in your spouse's account.

These limits lead to a couple of interesting consequences. First, the limits apply even if one spouse is not working and has no compensation.

> EXAMPLE: You are self-employed and you have net earnings from self-employment of $90,000. Your spouse has no compensation from employment. He stays home and cares for your seven children. You may contribute $2,000 to your own IRA and $2,000 to your husband's IRA.

Second, you are not required to contribute equal amounts to your own IRA and your nonworking spouse's IRA.

> EXAMPLE: You are self-employed and you have net earnings from self-employment of $3,000. Your spouse has no compensation from employment. The maximum combined amount you can contribute to your IRA and your spouse's IRA is $3,000. However, you are not required to contribute $1,500 to each. You may contribute $2,000 to your spouse's and $1,000 to yours, or vice versa. In fact you may divide the $3,000 between the IRAs any way you like, as long as you don't deposit more than $2,000 in either one of them.

b. Minimum

One of the most attractive features of an IRA is that you are not required to make a contribution every year. And if you do decide to make a contribution, you can contribute any amount you like, as long as you don't exceed the maximum.

2. Cash Only

All contributions to your IRA must be in cash. If you contribute property other than cash, it is treated as an excess contribution subject to penalties (see Section G.1, below, for more about excess contributions)—even if the value is below your contribution limit. Fortunately, that little mistake won't completely disqualify the IRA, as long as you correct it by removing the property from your IRA.

3. Deadlines

You may make your IRA contribution any time during the year, so long you do so prior to the due date of your tax return. Generally the earlier you make it, the better, because the money can be working for you—and all of that growth will be tax-deferred.

Unfortunately, you don't always know how much money you will make until late in the year, or even after the end of the year. If you make less than you expected, you might feel you cannot afford to make a contribution. That's why the government gives you until the due date of your tax return to make the precise contribution. However, you could make a partial contribution early in the year and contribute the remainder any time on or before the due date.

 You'll meet the contribution deadline so long as your contribution is post-marked by the due date of your tax return. In other words, you can write a check and take it to the post office on the day your tax return is due. The money doesn't actually have to be in the account by then. Just be sure to obtain proof of mailing.

 Suppose you are short of cash for making your IRA contribution but you are expecting a big tax refund—enough to cover the IRA contribution. You can file your tax return claiming your deduction (if you qualify for a deduction) and then make the contribution after you receive the refund. The only caveat is that you must receive the refund before the filing deadline, or you'll have to come up with another source of funds.

D. Deductions

After you have computed the maximum amount you can contribute to an IRA, you must perform a separate calculation to determine how much of the contribution you can deduct. That calculation will be affected by two factors: whether you are covered by an employer plan and how much income you report on your tax return.

1. No Employer Plan

If neither you nor your spouse (if you are married) is covered by an employer plan, you can deduct your entire IRA contribution. Period. There isn't even an income limit. You could make $500,000 a year and still deduct your IRA contribution.

For purposes of this rule, you are covered by an employer plan if you work for a corporation that provides a retirement plan to which an allocation is made on your behalf for the year. Similarly, if you are self-employed and you have established a Keogh, a SEP or a SIMPLE IRA for your business, then you are covered by the plan in the years for which a contribution or allocation is made to your account.

In the case of a defined benefit plan, you are considered covered by the plan if you are eligible to participate, whether or not you actually accrue a benefit in any given year.

2. Employer Plan

Your income becomes a factor only if you or your spouse (if you have one) are covered by an employer plan. When you are covered by a plan, the IRA deduction is reduced and eventually eliminated as your "modified adjusted gross income" (modified AGI) increases.

Your modified AGI is your adjusted gross income (from page 1 of your tax return) before it is reduced by any IRA deduction or any student loan interest deduction, and before excluding any of the following (less common) items:

- foreign earned income
- income an employer provided to you to cover foreign housing
- EE bond interest used to pay higher education expenses, and
- income an employer provided to you to cover adoption expenses.

a. If You Are Single

If you are single (and covered by an employer plan) and your modified AGI is $32,000 or less, you can deduct your entire IRA contribution. Once your modified AGI exceeds $32,000, however, you can deduct only part—or none—of your contribution. To determine how much you can deduct, use the following formula:

Step 1:
Subtract $32,000 from your modified AGI.

Step 2:
Multiply the result by 20% or .20.

Step 3:
Subtract the Step 2 result from $2,000.

Step 4:
Round the result from Step 3 to the next highest multiple of 10—not the nearest multiple of 10. For example, if the result is $722, round up to $730.

Step 5:
If Step 4 is less than $200 but greater than zero, use $200. Otherwise, use the result from Step 4.

Step 6:
Your deduction is the smaller of either the amount from Step 5 or your compensation from employment.

EXAMPLE: You are self-employed. You have a money purchase pension plan for your business to which you have contributed the maximum the law permits. Your net earnings from self employment for the year are $30,000. Your modified AGI is $35,415. You made a $2,000 contribution to your IRA. The deductible portion of your IRA contribution is computed as follows:

Step 1: Subtract $32,000 from your modified AGI.

$35,415 − $32,000 = $3,415.

Step 2: Multiply the result by 20% or .20.

$3,415 x .20 = $683.

Step 3: Subtract the result from $2,000.

$2,000 − $683 = $1,317.

Step 4: Round to the next highest multiple of 10.

$1,317 is rounded up to $1,320.

Step 5: If the answer in Step 4 is less than $200 but greater than zero, use $200. Otherwise, use the result from Step 4.

Phase-Out of Deduction When You Are Single		
Year	Deduction Starts to Phase Out When Modified AGI Is:	Deduction Completely Disappears Once Modified AGI Reaches:
2000	$32,000	$42,000
2001	$33,000	$43,000
2002	$34,000	$44,000
2003	$40,000	$50,000
2004	$45,000	$55,000
2005 and later	$50,000	$60,000

The result from Step 4 = $1,320.

Step 6: Your deduction is the smaller of the amount from Step 5 or your compensation from employment.

Compensation = $30,000

Step 4 amount = $ 1,320

The deductible portion of your IRA contribution is $1,320.

If you play around with the above formula (a favorite pastime?), you will discover that once your modified AGI reaches $42,000, you will not be able to deduct any of your IRA contribution. But don't fret, Congress tossed a few crumbs our way. Over the next few years, the ceiling on modified AGI is to be increased. Here's what the future holds:

b. If You Are Married Filing a Joint Tax Return

If you are married and filing a joint tax return with your spouse and if at least one of you is covered by an employer plan, the deductibility rules apply differently depending on which of you is covered. And remember that IRAs are individual accounts, so you and your spouse must make separate calculations for your respective IRAs.

Bear in mind that both of you will use the same modified AGI. Modified AGI is determined from the numbers on your joint tax return and therefore will be exactly the same for both of you.

i.   Both You and Your Spouse Are Covered

We'll start with the easy case. If each of you is covered by an employer plan, then for the years 2000 through 2006, each of you will calculate the deductible portion of your respective contributions as described in Section a, above. The only difference is the phase-out range. Because each of you will be using a modified AGI that combines your incomes, your phase-out numbers are higher than those for single people.

Phase-Out of Deduction When You Are Married		
Year	**Deduction Starts to Phase Out When Modified AGI Is:**	**Deduction Completely Disappears Once Modified AGI Reaches:**
2000	$52,000	$62,000
2001	$53,000	$63,000
2002	$54,000	$64,000
2003	$60,000	$70,000
2004	$65,000	$75,000
2005	$70,000	$80,000
2006	$75,000	$85,000
2007 and later	$80,000	$100,000

⚠️ **Note that beginning in the year 2007, the phase-out range** (that is, the difference between when the deduction starts to phase out and when the deduction disappears entirely) is $20,000 instead of $10,000. This will change the percentage described in Step 2 of the deduction calculation to 10% from 20%.

ii. You Are Covered; Your Spouse Is Not Covered

If you are covered by an employer plan but your spouse is not, you compute the deductible portion of your own contribution as described in Section i, above.

Your spouse will also follow the steps described in Section i, above. The only difference will be the phase-out range. Your spouse will be able to deduct all of his or her contribution if your joint modified AGI is $150,000 or less. Your spouse will not be able to deduct any of his or her contribution if your modified AGI is $160,000, or more.

iii. You Are Not Covered; Your Spouse Is Covered

If your spouse is covered but you are not, the calculation is identical to that described in Section ii, above, except this time you are the one with the higher phase-out threshold. Your deduction is phased out between $150,000 and $160,000 while your spouse is stuck with the phase-out range described in Section i, above.

c. If You Are Married Filing Separately

Woe unto those who are married but filing separate returns. Congress shows them little mercy on any tax front. The IRA rules illustrate the bias well. If you are married filing separately and you are covered by an employer plan, your IRA deduction starts phasing out with your first dollar of modified AGI. The deduction is completely gone when your modified AGI hits $10,000.

E. Ongoing Administration

Other than computing and depositing your IRA contribution every year and then claiming any deduction to which you might be entitled, you have little administrative responsibility for your IRA.

1. Reporting the Contribution and Deduction

You claim the deductible portion of your IRA contribution on page 1, line 23, of your individual income tax return (Form 1040). There's a separate line just for the IRA deduction. You can find a sample form in the Appendix.

If any part of your IRA contribution is not deductible, you must complete a Form 8606 and file it with your tax return. You can find a sample form in the Appendix.

2. Filing Tax Returns

Your IRA is a tax exempt entity. Therefore, it generally does not have to file a tax return or pay taxes on any income it produces.

But if your IRA engages in a business that produces more than $1,000 of income during the year, you must file a special tax return—Form 990-T—for the IRA. Income from a business inside a IRA is called unrelated business taxable income, or UBTI. Once UBTI exceeds $1,000 in a year, it is subject to tax, and the tax must be paid out of the IRA assets.

Most people invest their IRA assets in stocks, bonds and other standard investments that don't generate UBTI. But suppose you invest some of the assets in a limited partnership. Many limited partnerships are in fact businesses. And when the business (the limited partnership) starts throwing off income, it will be taxable, even though it is inside your IRA.

3. Preparing Statements

Your IRA custodian (the financial institution that holds your IRA assets) has a few additional administrative responsibilities related to your IRA. First the custodian must provide you with statements of your account from time to time, but no less frequently than annually. The institution is also required to report your annual contributions and the year-end value of the IRA

to the IRS each year on Form 5498. It must also report to the IRS, and to you, any distributions you take during the year.

4. Updating Documents

The IRA agreement you sign to establish your account with your financial institution is a prototype IRA. That means it is pre-approved by the IRS. Changes in the law might require your IRA agreement to be updated from time to time. The financial institution that provides the IRA documents and that serves as custodian will take responsibility for updating the plan.

If you want to change the beneficiary of your IRA, you don't have to complete an entirely new adoption agreement. Generally, you can simply request a "Change of Beneficiary Designation" form, drop in the name of the new beneficiary, sign and date the form and return it to the financial institution.

F. Distributions

In this section, we discuss the rules that govern when you can—and cannot—take money out of your traditional IRA.

When you put your money into a retirement plan, whether a qualified plan or an IRA, the government wants you to leave it there until retirement. That's the bargain you make for the tax deduction and the deferral of tax on the earnings. If you break that bargain and take the money out early, you could be subject to penalties.

Whenever you take a distribution from your traditional IRA—whether before or after retirement—you must pay income tax on it. There's no escaping it. And you must use ordinary tax rates. You cannot use capital gains rates on the distribution, even if some or all of the assets in the IRA represent gains from stock sales.

Thus, income taxes are inevitable. However, you can escape the penalty for taking money out early if the distribution falls into any one of the categories described in Section 1, below.

 This is not a book about retirement plan distributions. Although we provide an overview of the distribution rules, you must look elsewhere for the details. One source is *IRAs, 401(k)s & Other Retirement Plans: Taking Your Money Out*, by Twila Slesnick and John C. Suttle (Nolo).

1. Early Distributions and Exceptions to the Early Distribution Penalty

In general, distributions that you take from your IRA before you reach age 59½ are considered early distributions and are subject to both regular income tax and a 10% penalty. Distributions you take on or after the day you turn 59½ will be subject to income tax but no additional penalties.

Fortunately, if you need to gain access to your retirement savings prior to reaching age 59½, you might be able to do so—without penalty—because of the myriad exceptions to the early distribution penalty. We discuss those exceptions in the following sections.

 Remember that distributions are always subject to income tax. The following sections simply describe situations when you can avoid paying the early distribution penalty.

a. Death

Distributions from your IRA after you die are not subject to the early distribution penalty, no matter how old you are when you die or how old your beneficiaries are when they withdraw the money. They will still have to pay income tax on the distributions, though.

b. Disability

If you become disabled, you can take money from your IRA without penalty. But first you must satisfy the IRS's definition of disabled. Here's how it reads: You must be unable to "engage in any substantial gainful activity by reason of any medically determinable physical or mental impairment which can be expected to result in death or to be of long-continued and indefinite duration." However, the IRS's own regulations state that the gainful activity refers specifically to the type of work you were doing before becoming disabled. Thus it would seem that you need not be unfit for all work—just the work you customarily do. Even if you do qualify for this exception to the penalty, your distributions will be subject to income tax.

c. Periodic Payments

You can begin taking distributions from your IRA regardless of your age as long as you take them in equal annual installments over your life expectancy. These distributions are called "substantially equal periodic payments."

To compute substantially equal periodic payments, you must use one of the IRS-approved methods for computing the payments—you cannot simply choose a monthly or annual payment that suits you. (See IRS Notice 89-25 in the Appendix for more information about how to calculate substantially equal payments.)

You must continue the payments for at least five years or until you are at least age 59½, whichever comes later. For example, if you begin at age 58, you must continue the payments for at least five years even though you pass age 59½ in the meantime. Or if you begin at age 52, you must continue until at least age 59½, even though more than five years have passed.

d. Medical Expenses

Although you can take money out of your IRA prior to age 59½ to pay for medical expenses, you won't escape the penalty entirely. The exemption applies only to the portion of your medical expenses that would be deductible on Schedule A of your tax return if you were to itemize deductions (whether or not you actually do itemize deductions). The remainder is subject to penalty. All of it is subject to income tax.

EXAMPLE: Your adjusted gross income is $50,000. You had medical bills of $6,000 during the year, which you paid with funds you withdrew from your IRA. (The $6,000 distribution is included in the $50,000 of income.) For income tax purposes, you are permitted to deduct medical expenses that exceed 7.5% of your adjusted gross income. Thus,

Adjusted gross income (AGI), including the IRA distribution = $50,000;

7.5% of AGI (.075 x $50,000) = $3,750 in nondeductible expenses;

Excess ($6,000 – $3,750) = $2,250 in deductible expenses.

Although you took $6,000 from your IRA to pay medical expenses, only $2,250 will escape the early distribution penalty. The remaining $3,750 will be subject to the penalty (unless you qualify for another exception). And don't forget that the entire $6,000 is subject to regular income tax, as well.

e. Health Insurance Premiums

People who are unemployed, or were recently unemployed, may draw money from a IRA to pay health insurance premiums without penalty, as long as they satisfy the following conditions:

- They received unemployment compensation for at least 12 consecutive weeks.
- They received the funds from the IRA during a year in which they received unemployment compensation or during the following year.
- They received the IRA distribution no more than 60 days after they returned to work.

It might sound as though this won't work for you if you are self-employed. However, the rules specifically permit this exception if you were self-employed before you stopped working, as long as you would have qualified for unemployment compensation under state law except for the fact that you were self-employed.

f. Higher Education Expenses

If you use IRA distributions to pay higher education expenses, you will not be subject to the early distribution penalty, as long as you satisfy all of the following requirements:

- You must use the money to pay the higher education expenses of you, your spouse, your child or your grandchild.
- You must use the money to pay for tuition, fees, books, supplies and equipment. You may also use the money for room and board if the student is carrying at least half of a normal study load (or is considered at least a half-time student).
- The distributions cannot exceed the amount of the higher education expenses. Furthermore, when computing the amount of the distribution that is exempt from the penalty, you must reduce the total expenses (tuition, fees and so on) by any tax-free scholarships or other tax-free assistance the student receives, not including loans, gifts or inheritances.

g. First Home Purchase

You may take an early distribution without penalty if the money is used to buy a first home. Although the purpose of this exception is to make it easier for people to buy a home, there is a lifetime distribution limit of only $10,000. Other restrictions include the following:

- You must use the IRA money for the acquisition, construction or reconstruction of a home.
- You must use the funds within 120 days of receiving them. If the home purchase is canceled or delayed, you

may roll the funds back into the same IRA or into another IRA, as long as you complete the rollover within 120 days of the initial distribution.

- You must use the funds for the benefit of a first-time home buyer. A first-time home buyer is someone who has had no interest in a principal residence during the two years ending on the date of purchase of the new home. If the individual happens to be married, then neither the individual nor the spouse may have owned any part of a principal residence during the preceding two-year period.
- The first-time home buyer can be you or your spouse. The buyer can also be an ancestor (for example, a parent, grandparent, great grandparent and so on), a child or a grandchild of either you or your spouse.
- The lifetime limit of $10,000 applies regardless of whose home is purchased or improved. If you withdraw $10,000 and give it to your child, your lifetime limit is used up and you may not use the exception for any future distribution (from any IRA, no matter what type), even if it is to buy a house for a different relative or for yourself. The $10,000 does not have to be distributed all at once or even in a single year. For example, you could withdraw $5,000 one year, giving it to a qualified person for a home purchase, and then withdraw another $5,000 in a later year.

h. Federal Tax Levy

If you owe back taxes, you can be reasonably certain the government will try to collect them. If you have assets in an IRA, the government can take those assets (in other words, the IRS can levy on your IRA) to pay your debt. If it does, those amounts taken for taxes will not be subject to the early distribution penalty even if you happen to be younger than 59½.

2. Loans

You are not permitted to borrow from your IRA, no matter how old you are. If you do, you will have engaged in a prohibited transaction and you will be penalized accordingly. (See Section G.3, below, for more about prohibited transactions.)

But a special rule, called the 60-day rule, essentially allows you to borrow from your IRA for up to 60 days. You can take money out of your IRA without paying income tax and penalties, as long as you put the money into another IRA or back into the same one within 60 days. However, there are two restrictions:

- You may use this strategy with your IRA only once in each 12-month period.
- When you put the money back in, you must return exactly the amount you took out.

3. Hardship

You cannot take money out of your IRA in the event of hardship, unless the hardship fits into one of the exceptions described in Section 1, above.

4. Divorce Payments

If you and your spouse divorce and your divorce agreement states that you must give some or all of your IRA assets to your former spouse, don't simply withdraw the IRA funds and hand them over. If you do, you (not your spouse) will have to pay income tax on the distribution. And if you are younger than 59½ at the time, you'll owe penalties, as well, even though you are turning the money over to your former spouse.

It might be distressing to inadvertently become liable for your former spouse's taxes. Fortunately, there is a way to transfer the funds without incurring either income tax or penalties. As long as the distribution is required by a divorce or maintenance decree, or a written separation agreement, you may instruct the custodian of your IRA to transfer some or all of the IRA assets directly into an IRA in your former spouse's name. Alternatively, you can roll over your former spouse's share of the IRA into a new traditional IRA in your name and then change the name on the new IRA to your former spouse's name. The critical point in every case is to be sure your former spouse does not take possession of the funds before they are deposited into an IRA in his or her name.

 You would be wise to have a lawyer draft or review the transfer instructions to the custodian because of possible overlapping federal income tax and state family law rules. The lawyer should know which rules preempt which and can prepare the instructions accordingly.

5. Mandatory Distributions

Beginning in the year you turn 70½, you are required to start taking money out of your IRA, even if you are still working. The income tax regulations provide a formula for calculating the minimum required distribution. You may take more than the minimum, but you may not take less. If you do take less, you will be fined 50% of the amount that you should have taken out of the IRA but didn't.

For more information about mandatory distributions from IRAs and other retirement plans, see *IRAs, 401(k)s & Other Retirement Plans: Taking Your Money Out*, by Twila Slesnick and John C. Suttle (Nolo).

G. Penalties

Because the IRA rules are relatively simple, you have few opportunities to get into trouble. It's still possible, though. Perhaps you contributed too much one year, took a distribution too early or did something with the money that the IRS considered creative but inappropriate. Here are the consequences.

1. Excess Contributions

If you contribute too much to your IRA, you will be fined 6% of the excess over what you were permitted to contribute. The 6% will be assessed again for every year any excess remains in the account.

The penalty can never exceed 6% of the total value of the IRA, though, determined as of the end of the tax year.

If you take some corrective action, however, you can lessen how much you will have to pay in penalties and taxes. We describe your options for corrective action in the following sections.

a. Option One: Remove Excess Before Due Date

One way you can correct your error is to remove the excess contribution plus any earnings attributable to the excess by the due date of your tax return (plus extensions, if you requested and received an extension for filing your tax return).

When you remove the contribution and earnings, you must report the earnings,

Infractions and Their Consequences

Problem	Penalty
Excess contributions	6% of the excess
Early distributions	10% of the distribution
Prohibited transactions: • If IRA owner engages in prohibited transaction: • If another disqualified person engages in prohibited transaction:	Disqualification 15% of transaction
Required distributions	50% of the amount that should have been distributed but was not

but not the contribution, as income on your tax return. Report the earnings for the year you actually deposited the excess contribution in your IRA. (The year you remove the funds might be different from the year you made the excess contribution.) If you are not yet 59½, you will have to pay a 10% early distribution penalty on the earnings in addition to the income tax, but you won't pay any penalty or taxes on the excess contribution.

EXAMPLE: You contributed $2,000 to your IRA in February 2001. You did not contribute to any other IRAs or retirement plans during the year. At the end of the year, you discovered that the maximum you were permitted to contribute to your IRA was only $1,800. The excess contribution is $200.

If you earned $160 on the $2,000 IRA contribution, then $16 of it would be attributable to the $200 excess (200/2,000 x 160 = $16). Therefore, you must remove $216—the earnings of $16 plus the excess of $200.

If you remove the money by April 15, you won't owe an excess contribution penalty on the $216. (If you received an extension for filing your tax return, you have until the extended due date.) If you are younger than 59½, however, you might owe an early distribution penalty on the earnings (the $16), unless you can find an exception that applies. (See Section F.1, above.)

On your tax return you will report the $16 of earnings that you withdrew, and you will claim an IRA deduction for $1,800 on your tax return.

If you filed your return early and claimed an IRA deduction for too much, you can still prepare an amended return before the actual due date of your tax return and avoid the 6% penalty.

EXAMPLE: As in the previous example, you contributed $2,000 to your IRA in February 2001. The end of the year comes and goes. You file your tax return in February 2002 claiming a deduction of $2,000. In March, you dreamed that you computed your IRA contribution incorrectly. The next morning when you checked the computation, you discovered you should have contributed only $1,800. To avoid an excess contribution penalty, you must do all of the following before April 15:

Remove the $200 excess contribution.

Remove the $16 of earnings attributable to the $200.

File an amended tax return claiming an IRA deduction of only $1,800 and reporting the $16 of earnings.

If you follow these procedures, you will not owe a 6% excess contribution penalty. However, you might owe a 10% early distribution penalty on the $16 of earnings, if you are younger than 59½.

b. Option Two: Remove Excess After Due Date

Another way you can deal with the situation is to remove the excess contribution late—after the due date (or extended due date) of your tax return—and leave the earnings in the account.

You won't escape the 6% penalty on the excess contribution, but you will avoid a penalty on the earnings if you leave them in the IRA. (Presumably, Congress considers the 6% penalty adequate payback for any benefit you might derive from leaving the earnings in the account.)

> EXAMPLE: In 2001, you contributed $200 too much to your IRA. Although you knew about the excess before your filing deadline (and deducted only the correct amount on your tax return), you forgot to remove the excess from the IRA account. The earnings on the excess are $16. You remove the $200 after your tax filing deadline and leave the $16 of earnings in the account. You will owe a penalty of $12 (6% of $200), but no additional penalties and no income tax.

You will not have to pay any income tax on the excess contribution that you remove from the IRA as long as you did not take a deduction for the excess on your tax return. If you did, you will have to submit an amended tax return with the correct deduction and pay the additional income tax.

The preceding discussion assumes that you were only allowed to contribute to your IRA something less than the $2,000 ceiling. If, however, you were allowed to contribute the full $2,000 and if you contributed money in excess of that amount, you will be in a little more trouble. Congress assumes everyone knows you can't put more than $2,000 into an IRA. So if you do, the presumption is that you did it on purpose. When you correct the excess contribution, you will have to pay tax on the distribution even if you didn't take a deduction

c. Option Three: Leave Excess In, Deduct Next Year

Your third option is to leave the excess in the IRA and deduct it in the next tax year.

You still have to pay the 6% penalty on the excess for the first year, because the excess remained in the account after the due date of your tax return. But you won't pay any penalty the next year, as long as the excess does not exceed the amount you are permitted to deduct for that year. There are no penalties on the earnings for any year, as long as they stay inside the IRA.

> EXAMPLE: In 2001, you contributed $200 too much to your IRA. Again you deducted the correct amount but forgot to remove the excess. You decide to leave the excess in the account and deduct it the following year. In 2002 you have enough income to make a

$2,000 IRA contribution. You apply the $200 excess from the previous year and add an additional $1,800 in cash by the due date of your tax return to complete the $2,000 contribution. You must still pay a $12 penalty for 2001, but you will pay no penalty for 2002 or beyond.

⚠️ **If your excess contribution is not deductible in the second year, you must pay an excess contribution penalty for that year.** This is so even if you would have been permitted to make a nondeductible contribution and the carryover excess does not exceed that amount. In order to use the excess in a subsequent year, it must be used as part of a deductible contribution.

Report excess contributions to your IRA on IRS Form 5329 for the year the excess contribution was made. Do not use a subsequent year's Form 5329.

EXAMPLE: You made an excess contribution of $200 to your IRA in 2001. You discovered your error in June 2002 long after you filed your tax return. You should complete the year 2001 Form 5329 (not year 2002's Form 5329) even though you have already filed the rest of your tax return. Sign and date the form and send it in with your check for $12 (6% of $200), which is the amount of the excess contribution penalty.

2. Early Distributions

If you take money out of your IRA before you reach age 59½ and if the distribution does not fall into any of the permissible categories described in Section F.1, above, then you will have to pay a 10% early distribution penalty. That penalty is in addition to the income tax you will owe.

The IRS requires you to report the early distribution penalty on Form 5329 for the year of the early distribution. You can find a sample Form 5329 in the Appendix.

3. Prohibited Transactions

The Tax Code prohibits certain transactions involving your IRA assets. The prohibited transaction rules are part of Congress's strategy to protect your IRA assets for use during your retirement. The rules are designed to keep you or any other disqualified person (see below) from using the assets for personal gain or engaging in transactions that put the assets at risk.

A disqualified person is someone who might reasonably have access to your IRA assets. In addition to you, such persons include your spouse, your lineal descendants (such as children and grandchildren) and your ancestors (such as parents and grandparents). The list also includes fiduciaries—those responsible for handling the assets of the IRA, such as a custodian or money manager.

The penalties for engaging in a prohibited transaction are severe. If you (the IRA owner) or your beneficiary engage in the prohibited transaction, the IRA is disqualified and all of the assets are considered distributed as of the first day of the year in which the prohibited transaction took place. You will have to pay income tax on the entire account, and if you are not yet 59½, you will have to pay a 10% early distribution penalty.

If a disqualified person (other than you or your beneficiary) engages in the prohibited transaction, the penalty is generally 15% of the transaction. If the transaction is not corrected, an additional tax of 100% is imposed. That's a total of 115%. But the disqualified person must pay the tax—not you.

These are the transactions to avoid. Note that these all refer to transactions that occur inside your IRA or with the use of your IRA assets.

- The sale, exchange or lease of any property between a disqualified person and the IRA. For example, you cannot sell your house to your IRA.

- The furnishing of goods or services or facilities between a disqualified person and the IRA. For example, you cannot hire your spouse to manage the IRA and pay him a big salary out of the IRA assets.

- The lending of money or extending of credit between a disqualified person and the IRA. For example, you cannot borrow from the IRA to buy a car, even if you intend to return the money. If you want to use your IRA assets to buy that car, you must withdraw the money permanently and hope you can find an exception to the early distribution penalty that applies (if you are younger than 59½).

- The transfer to or use by a disqualified person of any assets or income of the IRA. For example, you cannot use IRA funds to invest in a house (held by the IRA) which you then occupy as your principal residence. Again, if you want to use the funds to buy yourself a house, you must withdraw the funds permanently and pay income tax on the distribution. But hopefully, you'll be able to use the $10,000 first-home exception to reduce any early distribution penalty that might apply. (See Section F.l, above, for more information about the first-home exception.)

- Any act of self-dealing, which occurs when a disqualified person uses the assets or income of the IRA for that person's own interest or account while the assets are still in the IRA. For example, if your money manager invests all of your IRA assets in the stock of a company of which she owns 80%, such an investment would clearly benefit her as a majority shareholder and, therefore, might be deemed a prohibited transaction.

- The receipt of payment by a fiduciary in connection with a transaction involving the income or assets of the plan. A kickback, for example.

If you engage in a prohibited transaction, you must file Form 5329 with the IRS. Furthermore, your IRA is disqualified from the moment of the transgression. That means all of the assets must be distributed, and you must pay income tax on the entire pre-tax portion of the IRA. You might also have to pay a 10% early distribution penalty if you are younger than 59½.

If another disqualified person engages in the prohibited transaction, he or she must complete IRS Form 5330 and pay the 15% penalty.

4. Life Insurance

You are not permitted to use assets in your IRA to purchase life insurance that you hold inside your IRA. If you do, the IRA becomes disqualified as of the first day of the year during which you made the purchase, and you must pay income tax and possibly an early distribution penalty on the entire amount in your IRA.

5. Collectibles

Although you can invest your IRA contributions in various securities—stocks, mutual funds, bonds—you cannot invest your contributions in certain tangible items known as collectibles. The Tax Code carefully lists all those items that are considered collectibles, followed of course, by a list of exceptions.

Collectibles include the following:

- works of art
- rugs or antiques
- metals or gems
- stamps or coins, and
- alcoholic beverages.

Exceptions include the following:

- certain U.S. minted gold, silver and platinum coins
- coins issued under the laws of any state, and
- gold, silver, platinum or palladium bullion equal to or exceeding the minimum fineness required by a contract market for metals delivered in satisfaction of a regulated futures contract (and only if the bullion is in the physical possession of the IRA custodian).

If you invest your IRA assets in an unacceptable collectible, the amount of IRA money you used to pay for it is considered a distribution—even if you don't actually withdraw the collectible (or any money) from your account. That means you will owe income tax on the amount that is considered a distribution. And you must report an early distribution penalty on Form 5329—unless you qualify for an exception. That's the bad news. The good news is that your mistake won't disqualify the IRA. Furthermore, you can keep the collectible in your IRA if you like. When it is ultimately distributed, the amount on which you have already paid tax will not be included in your income.

EXAMPLE: Last year, you purchased an antique Persian rug with $5,000 of your IRA funds. This year your accountant told you it was a prohibited transaction. You must pay income tax on $5,000, even though the IRA continues to hold title to the rug. You must also pay a 10% early distribution penalty of $500 ($5,000 x 10%) because you are younger than 59½—even though you did not actually take a distribution. When you turn 70½, the rug is distributed to you from the IRA. At the time of the distribution the fair market value of the rug is $20,000. You must pay income tax (and perhaps an early distribution penalty) on $15,000 (which is $20,000 reduced by the $5,000 on which you have already paid taxes).

6. Pledging the Account As Security

If any portion of your IRA is used as security for a loan to you (for example, you borrow money using your IRA as collateral), that portion is treated as a distribution, and you will pay income tax on it. You will also have to pay an early distribution penalty, unless you qualify for an exception. You report the distribution on your tax return and include Form 5329 if you owe an early distribution penalty. The IRA as a whole will not be disqualified. The rest of the assets can remain in the

IRA and continue their tax-deferred growth.

 This is different from actually borrowing the funds from the IRA. If you do that, the entire IRA is disqualified. (See Section F.2, above.)

7. Mandatory Distribution Penalty

You must begin taking money out of your IRA when you turn 70½. If you fail to do so, you will pay a penalty of 50% of the amount that you should have taken out but didn't. For example, if you were required to distribute $10,000 from your IRA for the year you turned 70½ but you forgot, you will owe a penalty of $5,000 ($10,000 x 50%).

Report this penalty on Form 5329.

H. Multiple IRAs and Qualified Plans

As discussed in Sections C and D, above, you can always contribute to a traditional IRA if you have compensation from employment, although the deduction for your contribution might be curtailed if you are covered by an employer plan.

It is only your contribution to other traditional IRAs and Roth IRAs that might affect your ability to make a contribution to a given traditional IRA. That's because the most you can contribute each year to all of your traditional and Roth IRAs combined is $2,000. If you contribute $2,000 to a Roth IRA (or to another traditional IRA), you cannot make a traditional IRA contribution. If you contribute $1,500 to a Roth, the most you can contribute to a traditional IRA is $500.

⚠️ **If your income from employment (including net self-employment income and other earnings from employment) is less than $2,000,** your total contribution to all traditional and Roth IRAs combined is limited to those earnings. (See Section C.1 for more information about contribution limits.)

For more information about Roth IRAs, including contribution requirements and limitations, see Chapter 9.

I. Terminating Your IRA

Terminating your IRA is easy. You just take all of the money out. Once all of the money has been distributed—for any reason—the IRA is terminated. You might terminate your IRA by withdrawing all funds for living expenses. Or perhaps you violated the prohibited transaction rules, which caused the IRA to be disqualified and all of the assets deemed distributed. In that case, too, the IRA is terminated.

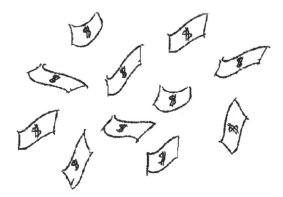

R310-page 1 of 4

+Retirement Resource Center

IRA Adoption Agreement

THE **Vanguard** GROUP®

Complete this form to establish a new or separate Vanguard traditional IRA *or* Vanguard Roth IRA.

- You can open only **one** type of IRA with this form. You must complete two IRA Adoption Agreements if you want to establish both a traditional IRA *and* a Roth IRA. You cannot use this form to convert a traditional IRA to a Roth IRA.
- If you will reach age 70½ during this calendar year, or are older and are required to take a minimum distribution from your retirement plan, please note:
    - **For asset transfers:** You can either take your required minimum distribution (RMD) before transferring the assets to us, or leave the amount of the RMD in your existing retirement plan and withdraw it prior to the distribution deadline (generally December 31).
    - **For rollovers:** You must take your RMD before rolling the assets over to us.

If you need assistance or other Vanguard forms, call us toll-free at **1-800-205-6** ___ All IRA forms are available on our website at **www.vanguard.com/?serviceforms**. Return this completed form a ___ any othe ___ uired documents in the enclosed postage-paid envelope, or mail to: **The Vanguard Group, P.O. Box 1110, V** ___ **e, PA 19** ___ **1110.** For overnight delivery, mail to: **The Vanguard Group, 455 Devon Park Drive, Wayne, PA 19** ___

Please print in capital letters, preferably in black ink.

1. **Type of IRA.** *(Check only one.)*   ☐ **Tradit** ___ **IRA**   **OR**   ☐ **Roth IRA**
        (___ *e al* ___ *ions except Section 4.)*   *(Complete all sections except Section 3.)*

2. **IRA Registration**
   If this IRA is ___ ing establi ___ nor who has earned income, write the minor's name, and next to the name, the wor ___ r."

   ☐☐☐-☐☐-☐☐☐☐   ☐☐-☐☐-☐☐☐☐
   Social Security Numbe ___   Birth Date *(month, day, year)*

   _____
   Name *(first, middle initial, last)*

   _____
   Street Address or Box Number

   _____ ☐☐   ☐☐☐☐☐-☐☐☐☐
   City   State   Zip

   ☐☐☐-☐☐☐-☐☐☐☐   ☐☐☐-☐☐☐-☐☐☐☐
   Daytime Telephone Number   Evening Telephone Number

3. **Traditional IRA Instructions** *(If you are establishing a traditional IRA, check all that apply in this section, then proceed to Section 5. You can find fund numbers and minimum initial investment amounts in Vanguard Funds for Retirement Investing, in Facts on Funds® for Retirement Investing, or on our website at www.vanguard.com.)*

   A. **By asset transfer from an existing traditional IRA.** *(If you are transferring assets to Vanguard from a traditional IRA held by another custodian, check one box below, and complete the enclosed Asset Transfer Authorization in addition to this adoption agreement. You will provide investment instructions in Section 3 of the Asset Transfer Authorization. Vanguard will contact your current custodian to arrange the transfer.)*

   ☐ **Asset transfer from an existing traditional IRA.** *(Check this box if your current traditional IRA contains either all personal contributions, or a combination of personal contributions and assets previously rolled over from an employer-sponsored retirement plan.)*

   ☐ **Asset transfer from an existing direct rollover traditional IRA.** *(Check this box if your current traditional IRA contains **only** assets previously rolled over from an employer-sponsored retirement plan.)*

R310-page 2 of 4

B. By check. (*Make your check payable to Vanguard Fiduciary Trust Company.*)

☐ **Annual contribution.** (*Contributions to all your traditional and Roth IRAs cannot exceed a total of $2,000 per year.*)

Dollar Amount
(*$1,000 minimum initial investment for most funds*)

Fund Number	Fund Name	For Tax Year	
☐☐☐☐	☐	☐☐☐☐	$ ☐,☐☐☐
☐☐☐☐	☐	☐☐☐☐	$ ☐,☐☐☐

Annual custodial fee of $10 for each fund selected* $ ☐☐

Total Amount $ ☐,☐☐☐

☐ **Rollover from a previously held traditional IRA.** (*Check this box if you have possession of the traditional IRA assets you had held at another institution. You must deposit the full value of your assets—including any taxes that were withheld—within 60 days for the rollover to remain tax-deferred. If you need more space, provide the information on a separate sheet.*)

Dollar Amount
(*$1,000 minimum initial investment for most funds*)

Fund Number	Fund Name	Total (or percentage)		Dollar Amount
☐☐☐☐	☐	☐%	OR	$ ☐,☐☐☐,☐☐☐
☐☐☐☐	☐	☐%	OR	$ ☐,☐☐☐,☐☐☐
☐☐☐☐	☐	☐%	OR	$ ☐,☐☐☐,☐☐☐

Percentages must total 100%.

Annual custodial fee of $10 for each fund selected* $ ☐☐

Total Amount $ ☐,☐☐☐,☐☐☐

4. Roth IRA Instructions (*Check all that apply. You can find fund numbers and minimum initial investment amounts in Vanguard Funds for Retirement Investing, in Facts on Funds® for Retirement Investing, or on our website at www.vanguard.com.*)

A. ☐ **By asset transfer from an existing Roth IRA.** (*If you are transferring assets to Vanguard from a Roth IRA held by another custodian, complete the enclosed Asset Transfer Authorization in addition to this adoption agreement. You will provide investment instructions in Section 3 of the Asset Transfer Authorization. Vanguard will contact your current custodian to arrange the transfer.*)

B. By check. (*Make your check payable to Vanguard Fiduciary Trust Company.*)

☐ **Annual contribution.** (*Contributions to all your traditional and Roth IRAs cannot exceed a total of $2,000 per year.*)

Dollar Amount
(*$1,000 minimum initial investment for most funds*)

Fund Number	Fund Name	For Tax Year	
☐☐☐☐	☐	☐☐☐☐	$ ☐,☐☐☐
☐☐☐☐	☐	☐☐☐☐	$ ☐,☐☐☐

Annual custodial fee of $10 for each fund selected* $ ☐☐

Total Amount $ ☐,☐☐☐

*The annual custodial fee of $10 is applied to each fund account having assets of less than $5,000. However, this fee is waived for those who have mutual fund and variable annuity assets at Vanguard totaling $50,000 or more.

R310-page 3 of 4

☐ **Rollover from a previously held Roth IRA.** *(Check this box if you have possession of the Roth IRA assets you had held at another institution. You must deposit the full value of your assets—including any taxes that were withheld—within 60 days for the rollover to remain tax-deferred. If you need more space, provide the information on a separate sheet.)*

Fund Number	Fund Name	% of Total *(whole percentages)*		Dollar Amount *($1,000 minimum initial investment for most funds)*
☐☐☐☐	☐☐☐☐☐☐☐☐☐☐☐☐	☐☐☐%	OR	$☐,☐☐☐,☐☐☐
☐☐☐☐	☐☐☐☐☐☐☐☐☐☐☐☐	☐☐☐%	OR	$☐,☐☐☐,☐☐☐
☐☐☐☐	☐☐☐☐☐☐☐☐☐☐☐☐	☐☐☐%	OR	$☐,☐☐☐,☐☐☐

Percentages must total 100%.

Annual custodial fee of $10 for each fund selected* $☐☐

Total Amount $☐,☐☐☐,☐☐☐

5. **Beneficiary Designation** *(Complete this section only if you are naming an individual, trust, or charity as your beneficiary. If your beneficiary designation is more complex or if you want information on why naming a beneficiary for your IRA is important, request a Vanguard Beneficiary Designation Option kit, and send the completed and signed Beneficiary Designation/Change Form for Retirement Accounts along with this adoption agreement.)*

Note: You must provide information on your beneficiary designations in the exact format that follows. To name more than two primary or three secondary beneficiaries, photocopy the appropriate sections (5A and/or 5B) before filling them out, and return the additional copies with this adoption agreement.

A. **Primary Beneficiaries**

Vanguard will transfer ownership of your IRA to your primary beneficiaries following your death. Your primary beneficiaries will share equally in your IRA unless you specify different percentages (totaling 100%) below. If a primary beneficiary dies before you, his or her share of your IRA will be divided equally among the surviving primary beneficiaries. *Important: If you designate more than one primary beneficiary without indicating percentages, equal percentages totaling 100% will be allocated to each beneficiary.*

☐☐☐☐☐☐☐☐☐☐☐☐☐☐☐☐☐☐
Individual *(first, middle initial, last)*, Trust Name, or Charity Name

Relationship: ☐ Spouse   ☐ Other   ☐☐☐% Percentage   ☐☐-☐☐-☐☐☐☐ Birth Date / Trust Date *(month, day, year)*

☐☐☐-☐☐-☐☐☐☐   **OR**   ☐☐-☐☐☐☐☐☐☐
Social Security Number *(for an individual)*   Employer Identification Number *(for a trust or charity)*

☐☐☐☐☐☐☐☐☐☐☐☐☐☐☐☐☐☐
Individual *(first, middle initial, last)*, Trust Name, or Charity Name

Relationship: ☐ Spouse   ☐ Other   ☐☐☐% Percentage   ☐☐-☐☐-☐☐☐☐ Birth Date / Trust Date *(month, day, year)*

☐☐☐-☐☐-☐☐☐☐   **OR**   ☐☐-☐☐☐☐☐☐☐
Social Security Number *(for an individual)*   Employer Identification Number *(for a trust or charity)*

SIGNATURE REQUIRED ON NEXT PAGE   *(over, please)*

*The annual custodial fee of $10 is applied to each fund account having assets of less than $5,000. However, this fee is waived for those who have mutual fund and variable annuity assets at Vanguard totaling $50,000 or more.

R310-page 4 of 4

B. Secondary Beneficiaries

Vanguard will transfer ownership of your IRA to your secondary beneficiaries only if there are no surviving primary beneficiaries at the time of your death. If this happens, your secondary beneficiaries will share equally in your IRA unless you specify different percentages (totaling 100%) below. If there are no surviving secondary beneficiaries at the time of your death, Vanguard will transfer ownership of your IRA to your estate.

Important: If you designate more than one secondary beneficiary without indicating percentages, equal percentages totaling 100% will be allocated to each beneficiary.

Individual *(first, middle initial, last)*, Trust Name, or Charity Name

Relationship: Spouse   Other   Percentage %   Birth Date / Trust Date *(month, day, year)*

Social Security Number *(for an individual)*   **OR**   Employer Identification Number *(for a trust or charity)*

Individual *(first, middle initial, last)*, Trust Name, or Charity Name

Relationship: Spouse   Other   Percentage %   Birth Date / Trust Date *(month, day, year)*

Social Security Number *(for an individual)*   **OR**   Employer Identification Number *(for a trust or charity)*

Individual *(first, middle initial, last)*, Trust Name, or Charity Name

Relationship: Spouse   Other   Percentage %   Birth Date / Trust Date *(month, day, year)*

Social Security Number *(for an individual)*   **OR**   Employer Identification Number *(for a trust or charity)*

6. Shareholder Signature—YOU MUST SIGN BELOW

I hereby adopt the Vanguard Individual Retirement Custodial Account Agreement that is incorporated herein by reference and acknowledge having received and read it. I further acknowledge having received and read the Vanguard IRA® Disclosure Statement and the prospectus for each Vanguard fund elected under this Agreement. Under penalty of perjury, I certify that my Social Security number on this form is correct.

Please sign here. Your IRA cannot be established without your signature.

Signature *(If the IRA owner is a minor, a legal guardian or custodian must sign.)*   Date *(month, day, year)*

Vanguard Fiduciary Trust Company, Custodian

Accepted by: _____   Title: _____Secretary_____

Chapter 9

Roth IRAs

A. What Is a Roth IRA? 9/3

   1. Who Can Establish a Roth IRA? 9/3

   2. Advantages 9/4

   3. Disadvantages 9/5

B. How to Establish a Roth IRA 9/5

   1. Trustee or Custodian 9/6

   2. Paperwork 9/6

   3. Beneficiary Designation 9/7

   4. Deadlines 9/8

C. Contributions 9/8

   1. Limits 9/8

   2. Conversions 9/12

   3. Cash Only 9/16

   4. Deadlines 9/16

D. Ongoing Administration 9/16

   1. Reporting the Contribution 9/16

   2. Filing Tax Returns 9/17

   3. Preparing Statements 9/17

   4. Updating Documents 9/17

E. Distributions **9/17**

   1. Distribution of Contributions 9/18

   2. Distribution of Converted Amounts 9/18

   3. Distribution of Investment Returns 9/19

   4. Ordering of Distributions.. 9/21

   5. Rollovers 9/22

   6. Loans 9/23

   7. Hardship 9/23

   8. Divorce Payments 9/23

   9. Mandatory Distributions 9/24

F. Penalties **9/24**

   1. Excess Contributions 9/25

   2. Early Distributions 9/28

   3. Prohibited Transactions.. 9/34

   4. Life Insurance 9/36

   5. Collectibles 9/36

   6. Pledging the Account As Security 9/36

   7. Mandatory Distribution Penalty 9/37

G. Multiple IRAs and Qualified Plans **9/37**

H. Terminating Your Roth IRA **9/37**

*I*n its eternal quest for the most effective way to encourage people to save for retirement, Congress has created one of the biggest sugarcoated carrots we've ever seen. It's called a Roth IRA, brought to us by the Taxpayer Relief Act of 1997.

A Roth IRA, like a traditional IRA, is a retirement plan for individuals. It is not an employer plan. That means, a Roth IRA must be established by an individual, not a business.

Although this book is about retirement plans for the self-employed, we have included this chapter on Roth IRAs and Chapter 8 on traditional IRAs because you might well qualify to establish one or both of these types of IRAs for yourself, even though you already have an employer plan for your business. And if you qualify to establish a Roth IRA, it is almost certainly to your advantage to do so.

A. What Is a Roth IRA?

Congress designed the Roth IRA to be much like a traditional IRA, but with a few attractive modifications. When the modifications began to fill pages rather than paragraphs, the new creature was given its own section in the Tax Code—Section 408A. The new section begins with the statement that all of the traditional IRA rules apply to Roth IRAs except as noted. In this chapter we'll focus on the exceptions that make a Roth IRA unique.

The two most prominent features of a Roth IRA are:

- contributions are never deductible, and
- all distributions, including the earnings on contributions, are potentially tax free.

The benefit an individual can derive from tax-free (as opposed to tax-deferred or delayed) growth of assets in a Roth IRA generally far outstrips the benefits of a traditional IRA—even if the traditional IRA contributions are deductible.

1. Who Can Establish a Roth IRA?

As is the case with a traditional IRA, you must have income from employment (earned income) to make a contribution to a Roth IRA. Your participation in an employer plan—whether sponsored by your business or by another employer—will not affect whether you can establish a Roth IRA

If you have a spouse who is not currently working, he or she might be able to establish a Roth IRA and make contributions based on your earnings. See Section C.l.a, below.

But unlike a traditional IRA, if your modified adjusted gross income is too high, you (or you and your spouse, if you are married) will not qualify to contribute to a Roth IRA at all.

Your modified adjusted gross income (modified AGI) is your adjusted gross income (from page 1 of your tax return) before it is reduced by any IRA deduction or any student loan interest deduction and before excluding any of the following less common items:

- foreign earned income
- income an employer provided to you to cover foreign housing
- EE bond interest used to pay higher education expenses, and
- income an employer provided to you to cover adoption expenses.

But you do not include in modified AGI any rollovers or conversions (discussed in Section C.2, below).

a. If You Are Single

If you are single, you may not contribute to a Roth IRA at all if your modified AGI exceeds $110,000.

If your modified AGI is $95,000 or less, you qualify to make a full Roth IRA contribution.

Between $95,000 and $110,000, the amount you can contribute is gradually reduced until it reaches zero. (See Section C.l, below for more information about this phase-out of the Roth IRA contribution.)

b. If You Are Married Filing a Joint Return

If you are married and you file a joint return with your spouse, you may not con-

tribute to a Roth IRA at all if your joint modified AGI exceeds $160,000.

If your modified AGI is $150,000 or less, you qualify to make a full Roth IRA contribution.

Between $150,000 and $160,000, the amount you can contribute is reduced until it reaches zero. (See Section C.l, below, for more information about the phase-out of the Roth IRA contribution.)

c. If You Are Married Filing a Separate Return

If you are married and filing a separate return from your spouse, you may not contribute to a Roth IRA at all if your modified AGI exceeds $10,000. Yes, $10,000—it's not a typo. Furthermore, the phase-out of your contribution begins with the first dollar of income you report on your tax return. (See Section C.l, below.)

2. Advantages

Because you can establish a Roth IRA for yourself even if you have an employer plan for your business, you do not have to choose between them. You can have both.

But you might have to choose between a traditional IRA and a Roth IRA. Although you can have both (assuming you qualify to establish a Roth) the annual limit on IRA contributions applies to all traditional and Roth IRAs combined. Typically, then, you would choose either a Roth or a traditional IRA to which you would make a maximum contribution for the year.

Some of the advantages of a Roth IRA over a traditional IRA are:

- You can remove the annual $2,000 contributions at any time without penalty. (For the nuances of this rule, see Section D, below.)
- You may continue to make contributions to a Roth IRA after age 70½ as long as you have earned income and your adjusted gross income doesn't exceed the limits described above.
- Earnings in a Roth are completely tax-free when distributed if certain requirements are satisfied. (See Section E, below.) Recall that earnings in a traditional IRA are tax-deferred, which means you will pay income tax on them when they are eventually distributed from the IRA.
- If you have a Roth IRA, you are not required to withdraw any amount during your lifetime. (See Section E.9, below.)

3. Disadvantages

There are few disadvantages of a Roth IRA, and they are not very troublesome at that.

- Contributions you make to a Roth IRA are never deductible.
- If your income is too high, you cannot make any contribution to a Roth IRA.

 Because the Tax Code limits contributions to all traditional and Roth IRAs combined to $2,000, your most pressing task is to choose among a deductible traditional IRA, a nondeductible traditional IRA and a Roth IRA. For the vast majority of individuals, the choice is an easy one. You should contribute to a Roth IRA if you can because the tax-free growth it offers is unbeatable. Your second choice should be to contribute to a deductible traditional IRA, if you can. If your contribution to the traditional IRA will not be deductible, you can contribute to a nondeductible traditional IRA, but the benefits are less dramatic. (See Chapter 8 for more information about traditional IRAs.)

It is a rare circumstance in which a deductible traditional IRA would be superior to a Roth IRA. The most likely situation would be if you need to draw on the Roth IRA (withdraw money to live on, for example) after a short time—before the Roth IRA has had time to accumulate a significant amount of tax-free earnings.

B. How to Establish a Roth IRA

As is the case with traditional IRAs, you can establish a Roth IRA at just about any bank, brokerage firm, mutual fund or insurance company.

1. Trustee or Custodian

Your Roth IRA must be funded through a trust or custodial account, which means the money you contribute must be held by a trustee or custodian, usually a custodian. The custodian is typically a bank, credit union, brokerage firm, mutual fund. You cannot serve as trustee or custodian of your own Roth IRA—nor can any of your friends or business associates. (See Chapter 1, Section C.2, for more information about trustees and custodians.) But as mentioned above, finding a custodian won't cause you much trouble. Your favorite financial institution is almost certainly qualified to serve as custodian of your Roth IRA.

2. Paperwork

Establishing a Roth IRA is no different from setting up a traditional IRA. In fact, many financial institutions use the same form for both. You simply check the appropriate box. To establish your Roth IRA, take these steps.

Step 1:
Identify the bank, brokerage firm or other financial institution that will hold your assets. This institution will serve as custodian of your Roth IRA.

Step 2:
Call the institution and ask for the documents to establish a Roth IRA. Alternatively, you can walk into a bank or brokerage firm and pick up the paperwork yourself. Sometimes, you'll find the forms sitting on a table along with other account applications and promotional material. You might even be able to download the forms from the financial institution's website.

Step 3:
Once you have the papers (called the Roth IRA Adoption Agreement), you simply fill in the blanks. The task is not nearly as difficult as completing the paperwork to establish a qualified plan. You can find a sample form at the end of this chapter. The following are instructions on how to complete that sample form:

- *Section 1, type of IRA:* Check the box next to "Roth IRA."
- *Section 2, IRA registration:* Enter your Social Security number, birth date, name, address and telephone number.
- *Section 3. traditional IRA instructions:* You can skip this section if you are establishing only a Roth IRA.
- *Section 4, Roth IRA instructions:* Because this is a new contribution, check the box next to "Annual contribution." (You can find it under Part B.) (Note: You would check another box—either in Part A or Part B—if you were rolling over or trans-

ferring money from another Roth IRA to this new Roth IRA.) When you establish your Roth IRA with a mutual fund, you must generally select one or more funds in which you would like to invest. The literature that accompanies the application will describe the various funds. You can then indicate how much of your Roth IRA contribution should go into each one. Next, total the amount of the contribution and add the custodial fee. In this case the fee is $10 for each fund in which you choose to invest. This low fee is not uncommon for a mutual fund. Brokerage firms generally charge more (from $30 to $100 per year), although the fee is often waived once your account balance reaches a specific threshold.

- *Section 5, beneficiary designation:* In Part A (primary beneficiaries), name the person or organization that should receive your Roth IRA assets when you die. (See Section 3, below, for more information about naming beneficiaries.) Indicate whether or not the person is your spouse (spouses have special privileges), the percentage of the Roth IRA each person should receive and the person's birth date and Social Security number. Not all forms treat a deceased beneficiary's share the same way, so be sure to read the fine print. On this particular form, if you name more

than one beneficiary and one dies before you do, his or her share will be divided among the remaining primary beneficiaries. In Part B (secondary beneficiaries), name the individuals or organizations that should receive your Roth IRA assets if all of the primary beneficiaries die before you do.

- *Section 6, signature:* Sign and date the form.

Step 4:

Make a copy of the Adoption Agreement for your files and send the original to the financial institution, along with a check for your contribution plus the custodial fee. If you do not know the precise amount of your contribution yet, you can send in enough money to open the account and deposit the rest later.

3. Beneficiary Designation

When you name a beneficiary of your Roth IRA, you are identifying the person or organization you want to receive your Roth IRA assets when you die. That's important, certainly. But the person or organization you name as beneficiary can be crucial for other reasons, as well. For example, your choice of beneficiary will determine how quickly the assets must be distributed from your Roth IRA after your death.

If you are married and you name your spouse as beneficiary, he or she will have options that other beneficiaries do not have. Your spouse can roll over your Roth IRA into a Roth IRA in his or her own name, pick new beneficiaries and generally delay distributions until his or her death. (Remember, when you delay distributions from a Roth IRA, the assets can continue to grow tax-free—a big benefit!)

And it is almost never right to simply name your "estate" as beneficiary. Doing so could accelerate distributions upon your death and perhaps increase probate fees, as well.

For most married individuals, naming a spouse as beneficiary is the best option. But if you are single or if your situation is unusual, choosing a beneficiary can be quite complex and you might want to seek help from a knowledgeable accountant or lawyer.

 For more information about the effect of your beneficiary designation on your retirement plan, see *IRAs, 401(k)s & Other Retirement Plans: Taking Your Money Out*, by Twila Slesnick and John Suttle (Nolo).

4. Deadlines

You must establish your Roth IRA by your original tax filing due date. For most people, that is April 15 after the end of the tax year. And there are no extensions. If you receive an extension of time for filing your tax return, you must still set up (and contribute to) the Roth IRA by April 15. (See Section C.4, below for more about contribution deadlines.) Of course, you can establish the Roth IRA earlier, if you like—any time between January 1 of the tax year and April 15 after the tax year.

C. Contributions

Once you confirm that you qualify to make a contribution to a Roth IRA, you must determine if the contribution is limited.

1. Limits

The general rule is that you cannot contribute more than $2,000 a year to your own Roth IRA. And under certain circumstances, the $2,000 ceiling must be reduced (see Section a, below).

 There are two circumstances under which you can contribute more than $2,000 to your Roth IRA. One is when you convert a traditional IRA to a Roth IRA (see Section 2, below). The other is when you transfer or roll over the assets of one Roth IRA into another (see Section E.5, below). In both cases, the $2,000 limit is waived, provided you qualify for the conversion or rollover.

a. Maximum

The contribution rules are slightly different for single individuals, married individuals who file a joint return and married individuals who file separate returns.

i. If You Are Single

If you are single and your modified AGI is $95,000 or less, your maximum Roth IRA contribution is the smaller of:

- your compensation from employment, or
- $2,000.

⚠ **When you are self-employed, your compensation from employment for Roth IRA purposes is net earnings from self-employment.** That is, your business revenue reduced by business expenses, including the self-employment tax deduction and any contributions you made to a retirement plan you set up for your business. (See Chapter 1, Section B.1.c.i, for more information about calculating net earnings from self-employment.)

If your modified AGI is greater than $95,000, your maximum Roth IRA contribution is reduced gradually until it reaches zero—which occurs when your modified AGI reaches $110,000. The amount of the reduction is computed according to the following formula:

Step 1:
Subtract $95,000 from your modified AGI (see Section A.1, above, for the definition of modified AGI).

Step 2:
Divide the result by $15,000 (which is $110,000 – $95,000).

Step 3:
Multiply the result from Step 2 by the lesser of your net earnings from self-employment or $2,000.

Step 4:
Subtract Step 3 from the lesser of your net earnings from self-employment or $2,000.

Step 5:
Round the result from Step 4 to the next highest multiple of 10 (not the nearest multiple of 10). For example, if the result is $722, round up to $730.

Step 6:
If Step 5 is less than $200 but greater than zero, use $200. Otherwise, use the result from Step 5.

Step 7:
Your maximum Roth IRA contribution is the smaller of the amount from Step 6 or your net earnings from self-employment.

EXAMPLE: You are single and your modified AGI is $100,000. You have $70,000 of net earnings from self-employment. You compute your maximum Roth IRA contribution as follows:

Step 1: Subtract $95,000 from your modified AGI:

$100,000 - $95,000 = $5,000.

Step 2: Divide the result by $15,000;

$5,000 / $15,000 = .3333.

Step 3: Multiply the result by the lesser of your net earnings from self-employment or $2,000:

.3333 x $2000 = $667.

Step 4: Subtract the result from the lesser of your net earnings from self-employment or $2,000:

$2,000 − 667 = $1,333.

Step 5: Round to the next highest multiple of 10:

$1,333 is rounded up to $1,340.

Step 6: If the answer in Step 5 is less than $200 but greater than zero, use $200. Otherwise, use the result from Step 5.

$1,340 is greater than $200, so use $1,340.

Step 7: Your maximum contribution is the smaller of your net earnings from self-employment or the amount from Step 6.

Net earnings from self-employment = $70,000, which is greater than the Step 6 amount of $1,340.

Therefore, the most you may contribute to your Roth IRA is $1,340.

ii. If You Are Married Filing a Joint Return

If you are married and filing a joint return with your spouse, and if your modified AGI is $150,000 or less, the maximum you and your spouse can contribute to both of your Roth IRAs combined is the smaller of:

- you and your spouse's combined earned income; or
- $4,000.

As is the case with a traditional IRA, however, the limit of $2,000 per individual still applies. For example, if your combined compensation is $40,000, your maximum contribution to both IRAs combined is $4,000, but you cannot put more than $2,000 into your account, and you cannot put more than $2,000 into your spouse's account.

These same rules apply even if your spouse is not working and has no compensation.

EXAMPLE: You are self-employed, and you have net earnings from self-employment of $90,000. Your spouse has no compensation from employment. She stays home and cares for your seven children. You may contribute $2,000 to your own Roth IRA and $2,000 to your wife's Roth IRA.

Also, you are not required to contribute equal amounts to your own Roth IRA and your nonworking spouse's Roth IRA.

EXAMPLE: You are self-employed, and you have net earnings from self-employment of $3,000. Your modified AGI is $25,000. Your spouse has no compensation from employment. The maximum combined amount you can contribute to your Roth IRA and your spouse's Roth IRA is $3,000. However, you are not required to contribute $1,500 to each. You may contribute $2,000 to your spouse's and $1,000 to yours, or vice versa. In fact you may divide the $3,000 between the IRAs any way you like, as long as you don't deposit more than $2,000 in either one of them.

You and your spouse's maximum Roth IRA contribution is gradually phased out when your modified AGI is between $150,000 and $160,000. You compute the allowable contribution as described in Section i, above, but with two changes:

- In Step 1, change $95,000 to $150,000.
- In Step 2, change $15,000 to $10,000.
- All other steps are the same.

iii. If You Are Married Filing a Separate Return

If you are married and filing a separate return from your spouse, your Roth IRA contribution begins to phase out with your first dollar of modified AGI and is completely phased out when your modified AGI reaches $10,000. To compute your allowable contribution for the year:

Step 1:
Divide your modified AGI by $10,000. (Remember your modified AGI cannot be greater than $10,000 or you do not qualify to make a contribution.)

Step 2:
Multiply the result from Step 1 by the lesser of your net earnings from self-employment or $2,000.

Step 3:
Subtract Step 2 from the lesser of your net earnings from self-employment or $2,000.

Step 4:
Round the result from Step 3 to the next highest multiple of 10 (not the nearest multiple of 10). For example, if the result is $722, round up to $730

Step 5:
If Step 4 is less than $200 but greater than zero, use $200. Otherwise, use the result from Step 4.

Step 6:
Your maximum Roth IRA contribution is the smaller of the amount from Step 5 or your net earnings from self-employment.

b. Minimum

You are not required to make a contribution to your Roth IRA every year that you qualify. If you do decide to make a contribution, you can contribute any amount you like, as long as you don't exceed the maximum.

c. After You Reach Age 70½

You are permitted to contribute to a Roth IRA even after you reach age 70½, as long as you have earned income and your modified AGI is not above the limit. (Note: This is not true for a traditional IRA.)

2. Conversions

There's another way to put money into a Roth IRA, aside from making annual contributions. You can transfer, or roll over, assets from a traditional IRA to a Roth IRA. This type of rollover is called a conversion. To make a conversion, you must be eligible (see Section b, below). And then you must face the consequences (see Section a, below).

a. Consequences of Converting a Traditional IRA to a Roth IRA

If you determine that you are eligible to roll over your traditional IRA to a Roth IRA (see Section b, below, for an explanation of who is eligible) and if you elect to do so, you must pay the piper. Specifically, you will have to pay income tax at ordinary rates on the entire amount of the rollover. Once you've ponied up the money and rolled over the assets, however, all future distributions of the rolled amount will be free of income tax. Furthermore, distributions of future earnings on the rollover will be tax-free as long as those distributions satisfy a five-year holding period and are qualified. (See Section E.3, below, for information about qualified distributions and the five-year holding period.)

To Convert or Not to Convert

The rollover or conversion of a traditional IRA to a Roth IRA can be a real boon to young investors who have years of tax-free compounding ahead of them and who can afford to pay the tax from non-IRA funds. If the tax is paid out of IRA funds, the advantage of the conversion declines.

As a practical matter, it might be difficult for people with sizable traditional IRAs to convert the entire account to a Roth IRA unless they have large amounts of cash outside the IRA. Imagine paying regular income tax on a $100,000 IRA. In 1998, at the top federal income tax bracket, for example, you would have to come up with about $40,000. One way around this problem is to roll over the traditional IRA to a Roth IRA in bits and pieces over a number of years to keep the tax at a manageable level. Nothing in the law prevents you from converting part of your traditional IRA instead of the whole thing.

For older IRA participants, rolling over a traditional IRA to a Roth IRA is not necessarily the correct decision. If you must include a large IRA in income, some or all of it could easily be taxed at the maximum tax rate, and you might not recover from that financial outlay (through tax-free compounded growth) before your death. If your primary concern is passing wealth to your beneficiaries, however, a rollover could save estate taxes and also give your beneficiaries an opportunity for additional tax-free growth after your death.

The decision to roll or not to roll a traditional IRA to a Roth IRA can involve some complex calculations. You must factor in age, health, income and estate tax rates and investment returns. If you are young, healthy and able to pay the taxes with money outside the IRA, the rollover is likely to pay off for you.

But watch out: If you are younger than $59\frac{1}{2}$ and if you elect to pay the tax out of the rollover itself, instead of rolling over the entire amount, the portion that goes to taxes could be subject to the early distribution penalty. (See Section F.2, below.)

b. Determining If You Are Eligible to Convert a Traditional IRA to a Roth IRA

Even if it makes sense for you to roll over, or convert, a traditional IRA to a Roth IRA, you must determine whether you are eligible to do so. You are *not* eligible if either of the following is true.

- You are a married person using the "married filing separate" status (instead of the "married filing joint" status) on your tax return.

- Your modified AGI (see Section A.l, above), not including the converted amount, exceeds $100,000. This income cap applies whether you are married or single. Recall that when calculating your modified AGI for this purpose, you may not take into account any deduction for a traditional IRA (which would ordinarily reduce your adjusted gross income). However, you may exclude the converted amount, but again, only for purposes of determining whether or not you qualify for the rollover.

EXAMPLE: Your modified AGI for the year 2001 is $90,000. You have accumulated $25,000 in a traditional IRA and would like to roll it over into a Roth IRA before the end of the year. Because your modified AGI (not including the $25,000 conversion) is less than $100,000, you qualify to convert your traditional IRA to a Roth IRA. On your tax return for the year 2001, you will report income of $115,000 (which is $90,000 plus $25,000).

 The income threshold for converting a traditional IRA to a Roth IRA is more restrictive than the threshold for making annual contributions to a Roth IRA. You may set up and contribute some amount to a Roth IRA as long as you have earnings from employment and your modified AGI does not exceed $160,000 (if you are filing a joint return) or $110,000 (if you are single).

c. Related Conversion Rules

If you decide to proceed with the conversion of a traditional IRA to a Roth IRA, here are some additional rules you should know about.

i. No Need to Move the Assets

You can convert your traditional IRA to a Roth IRA without moving the assets. You can simply instruct your custodian to change the title on the account to show that it is now a Roth IRA. Even though the funds aren't technically moved from one account to another, you are deemed to have converted the assets. Whether you convert your traditional IRA by changing title or by moving the assets to a new account, the law identifies the assets as "converted" amounts, meaning they were once in a traditional IRA but are now in a Roth IRA.

ii. Early Distribution Penalty Does Not Apply

Even if you are younger than 59½ when you roll over or convert a traditional IRA to a Roth IRA, you will not have to pay an early distribution penalty on the converted amount, as long as the entire taxable portion is rolled over. If you roll over less, the portion not rolled over but taken out of the traditional IRA is subject to the early distribution penalty. And beware of using part of the rollover to pay income tax. (See Section F.2.b.iii, below.)

iii. You Pay Tax Only on Earnings

For income tax purposes, the converted portion will not be subject to income tax when it is distributed in future years, but the earnings will be subject to tax unless they are part of a qualified distribution. (See Section E.3, below, for the definition of a qualified distribution.)

iv. You Can Convert SIMPLE IRAs and SEPs

If you have a SEP, you can convert it to a Roth IRA.

If you have a SIMPLE IRA, you can also convert it to a Roth IRA, but only after two years from the date you first established that SIMPLE IRA or any other SIMPLE IRA.

d. If You Convert in Error

If you convert a traditional IRA to a Roth IRA during the year and discover at the end of the year that your modified AGI is so high that it makes you ineligible for conversion (see Section b, above), you won't be in serious trouble. The law allows you to transfer the funds back out of the Roth IRA and into the same or even a different traditional IRA before the due date of your tax return (or the extended due date, if you request and receive an extension of time for filing your return). This is called a recharacterization.

In a proper recharacterization, the custodian of the Roth IRA must transfer the errant funds plus any investment earnings on those funds directly to the custodian of the traditional IRA. If this is all done in timely fashion, there will be no income tax or penalties.

If you recharacterize a converted amount (meaning you undo a conversion from a traditional IRA to a Roth IRA by putting the money back into a traditional IRA), you may not reconvert those recharacterized funds to a Roth IRA until the following tax year or until 30 days have passed, if that period of time is longer. For example, if you recharacterize in June, you must wait until the next January to reconvert. But if you recharacterize on December 31, you cannot reconvert until January 30 of the next year.

The waiting period for reconverting was added to the Roth IRA laws somewhat belatedly to quash a tax-saving maneuver that was spreading like wildfire. Smart taxpayers were converting and recharacterizing several times during a year to take advantage of dips in the market. When the market dips, the value of an IRA drops—and so does the tax cost of conversion.

3. Cash Only

All contributions to your Roth IRA must be in cash. If you contribute property other than cash, the transaction is treated as an excess contribution (see Section F.1, below, for more about excess contributions)—even if the value is below your contribution limit—and you could be subject to penalties. Fortunately, that little mistake won't completely disqualify the Roth IRA, as long as you correct it by removing the property from the IRA.

 This cash requirement does not apply to rollovers or conversions. In those cases, you simply transfer the contents of one IRA to the other, even if it contains non-cash items such as stocks or bonds.

4. Deadlines

You may make your Roth IRA contribution any time during the year. Generally, the earlier you make it, the better, because the money can be earning tax free income for you. Unfortunately you don't always know if you will qualify to make a contribution until late in the year, or even after the end of the year. That's why the government gives you until the due date of your tax return to make the precise contribution.

 You'll meet the deadline if your contribution is postmarked by the due date of your tax return. In other words, you can write a check and take it to the post office on the day your tax return is due. The money doesn't actually have to be in the account by then. Just be sure to obtain proof of mailing.

 Suppose you are short of cash for making your IRA contribution but you are expecting a big tax refund—enough to cover the Roth IRA contribution. You can file your tax return, and then make the contribution after you receive your refund. The only caveat is that you must receive the refund before the filing deadline, or you'll have to come up with another source of funds for the contribution.

D. Ongoing Administration

You have little administrative responsibility for your Roth IRA. In fact, most of the tasks described below fall to the custodian of your Roth IRA.

1. Reporting the Contribution

Because your Roth IRA contribution is not deductible, you do not report it on your tax return.

2. Filing Tax Returns

As is the case with a traditional IRA, your Roth IRA is a tax exempt entity, which is why it generally doesn't have to pay tax each year on the income it produces—or file a tax return.

But if your Roth IRA engages in a business that produces more than $1,000 of income during the year, you must file a special tax return—IRS Form 990-T—for the Roth IRA. (You can find a sample Form 990-T in the Appendix.) Income from a business inside a Roth IRA is called unrelated business taxable income, or UBTI. Once UBTI exceeds $1,000 in a year, it is subject to tax and the tax must be paid out of the Roth IRA assets.

Most people invest their Roth IRA assets in stocks, bonds and other standard investments that don't generate UBTI. But suppose you invest some of the assets in a limited partnership. Many limited partnerships are in fact businesses. And when the business (the limited partnership) starts throwing off income, it will be taxable, even though it is inside your Roth IRA.

3. Preparing Statements

Your Roth IRA custodian (the financial institution) has a few administrative responsibilities. First, the custodian must provide you with statements of your account from time to time, but no less frequently than annually. The institution is also required to report your annual contributions and the year-end value of the Roth IRA to the IRS each year on Form 5498. It must also report to the IRS, and to you, any distributions you take during the year.

4. Updating Documents

The Roth IRA agreement you sign to establish your account with your financial institution is a prototype. That means it is pre-approved by the IRS as a qualified Roth IRA. Changes in the law might require the agreement to be updated from time to time, but the financial institution that provides the documents and serves as custodian will take responsibility for those updates.

If you want to change the beneficiary of your Roth IRA, you don't have to complete an entirely new adoption agreement. Generally, you can simply request a "Change of Beneficiary Designation" form, drop in the name of the new beneficiary, sign and date the form and return it to the financial institution.

E. Distributions

The key to squeezing the maximum benefit from a Roth IRA is to be aware of which distributions are taxable and which are not. Maintaining that vigilance is not difficult; you must simply view your Roth IRA as the sum of three distinct parts. The first part consists of the contributions you have made (see Section 1, below). The second part consists of amounts you have converted from a traditional IRA (if any) (see Section 2, below). The third part consists of the earnings that have accumulated in the account, such as interest earned on bond investments or gains from stock sales (see Section 3, below).

1. Distribution of Contributions

The portion of your Roth IRA that consists of your contributions is never subject to income tax when it comes out. Never. Even if you take it out the day after you put it in. That's because all contributions you made were nondeductible, which means you have already paid tax on the money. You don't have to pay tax a second time when you take it out. Fair is fair.

Furthermore, any distribution you take from a Roth IRA is presumed to be a return of your contributions until you have withdrawn the total amount of contributions you have made to it over the years (or to all Roth IRAs, if you have more than one). In other words, all contributions are recovered before earnings are recovered. This simple rule gives the Roth IRA an advantage over a traditional IRA. It means you may retrieve your contributions whenever you want without incurring any income tax. In this way, the contributions can serve as an emergency fund.

EXAMPLE: You began making contributions to a Roth IRA in 1998, contributing $2,000 every year. By the end of the year 2001, the Roth IRA had grown to $11,000. Of that amount, $8,000 was from your annual contributions and $3,000 was from investment returns. In 2002, you have an auto accident and total your car. You need to purchase a new car but don't have any resources other than your Roth IRA. You withdraw $8,000 from your Roth IRA. The $8,000 is not subject to tax (or penalties) because your distribution is deemed to be a return of your contributions.

2. Distribution of Converted Amounts

Distributions of converted amounts are given unique treatment. The distribution will not be subject to income tax, because you paid the tax when you converted the assets of the traditional IRA to a Roth IRA. But if the distribution occurs within five years of the conversion, it could be subject to an early distribution penalty, if you are younger than 59½. (See Section F.2, below, for more information about this penalty.)

3. Distribution of Investment Returns

When you put money into a Roth IRA (either through contribution or conversion), you ordinarily use the funds to purchase investments that will earn money for you. For example, you might invest in bonds or CDs to generate interest. Or you might buy stock, hoping the price will shoot up so you can make a bundle on a later sale. As long as those earnings—the interest and the stock proceeds—stay inside the Roth IRA, they are not taxed. But what happens when they come out? In the case of a traditional IRA, all of the earnings are subject to ordinary income tax. The advantage of a Roth IRA is that when you distribute earnings, they are tax-free—even though they have never before been taxed—as long as the distribution is considered a "qualified" distribution.

a. Qualified Distributions

To be qualified—and therefore totally tax free—a distribution must satisfy two requirements. First, it must satisfy a holding period requirement, and second, it must fall into one of four categories (see below).

i. Requirement One: Five-Year Holding Period

To be qualified, the distribution must satisfy a five-year holding period requirement. A distribution that you take within five calendar years of the year you first established a Roth IRA can never be a qualified distribution.

 The distribution must satisfy this holding period requirement even if you—the owner of the Roth IRA—die before the five years is up. In that case, your beneficiary must wait until you would have satisfied the holding period for the distribution to be qualified.

Counting the year of your first contribution as year one, you will satisfy the five-year requirement if you wait until the sixth year before withdrawing any earnings.

> **EXAMPLE:** You opened a Roth IRA in June 2001 and made a $2,000 contribution in each of the years 2001 through 2004. At the end of 2004, your account was worth $15,000, of which $8,000 was from contributions and $7,000 was from investment earnings. In June 2005, you withdrew $10,000 to pay for a trip to China. Of that amount, $8,000 is deemed to be from contributions and will not be subject to income tax. The remaining $2,000 is deemed to come from earnings. Because the distribution does not satisfy the five-year holding requirement, you will pay income tax on the $2,000. (You might also have to pay an early distribution penalty. See Section F.2, below.)

Although you are permitted to make a contribution to a Roth IRA after the end of the year (until April 15), the five-year holding period for a qualified distribution begins on the first day of the calendar year to which your very first contribution relates. This means that the first year might be an earlier year than the one during which you actually made the contribution.

> EXAMPLE: You wanted to set up a Roth IRA and make a contribution for 2001. You finally got around to doing so in February 2002, well before the April 15, 2002, deadline. Because the contribution is for 2001, you will count 2001 as year one when computing the five-year holding period, even though you didn't actually make the contribution until 2002.

ii. Requirement Two: Categories

In addition to satisfying the holding period described above, the distribution must fall into one of the following categories to be qualified and therefore, tax free:

- distributions you take after reaching age 59½
- distributions you take after becoming disabled
- distributions to your beneficiary or your estate after your death, or
- distributions you take to purchase a first home (up to a lifetime withdrawal limit of $10,000).

 Recall that contributions and converted amounts are never subject to income tax when they come out of a Roth IRA. So even if they are part of a nonqualified distribution, they are tax free. Only the earnings will be taxed if they are part of a nonqualified distribution.

> EXAMPLE: You began making contributions to a Roth IRA in 2001. By June 2003, you had accumulated $6,500. Of that amount, $6,000 was from contributions you made in the years 2001, 2002 and 2003. The remaining $500 was from earnings on your investments. In December 2003, you withdrew $6,200 from the IRA. The distribution is a nonqualified distribution because it occurred within five years of your initial contribution. Only $200 is subject to tax, however, because your contributions, which total $6,000, are deemed to come out first, and they are never subject to income tax.

b. Nonqualified Distributions

Any distribution from a Roth IRA that does not meet the requirements described in Section a, above, is automatically a nonqualified distribution. You might have to pay income tax on the distribution depending on whether it consists of contributions or earnings. Remember, the rule is that any nonqualified distribution (or portion thereof) that consists of contributions to the IRA will not be taxed, but any nonqualified distribution (or portion thereof) that consists of earnings in the IRA will be taxed. As explained above, the law presumes (to your advantage) that contributions come out before earnings. That means that some or all of your nonqualified distribution will escape income tax as long as you have not previously withdrawn all of your contributions.

> **EXAMPLE:** You have contributed $2,000 to a Roth IRA in each of the years 2001, 2002 and 2003. By June 2003, you had accumulated $7,000, of which $6,000 was from contributions and $1,000 was from earnings. In December, you withdrew $6,000 from your IRA. Although the distribution was nonqualified (because it did not meet the five-year requirement), the $6,000 was nontaxable because it was all attributable to your contributions. In April 2004, you contributed another $2,000 to your Roth IRA. By December, you had a total of $3,200 in the IRA. Only $2,000 was attributable to contributions because you had already withdrawn the contributions for prior years. The remaining $1,200 represented earnings. You decided to withdraw $3,000. The entire distribution is nonqualified, but the $2,000 attributable to contributions would be tax-free. Only $1,000 of the distribution is attributable to earnings, and that portion will be subject to income tax.

4. Ordering of Distributions

You might think you should be able to pick and choose which amounts come out of your Roth IRA first. For example if you take a distribution before the five-year holding period is up, you would want to take your contributions first because they are not subject to tax or penalties. Or if you converted one of your traditional IRAs six years ago and another one of your traditional IRAs two years ago, you would want to take a distribution from the one that you converted six years ago because those converted amounts satisfy the five-year holding period.

Sadly, you cannot pick and choose the origin of each distribution you take. Instead, the distributions come out according to certain ordering rules set out in the Tax Code. Serendipitously, those ordering rules are quite favorable to you and your pocketbook. Distributions are deemed to come out of your Roth IRA in the following order.

- Regular Roth IRA contributions come out first.
- Converted amounts, starting with the amounts first converted, come out next.
- Earnings come out last.

> **EXAMPLE:** You have two traditional IRAs: IRA #1 and IRA #2. In 2001, you convert IRA #1, then valued at $10,000, to a Roth IRA. In 2005, you convert IRA #2, valued at $20,000, to a

Roth IRA. You also have a separate contributory Roth IRA, which you established in 2001 and to which you have been making annual contributions of $2,000. By 2009, the contributory Roth IRA has grown to $15,000, of which $8,000 are contributions and $7,000 are earnings. In November 2009 on your 40th birthday, you withdraw $25,000 to pay for your trip to India. The source of the distribution is deemed to be:

$8,000 from Roth IRA contributions;

$10,000 from the oldest converted amount (IRA #1);

$7,000 from the next oldest converted amount (IRA #2).

The $8,000 of contributions are not subject to either income tax or the early distribution penalty because they are all from nondeductible after-tax contributions.

The $10,000 deemed to be from IRA #1 is also not subject to either income tax (which you already paid in the year of conversion) or the early distribution penalty (because the conversion occurred more than five years before).

The remaining $7,000 will not be subject to income tax because it was converted from a traditional IRA and you already paid tax on it in 2005. However, it will be subject to an early distribution penalty of $700 (10% of $7,000) because it was distributed within five years of the conversion and

you are younger than 59½. (See Section F.2, below, for more information about the early distribution penalty.)

5. Rollovers

If you take a distribution from a Roth IRA with the intention of rolling it over (transferring it to another IRA), you may roll it over only to another Roth IRA. This is logical when you think about it. Distributions from a Roth IRA are all potentially tax-free, whereas most, if not all, distributions from a traditional IRA or a qualified plan are taxable. If you were allowed to mix plans indiscriminately, the IRS would have a hard time tracking the source of the various distributions to determine which funds are taxable.

Except for the fact that you may only roll a Roth IRA to another Roth IRA, all the rules governing rollovers between IRAs apply to rollovers between Roth IRAs. Among the most important of those rules are the following:

- Once you take a distribution from a Roth IRA, you have only 60 days to complete the rollover to another Roth IRA.
- You may only make one Roth-to-Roth rollover in any 12-month period.

6. Loans

You may not borrow from your Roth IRA. Such a transaction is considered a prohibited transaction. (See Section F.3, below, for more about prohibited transactions.)

But a special rule, called the 60-day rule, essentially allows you to borrow from your Roth IRA for up to 60 days. The rule allows you to take money out of your Roth IRA without paying income tax or penalties, as long as you put the money into another Roth IRA or back into the same one within 60 days.

This strategy is subject to two restrictions:

- you may use this strategy with your Roth IRA only once in each 12-month period, and
- when you put the money back in, you must return exactly the amount you took out. If you retain some but not all of the amount withdrawn beyond the 60-day window, the retained amount will be treated as a distribution (see the ordering rules, above).

7. Hardship

There is no such thing as a hardship distribution from a Roth IRA.

8. Divorce Payments

If your divorce agreement states that you must give some or all of your Roth IRA assets to your former spouse, don't simply withdraw the funds and hand them over. If you do, any income tax or penalties that would apply if you were taking distributions for yourself will still apply, even though you are turning the money over to your former spouse.

But there is a way to transfer the funds and not incur either income tax or penalties. As long as the distribution is required by a divorce decree or separate maintenance decree or a written separation agreement, you may instruct the custodian of your Roth IRA to transfer some or all of the assets directly into a Roth IRA in your former spouse's name. Alternatively, you can roll over your former spouse's share into a new Roth IRA in your name and then change the name on the new Roth IRA to your former spouse's name. The critical point in each case is to be sure your former spouse does not take possession of the funds before they are deposited into a Roth IRA in his or her name.

 You would be wise to have a lawyer draft or review the transfer instructions to the custodian because of possible overlapping federal income tax and state family law rules. The lawyer should know whether the federal rules preempt the state or vice versa—and can prepare the instructions accordingly.

9. Mandatory Distributions

During your lifetime, you are not required to take distributions from a Roth IRA. Ever. In fact, you could die without ever having removed a cent.

After you die, however, your beneficiaries must begin taking distributions, unless your beneficiary is your spouse. Your spouse can continue to defer distributions until his or her death.

 For more information about mandatory distributions from Roth IRAs and other retirement plans, see is *IRAs, 401(k)s & Other Retirement Plans: Taking Your Money Out*, by Twila Slesnick and John C. Suttle (Nolo).

F. Penalties

Roth IRAs are subject to virtually the same penalties as traditional IRAs, whether you contribute too much one year, take a distribution too early or do something inappropriate with the money. Here are the consequences.

Infractions and Their Consequences	
Problem	**Penalty**
Excess Contributions	6% of the excess
Early Distributions	10% of the distribution
Prohibited Transactions:	
• If you, as the owner of the Roth IRA, engage in the transaction:	Disqualification
• If someone other than owner engages in the transaction:	15% of transaction
Required Distributions:	
• During your lifetime:	No penalty, because you as the owner are never required to take a distribution from your Roth IRA
• After your death:	Fifty percent of the amount your beneficiaries should have taken out, but didn't

1. Excess Contributions

If you contribute too much to your Roth IRA, you will be fined 6% of the excess over what you were permitted to contribute. The 6% will be assessed again for every year any excess remains in the account. The penalty can never exceed 6% of the total value of the Roth IRA, though, determined as of the end of the tax year.

Suppose you contribute the maximum $2,000 to your Roth IRA in February. December comes and goes. In April, you slave over your records as you begin to prepare your tax return, and you discover that you are eligible to contribute only $1,800 to your Roth IRA. Now what?

You will have to take some corrective action or pay a penalty. Here are your options:

a. Option One: Remove Excess Before Due Date

One way you can correct the error is to remove the excess contribution plus any earnings attributable to the excess by the due date of your tax return (plus extensions, if you requested and received an extension for filing your tax return).

When you remove the contribution and earnings, you must report the earnings, but not the contribution, as income on your tax return. Report the earnings for the year you actually deposited the excess contribution in your Roth IRA. (The year you remove the funds might be different from the year you made the excess contribution.) If you are not yet 59½, you will have to pay a 10% early distribution penalty on the earnings, but not on the excess contribution.

EXAMPLE: You contributed $2,000 to your Roth IRA in February 2001. You did not contribute to any other IRAs or retirement plans during the year. At the end of the year, you discovered that the maximum you were permitted to contribute to your Roth IRA was only $1,800. The excess contribution is $200.

If you earned $160 on the $2,000 Roth IRA contribution, then $16 of it would be attributable to the $200 excess. (200/2,000 x 160 = $16). Therefore you must remove $216—the earnings of $16 plus the excess of $200.

If you remove the money by April 15, you won't owe an excess contribution penalty on the $216. (If you received an extension for filing your tax return, you have until the extended due date.) If you are younger than 59½, however, you might owe an early distribution penalty on the earnings (the $16), unless you can find an exception that applies. (See Section 2.c, below, for more about the early distribution penalty and its exceptions.)

On your tax return you will report the $16 of earnings that you withdrew.

b. Option Two: Transfer Excess to Traditional IRA

A second option is to transfer the ineligible Roth IRA contribution, plus any earnings attributable to the excess, to a traditional IRA by the due date of your tax return (plus extensions, if you requested and received an extension for filing your tax return). This works as long as you qualify to make a traditional IRA contribution. (See Chapter 8, Section A.1, for a discussion of who qualifies to make a traditional IRA contribution.) You cannot simply withdraw the funds from the Roth IRA and then deposit them into your traditional IRA. The transaction has to be performed by the custodian; you cannot take possession of the funds.

As long as the excess contribution and the earnings are transferred directly from one account to the other, there will be no income tax or penalties.

EXAMPLE: In 2001, you contributed $2,000 to your Roth IRA and nothing to your traditional IRA. In February 2002, as you were preparing your tax return for the year 2001, you discovered that your modified AGI was $200,000, which means you didn't qualify to make a Roth IRA contribution. You calculated that your earnings on the $2,000 were $18. You called the bank that is serving as custodian of both your Roth IRA and your traditional IRA and instructed the person in charge of your accounts to transfer the $2,018 from your Roth IRA to your traditional IRA. As long as the transfer is completed before the due date of your tax return, there will be no excess contribution penalty.

Note that in the above example, you transferred more than $2,000 into the traditional IRA. (It was $2,000 plus $18 of earnings.) However, the law treats the entire transaction as though the $2,000 contribution was originally made to the traditional IRA—as though you never made the Roth IRA contribution in the first place. The $18 of earnings is presumed to be the amount the $2,000 would have earned if it had been in the traditional IRA all along.

c. Option Three: Remove Excess After Due Date

Another option is to remove the excess funds late—after the due date (or extended due date) of your tax return—and leave the earnings in the account.

You must pay a 6% penalty on the excess contribution, but no penalty on the earnings if you leave them in the Roth IRA. Presumably, Congress considers the 6% penalty on the contribution an adequate payback for any benefit you might derive from leaving the earnings in the account.

EXAMPLE: In 2001, you contributed $200 too much to your Roth IRA, and you forgot to remove the excess before the due date of your tax return. The earnings on the excess are $16. You remove the $200 after your tax filing deadline and leave the $16 of earnings in the account. You will owe a penalty of $12 on the contribution (6% of $200), but no income tax or penalties on the earnings.

d. Option Four: Leave Excess In, Apply to Next Year

Your fourth option is to leave the excess in the Roth IRA and apply it to the next year's contribution.

If you choose this option, you will still have to pay the 6% excise tax on the contribution for the first year, because the excess remained in the account after the due date of your tax return. But as long as the excess does not exceed the amount you are permitted to contribute in the second year, there will be no penalty for that year.

EXAMPLE: In 2001, you contributed $200 too much to your Roth IRA. You left the excess in the account. In 2002 you qualify to make a $2,000 Roth IRA contribution. You apply the $200 excess from the previous year and add an additional $1,800 in cash by the due date of your tax return to complete the $2,000 contribution. You

must still pay a $12 penalty for 2001 (6% of $200), but no penalty will be assessed for 2002 or beyond.

If you contribute to both a traditional IRA and a Roth IRA in the same year, and if you make an excess combined contribution (for example, the combined contributions total more than $2,000), your traditional IRA contribution is deemed to have been made first, which means that the excess contribution is generally deemed made to the Roth IRA.

EXAMPLE: In 2002, you contribute $2,000 to a Roth IRA and $2,000 to a traditional IRA, not realizing that your combined contribution to both IRAs is limited to $2,000. Because the traditional IRA contribution is deemed to be made first, you have made an excess contribution of $2,000 to your Roth IRA.

Report excess contributions on IRS Form 5329 for the year you made the excess contribution. Do not use a subsequent year's Form 5329. You can find a sample copy of Form 5329 in the Appendix.

EXAMPLE: You made an excess contribution of $200 to your Roth IRA in 2001. You discovered your error in June 2002 long after you filed your tax return. You should complete a year 2001 Form 5329—and not a year 2002 Form—even though you have already filed the rest of your tax return. Sign and date the form and send it in with your check for $12 (6% of $200), which is the amount of the excess contribution penalty.

2. Early Distributions

The government's goal in creating the Roth IRA was to encourage people to save for retirement. Like all retirement plan rules, the Roth IRA rules are designed to encourage you to leave your contributions alone until you are within striking distance of retirement age. If you take money out of your Roth IRA too early, you could be subject to penalties.

In general, distributions from retirement plans before age 59½ are considered early distributions and are subject to both regular income tax and a 10% early distribution penalty. Roth IRA distributions are different, primarily because some of the distributions are not subject to income tax. Distributions that are not subject to income tax are generally—but not always—exempt from the early distribution penalty, as well.

Understanding how the early distribution penalty applies to Roth IRAs is complicated by the fact that there are two types of distributions (qualified and nonqualified) and a special set of rules for converted amounts.

 As you will see from the discussion below, determining whether you will have to pay an early distribution penalty requires you to know whether your distribution is qualified or nonqualified. Those terms were discussed in Section E.3, above, in the context of income taxation of distributions. In this section, the context is early distributions. However, the definitions of qualified and nonqualified distributions, as well as the rules that govern them, are the same in both contexts.

a. Qualified Distributions

Qualified distributions from Roth IRAs are not subject to the early distribution penalty no matter when you take them. It's as simple as that. As mentioned above, the early distribution penalty applies only to distributions that are included in income—those that are required to be reported on your tax return. Because all qualified distributions from Roth IRAs are tax-free, they are all exempt from the early distribution penalty.

b. Nonqualified Distributions

Whether or not you will pay an early distribution penalty on a nonqualified distribution depends on what the distribution consists of: contributions, earnings or converted amounts.

i. Distributions of Contributions

Distributions of contributions that you have made to your Roth IRA are never subject to the early distribution penalty. Period. This is true whether or not the distribution is qualified. That's because the distributions are not taxed (remember— these were nondeductible contributions, which means you paid tax on them before putting them in the Roth IRA in the first place), and the early distribution penalty generally applies only to taxable distributions.

ii. Distributions of Earnings

You will have to pay an early distribution penalty on any earnings that are part of a nonqualified distribution from your Roth IRA—unless an exception applies (see Section c, below, for a discussion of exceptions).

 Recall that contributions are deemed to come out of your Roth IRA first—before earnings. That means some or all of your nonqualified distributions will escape the early distribution penalty, as long as you have not previously withdrawn all of your contributions.

EXAMPLE: In 2001, you established a Roth IRA. You contributed $2,000 in 2001, 2002 and 2003. By November of the year 2004, the account had grown to $6,600. Finding yourself a little strapped for cash, you withdraw $4,000 from the account in late No-

vember. Because the distribution is less than your total contributions of $6,000, the $4,000 will not be subject to either income tax or the early distribution penalty.

iii. Distributions of Converted Amounts

A special rule exempts converted amounts—amounts that you contribute to a Roth IRA by converting or rolling over a traditional IRA—from the early distribution penalty in the year of the conversion or rollover, as long as you roll over the entire amount of the distribution.

But be careful: There are still two ways to get caught by the early distribution penalty. You might use some of the converted amount to pay the income tax you owe on the conversion, or you might withdraw the converted amount too soon after the rollover was completed. But remember, the early distribution penalty never applies if you are older than 59½ at the time of the distribution—or if another exception applies. (See Section c, below, for a list of exceptions to the early distribution penalty.)

Paying income tax with converted amounts: If you qualify to convert a traditional IRA to a Roth IRA (see Section C.2, above), any portion of the converted amount that is actually rolled over (contributed) to the Roth IRA will not be subject to an early distribution penalty. Even though the converted amount is included on your tax return and you pay income tax on it, you are spared the early distribution penalty if you roll over everything. But if you use some of the converted amount to pay the income tax liability instead of rolling it over, the portion used for taxes will be subject to the early distribution penalty—unless you are older than 59½ or an exception applies. (See Section c, below, for a list of exceptions to the early distribution penalty.)

Withdrawing converted amounts too soon: Even though converted amounts in a Roth IRA are after-tax amounts (because you paid tax in the year of conversion), if you withdraw any converted amounts within five years of the conversion, that portion of the distribution will be treated as though it is taxable, but only for purposes of determining the early distribution penalty (they will remain tax free).

EXAMPLE: You have a traditional IRA to which you have been making $2,000 deductible contributions each year. By 2001, when you are 50, the account has grown to $15,000. You convert the IRA to a Roth IRA, paying tax on the entire $15,000. The following year, you withdraw $10,000 to bail your son out of jail. Because you are younger than 59½ and you withdrew the $10,000 within five years of converting your traditional IRA to a Roth IRA, you must pay an early distribution penalty of $1,000 ($10,000 x 10%). You will not owe regular income tax on the $10,000, however.

The portion of a distribution that is subject to the early distribution penalty is limited to the amount that you included in your taxable income and reported on your tax return in the year of conversion.

EXAMPLE: You have a traditional IRA to which you have made deductible contributions of $4,000 and nondeductible (after-tax) contributions of $6,000. By 2001, the account has grown to $17,000. You convert the IRA to a Roth IRA, paying tax on $11,000. (You don't have to pay tax on the $6,000 of nondeductible contributions.) In the year 2002 when you are 52, you withdraw $17,000 to help your daughter start a new business. You must pay an early distribution penalty on the $11,000 because that is the amount that was included on your income tax return in the year of conversion. The early distribution penalty is $1,100 ($11,000 x 10%).

The earnings on converted amounts are treated exactly the same as earnings on contributory amounts. Only qualified distributions of earnings escape the early distribution penalty, unless an exception to the early distribution penalty applies. (See Section c, below, for a list of exceptions.)

c. Exceptions to the Early Distribution Penalty

Once you reach age 59½, none of the distributions you take from your Roth IRA will be subject to an early distribution penalty. This is, quite simply, because they won't be early distributions. That is true whether the distribution is a qualified distribution or not. It is also true regardless of the source of the funds—whether from converted amounts, regular contributions or earnings.

 Bear in mind, however, that if the distribution is a nonqualified distribution, the portion attributable to earnings could be subject to regular income tax, even though it might not be subject to an early distribution penalty.

But if you are not yet 59½, distributions that you take from your Roth IRA will be considered early. Although you won't have to pay a penalty on the portion that consists of earnings, you will have to pay a penalty on other portions (earnings, for example, or converted amounts that you withdraw prematurely) unless an exception applies. These are the exceptions:

i. Death

None of the distributions from your Roth IRA after you die are subject to the penalty, no matter how old you are when you die or how old your beneficiaries are when they withdraw the money. Your heirs will still have to pay income tax on the earnings portion of the distribution, though, if the five-year holding period was not met.

ii. Disability

If you become disabled, you can take any amount of money from your Roth IRA without penalty. But first you must satisfy the IRS's definition of disabled. Here's how it reads: You must be unable to "engage in any substantial gainful activity by reason of any medically determinable physical or mental impairment which can be expected to result in death or to be of long-continued and indefinite duration." However, the IRS's own regulations state that the gainful activity refers specifically to the type of work you were doing before becoming disabled. Thus it would seem that you need not be unfit for all work—just the work you customarily do.

iii. Periodic Payments

You can begin taking distributions from your Roth IRA regardless of your age as long as you take them in equal annual installments over your life expectancy. These distributions are called "substantially equal periodic payments."

To compute substantially equal periodic payments, you must use one of the IRS-approved methods for computing the payments—you cannot simply choose a monthly or annual payment that suits you. (See IRS Notice 89-25 in the Appendix for more information about how to calculate substantially equal payments.)

You must continue the payments for at least five years or until you are at least age 59½, whichever comes later. For example, if you begin at age 58, you must continue the payments for at least five years even though you pass age 59½ in the meantime. Or if you begin at age 52, you must continue until at least age 59½, even though more than five years have passed.

iv. Medical Expenses

Although you can take money out of your Roth IRA prior to age 59½ to pay for medical expenses, you won't escape the early distribution penalty entirely. The exemption applies only to the portion of your medical expenses that would be deductible on Schedule A of your tax return if you were to itemize deductions (whether or not you actually do itemize deductions). The remainder is subject to penalty.

> EXAMPLE: Your adjusted gross income is $50,000. You had medical bills of $6,000 during the year, which you paid with funds you withdrew from your Roth IRA. For income tax purposes, you are permitted to deduct medical expenses that exceed 7.5% of your adjusted gross income. Thus,
>
> Adjusted gross income (AGI) = $50,000;
>
> 7.5% of AGI (.075 x $50,000) = $3,750 nondeductible expenses;

Excess ($6,000 − $3,750) = $2,250 deductible expenses.

Although you took $6,000 from your Roth IRA to pay medical expenses, only $2,250 will escape the early distribution penalty. The remaining $3,750 will be subject to the penalty (unless you qualify for another exception). And that same portion that might be subject to the early distribution penalty could be subject to regular income tax, as well.

v. Health Insurance Premiums

People who are unemployed, or were recently unemployed, may draw money from a Roth IRA to pay health insurance premiums without penalty, as long as they satisfy the following conditions:

- They received unemployment compensation for at least 12 consecutive weeks.
- They received the funds from the Roth IRA during a year in which they received unemployment compensation or during the following year.
- They received the Roth IRA distribution no more than 60 days after they returned to work.

It might sound as though this won't work for you if you are self-employed. However, the rules specifically permit this exception if you were self-employed before you stopped working, as long as you would have qualified for unemployment compensation under state law except for the fact that you were self-employed.

vi. Higher Education Expenses

If you use Roth IRA distributions to pay higher education expenses, you will not have to pay the early distribution penalty if you satisfy the following requirements:

- You must use the money to pay the higher education expenses of you, your spouse, your child or your grandchild.
- You must use the money to pay for tuition, fees, books, supplies and equipment. You may also use the money for room and board if the student is carrying at least half of a normal study load (or is considered at least a half-time student).
- The distributions cannot exceed the amount of the higher education expenses. Furthermore, when computing the amount of the distribution that is exempt from the penalty, you must reduce the total expenses (tuition, fees and so on) by any tax-free scholarships or other tax-free assistance the student receives, not including loans, gifts or inheritances.

vii. Purchasing a First Home

You may take a distribution without penalty if the money is used to buy a first home. Although the purpose of this exception is to make it easier for people to buy a home, there is a lifetime distribution limit of only $10,000. Other restrictions include the following:

- You must use the Roth IRA money for the acquisition, construction or reconstruction of a home.
- You must use the funds within 120 days of receiving them. If the home purchase is canceled or delayed, you may roll the funds back into the same Roth IRA or into another Roth IRA, as long as you complete the rollover within 120 days of the initial distribution.
- You must use the funds for the benefit of a first-time home buyer. A first-time home buyer is someone who has had no interest in a principal residence during the two years ending on the date of purchase of the new home. If the individual happens to be married, then neither the individual nor the spouse may have owned any part of a principal residence during the preceding two-year period.
- The first-time home buyer can be you or your spouse. The buyer can also be an ancestor (for example, a parent, grandparent, great grandparent and so on), a child or a grandchild of either you or your spouse.
- The lifetime limit of $10,000 applies regardless of whose home is purchased or improved. If you withdraw $10,000 and give it to your child, your lifetime limit is used up and you may not use the exception for any future distribution (from any IRA, no matter what type), even if it

is to buy a house for a different relative or for yourself. The $10,000 does not have to be distributed all at once or even in a single year. For example, you could withdraw $5,000 one year, giving it to a qualified person for a home purchase, and then withdraw another $5,000 in a later year.

viii. Federal Tax Levy

If you owe back taxes, you can be reasonably certain the government will try to collect them. If you have assets in a Roth IRA, the government can take those assets (in other words, the IRS can levy on your Roth IRA) to pay your debt. If it does, those amounts taken for taxes will not be subject to the early distribution penalty even if you happen to be younger than 59½.

The IRS requires you to report the early distribution penalty on Form 5329 for the year of the early distribution. You can find a sample copy of the form in the Appendix.

3. Prohibited Transactions

The prohibited transaction rules for Roth IRAs are virtually identical to those for traditional IRAs. The rules are designed to keep you or any other disqualified person (see below) from using the assets for personal gain or from engaging in transactions that put the assets at risk.

A disqualified person is someone who might reasonably have access to your Roth IRA assets. In addition to you, such persons include your spouse, your lineal descendants (such as children and grandchildren) and your ancestors (such as parents and grandparents). The list also includes fiduciaries, who are the people responsible for handling the assets of the Roth IRA, such as a custodian or money manager.

The penalties for engaging in a prohibited transaction are severe. If you (the Roth IRA owner) or your beneficiary engages in the prohibited transaction, the Roth IRA is disqualified and all of the assets are considered distributed as of the first day of the year in which the prohibited transaction took place. You will have to pay income tax on the taxable portion of the entire account, and if you are not yet 59½, you will have to pay a 10% early distribution penalty, as well.

If a disqualified person (other than you or your beneficiary) engages in the prohibited transaction, the penalty is generally 15% of the transaction. If the transaction is not corrected, an additional tax of 100% is imposed. That's a total of 115%. But the disqualified person has to pay the penalty—not you.

These are the transactions to avoid. Note that these all refer to transactions that occur inside your Roth IRA or with the use of your Roth IRA assets.

- The sale, exchange or lease of any property between a disqualified person and the Roth IRA. For example, you cannot sell your house to your Roth IRA.

- The furnishing of goods or services or facilities between a disqualified person and the Roth IRA. For example, you cannot hire your spouse to manage the Roth IRA and pay him a big salary out of the Roth IRA assets.

- The lending of money or extending of credit between a disqualified person and the Roth IRA. For example, you cannot borrow from the Roth IRA to buy a car, even if you intend to return the money. If you want to use your Roth IRA assets to buy that car, you must withdraw the money permanently and hope you can find an exception to the early distribution penalty that applies (if you are younger than 59½).

- The transfer to or use by a disqualified person of any assets or income of the Roth IRA. For example, you cannot use Roth IRA funds to invest in a house (held by the Roth IRA) that you then occupy as your principal residence. Again, if you want to use the funds to buy yourself a house, you must withdraw the funds permanently. You must pay income tax on the distribution. But hopefully, you'll be able to use the $10,000 first-home exception to re-

duce any early distribution penalty that might apply. (See Section 2, above, for more information about the first-home exception.)

- Any act of self-dealing, which occurs when a disqualified person uses the assets or income of the Roth IRA for that person's own interest or benefit while the assets are still in the Roth IRA. For example, if your money manager invests all of your Roth IRA assets in the stock of a company of which she owns 80%, such an investment would clearly benefit her as a majority shareholder and, therefore, might be deemed a prohibited transaction.

- The receipt of payment by a fiduciary in connection with a transaction involving the income or assets of the plan. A kickback, for example.

If you engage in a prohibited transaction, you must file IRS Form 5329 with the IRS. (You can find a sample copy of Form 5329 in the Appendix.) Furthermore, your Roth IRA is disqualified from the moment of the transgression. All of the assets must be distributed and the taxable portion must be reported on your tax return, along with any early distribution penalty that applies.

If another disqualified person engages in the prohibited transaction, he or she must complete Form 5330 and pay the 15% penalty.

4. Life Insurance

You are not permitted to use assets in your Roth IRA to purchase life insurance that you hold inside your Roth IRA. If you do, the Roth IRA becomes disqualified as of the first day of the year during which you made the purchase, and you must pay income tax and possibly an early distribution penalty on the taxable portion of your Roth IRA.

5. Collectibles

Although you can invest your Roth IRA contributions in various securities—stocks, mutual funds and bonds, for example—you cannot invest your contributions in certain tangible items known as collectibles. The Tax Code carefully lists all those items that are considered collectibles, followed of course, by a list of exceptions.

Collectibles include the following:
- works of art
- rugs or antiques
- metals or gems
- stamps or coins, and
- alcoholic beverages.

Exceptions include the following:
- certain U.S. minted gold, silver and platinum coins
- coins issued under the laws of any state, and
- gold, silver, platinum or palladium bullion equal to or exceeding the minimum fineness required by a contract market for metals delivered in satisfaction of a regulated futures contract (and only if the bullion is in the physical possession of the Roth IRA custodian).

If you invest your Roth IRA assets in an unacceptable collectible, the amount of Roth IRA money you used to pay for it is considered a distribution—even if you don't actually withdraw the collectible (or any money) from your account. That means you will owe income tax on the amount that is considered a distribution (to the extent that amount would have been taxable, if distributed) and you must report an early distribution penalty on Form 5329 (unless you qualify for an exception). That's the bad news. The good news is that your mistake won't disqualify the Roth IRA. Furthermore, you can keep the collectible in your Roth IRA if you like. When it is ultimately distributed, the amount on which you have already paid tax will not be included in your income.

6. Pledging the Account As Security

If any portion of your Roth IRA is used as security for a loan to you (for example, you borrow money using your Roth IRA as collateral), that portion is treated as a distribution and it might be subject to income tax and an early distribution penalty (unless you qualify for an exception). You report the distribution on your tax return and include Form 5329 if you owe an early distribution penalty. The entire Roth IRA will not be disqualified, however.

 This is different from actually borrowing the funds from the Roth IRA. If you do that, the entire Roth IRA is disqualified. (See Section E.6, above.)

7. Mandatory Distribution Penalty

Although you are not required to take distributions from your Roth IRA during your lifetime, your beneficiaries must begin taking distributions after your death. Failure to do so will result in a penalty of 50% of the amount that they should have taken out but didn't.

 For more information about mandatory distributions from your Roth IRA see *IRAs, 401(k)s & Other Retirement Plans: Taking Your Money Out*, by Twila Slesnick and John Suttle (Nolo).

G. Multiple IRAs and Qualified Plans

It is only your income and your contribution to a traditional IRA that might affect your ability to make a contribution to a Roth IRA. Contributions to other types of retirement plans are irrelevant.

The most you can contribute each year to all of your traditional and Roth IRAs combined is $2,000. If you contribute $2,000 to a traditional IRA, you cannot make a Roth IRA contribution. If you contribute $1,500 to a Roth IRA, the most you can contribute to a traditional IRA is $500.

If your income from employment (including net self-employment income and other earnings from employment) is less than $2,000, your total contribution to all traditional and Roth IRAs combined is limited to those earnings. (See Section C.1.a, above, for more information about contribution limits.)

H. Terminating Your Roth IRA

Terminating your Roth IRA is easy. You just take all the money out. Once all the money has been distributed—for any reason—the Roth IRA is terminated. You might terminate your Roth IRA because you had to withdraw all of the funds to live on. Or perhaps you violated the prohibited transaction rules, which caused the Roth IRA to be disqualified and all of the assets deemed distributed.

R310-page 1 of 4

+ Retirement Resource Center

IRA Adoption Agreement

THE **Vanguard** GROUP.

Complete this form to establish a new or separate Vanguard traditional IRA *or* Vanguard Roth IRA.

- You can open only **one** type of IRA with this form. You must complete two IRA Adoption Agreements if you want to establish both a traditional IRA *and* a Roth IRA. You cannot use this form to convert a traditional IRA to a Roth IRA.
- If you will reach age 70½ during this calendar year, or are older and are required to take a minimum distribution from your retirement plan, please note:
  - **For asset transfers:** You can either take your required minimum distribution (RMD) before transferring the assets to us, or leave the amount of the RMD in your existing retirement plan and withdraw it prior to the distribution deadline (generally December 31).
  - **For rollovers:** You must take your RMD before rolling the assets over to us.

If you need assistance or other Vanguard forms, call us toll-free at **1-800-205-6189.** All IRA forms are available on our website at **www.vanguard.com/?serviceforms**. Return this completed form and any other required documents in the enclosed postage-paid envelope, or mail to: **The Vanguard Group, P.O. Box 1110, Valley Forge, PA 19482-1110.** For overnight delivery, mail to: **The Vanguard Group, 455 Devon Park Drive, Wayne, PA 19087.**

Please print in capital letters, preferably in black ink.

1. Type of IRA. *(Check only one.)* ☐ Traditional IRA *(Complete all sections except Section 4.)*   ☐ Roth IRA *(Complete all sections except Section 3.)*

2. IRA Registration

If this IRA is being established for a minor who has earned income, write the minor's name, and next to the name, the word *a minor.*

Social Security Number

Birth Date *(month, day, year)*

Name *(first, middle initial, last)*

Street Address or Box Number

City   State   Zip

Daytime Telephone Number

Evening Telephone Number

3. Traditional IRA Instructions *(If you are establishing a traditional IRA, check all that apply in this section, then proceed to Section 5. You can find fund numbers and minimum initial investment amounts in* Vanguard Funds for Retirement Investing, *in* Facts on Funds® for Retirement Investing, *or on our website at* **www.vanguard.com**.*)*

A. By asset transfer from an existing traditional IRA. *(If you are transferring assets to Vanguard from a traditional IRA held by another custodian, check one box below, and complete the enclosed Asset Transfer Authorization in addition to this adoption agreement. You will provide investment instructions in Section 3 of the Asset Transfer Authorization. Vanguard will contact your current custodian to arrange the transfer.)*

☐ **Asset transfer from an existing traditional IRA.** *(Check this box if your current traditional IRA contains either all personal contributions, or a combination of personal contributions and assets previously rolled over from an employer-sponsored retirement plan.)*

☐ **Asset transfer from an existing direct rollover traditional IRA.** *(Check this box if your current traditional IRA contains **only** assets previously rolled over from an employer-sponsored retirement plan.)*

B. **By check.** *(Make your check payable to Vanguard Fiduciary Trust Company.)*

R310-page 2 of 4

☐ **Annual contribution.** *(Contributions to all your traditional and Roth IRAs cannot exceed a total of $2,000 per year.)*

Fund Number	Fund Name	For Tax Year	Dollar Amount *($1,000 minimum initial investment for most funds)*
☐☐☐☐	☐	☐☐☐☐	$☐,☐☐☐
☐☐☐☐	☐	☐☐☐☐	$☐,☐☐☐

Annual custodial fee of $10 for each fund selected* $☐☐

Total Amount $☐,☐☐☐

☐ **Rollover from a previously held traditional IRA.** *(Check this box if you have possession of the traditional IRA assets you had held at another institution. You must deposit the full value of your assets—including any taxes that were withheld—within 60 days for the rollover to remain tax deferred. If you need more space, provide the information on a separate sheet.)*

Fund Number	Fund Name	% of Total *(whole percentage)*		Dollar Amount *($1,000 minimum initial investment for most funds)*
☐☐☐☐	☐	☐☐%	OR	$☐,☐☐☐,☐☐☐
☐☐☐☐	☐	☐☐%	OR	$☐,☐☐☐,☐☐☐
☐☐☐☐	☐	☐☐%	OR	$☐,☐☐☐,☐☐☐

Percentages must total 100%.

Annual custodial fee of $10 for each fund selected* $☐☐

Total Amount $☐,☐☐☐,☐☐☐

4. **Roth IRA Instructions** *(Check all that apply. You can find fund numbers and minimum initial investment amounts in Vanguard Funds for Retirement Investing, in Facts on Funds® for Retirement Investing, or on our website at www.vanguard.com.)*

A. ☐ **By asset transfer from an existing Roth IRA.** *(If you are transferring assets to Vanguard from a Roth IRA held by another custodian, complete the enclosed Asset Transfer Authorization in addition to this adoption agreement. You will provide investment instructions in Section 3 of the Asset Transfer Authorization. Vanguard will contact your current custodian to arrange the transfer.)*

B. **By check.** *(Make your check payable to Vanguard Fiduciary Trust Company.)*

☐ **Annual contribution.** *(Contributions to all your traditional and Roth IRAs cannot exceed a total of $2,000 per year.)*

Fund Number	Fund Name	For Tax Year	Dollar Amount *($1,000 minimum initial investment for most funds)*
☐☐☐☐	☐	☐☐☐☐	$☐,☐☐☐
☐☐☐☐	☐	☐☐☐☐	$☐,☐☐☐

Annual custodial fee of $10 for each fund selected* $☐☐

Total Amount $☐,☐☐☐

*The annual custodial fee of $10 is applied to each fund account having assets of less than $5,000. However, this fee is waived for those who have mutual fund and variable annuity assets at Vanguard totaling $50,000 or more.

R310-page 3 of 4

☐ **Rollover from a previously held Roth IRA.** *(Check this box if you have possession of the Roth IRA assets you had held at another institution. You must deposit the full value of your assets—including any taxes that were withheld—within 60 days for the rollover to remain tax-deferred. If you need more space, provide the information on a separate sheet.)*

Fund Number	Fund Name	% of Total *(whole percentages)*		Dollar Amount *($1,000 minimum initial investment for most funds)*
☐☐☐☐☐	☐	☐☐☐%	OR	$☐,☐☐☐,☐☐☐
☐☐☐☐☐	☐	☐☐☐%	OR	$☐,☐☐☐,☐☐☐
☐☐☐☐☐	☐	☐☐☐%	OR	$☐,☐☐☐,☐☐☐

Percentages must total 100%.

Annual custodial fee of $10 for each fund selected* $☐☐

Total Amount $☐,☐☐☐,☐☐☐

5. **Beneficiary Designation** *(Complete this section only if you are naming an individual, trust, or charity as your beneficiary. If your beneficiary designation is more complex or if you want information on why naming a beneficiary for your IRA is important, request a Vanguard Beneficiary Designation Option kit and send the completed and signed Beneficiary Designation/Change Form for Retirement Accounts along with this adoption agreement.)*

Note: You must provide information on your beneficiary designations in the exact format that follows. To name more than two primary or three secondary beneficiaries, photocopy the appropriate sections (5A and/or 5B) before filling them out, and return the additional copies with this adoption agreement.

A. **Primary Beneficiaries**

Vanguard will pass ownership of your IRA to your primary beneficiaries following your death. Your primary beneficiaries will share equally in your IRA unless you specify different percentages (totaling 100%) below. If a primary beneficiary dies before you, his or her share of your IRA will be divided equally among the surviving primary beneficiaries. *Important:* If you designate more than one primary beneficiary without indicating percentages, equal percentages totaling 100% will be allocated to each beneficiary.

☐

Individual *(first, middle initial, last)*, Trust Name, or Charity Name

Relationship: ☐ ☐ ☐☐☐%   ☐☐-☐☐-☐☐☐☐
Spouse Other Percentage   Birth Date / Trust Date *(month, day, year)*

☐☐☐-☐☐-☐☐☐☐ **OR** ☐☐-☐☐☐☐☐☐☐
Social Security Number *(for an individual)*   Employer Identification Number *(for a trust or charity)*

☐

Individual *(first, middle initial, last)*, Trust Name, or Charity Name

Relationship: ☐ ☐ ☐☐☐%   ☐☐-☐☐-☐☐☐☐
Spouse Other Percentage   Birth Date / Trust Date *(month, day, year)*

☐☐☐-☐☐-☐☐☐☐ **OR** ☐☐-☐☐☐☐☐☐☐
Social Security Number *(for an individual)*   Employer Identification Number *(for a trust or charity)*

SIGNATURE REQUIRED ON NEXT PAGE   *(over, please)*

*The annual custodial fee of $10 is applied to each fund account having assets of less than $5,000. However, this fee is waived for those who have mutual fund and variable annuity assets at Vanguard totaling $50,000 or more.

R310-page 4 of 4

B. Secondary Beneficiaries

Vanguard will transfer ownership of your IRA to your secondary beneficiaries only if there are no surviving primary beneficiaries at the time of your death. If this happens, your secondary beneficiaries will share equally in your IRA unless you specify different percentages (totaling 100%) below. If there are no surviving secondary beneficiaries at the time of your death, Vanguard will transfer ownership of your IRA to your estate.

Important: If you designate more than one secondary beneficiary without indicating percentages, equal percentages totaling 100% will be allocated to each beneficiary.

Individual *(first, middle initial, last)*, Trust Name, or Charity Name

Relationship: Spouse Other Percentage %

Birth Date / Trust Date *(month, day, year)*

Social Security Number *(for an individual)* OR Employer Identification Number *(for a trust or charity)*

Individual *(first, middle initial, last)*, Trust Name, or Charity Name

Relationship: Spouse Other Percentage %

Birth Date / Trust Date *(month, day, year)*

Social Security Number *(for an individual)* OR Employer Identification Number *(for a trust or charity)*

Individual *(first, middle initial, last)*, Trust Name, or Charity Name

Relationship: Spouse Other Percentage %

Birth Date / Trust Date *(month, day, year)*

Social Security Number *(for an individual)* OR Employer Identification Number *(for a trust or charity)*

6. Shareholder Signature—YOU MUST SIGN BELOW

I hereby adopt the Vanguard Individual Retirement Custodial Account Agreement that is incorporated herein by reference and acknowledge having received and read it. I further acknowledge having received and read the Vanguard IRA® Disclosure Statement and the prospectus for each Vanguard fund elected under this Agreement. Under penalty of perjury, I certify that my Social Security number on this form is correct.

Please sign here. Your IRA cannot be established without your signature.

Signature *(If the IRA owner is a minor, a legal guardian or custodian must sign.)*

Date *(month, day, year)*

Vanguard Fiduciary Trust Company, Custodian

Accepted by: _____ Title: ___Secretary___

Glossary

Accrued benefit: In the case of a defined benefit plan, a benefit is the amount a participant receives at retirement. Generally, the participant receives the benefit as a monthly payment for the remainder of his or her life. An accrued benefit is the amount of a participant's benefit as of a particular point in time.

Adjusted gross income (AGI): A person's AGI is his or her total taxable income after it has been reduced by certain expenses such as qualified plan contributions or IRA contributions or alimony payments. AGI does not take into account any itemized deductions.

Affiliated service group: A group of organizations that, by virtue of business relationships, are treated as a single employer for retirement plan purposes.

After-tax dollars: The amount of income left after all income taxes have been withheld or paid.

C corporation: A regular corporation. The "C" refers to the chapter of the Tax Code that governs corporations. A C corporation is a separate legal entity (an artificial person), subject to tax and characterized primarily by the following: i) limited liability (owners lose only what they invest), ii) easy transferability of ownership (through the sale of stock), iii) continuity of life, and iv) centralized management. If your business is organized as a corporation, you are not self-employed.

Commonly controlled businesses: All partnerships, sole proprietorships, and other businesses that are under common ownership are commonly controlled business. Also, all corporations that are members of a controlled group (see entry, below) are considered a commonly controlled business. Commonly controlled businesses are treated as a single employer for retirement plan purposes.

Compensation: The amount of a participant's taxable and non-taxable remuneration that is considered for retirement plan purposes. Different definitions of compensation are used for deduction purposes, for calculation of maximum benefits and contributions, and for nondiscrimination purposes.

Controlled group of corporations: Two or more corporations that, by virtue of their common ownership, are treated as a single entity for retirement plan purposes.

Conversion: A rollover contribution to a Roth IRA from a non-Roth IRA. Also called a qualified rollover contribution.

Custodian: A person or entity who is in possession of property belonging to another. For example, the custodian of an IRA is the institution that holds the stocks, bonds, cash or other property of the IRA, even though the assets actually belong to the individual who established and funded the IRA.

Defined benefit plan: A type of qualified plan that promises to pay each participant a specific dollar amount as an annuity (usually in monthly payments) at retirement. The employer contributions for all participants are pooled into one account; payments to all participants are paid out of that account.

Defined contribution plan: A type of qualified plan in which contributions are allocated to a separate account for each participant. Although the amount of the contribution is set by the plan, the amount that the participant will receive upon retirement is not guaranteed—it depends on how the money is managed.

Discretionary contribution: An employer contribution that is not fixed in amount and is not required to be made every year. The employer makes the contribution at its discretion.

Distribution: A payout of property (such as shares of stock) or cash from a retirement plan or IRA to the participant or beneficiary.

Earned income: Income received for providing goods or services. Earned income might be wages or salary or net profit from a business.

Elective contribution or elective deferral: These terms are used interchangeably to refer to a retirement plan option that allows an employee to have part of his or her pay contributed by the employer to a retirement plan rather than included in current wages and paid in cash. The deferred pay is not taxable to the employee until it is distributed from the retirement plan.

Employer plan: A retirement plan that must be established by an employer—a business—rather than by an individual. For example, profit sharing plans, money purchase pension plans, defined benefit plans, SEPs and SIMPLE IRAs are all employer plans. Traditional IRAs and Roth IRAs are not employer plans; they must be established by individuals.

Experience losses: In a defined benefit plan, experience losses are those resulting from differences between predicted outcomes and actual outcomes—for example, a lower-than-expected return on investments.

Hardship distribution: A distribution from a profit sharing plan that is made because of the plan participant's immediate and heavy financial need. The distribution must be used to pay for medical expenses or post-secondary tuition, or to avoid foreclosure on a principal residence. The distribution cannot exceed the amount necessary to satisfy the need. If a plan participant receives a hardship distribution, he or she is prohibited from making contributions to the plan for at least 12 months after the distribution.

Inservice distribution: A distribution from an employer plan that a participant takes while he or she is still working for the employer that sponsors the plan.

Matching contribution: An employer contribution to a participant's account that is based on the participant's elective deferral.

Minimum funding requirement: The minimum amount an employer must contribute to properly fund a money purchase pension plan or a defined benefit plan in a given year.

Net earnings from self-employment: All self-employment income reduced by self-employment business expenses, including half of the self-employment tax and any Keogh or SEP contribution.

Net profit: Business income reduced by all deductible business expenses, except the self-employment tax deduction and the retirement plan deduction. If you are a sole proprietor who reports business income on Schedule C of your income tax return, your net profit is the number on the last line of Schedule C.

Nonelective contribution: An employer contribution that is not a matching or elective contribution and that the employee cannot elect to receive in cash.

One-participant plan: A plan that covers only owners, partners and their spouses who work in the business.

Participant (or active participant): An employee for whom an employer makes a retirement plan contribution.

Present value of accrued benefit: The value in today's dollars of the benefit a participant will receive at retirement.

Pre-tax dollars: Total taxable income before income taxes have been paid.

Prototype plan: An employer plan that has been approved by the IRS. Using the prototype plan of the financial institution that will hold the assets of the plan saves employers the cost of drafting a plan from scratch and seeking approval of the plan from the IRS. Although prototype plans contain certain design restrictions that make them less flexible than custom plans, they are appropriate for self-employed individuals with no employees.

Recharacterization: The movement of assets from one type of IRA to another, such as from a Roth IRA to a traditional IRA or vice versa, in a transaction that reverses or cancels a previous transaction. For example, if a traditional IRA is converted to a Roth IRA and later unconverted and put back into a traditional IRA, the process of undoing the conversion is a recharacterization. The law views such a transaction as though the assets had originally gone into the traditional IRA and not the Roth IRA.

Rollover: An employee's transfer of retirement funds from one retirement plan to another plan of the same type—or to an IRA—without incurring a tax liability.

S corporation: A corporation that has made an election (an election under "subchapter S" of the Tax Code—hence the name) not to be taxed as a regular corporation. Instead, shareholders (owners) include on their personal tax returns the income from the corporation, which might include capital gains, ordinary income and various deductions. By making an S election, shareholders enjoy the liability protection a regular corporation does, but also avoid a double tax. If your business is organized as an S corporation, you are not self-employed.

Salary reduction contribution: Same as elective contribution or elective deferral (see entry, above).

Self-employment tax deduction: The amount of the self-employment tax that you can deduct on your tax return. One half of the self-employment tax is deductible.

Tax deduction: An item of expense that may be used to offset income on a tax return.

Tax deferral: The postponement of tax payments until a future year.

Trustee: A person or entity that holds legal title to the property in a trust. For example, a qualified retirement plan is a trust that is administered by a trustee who manages the trust property for the plan participant.

Unrelated business taxable income (UBTI): The income earned by a tax-exempt entity from a trade or business that is unrelated to its tax-exempt purpose. A retirement plan (which is a tax-exempt entity) earns UBTI when it owns an interest in a trade or business that produces income to the plan. If your retirement plan earns UBTI, you must file a tax return for it.

Vested benefit: The portion of a participant's retirement plan accumulation that is not forfeitable. In other words, the portion that a participant may keep after leaving the business that sponsors the plan; or the portion that goes to a participant's beneficiary if the participant dies. ■

Appendix

IRS Forms and Notices

Form 1040   U.S. Individual Income Tax Return A/3

Schedule SE   Self-Employment Tax A/5

Notice 89-25   Question and Answer 12 .... A/7

Form 5500-EZ   Annual Return of One-Participant (Owners and Their
                   Spouses) Retirement Plan A/9

Form 990-T   Exempt Organization Business Income Tax Return A/23

Form 5330   Return of Excise Taxes Related to Employee Benefit Plans A/25

Form 5329   Additional Taxes Attributable to IRAs, Other Qualified
                   Retirement Plans, Annuities, Modified Endowment
                   Contracts, and MSAs A/29

Form SS-4   Application for Employer Identification Number A/31

Form 8606   Non deductible IRAs A/35

Form 1040

Department of the Treasury—Internal Revenue Service

U.S. Individual Income Tax Return 2000

(99)   IRS Use Only—Do not write or staple in this space.

For the year Jan. 1–Dec. 31, 2000, or other tax year beginning   , 2000, ending   , 20   OMB No. 1545-0074

Label

(See instructions on page 19.)

Use the IRS label. Otherwise, please print or type.

LABEL HERE

Your first name and initial   Last name   **Your social security number**

If a joint return, spouse's first name and initial   Last name   **Spouse's social security number**

Home address (number and street). If you have a P.O. box, see page 19.   Apt. no.

City, town or post office, state, and ZIP code. If you have a foreign address, see page 19.

▲ **Important!** ▲

You **must** enter your SSN(s) above.

Presidential Election Campaign

(See page 19.)

Note. Checking "Yes" will not change your tax or reduce your refund.

Do you, or your spouse if filing a joint return, want $3 to go to this fund? . . . ▶

	You		Spouse	
	☐ Yes	☐ No	☐ Yes	☐ No

Filing Status

Check only one box.

1. ☐ Single
2. ☐ Married filing joint return (even if only one had income)
3. ☐ Married filing separate return. Enter spouse's social security no. above and full name here. ▶ _____
4. ☐ Head of household (with qualifying person). (See page 19.) If the qualifying person is a child but not your dependent, enter this child's name here. ▶ _____
5. ☐ Qualifying widow(er) with dependent child (year spouse died ▶ _____). (See page 19.)

Exemptions

If more than six dependents, see page 20.

6a ☐ **Yourself.** If your parent (or someone else) can claim you as a dependent on his or her tax return, **do not** check box 6a . . . .

b ☐ **Spouse** . . . .

c **Dependents:**

(1) First name Last name	(2) Dependent's social security number	(3) Dependent's relationship to you	(4)✔ if qualifying child for child tax credit (see page 20)
			☐
			☐
			☐
			☐
			☐
			☐

No. of boxes checked on 6a and 6b _____

No. of your children on 6c who:
• lived with you _____
• did not live with you due to divorce or separation (see page 20) _____

Dependents on 6c not entered above _____

Add numbers entered on lines above ▶ ☐

d Total number of exemptions claimed . . . .

Income

Attach Forms W-2 and W-2G here. Also attach Form(s) 1099-R if tax was withheld.

If you did not get a W-2, see page 21.

Enclose, but do not attach, any payment. Also, please use Form 1040-V.

7	Wages, salaries, tips, etc. Attach Form(s) W-2	7
8a	**Taxable interest.** Attach Schedule B if required	8a
b	**Tax-exempt interest. Do not** include on line 8a . . .	8b
9	Ordinary dividends. Attach Schedule B if required	9
10	Taxable refunds, credits, or offsets of state and local income taxes (see page 22) . .	10
11	Alimony received	11
12	Business income or (loss). Attach Schedule C or C-EZ	12
13	Capital gain or (loss). Attach Schedule D if required. If not required, check here ▶ ☐	13
14	Other gains or (losses). Attach Form 4797	14
15a	Total IRA distributions . 15a _____ b Taxable amount (see page 23)	15b
16a	Total pensions and annuities 16a _____ b Taxable amount (see page 23)	16b
17	Rental real estate, royalties, partnerships, S corporations, trusts, etc. Attach Schedule E	17
18	Farm income or (loss). Attach Schedule F	18
19	Unemployment compensation	19
20a	Social security benefits . 20a _____ b Taxable amount (see page 25)	20b
21	Other income. List type and amount (see page 25) ------------------------	21
22	Add the amounts in the far right column for lines 7 through 21. This is your **total income** ▶	22

Adjusted Gross Income

23	IRA deduction (see page 27)	23
24	Student loan interest deduction (see page 27)	24
25	Medical savings account deduction. Attach Form 8853 .	25
26	Moving expenses. Attach Form 3903	26
27	One-half of self-employment tax. Attach Schedule SE .	27
28	Self-employed health insurance deduction (see page 29)	28
29	Self-employed SEP, SIMPLE, and qualified plans . .	29
30	Penalty on early withdrawal of savings	30
31a	Alimony paid b Recipient's SSN ▶ _____	31a
32	Add lines 23 through 31a	32
33	Subtract line 32 from line 22. This is your **adjusted gross income** . . . . ▶	33

For Disclosure, Privacy Act, and Paperwork Reduction Act Notice, see page 56.   Cat. No. 11320B   Form **1040** (2000)

Tax and Credits	**34** Amount from line 33 (adjusted gross income)	**34**
	35a Check if: ☐ **You** were 65 or older, ☐ Blind; ☐ **Spouse** was 65 or older, ☐ Blind. Add the number of boxes checked above and enter the total here . . . . ▶ **35a**	
	b If you are married filing separately and your spouse itemizes deductions, or you were a dual-status alien, see page 31 and check here . . . . . . ▶ **35b** ☐	
Standard Deduction for Most People	**36** Enter your **itemized deductions** from Schedule A, line 28, **or standard deduction** shown on the left. **But** see page 31 to find your standard deduction if you checked any box on line 35a or 35b **or** if someone can claim you as a dependent	**36**
Single: $4,400	**37** Subtract line 36 from line 34	**37**
Head of household: $6,450	**38** If line 34 is $96,700 or less, multiply $2,800 by the total number of exemptions claimed on line 6d. If line 34 is over $96,700, see the worksheet on page 32 for the amount to enter .	**38**
Married filing jointly or Qualifying widow(er): $7,350	**39 Taxable income.** Subtract line 38 from line 37. If line 38 is more than line 37, enter -0- .	**39**
	40 Tax (see page 32). Check if any tax is from **a** ☐ Form(s) 8814 **b** ☐ Form 4972 . . .	**40**
	41 Alternative minimum tax. Attach Form 6251	**41**
Married filing separately: $3,675	**42** Add lines 40 and 41 . . . . ▶	**42**
	43 Foreign tax credit. Attach Form 1116 if required	**43**	
	44 Credit for child and dependent care expenses. Attach Form 2441	**44**	
	45 Credit for the elderly or the disabled. Attach Schedule R . .	**45**	
	46 Education credits. Attach Form 8863	**46**	
	47 Child tax credit (see page 36)	**47**	
	48 Adoption credit. Attach Form 8839	**48**	
	49 Other. Check if from **a** ☐ Form 3800 **b** ☐ Form 8396 **c** ☐ Form 8801 **d** ☐ Form (specify) _____	**49**	
	50 Add lines 43 through 49. These are your **total credits**	**50**
	51 Subtract line 50 from line 42. If line 50 is more than line 42, enter -0- . . . . . ▶	**51**
Other Taxes	**52** Self-employment tax. Attach Schedule SE	**52**
	53 Social security and Medicare tax on tip income not reported to employer. Attach Form 4137	**53**
	54 Tax on IRAs, other retirement plans, and MSAs. Attach Form 5329 if required . . .	**54**
	55 Advance earned income credit payments from Form(s) W-2	**55**
	56 Household employment taxes. Attach Schedule H	**56**
	57 Add lines 51 through 56. This is your **total tax** . . . . ▶	**57**
Payments	**58** Federal income tax withheld from Forms W-2 and 1099 . .	**58**	
	59 2000 estimated tax payments and amount applied from 1999 return	**59**	
If you have a qualifying child, attach Schedule EIC.	**60a Earned income credit (EIC)**	**60a**	
	b Nontaxable earned income: amount . . ▶ [____] and type ▶ _____		
	61 Excess social security and RRTA tax withheld (see page 50)	**61**	
	62 Additional child tax credit. Attach Form 8812	**62**	
	63 Amount paid with request for extension to file (see page 50)	**63**	
	64 Other payments. Check if from **a** ☐ Form 2439 **b** ☐ Form 4136	**64**	
	65 Add lines 58, 59, 60a, and 61 through 64. These are your **total payments** . . . . ▶	**65**
Refund	**66** If line 65 is more than line 57, subtract line 57 from line 65. This is the amount you **overpaid**	**66**
Have it directly deposited! See page 50 and fill in 67b, 67c, and 67d.	**67a** Amount of line 66 you want **refunded to you** . . . . ▶	**67a**
	▶ **b** Routing number [_____] ▶ **c** Type: ☐ Checking ☐ Savings	
	▶ **d** Account number [_____]	
	68 Amount of line 66 you want **applied to your 2001 estimated tax** . ▶ **68**	
Amount You Owe	**69** If line 57 is more than line 65, subtract line 65 from line 57. This is the **amount you owe**. For details on how to pay, see page 51 . . . . ▶	**69**
	70 Estimated tax penalty. Also include on line 69 . . . **70**	

Sign Here

Under penalties of perjury, I declare that I have examined this return and accompanying schedules and statements, and to the best of my knowledge and belief, they are true, correct, and complete. Declaration of preparer (other than taxpayer) is based on all information of which preparer has any knowledge.

Joint return? See page 19.

Keep a copy for your records.

Your signature	Date	Your occupation	Daytime phone number ( )
Spouse's signature. If a joint return, **both** must sign.	Date	Spouse's occupation	May the IRS discuss this return with the preparer shown below (see page 52)? ☐ Yes ☐ No

Paid Preparer's Use Only

Preparer's signature ▶	Date	Check if self-employed ☐	Preparer's SSN or PTIN
Firm's name (or yours if self-employed), address, and ZIP code ▶		EIN	
		Phone no. ( )	

SCHEDULE SE	Self-Employment Tax	OMB No. 1545-0074
(Form 1040)	▶ See Instructions for Schedule SE (Form 1040).	**2000**
Department of the Treasury Internal Revenue Service (99)	▶ Attach to Form 1040.	Attachment Sequence No. **17**

Name of person with **self-employment** income (as shown on Form 1040)	Social security number of person with **self-employment** income ▶	: :

Who Must File Schedule SE

You must file Schedule SE if:

- You had net earnings from self-employment from **other than** church employee income (line 4 of Short Schedule SE or line 4c of Long Schedule SE) of $400 or more **or**
- You had church employee income of $108.28 or more. Income from services you performed as a minister or a member of a religious order **is not** church employee income. See page SE-1.

Note. Even if you had a loss or a small amount of income from self-employment, it may be to your benefit to file Schedule SE and use either "optional method" in Part II of Long Schedule SE. See page SE-3.

Exception. If your only self-employment income was from earnings as a minister, member of a religious order, or Christian Science practitioner **and** you filed Form 4361 and received IRS approval not to be taxed on those earnings, **do not** file Schedule SE. Instead, write "Exempt-Form 4361" on Form 1040, line 52.

May I Use Short Schedule SE or Must I Use Long Schedule SE?

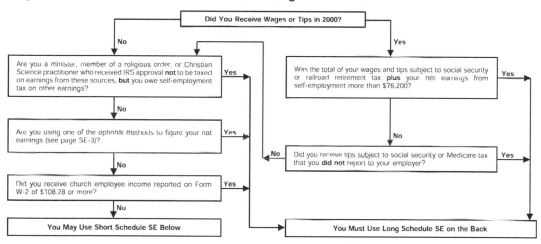

Section A—Short Schedule SE. Caution: *Read above to see if you can use Short Schedule SE.*

1	Net farm profit or (loss) from Schedule F, line 36, and farm partnerships, Schedule K-1 (Form 1065), line 15a	**1**
2	Net profit or (loss) from Schedule C, line 31; Schedule C-EZ, line 3; Schedule K-1 (Form 1065), line 15a (other than farming); and Schedule K-1 (Form 1065-B), box 9. Ministers and members of religious orders, see page SE-1 for amounts to report on this line. See page SE-2 for other income to report	**2**
3	Combine lines 1 and 2	**3**
4	**Net earnings from self-employment.** Multiply line 3 by 92.35% (.9235). If less than $400, **do not** file this schedule; you do not owe self-employment tax . . . . ▶	**4**
5	Self-employment tax. If the amount on line 4 is: • $76,200 or less, multiply line 4 by 15.3% (.153). Enter the result here and on **Form 1040, line 52.** • More than $76,200, multiply line 4 by 2.9% (.029). Then, add $9,448.80 to the result. Enter the total here and on **Form 1040, line 52.**	**5**
6	**Deduction for one-half of self-employment tax.** Multiply line 5 by 50% (.5). Enter the result here and on **Form 1040, line 27** . . . . | **6** |	

For Paperwork Reduction Act Notice, see Form 1040 instructions.   Cat. No. 11358Z   Schedule SE (Form 1040) 2000

Schedule SE (Form 1040) 2000	Attachment Sequence No. **17**	Page **2**

Name of person with **self-employment** income (as shown on Form 1040)	Social security number of person with **self-employment** income ▶	: :

Section B—Long Schedule SE

Part I   Self-Employment Tax

Note. If your only income subject to self-employment tax is **church employee income,** skip lines 1 through 4b. Enter -0- on line 4c and go to line 5a. Income from services you performed as a minister or a member of a religious order **is not** church employee income. See page SE-1.

A   If you are a minister, member of a religious order, or Christian Science practitioner **and** you filed Form 4361, but you had $400 or more of **other** net earnings from self-employment, check here and continue with Part I . . . . ▶ ☐

1	Net farm profit or (loss) from Schedule F, line 36, and farm partnerships, Schedule K-1 (Form 1065), line 15a. **Note.** Skip this line if you use the farm optional method. See page SE-3 . .	**1**	
2	Net profit or (loss) from Schedule C, line 31; Schedule C-EZ, line 3; Schedule K-1 (Form 1065), line 15a (other than farming); and Schedule K-1 (Form 1065-B), box 9. Ministers and members of religious orders, see page SE-1 for amounts to report on this line. See page SE-2 for other income to report. **Note.** Skip this line if you use the nonfarm optional method. See page SE-3.	**2**	
3	Combine lines 1 and 2	**3**	
4a	If line 3 is more than zero, multiply line 3 by 92.35% (.9235). Otherwise, enter amount from line 3	**4a**	
b	If you elect one or both of the optional methods, enter the total of lines 15 and 17 here . . .	**4b**	
c	Combine lines 4a and 4b. If less than $400, **do not** file this schedule; you do not owe self-employment tax. **Exception.** If less than $400 and you had **church employee income,** enter -0- and continue ▶	**4c**	
5a	Enter your **church employee income** from Form W-2. **Caution:** See page SE-1 for definition of church employee income **5a**		
b	Multiply line 5a by 92.35% (.9235). If less than $100, enter -0-	**5b**	
6	**Net earnings from self-employment.** Add lines 4c and 5b	**6**	
7	Maximum amount of combined wages and self-employment earnings subject to social security tax or the 6.2% portion of the 7.65% railroad retirement (tier 1) tax for 2000	**7**	76,200 00
8a	Total social security wages and tips (total of boxes 3 and 7 on Form(s) W-2) and railroad retirement (tier 1) compensation **8a**		
b	Unreported tips subject to social security tax (from Form 4137, line 9) **8b**		
c	Add lines 8a and 8b	**8c**	
9	Subtract line 8c from line 7. If zero or less, enter -0- here and on line 10 and go to line 11 . ▶	**9**	
10	Multiply the **smaller** of line 6 or line 9 by 12.4% (.124)	**10**	
11	Multiply line 6 by 2.9% (.029)	**11**	
12	**Self-employment tax.** Add lines 10 and 11. Enter here and on **Form 1040, line 52**	**12**	
13	**Deduction for one-half of self-employment tax.** Multiply line 12 by 50% (.5). Enter the result here and on **Form 1040, line 27** **13**		

Part II   Optional Methods To Figure Net Earnings (See page SE-3.)

Farm Optional Method. You may use this method **only** if:
- Your gross farm income[1] was not more than $2,400 **or**
- Your net farm profits[2] were less than $1,733.

14	Maximum income for optional methods	**14**	1,600 00
15	Enter the **smaller** of: two-thirds (⅔) of gross farm income[1] (not less than zero) **or** $1,600. Also include this amount on line 4b above	**15**	

Nonfarm Optional Method. You may use this method **only** if:
- Your net nonfarm profits[3] were less than $1,733 and also less than 72.189% of your gross nonfarm income[4] **and**
- You had net earnings from self-employment of at least $400 in 2 of the prior 3 years.

Caution: You may use this method no more than five times.

16	Subtract line 15 from line 14	**16**	
17	Enter the **smaller** of: two-thirds (⅔) of gross nonfarm income[4] (not less than zero) **or** the amount on line 16. Also include this amount on line 4b above	**17**	

[1]From Sch. F, line 11, and Sch. K-1 (Form 1065), line 15b.   [3]From Sch. C, line 31; Sch. C-EZ, line 3; Sch. K-1 (Form 1065), line 15a; and Sch. K-1 (Form 1065-B), box 9.
[2]From Sch. F, line 36, and Sch. K-1 (Form 1065), line 15a.   [4]From Sch. C, line 7; Sch. C-EZ, line 1; Sch. K-1 (Form 1065), line 15c; and Sch. K-1 (Form 1065-B), box 9.

Notice 89-25, Question and Answer 12

Q-12: In the case of an IRA or individual account plan, what constitutes a series of substantially equal periodic payments for purposes of section 72(t)(2)(A)(iv)?

A-12: Section 72(t)(1) imposes an additional tax of 10 percent on the portion of early distributions from qualified retirement plans (including IRAs) includible in gross income. However, section 72(t)(2)(A)(iv) provides that this tax shall not apply to distributions which are part of a series of substantially equal periodic payments (not less frequently than annually) made for the life (or life expectancy) of the employee or the joint lives (or joint life expectancies) of the employee and beneficiary. Section 72(t)(4) provides that, if the series of periodic payments is subsequently modified within five years of the date of the first payment, or, if later, age 59½, the exception to the 10 percent tax under section 72(t)(2)(A)(iv) does not apply, and the taxpayer's tax for the year of modification shall be increased by an amount, determined under regulations, which (but for the 72(t)(2)(A)(iv) exception) would have been imposed, plus interest.

Payments will be considered to be substantially equal periodic payments within the meaning of section 72(t)(2)(A)(iv) if they are made according to one of the methods set forth below.

Payments shall be treated as satisfying section 72(t)(2)(A)(iv) if the annual payment is determined using a method that would be acceptable for purposes of calculating the minimum distribution required under section 401(a)(9). For this purpose, the payment may be determined based on the life expectancy of the employee or the joint life and last survivor expectancy of the employee and beneficiary.

Payments will also be treated as substantially equal periodic payments within the meaning of section 72(t)(2)(A)(iv) if the amount to be distributed annually is determined by amortizing the taxpayer's account balance over a number of years equal to the life expectancy of the account owner or the joint life and last survivor expectancy of the account owner and beneficiary (with life expectancies determined in accordance with proposed section 1.401(a)(9)-1 of the regulations) at an interest rate that does not exceed a reasonable interest rate on the date payments commence. For example, a 50 year old individual with a life expectancy of 33.1, having an account balance of $100,000, and assuming an interest rate of 8 percent, could satisfy section 72(t)(2)(A)(iv) by distributing $9,679 annually, derived by amortizing $100,000 over 33.1 years at 8 percent interest.

Notice 89-25, Question and Answer 12 (continued)

Finally, payments will be treated as substantially equal periodic payments if the amount to be distributed annually is determined by dividing the taxpayer's account balance by an annuity factor (the present value of an annuity of $1 per year beginning at the taxpayer's age attained in the first distribution year and continuing for the life of the taxpayer) with such annuity factor derived using a reasonable mortality table and using an interest rate that does not exceed a reasonable interest rate on the date payments commence. If substantially equal monthly payments are being deter-

mined, the taxpayer's account balance would be divided by an annuity factor equal to the present value of an annuity of $1 per month beginning at the taxpayer's age attained in the first distribution year and continuing for the life of the taxpayer. For example, if the annuity factor for a $1 per year annuity for an individual who is 50 years old is 11.109 (assuming an interest rate of 9 percent and using the UP-1984 Mortality Table), an individual with a $100,000 account balance would receive an annual distribution of $9,002 ($100,000/ 11.109 = $9,002).

Form **5500-EZ**

Department of the Treasury
Internal Revenue Service

Annual Return of One-Participant
(Owners and Their Spouses) Retirement Plan

This form is required to be filed under
section 6058(a) of the Internal Revenue Code.

▶ **Type or print all entries in accordance with
the instructions to the Form 5500-EZ.**

Official Use Only

OMB No. 1545-0956

2000

This Form is Open to
Public Inspection.

Part I   **Annual Return Identification Information**

**For the calendar plan year 2000
or fiscal plan year beginning**   MM / DD / YYYY   **and ending**   MM / DD / YYYY

A This return is:

(1) ☐ the first return filed for the plan;

(2) ☐ an amended return;

(3) ☐ the final return filed for the plan;

(4) ☐ a short plan year return
(less than 12 months).

B If you filed for an extension of time to file, check the box and attach a copy of the extension application .... ▶ ☐

Part II   **Basic Plan Information** -- enter all requested information.

1a Name of plan

1b Three-digit plan number (PN) ▶

1c Date plan first
became effective   MM / DD / YYYY

Caution: *A penalty for the late or incomplete filing of this return will be assessed unless reasonable cause is established.*

Under penalties of perjury and other penalties set forth in the instructions, I declare that I have examined this return, including accompanying schedules, statements, and attachments, and to the best of my knowledge and belief, it is true, correct, and complete.

Signature of employer or plan administrator

Date   MM / DD / YYYY

Typed or printed name of individual signing as employer or plan administrator

For Paperwork Reduction Act Notice, see the instructions for Form 5500-EZ.

Cat. No. 63263R

Form **5500-EZ** (2000)

0 3 0 0 0 0 0 1 0 4

v3.2

Form 5500-EZ (2000)   Page 2

Official Use Only

2a Employer's name and address (Address should include room or suite no.)

1)   Name

     Name Continued

     Name Continued Add'l Name

2)   c / o   Name

     Mailing Street Address (or Foreign Street)

3)

4)   Location Address

     Location Address Continued

5)   Foreign Routing Code/Zip Code

6)   Foreign Mailing Country

7)   City (or Foreign City)

8)   State   Zip Code

2b Employer Identification Number (EIN)
       (Do not enter your Social Security Number)

2c Employer's telephone number

2d Business code
       (see instructions)

3a Plan administrator's name and address (If same as employer, enter "Same")

1)   Name

     Name Continued

     c / o   Name

2)   Street Address (or Foreign Street)

3)   Foreign Routing Code/ Zip Code

4)   Foreign Mailing Country

5)   City (or Foreign City)

6)   State   Zip Code

3b Administrator's EIN

3c Administrator's telephone number

4   If the name and/or EIN of the employer has changed since the last return filed for this plan, enter the name, EIN and the plan number from the last return below:

a   Employer's name

b   EIN   **c** PN

0 3 0 0 0 0 0 2 0 5

Form 5500-EZ (2000)   Page **3**

Official Use Only

5 Preparer information (optional)

a Name (including firm name, if applicable) and address

1)

2)

3)   **b** EIN

4)

5)   **c** Telephone number

6)

6 Type of plan: **(a)** ☐   Defined benefit pension plan (attach Schedule B (Form 5500))

(b) ☐   Money purchase pension plan (see instructions)   **(d)** ☐   Stock bonus plan

(c) ☐   Profit-sharing plan   **(e)** ☐   ESOP plan (attach Schedule E (Form 5500))

7a If this is a master/prototype, or regional prototype plan, enter the opinion/notification letter number .... ▶

b Check if this plan covers:

(1) ☐   Self-employed individuals,   *(2)* ☐   Partner(s) in a partnership, or   *(3)* ☐   100% owner of corporation

8a Enter the number of qualified pension benefit plans maintained by the employer (including this plan) .... ▶

b Check here if you have more than one plan and the total assets of all plans are more than $100,000 (see instructions) .... ▶ ☐

Number

9 Enter the number of participants in each category listed below:

a Under age 59 1/2 at the end of the plan year ....

b Age 59 1/2 or older at the end of the plan year, but under age 70 1/2 at the beginning of the plan year ....

c Age 70 1/2 or older at the beginning of the plan year ....

03000000306

Form 5500-EZ (2000)   Page **4**

10a *(1)* Is this a fully insured pension plan which is funded entirely by insurance or annuity contracts? ▶

       If "Yes," complete lines 10a*(2)* through 10f and skip lines 10g through 13d.

     (2) If 10a*(1)* is "Yes," are the insurance contracts held: .... ▶ **(1)**

	Yes		No
	under a trust	**(2)**	with no trust

b Cash contributions received by the plan for this plan year ....

c Noncash contributions received by the plan for this plan year ....

d Total plan distributions to participants or beneficiaries (see instructions) ....

e Total nontaxable plan distributions to participants or beneficiaries ....

f Transfers to other plans ....

g Amounts received by the plan other than from contributions ....

h Plan expenses other than distributions ....

	(a) Beginning of Year	**(b)** End of Year
11a Total plan assets		
b Total plan liabilities		

12 Specific Assets: If the plan held assets at any time during the plan year in any of the following categories, check "Yes" and enter the current value of any assets remaining in the plan as of the end of the plan year. Otherwise, check "No."

	Yes	No	Amount
a Partnership/joint venture interests			
b Employer real property..			
c Real estate (other than employer real property)			

0 3 0 0 0 0 0 4 0 7

Form 5500-EZ (2000)   Page **5**

		Yes	No	Amount
d	Employer securites	☐	☐	
e	Participant loans (see instructions)	☐	☐	
f	Loans (other than to participants)	☐	☐	
g	Tangible personal property	☐	☐	

13 Check "Yes" and enter amount involved if any of the following transactions took place between the plan and a disqualified person during this plan year. Otherwise, check "No."

		Yes	No	Amount
a	Sale, exchange, or lease of property	☐	☐	
b	Payment by the plan for services	☐	☐	
c	Acquisition or holding of employer securities	☐	☐	
d	Loan or extension of credit	☐	☐	

If 14a is "No," do not complete line 14b and line 14c. See the specific instructions for line 14b and line 14c.

			Yes	No
14a	Does your business have any employees other than you and your spouse (and your partners and their spouses)? .... ▶		☐	☐
b	Total number of employees (including you and your spouse and your partners and their spouses) .... ▶			
c	Does this plan meet the coverage requirements of Code section 410(b)? .... ▶		☐	☐
15a	Did the plan distribute any annuity contracts this plan year? .... ▶		☐	☐
b	During this plan year, did the plan make distributions to a married participant in a form other than a qualified joint and survivor annuity or were any distributions on account of the death of a married participant made to beneficiaries other than the spouse of that participant? .... ▶		☐	☐
c	During this plan year, did the plan make loans to married participants? .... ▶		☐	☐

0 3 0 0 0 0 0 5 0 8

19**99**

Department of the Treasury
Internal Revenue Service

Instructions for
Form 5500-EZ

Annual Return of One-Participant
(Owners and Their Spouses) Retirement Plan

Section references are to the Internal Revenue Code.

Changes To Note for 1999

• The Form 5500-EZ has been revised to take advantage of a new computerized system that will process the form (the ERISA Filing Acceptance System or "EFAST"). The new form is printed on special paper with green drop-out ink. Filers should not substitute a reproduction of these machine readable pages. A copy of the hand printed form is available in **Package 5500-EZ**.
• For the first time you will file your Form 5500-EZ with the U.S. Department of Labor's Pension and Welfare Benefits Administration **(PWBA)** rather than the Internal Revenue Service (see **Where To File** on page 2 for the new mailing and private delivery addresses).

Telephone Assistance

If you have questions and/or need help completing this form, please call **1-877-829-5500**. This toll-free telephone service is available Monday through Friday from 8:00am to 9:30pm EST.

How To Get Forms and Publications

Personal computer
You can access the IRS's Internet Web Site 24 hours a day, 7 days a week at **www.irs.gov** to:
• Download forms, instructions, and publications.
• See answers to frequently asked tax questions.
• Search publications on-line by topic or keyword.
• Send us comments or request help by e-mail.
• Sign up to receive local and national tax news by e-mail.
You can also reach us using file transfer protocol at **ftp.irs.gov**
By phone and in person.
You can order forms and publications 24 hours a day, 7 days a week, by calling **1-800-TAX-FORM** (1-800-829-3676). You can also get most forms and publications at your local IRS office.

General Instructions

Reminder

For 1994 and prior years, one-participant plan(s) that held $100,000 or less in total plan assets at the end of any plan year did not have to file Form 5500-EZ (or any other annual information return) for that plan year. For Forms 5500-EZ filed in 1995 and later years, one-participant plans that held more than $100,000 at the end of any plan year beginning on or after January 1, 1994, must file a Form 5500-EZ for the year the assets exceeded $100,000 and for each year thereafter, even if total plan assets were reduced to $100,000 or less. For example, if plan assets in a plan that otherwise satisfies the requirements for filing the Form 5500-EZ totaled $110,000 at the end of the 1998 plan year, and a distribution occurred in 1999 so that total plan assets were $85,000 at the end of the 1999 plan year, a Form 5500-EZ must be filed for the 1999 plan year and for all following years.

Purpose of Form

Form 5500-EZ is a simpler form that you can use if you have a one-participant retirement plan and you meet the five conditions listed under **Who May File Form 5500-EZ**. If you do not meet the five conditions, see **Form 5500**, Return/Report of Employee Benefit Plan, for reporting requirements.

Retirement plans can be either defined contribution plans (which include profit-sharing plans, money purchase pension plans, stock bonus plans, and employee stock ownership plans (ESOPs)) or defined benefit pension plans.

Who May File Form 5500-EZ

You may file Form 5500-EZ instead of Form 5500 if you meet **ALL** of the following conditions:

1. The plan is a one-participant plan. This means that as of the 1st day of the plan year for which this form is filed, either:

a. The plan only covers you (or you and your spouse) and you (or you and your spouse) own the entire business. (The business may be incorporated or unincorporated); OR

b. The plan only covers one or more partners (or partner(s) and spouse(s)) in a business partnership.

2. The plan meets the minimum coverage requirements of section 410(b) without being combined with any other plan you may have that covers other employees of your business. See the instructions for line 14c for more information.

3. The plan does not provide benefits for anyone except you, or you and your spouse, or one or more partners and their spouses.

4. The plan does not cover a business that is a member of:

a. An affiliated service group,

b. A controlled group of corporations, or

c. A group of businesses under common control.

5. The plan does not cover a business that leases employees. For an explanation of the technical terms above, see **Definitions** on page 3.

If you do not meet all five of the conditions listed above, file Form 5500 instead of Form 5500-EZ. If you meet all five of the conditions, read **Who May Not Have To File**.

Who May Not Have To File

You do not have to file Form 5500-EZ (or Form 5500) for 1999 if you meet the five conditions above, **AND**

You have a one-participant plan that had total plan assets of $100,000 or less at the end of every plan year beginning on or after January 1, 1994, **OR**

You have two or more one-participant plans that together had total plan assets of $100,000 or less at the end of every plan year beginning on or after January 1, 1994.

Note: *All one-participant plans* **must** *file a Form 5500-EZ for their* **final** *plan year even if the total plan assets have always been less than $100,000. The final plan year is the year in which distribution of all plan assets is completed. Check the "final return" box at the top of Form 5500-EZ if all assets under the* plan(s) (including insurance/annuity contracts) have been distributed to the participants and beneficiaries or distributed to another plan.

What To File

One-participant retirement plans that are required to file should complete and file Form 5500-EZ for the first year that it is required to be filed and for every plan year thereafter.

When To File

File the 1999 return for plan years that started in 1999. All required forms, schedules, statements, and attachments must be filed by the last day of the 7th calendar month after the end of the plan year that began in 1999 (not to exceed 12 months in length).

Note: If the filing due date falls on a Saturday, Sunday, or Federal holiday, the return may be filed on the next day that is not a Saturday, Sunday, or Federal holiday.

Private Delivery Service

You can use certain private delivery services designated by the IRS to meet the "timely mailing as timely filing/paying" rule for tax returns and payments. The most recent list of designated private delivery services was published by the IRS in August 1999 and includes only the following:

● Airborne Express (Airborne): Overnight Air Express Service, Next Afternoon Service, Second Day Service.
● DHL Worldwide Express (DHL): DHL "Same Day" Service, DHL USA Overnight.
● Federal Express (FedEx): FedEx Priority Overnight, FedEx Standard Overnight, FedEx 2Day.
● United Parcel Service (UPS): UPS Next Day Air, UPS Next Day Air Saver, UPS 2nd Day Air, UPS 2nd Day Air A.M.

The private delivery service can tell you how to get written proof of the mailing date.

See **Where To File** for the street address, when using a private delivery service.

Extension of Time To File

A one-time extension of time to file Form 5500-EZ (up to 2½ months) may be obtained by filing **Form 5558,** Application for Extension of Time To File Certain Employee Plan Returns, **before** the normal due date (not including any extensions) of the return. **You must continue to file Form 5558 with the IRS..**

Approved copies of the Form 5558 will not be returned to the filer. However, a photocopy of the extension request that was filed must be attached to the Form 5500-EZ.

The address for requesting a one-time extension of time to file the Form 5500-EZ (filing Form 5558) remains:

Internal Revenue Service Center

Memphis, TN 37501

Exception. One-participant plans are automatically granted an extension of time to file Form 5500-EZ until the extended due date of the Federal income tax return of the employer (and are not required to file Form 5558) if all the following conditions are met: **(1)** the plan year and the employer's tax year are the same, **(2)** the employer has been granted an extension of time to file its Federal income tax return to a date later than the normal due date for filing the Form 5500-EZ, and **(3)** a copy of the application for extension of time to file the Federal income tax return is attached to the Form 5500-EZ. Be sure to check box B at the top of the form. An extension granted by using this exception CANNOT be extended further by filing a Form 5558 after the normal due date (without extension) of Form 5500-EZ.

Short Plan Year

For a short plan year, file a return and all applicable schedules by the last day of the 7th month following the end of the short plan year. Modify the heading of the form to show the beginning and ending dates of your short plan year and check box A(4) for a short plan year. If this is also the first or final return, check the appropriate box (box A(1) or A(3)).

Amended Return

If you file an amended return, check box A(2) at the top of the return. Be sure to circle the amended line numbers.

Where To File

File Form 5500-EZ with any required schedules, statements, and attachments, at the address indicated below.
by mail:

PWBA

P.O. Box 7042

Lawrence, KS 66044-7042

by private delivery service:

PWBA / NCS

Attn: EFAST

3833 Greenway Drive

Lawrence, KS 66046-1290

Electronic Filing

You may file Form 5500-EZ using 4mm DAT, 8mm DAT, 3½ inch diskette, CD-ROM, 3490 Tape or 9-Track Tape at the above address or via modem. If the Form 5500-EZ is filed in this manner, the filer must obtain an electronic signature and a transmission encryption key. For more information regarding electronic filing and how to obtain electronic signatures and transmission encryption keys, check the EFAST Web Site at **www.efast.dol.gov** periodically, beginning in late March, 2000 for updates.

Paper Filing

Completion by Computer. If Electronic Filing is not used, print out the Form 5500-EZ on standard 8½ by 11 inch paper using EFAST approved computer software.

Completion by Hand. Enter one letter or number within each green box without any overlapping of characters. If entering a negative number, enter a minus sign "–" in a box to the left of the number.

Completion by Typewriter. Ignore the vertical lines and type directly through the boxes. Do NOT type more characters than the number of boxes. Do NOT use commas. See example below. If entering a negative number, enter a minus sign "–" within the boxes to the left of the number.

If you did not receive Form 5500-EZ in the mail, call **1-800-TAX-FORM** (1-800-829-3676) to order forms to be used for completion by hand or typewriter since these forms use special paper, special green drop-out ink, and are printed within precise specifications.

Signature and Date

The plan administrator or employer (owner) must sign and date Form 5500-EZ.

Penalties

The Internal Revenue Code imposes a penalty of $25 a day (up to $15,000) for not filing returns in connection with pension, profit-sharing, etc., plans by the required due date.

Schedules

• Actuaries of defined benefit plans subject to the minimum funding standards for this plan year must complete **Schedule B (Form 5500),** Actuarial Information, and attach it to Form 5500-EZ. See the instructions for Schedule B (Form 5500).

• **Schedule E (Form 5500),** ESOP Annual Information, is required for all pension benefit plans with ESOP benefits. For additional information, see the instructions for Schedule E (Form 5500).

• **Schedule P (Form 5500),** Annual Return of Fiduciary of Employee Benefit Trust, can be filed as an attachment to Form 5500-EZ for a one-participant plan that is funded by a trust by any trustee or custodian to start the running of the statute of limitations for the trust. See the instructions for Schedule P (Form 5500).

Definitions

Organizations defined in **Affiliated Service Group** or **Controlled Group of Corporations and a Group of Trades or Businesses Under Common Control** must file Form 5500 rather than Form 5500-EZ.

Affiliated Service Group

In general, two or more businesses may be an affiliated service group if: **(a)** one or more of the businesses (or the shareholders, officers, or highly compensated employees of one or more of the businesses) has an ownership interest in any of the other businesses, and **(b)** any of the businesses provide services to any of the other businesses (or the businesses are associated to provide services to third parties). If this applies to your business, read the rest of this definition for more details.

Section 414(m)(2) defines an affiliated service group as a group consisting of a service organization (referred to below as the "first service organization" (FSO)) and:

1. A service organization (A-ORG) that is a shareholder or partner in the FSO and that regularly performs services for the FSO or is regularly associated with the FSO in performing services for third persons, and/or

2. Any other organization (B-ORG) if:

a. A significant portion of the business of that organization consists of performing services for the FSO or A-ORG of a type historically performed by employees in the service field of the FSO or A-ORG, and

b. 10% or more of the interest of the B-ORG is held by persons who are officers, highly compensated employees, or owners of the FSO or A-ORG.

An affiliated service group also includes a group consisting of: **(a)** an organization whose principal business is performing management functions on a regular and continuous basis for another organization (or one organization and other related organizations), and **(b)** the organization (and related organizations) for which such functions are performed. See section 414(m)(5).

Controlled Group of Corporations and a Group of Trades or Businesses under Common Control

These are corporations or unincorporated businesses in which there is common ownership by one or more individuals or persons. See sections 414(b) and 414(c).

Leased Employee

Under section 414(n), a leased employee provides employee services for you that are performed under your primary direction and control, the individual provides services on a substantially full-time basis for at least a year, and the services are provided pursuant to an agreement between you and a leasing organization.

Disqualified Person

Generally, a disqualified person in the case of a sole proprietorship or partnership includes you, your partners, your

relatives and your partner's relatives, and other businesses in which you, your partners, or the partnership have an interest. In the case of a corporation, another corporation in which your corporation has an interest may be a disqualified person.

Specifically, the term "disqualified person" means:

1. Any fiduciary (including, but not limited to, any administrator, officer, trustee, or custodian), or counsel;

2. A person providing services to the plan;

3. An employer any of whose employees are covered by the plan;

4. An employee organization any of whose members are covered by the plan;

5. An owner, direct or indirect, of 50% or more of: **(a)** the combined voting power of all classes of stock entitled to vote or the total value of shares of all classes of stock of a corporation, **(b)** the capital interest or the profits interest of a partnership, or **(c)** the beneficial interest of a trust or unincorporated enterprise, which is an employer or an employee organization described in paragraph **3** or **4;**

6. A relative of any individual, described in paragraph **1, 2, 3,** or **5;**

7. A corporation, partnership, or trust or estate of which (or in which) 50% or more of: **(a)** the combined voting power of all classes of stock entitled to vote or the total value of shares of all classes of stock of such corporation, **(b)** the capital interest or profits interest of such partnership, or **(c)** the beneficial interest of such trust or estate is owned directly or indirectly, or held by persons described in paragraph **1, 2, 3, 4,** or **5;**

8. An officer, director (or an individual having power or responsibilities similar to those of officers or directors), or a 10% or more shareholder, directly or indirectly, of a person described in paragraph **3, 4, 5,** or **7;** or

9. A 10% or more (directly or indirectly in capital or profits) partner or joint venturer of a person described in paragraph **3, 4, 5,** or **7.**

Specific Instructions

Information at the Top of the Form

Check box A(1) if this is the first filing for this plan. Do not check this box if you have ever filed for this plan, even if it was a different form (e.g., Form 5500 or Form 5500-C/R).

Check box A(2) if you have already filed for the 1999 plan year and are now filing an amended return to correct errors and/or omissions on the previously filed return.

Check box A(3) if all assets under the plan(s) (including insurance/annuity contracts) have been distributed to the participants and beneficiaries or distributed to another plan. The final plan year is the year in which distribution of all plan assets is completed.

Check box A(4) if this form is filed for a period of less than 12 months. Show the dates at the top of the form.

Line 1a. Enter the formal name of the plan or sufficient information to identify the plan.

Line 1b. Enter the three-digit number the employer assigned to the plan. Plans should be numbered consecutively starting with 001.

Once a plan number is used for a plan, it must be used as the plan number for all future filings of returns for the plan, and this number may not be used for any other plan even after the plan is terminated.

Line 1c. Enter the date the plan first became effective.

Line 2a. Enter the employer's name and address. Include the suite, room, or other unit number after the street address. If the Post Office does not deliver mail to the street address and the employer has a P.O. box, show the box number instead of the street address.

Line 2b. Enter the employer's nine-digit employer identification number (EIN). For example, 00-1234567. **Do Not Enter Your Social Security Number.**

Employers who do not have an EIN should apply for one on **Form SS-4,** Application for Employer Identification Number, as soon as possible. Form SS-4 can be obtained at most IRS or Social Security Administration (SSA) offices. The PWBA does NOT issue EINs.

You may also apply for an EIN before you are required to file Form 5500-EZ by filing a completed Form SS-4 with the IRS Service Center, Memphis, TN 37501. If you do not receive your EIN in time to enter it on the Form 5500-EZ you file, enter "Applied For" on line 2b.

Note: *Although EINs for funds (trusts or custodial accounts) associated with plans are generally not required to be furnished on the Form 5500 series returns/reports (except on Schedule P (Form 5500)), the IRS will issue EINs for such funds for other reporting purposes. EINs may be obtained by filing Form SS-4 as explained above.*

The plan administrator or employer should use the trust's EIN described in the **Note** above when opening a bank account or conducting other transactions for a plan that requires an EIN.

Line 2d. From the list of business activity codes on pages 6 through 8, enter the one that best describes the nature of your business.

Line 3a. Enter the name and address of the plan administrator unless the administrator is the employer identified in line 2a. If this is the case, enter the word "same" on line 3a and leave lines 3b and 3c blank.

Line 3b. Enter the plan administrator's nine-digit EIN. A plan administrator must have an EIN for Form 5500-EZ reporting purposes. If the plan administrator does not have an EIN, apply for one as explained in the instructions for line 2b.

Line 4. If the employer's name and/or EIN have changed since the last return was filed for this plan enter the employer's name, EIN, and the plan number as it appeared on the last return filed for this plan.

Line 5. If the person who prepared the annual return is not the employer named in line 2a or the plan administrator named in line 3a, you may identify the person on line 5.

Line 6. Check one box on this line. Profit-sharing, employee stock ownership (ESOP), stock bonus, and money purchase pension plans are types of defined contribution plans. A "defined contribution plan" is a plan that provides for an individual account for each participant and for benefits based solely on the amount in such account. If a plan is not a defined contribution plan, it is a defined benefit plan.

Line 6a. Any defined benefit pension plan subject to the minimum funding standards must complete and attach Schedule B (Form 5500) to this form. All defined benefit pension plans are subject to the minimum funding standards, except certain insurance contract plans described in section 412(i), church plans, governmental plans, and certain other plans described in section 412(h).

Line 6b. If this is a defined contribution plan for which a waived funding deficiency is being amortized in the current plan year, attach Schedule B (Form 5500) to this form. Complete only lines 3, 8a, 9, and 10 of Schedule B. An enrolled actuary does not have to sign the Schedule B under these circumstances.

Line 7a. If this plan is a master/prototype plan, enter the latest opinion letter number issued for the master/prototype plan. If this plan is a regional prototype plan, enter the latest notification letter number issued for the regional prototype plan. Leave line 7a blank if this plan is not a master/prototype plan or a regional prototype plan.

Line 7b. Check box **(1)** if you, or you and your spouse together, own 100% of the business which maintains the plan, and the business is unincorporated. Check box **(2)** if you are a partner in the partnership which maintains the plan. Check box **(3)** if you, or you and your spouse jointly, own 100% of the shares of the corporation which maintains the plan.

Line 8b. File a separate Form 5500-EZ for each plan if you have two or more one-participant plans with combined total plan assets that exceeded $100,000 at the end of any plan year beginning on or after January 1, 1994.

Line 9. In general, distributions received by participants from any qualified plan prior to attainment of age 59½, death, or disability will be subject to a 10% tax on the amount of the distributions (in addition to the income tax owed on the amount distributed). In addition, individuals generally must begin to receive distributions from qualified plans by April 1 of the calendar year following the calendar year in which they reach age 70½.

For more details on early distributions and excess accumulations in qualified retirement plans, see **Pub. 560,** Retirement Plans for Small Business, and **Pub. 590,** Individual Retirement Arrangements (IRAs). In addition, **Form 5329,** Additional Taxes Attributable to Qualified Retirement Plans (Including IRAs), Annuities, and Modified Endowment Contracts, contains detailed information on how to report any excise tax or additional income tax in connection with your plan. These publications and the form can be downloaded at the IRS Web Site **(www.irs.gov)**.

Line 10. Do not include transfers received or rollovers received from other plans on lines 10b and 10c. Those should be included on line 11a.

Line 10b. Enter the total cash contributions received by the plan during the year and the contributions owed to the plan at the end of the plan year including contributions for administrative expenses.

Line 10d. Enter the total plan distributions made to participants or beneficiaries (including those distributions that are rolled over, whether or not in a direct transfer under section 401(a)(31)). If distributions include securities or other property, include the current value of the securities or other property at the date these assets were distributed. For distributions of insurance or annuity contracts to participants, enter the cash value of the contract when distributed.

Also report on line 10d a participant loan that is included in line 11a, column (a) (total plan assets - beginning of year) and that has been deemed distributed during the plan year or any prior year under the provisions of Code section 72(p) and proposed IRS regulation section 1.72(p)-1 provided both of the following circumstances apply:

• Under the plan, the participant loan is treated as a directed investment solely of the participant's individual account; and

• As of the end of the plan year, the participant is not continuing repayment under the loan.

If either of these circumstances does not apply, a deemed distribution of a participant loan should not be reported on line 10d. Instead, the current value of the participant loan (including interest accruing thereon after the deemed distribution) should be included on line 11a, column (b) (plan assets - end of year) and on line 12e (participant loans), without regard to the occurrence of a deemed distribution.

Note: *Although certain participant loans that are deemed distributions are to be reported on line 10d and are not to be reported as an asset thereafter, they are still considered outstanding loans and are not treated as actual distributions for certain purposes. See Q&As 12 and 19 of proposed IRS regulation section 1.72(p)-1.*

Line 10e. Enter the total plan distributions made during the year attributable to employee contributions or other basis under the plan.

Line 10f. Enter the amount of assets transferred (under section 414(l)) from this plan to another plan, if any. Do not include rollovers or direct transfers under section 401(a)(31) included on line 10d.

Line 10g. Include rollovers, direct transfers under section 401(a)(31), transfers under section 414(l), and net income received by the plan for the year. Do not include unrealized gains or losses.

Line 11a. "Total plan assets" includes rollovers and transfers received from other plans, and unrealized gains and losses such as appreciation/depreciation in assets.

Note: *Do not include in column (b) a participant loan that has been deemed distributed if the loan has been reported on line 10d in accordance with the instructions for line 10d.*

Line 11b. Do not include the value of future distributions that will be made to participants.

Line 12a. Enter the value of the plan's participation in a partnership or joint venture.

Line 12b. The term "employer real property" means real property (and related personal property) that is leased to an employer of employees covered by the plan, or to an affiliate of such employer. For purposes of determining the time at which a plan acquires employer real property for purposes of this line, such property shall be deemed to be acquired by the plan on the date on which the plan acquires the property or on the date on which the lease to the employer (or affiliate) is entered into, whichever is later.

Line 12d. An employer security is any security issued by an employer (including affiliates) of employees covered by the plan. These may include common stocks, preferred stocks, bonds, zero coupon bonds, debentures, convertible debentures, notes and commercial paper.

Line 12e. Enter on this line all loans to participants including residential mortgage loans that are subject to section 72(p). Include the sum of the value of the unpaid principal balances, plus accrued but unpaid interest, if any, for participant loans made under an individual account plan with investment experience segregated for each account made in accordance with 29 CFR 2550.408b-1 and which are secured solely by a portion of the participant's vested accrued benefit. When applicable, combine this amount with the current value of any other participant loans.

Note: *Do not include on line 12e a participant loan that has been deemed distributed if the loan has been reported on line 10d in accordance with the instructions for line 10d.*

After a participant loan that has been deemed distributed is reported on line 10d, it is no longer to be reported as an asset unless the participant resumes repayment under the loan in a later year. However, such a loan (including interest accruing thereon after the deemed distribution) that has not been repaid is still considered outstanding for purposes of applying Code section 72(p)(2)(A) to determine the maximum amount of subsequent loans. The loan is also considered outstanding for other purposes, such as the qualification requirements of section 401(a), including, for example, the determination of top-heavy status under Code section 416. See Q&As 12 and 19 of proposed IRS regulation 1.72(p)-1.

Line 12f. Enter all loans made by the plan except participant loans reported on line 12e. These include loans for construction, securities loans, mortgage loans (either by making or participating in the loans directly or by purchasing loans originated by a third party), and other miscellaneous loans. Include on this line residential mortgage loans that are not subject to section 72(p).

Line 12g. Include all property that has concrete existence and is capable of being processed, such as goods, wares, merchandise, furniture, machines, equipment, animals, automobiles, etc. This includes collectibles, such as works of art, rugs, antiques, metals, gems, stamps, coins, alcoholic beverages, musical instruments, and historical objects (documents, clothes, etc.). Do not include the value of a plan's interest in property reported on lines 12a through 12f, or intangible property, such as patents, copyrights, goodwill, franchises, notes, mortgages, stocks, claims, interests, or other property that embodies intellectual or legal rights.

Line 13. Section 4975 prohibits certain transactions between a plan and any disqualified person and imposes an excise tax on each prohibited transaction.

The section 4975 tax is paid with the filing of **Form 5330,** Return of Excise Taxes Related to Employee Benefit Plans. References to disqualified person transactions refer to all such transactions, not only those that are prohibited.

See **Definitions** for the meaning of "disqualified person."

Line 14b. Count your spouse and your partners' spouses only if they work in the business and benefit under the plan.

Line 14c. Your plan meets the minimum coverage requirements of section 410(b), for purposes of Form 5500-EZ, if the employees of your business (other than those benefiting under the plan) are:

1. Covered by a collective-bargaining agreement, under which retirement benefits were subject to good-faith bargaining,

2. Nonresident aliens who receive no earned income from you that constitutes income from sources within the United States, or

3. Not eligible because they do not meet the plan's minimum age or years-of-service requirements.

Note: You cannot use Form 5500-EZ if you have employees covered by another plan and this one-participant plan relies on that plan to meet the minimum coverage requirements. Use Form 5500 instead.

Line 15b. A qualified joint and survivor annuity is an immediate annuity for the life of the participant, with a survivor annuity for the life of the spouse that is not less than 50% of, and is not greater than 100% of, the amount of the annuity that is payable during the joint lives of the participant and the spouse. The qualified joint and survivor annuity may be provided either by the purchase of an annuity contract from an insurance company or directly from the plan's trust. See section 417(b).

Privacy Act and Paperwork Reduction Act Notice

We ask for the information on this form to carry out the Internal Revenue laws of the United States. This form is required to be filed under section 6058(a) of the Internal Revenue Code. Section 6109 requires you to provide your taxpayer identification number (SSN or EIN). If you fail to provide this information in a timely manner, you may be liable for penalties and interest. Section 6104(b) makes the information contained in this form publicly available. Therefore, the information will be given to anyone who asks for it and may be given to the Pension Benefit Guaranty Corporation (PBGC), Department of Justice for civil and criminal litigation, and cities, states and the District of Columbia for use in administering their tax laws.

You are not required to provide the information requested on a form that is subject to the Paperwork Reduction Act unless the form displays a valid OMB control number. Books or records relating to a form or its instructions must be retained as long as their contents may become material in the administration of ERISA or the Internal Revenue Code. Generally, the Form 5500 series return/reports and some of the related schedules are open to public inspection.

The time needed to complete and file this form will vary depending on individual circumstances. The estimated average time is:

Recordkeeping	18 hr., 11 min.
Learning about the law or the form	2 hr., 13 min
Preparing the form	4 hr., 35 min.
Copying, assembling, and sending the form	32 min.

If you have comments concerning the accuracy of these time estimates or suggestions for making this form simpler, we would be happy to hear from you. You can write to the Tax Forms Committee, Western Area Distribution Center, Rancho Cordova, CA 95743-0001. **DO NOT** send this form to this address. Instead, see **Where To File** on page 2.

Forms 5500 and 5500-EZ

Codes for Principal Business Activity

This list of principal business activities and their associated codes is designed to classify an enterprise by type of activity in which it is engaged. These principal activity codes are based on the North American Industry Classification System.

Agriculture, Forestry, Fishing and Hunting

Code

Crop Production
111100 Oilseed & Grain Farming
111210 Vegetable & Melon Farming (including potatoes & yams)
111300 Fruit & Tree Nut Farming
111400 Greenhouse, Nursery, & Floriculture Production
111900 Other Crop Farming (including tobacco, cotton, sugarcane, hay, peanut, sugar beet & all other crop farming)

Animal Production
112111 Beef Cattle Ranching & Farming
112112 Cattle Feedlots
112120 Dairy Cattle & Milk Production
112210 Hog & Pig Farming
112300 Poultry & Egg Production
112400 Sheep & Goat Farming
112510 Animal Aquaculture (including shellfish & finfish farms & hatcheries)
112900 Other Animal Production

Forestry and Logging
113110 Timber Tract Operations
113210 Forest Nurseries & Gathering of Forest Products
113310 Logging

Fishing, Hunting and Trapping
114110 Fishing
114210 Hunting & Trapping

Support Activities for Agriculture and Forestry
115110 Support Activities for Crop Production (including cotton ginning, soil preparation, planting, & cultivating)
115210 Support Activities for Animal Production
115310 Support Activities For Forestry

Mining
211110 Oil & Gas Extraction
212110 Coal Mining
212200 Metal Ore Mining
212310 Stone Mining & Quarrying
212320 Sand, Gravel, Clay, & Ceramic & Refractory Minerals Mining & Quarrying
212390 Other Nonmetallic Mineral Mining & Quarrying
213110 Support Activities for Mining

Utilities
221100 Electric Power Generation, Transmission & Distribution
221210 Natural Gas Distribution
221300 Water, Sewage & Other Systems

Construction

Code

Building, Developing, and General Contracting
233110 Land Subdivision & Land Development
233200 Residential Building Construction
233300 Nonresidential Building Construction

Code

Heavy Construction
234100 Highway, Street, Bridge, & Tunnel Construction
234900 Other Heavy Construction

Special Trade Contractors
235110 Plumbing, Heating, & Air-Conditioning Contractors
235210 Painting & Wall Covering Contractors
235310 Electrical Contractors
235400 Masonry, Drywall, Insulation, & Tile Contractors
235500 Carpentry & Floor Contractors
235610 Roofing, Siding, & Sheet Metal Contractors
235710 Concrete Contractors
235810 Water Well Drilling Contractors
235900 Other Special Trade Contractors

Manufacturing

Food Manufacturing
311110 Animal Food Mfg
311200 Grain & Oilseed Milling
311300 Sugar & Confectionery Product Mfg
311400 Fruit & Vegetable Preserving & Specialty Food Mfg
311500 Dairy Product Mfg
311610 Animal Slaughtering and Processing
311710 Seafood Product Preparation & Packaging
311800 Bakeries & Tortilla Mfg
311900 Other Food Mfg (including coffee, tea, flavorings & seasonings)

Beverage and Tobacco Product Manufacturing
312110 Soft Drink & Ice Mfg
312120 Breweries
312130 Wineries
312140 Distilleries
312200 Tobacco Manufacturing

Textile Mills and Textile Product Mills
313000 Textile Mills
314000 Textile Product Mills

Apparel Manufacturing
315100 Apparel Knitting Mills
315210 Cut & Sew Apparel Contractors
315220 Men's & Boys' Cut & Sew Apparel Mfg
315230 Women's & Girls' Cut & Sew Apparel Mfg
315290 Other Cut & Sew Apparel Mfg
315990 Apparel Accessories & Other Apparel Mfg

Leather and Allied Product Manufacturing
316110 Leather & Hide Tanning & Finishing
316210 Footwear Mfg (including rubber & plastics)
316990 Other Leather & Allied Product Mfg

Wood Product Manufacturing
321110 Sawmills & Wood Preservation
321210 Veneer, Plywood, & Engineered Wood Product Mfg

Code

321900 Other Wood Product Mfg

Paper Manufacturing
322100 Pulp, Paper, & Paperboard Mills
322200 Converted Paper Product Mfg

Printing and Related Support Activities
323100 Printing & Related Support Activities

Petroleum and Coal Products Manufacturing
324110 Petroleum Refineries (including integrated)
324120 Asphalt Paving, Roofing, & Saturated Materials Mfg
324190 Other Petroleum & Coal Products Mfg

Chemical Manufacturing
325100 Basic Chemical Mfg
325200 Resin, Synthetic Rubber, & Artificial & Synthetic Fibers & Filaments Mfg
325300 Pesticide, Fertilizer, & Other Agricultural Chemical Mfg
325410 Pharmaceutical & Medicine Mfg
325500 Paint, Coating, & Adhesive Mfg
325600 Soap, Cleaning Compound, & Toilet Preparation Mfg
325900 Other Chemical Product & Preparation Mfg

Plastics and Rubber Products Manufacturing
326100 Plastics Product Mfg
326200 Rubber Product Mfg

Nonmetallic Mineral Product Manufacturing
327100 Clay Product & Refractory Mfg
327210 Glass & Glass Product Mfg
327300 Cement & Concrete Product Mfg
327400 Lime & Gypsum Product Mfg
327900 Other Nonmetallic Mineral Product Mfg

Primary Metal Manufacturing
331110 Iron & Steel Mills & Ferroalloy Mfg
331200 Steel Product Mfg from Purchased Steel
331310 Alumina & Aluminum Production & Processing
331400 Nonferrous Metal (except Aluminum) Production & Processing
331500 Foundries

Fabricated Metal Product Manufacturing
332110 Forging & Stamping
332210 Cutlery & Handtool Mfg
332300 Architectural & Structural Metals Mfg
332400 Boiler, Tank, & Shipping Container Mfg
332510 Hardware Mfg
332610 Spring & Wire Product Mfg
332700 Machine Shops; Turned Product; & Screw, Nut, & Bolt Mfg
332810 Coating, Engraving, Heat Treating, & Allied Activities
332900 Other Fabricated Metal Product Mfg

Machinery Manufacturing
333100 Agriculture, Construction, & Mining Machinery Mfg
333200 Industrial Machinery Mfg
333310 Commercial & Service Industry Machinery Mfg
333410 Ventilation, Heating, Air-Conditioning, & Commercial Refrigeration Equipment Mfg
333510 Metalworking Machinery Mfg
333610 Engine, Turbine & Power Transmission Equipment Mfg

Code

333900 Other General Purpose Machinery Mfg

Computer and Electronic Product Manufacturing
334110 Computer & Peripheral Equipment Mfg
334200 Communications Equipment Mfg
334310 Audio & Video Equipment Mfg
334410 Semiconductor & Other Electronic Component Mfg
334500 Navigational, Measuring, Electromedical, & Control Instruments Mfg
334610 Manufacturing & Reproducing Magnetic & Optical Media

Electrical Equipment, Appliance, and Component Manufacturing
335100 Electric Lighting Equipment Mfg
335200 Household Appliance Mfg
335310 Electrical Equipment Mfg
335900 Other Electrical Equipment & Component Mfg

Transportation Equipment Manufacturing
336100 Motor Vehicle Mfg
336210 Motor Vehicle Body & Trailer Mfg
336300 Motor Vehicle Parts Mfg
336410 Aerospace Product & Parts Mfg
336510 Railroad Rolling Stock Mfg
336610 Ship & Boat Building
336990 Other Transportation Equipment Mfg

Furniture and Related Product Manufacturing
337000 Furniture & Related Product Manufacturing

Miscellaneous Manufacturing
339110 Medical Equipment & Supplies Mfg
339900 Other Miscellaneous Manufacturing

Wholesale Trade

Wholesale Trade, Durable Goods
421100 Motor Vehicle & Motor Vehicle Parts & Supplies Wholesalers
421200 Furniture & Home Furnishing Wholesalers
421300 Lumber & Other Construction Materials Wholesalers
421400 Professional & Commercial Equipment & Supplies Wholesalers
421500 Metal & Mineral (except Petroleum) Wholesalers
421600 Electrical Goods Wholesalers
421700 Hardware, & Plumbing & Heating Equipment & Supplies Wholesalers
421800 Machinery, Equipment, & Supplies Wholesalers
421910 Sporting & Recreational Goods & Supplies Wholesalers
421920 Toy & Hobby Goods & Supplies Wholesalers
421930 Recyclable Material Wholesalers
421940 Jewelry, Watch, Precious Stone, & Precious Metal Wholesalers
421990 Other Miscellaneous Durable Goods Wholesalers

Code

Wholesale Trade, Nondurable Goods
422100 Paper & Paper Product Wholesalers
422210 Drugs & Druggists' Sundries Wholesalers
422300 Apparel, Piece Goods, & Notions Wholesalers
422400 Grocery & Related Product Wholesalers
422500 Farm Product Raw Material Wholesalers
422600 Chemical & Allied Products Wholesalers
422700 Petroleum & Petroleum Products Wholesalers
422800 Beer, Wine, & Distilled Alcoholic Beverage Wholesalers
422910 Farm Supplies Wholesalers
422920 Book, Periodical, & Newspaper Wholesalers
422930 Flower, Nursery Stock, & Florists' Supplies Wholesalers
422940 Tobacco & Tobacco Product Wholesalers
422950 Paint, Varnish, & Supplies Wholesalers
422990 Other Miscellaneous Nondurable Goods Wholesalers

Retail Trade
Motor Vehicle and Parts Dealers
441110 New Car Dealers
441120 Used Car Dealers
441210 Recreational Vehicle Dealers
441221 Motorcycle Dealers
441222 Boat Dealers
441229 All Other Motor Vehicle Dealers
441300 Automotive Parts, Accessories, & Tire Stores
Furniture and Home Furnishings Stores
442110 Furniture Stores
442210 Floor Covering Stores
442291 Window Treatment Stores
442299 All Other Home Furnishings Stores
Electronics and Appliance Stores
443111 Household Appliance Stores
443112 Radio, Television, & Other Electronics Stores
443120 Computer & Software Stores
443130 Camera & Photographic Supplies Stores
Building Material and Garden Equipment and Supplies Dealers
444110 Home Centers
444120 Paint & Wallpaper Stores
444130 Hardware Stores
444190 Other Building Material Dealers
444200 Lawn & Garden Equipment & Supplies Stores
Food and Beverage Stores
445110 Supermarkets and Other Grocery (except Convenience) Stores
445120 Convenience Stores
445210 Meat Markets
445220 Fish & Seafood Markets
445230 Fruit & Vegetable Markets
445291 Baked Goods Stores
445292 Confectionery & Nut Stores
445299 All Other Specialty Food Stores
445310 Beer, Wine, & Liquor Stores
Health and Personal Care Stores
446110 Pharmacies & Drug Stores
446120 Cosmetics, Beauty Supplies, & Perfume Stores
446130 Optical Goods Stores
446190 Other Health & Personal Care Stores
Gasoline Stations
447100 Gasoline Stations (including convenience stores with gas)

Code

Clothing and Clothing Accessories Stores
448110 Men's Clothing Stores
448120 Women's Clothing Stores
448130 Children's & Infants' Clothing Stores
448140 Family Clothing Stores
448150 Clothing Accessories Stores
448190 Other Clothing Stores
448210 Shoe Stores
448310 Jewelry Stores
448320 Luggage & Leather Goods Stores
Sporting Goods, Hobby, Book, and Music Stores
451110 Sporting Goods Stores
451120 Hobby, Toy, & Game Stores
451130 Sewing, Needlework, & Piece Goods Stores
451140 Musical Instrument & Supplies Stores
451211 Book Stores
451212 News Dealers & Newsstands
451220 Prerecorded Tape, Compact Disc, & Record Stores
General Merchandise Stores
452110 Department stores
452900 Other General Merchandise Stores
Miscellaneous Store Retailers
453110 Florists
453210 Office Supplies & Stationery Stores
453220 Gift, Novelty, & Souvenir Stores
453310 Used Merchandise Stores
453910 Pet & Pet Supplies Stores
453920 Art Dealers
453930 Manufactured (Mobile) Home Dealers
453990 All Other Miscellaneous Store Retailers (including tobacco, candle, & trophy shops)
Nonstore Retailers
454110 Electronic Shopping & Mail-Order Houses
454210 Vending Machine Operators
454311 Heating Oil Dealers
454312 Liquefied Petroleum Gas (Bottled Gas) Dealers
454319 Other Fuel Dealers
454390 Other Direct Selling Establishments (including door-to-door retailing, frozen food plan providers, party plan merchandisers, & coffee-break service providers)

Transportation and Warehousing
Air, Rail, and Water Transportation
481000 Air Transportation
482110 Rail Transportation
483000 Water Transportation
Truck Transportation
484110 General Freight Trucking, Local
484120 General Freight Trucking, Long-distance
484200 Specialized Freight Trucking
Transit and Ground Passenger Transportation
485110 Urban Transit Systems
485210 Interurban & Rural Bus Transportation
485310 Taxi Service
485320 Limousine Service
485410 School & Employee Bus Transportation
485510 Charter Bus Industry
485990 Other Transit & Ground Passenger Transportation
Pipeline Transportation
486000 Pipeline Transportation
Scenic & Sightseeing Transportation
487000 Scenic & Sightseeing Transportation

Code

Support Activities for Transportation
488100 Support Activities for Air Transportation
488210 Support Activities for Rail Transportation
488300 Support Activities for Water Transportation
488410 Motor Vehicle Towing
488490 Other Support Activities for Road Transportation
488510 Freight Transportation Arrangement
488990 Other Support Activities for Transportation
Couriers and Messengers
492110 Couriers
492210 Local Messengers & Local Delivery
Warehousing and Storage
493100 Warehousing & Storage (except lessors of miniwarehouses & self-storage units)

Information
Publishing Industries
511110 Newspaper Publishers
511120 Periodical Publishers
511130 Book Publishers
511140 Database & Directory Publishers
511190 Other Publishers
511210 Software Publishers
Motion Picture and Sound Recording Industries
512100 Motion Picture & Video Industries (except video rental)
512200 Sound Recording Industries
Broadcasting and Telecommunications
513100 Radio & Television Broadcasting
513200 Cable Networks & Program Distribution
513300 Telecommunications (including paging, cellular, satellite, & other telecommunications)
Information Services and Data Processing Services
514100 Information Services (including news syndicates, libraries, & on-line information services)
514210 Data Processing Services

Finance and Insurance
Depository Credit Intermediation
522110 Commercial Banking
522120 Savings Institutions
522130 Credit Unions
522190 Other Depository Credit Intermediation
Nondepository Credit Intermediation
522210 Credit Card Issuing
522220 Sales Financing
522291 Consumer Lending
522292 Real Estate Credit (including mortgage bankers & originators)
522293 International Trade Financing
522294 Secondary Market Financing
522298 All Other Nondepository Credit Intermediation
Activities Related to Credit Intermediation
522300 Activities Related to Credit Intermediation (including loan brokers)
Securities, Commodity Contracts, and Other Financial Investments and Related Activities
523110 Investment Banking & Securities Dealing
523120 Securities Brokerage
523130 Commodity Contracts Dealing
523140 Commodity Contracts Brokerage

Code

523210 Securities & Commodity Exchanges
523900 Other Financial Investment Activities (including portfolio management & investment advice)
Insurance Carriers and Related Activities
524140 Direct Life, Health, & Medical Insurance & Reinsurance Carriers
524150 Direct Insurance & Reinsurance (except Life, Health & Medical) Carriers
524210 Insurance Agencies & Brokerages
524290 Other Insurance Related Activities
Funds, Trusts, and Other Financial Vehicles
525100 Insurance & Employee Benefit Funds
525910 Open-End Investment Funds (Form 1120-RIC)
525920 Trusts, Estates, & Agency Accounts
525930 Real Estate Investment Trusts (Form 1120-REIT)
525990 Other Financial Vehicles

Real Estate and Rental and Leasing
Real Estate
531110 Lessors of Residential Buildings & Dwellings
531120 Lessors of Nonresidential Buildings (except Miniwarehouses)
531130 Lessors of Miniwarehouses & Self-Storage Units
531190 Lessors of Other Real Estate Property
531210 Offices of Real Estate Agents & Brokers
531310 Real Estate Property Managers
531320 Offices of Real Estate Appraisers
531390 Other Activities Related to Real Estate
Rental and Leasing Services
532100 Automotive Equipment Rental & Leasing
532210 Consumer Electronics & Appliances Rental
532220 Formal Wear & Costume Rental
532230 Video Tape & Disc Rental
532290 Other Consumer Goods Rental
532310 General Rental Centers
532400 Commercial & Industrial Machinery & Equipment Rental & Leasing
Lessors of Nonfinancial Intangible Assets (except copyrighted works)
533110 Lessors of Nonfinancial Intangible Assets (except copyrighted works)

Professional, Scientific, and Technical Services
Legal Services
541110 Offices of Lawyers
541190 Other Legal Services
Accounting, Tax Preparation, Bookkeeping, and Payroll Services
541211 Offices of Certified Public Accountants
541213 Tax Preparation Services
541214 Payroll Services
541219 Other Accounting Services
Architectural, Engineering, and Related Services
541310 Architectural Services
541320 Landscape Architecture Services
541330 Engineering Services
541340 Drafting Services
541350 Building Inspection Services

Code

541360 Geophysical Surveying & Mapping Services
541370 Surveying & Mapping (except Geophysical) Services
541380 Testing Laboratories

Specialized Design Services
541400 Specialized Design Services (including interior, industrial, graphic, & fashion design)

Computer Systems Design and Related Services
541511 Custom Computer Programming Services
541512 Computer Systems Design Services
541513 Computer Facilities Management Services
541519 Other Computer Related Services

Other Professional, Scientific, and Technical Services
541600 Management, Scientific, & Technical Consulting Services
541700 Scientific Research & Development Services
541800 Advertising & Related Services
541910 Marketing Research & Public Opinion Polling
541920 Photographic Services
541930 Translation & Interpretation Services
541940 Veterinary Services
541990 All Other Professional, Scientific, & Technical Services

Management of Companies (Holding Companies)
551111 Offices of Bank Holding Companies
551112 Offices of Other Holding Companies

Administrative and Support and Waste Management and Remediation Services

Administrative and Support Services
561110 Office Administrative Services
561210 Facilities Support Services
561300 Employment Services
561410 Document Preparation Services
561420 Telephone Call Centers
561430 Business Service Centers (including private mail centers & copy shops)
561440 Collection Agencies
561450 Credit Bureaus
561490 Other Business Support Services (including repossession services, court reporting, & stenotype services)

Code

561500 Travel Arrangement & Reservation Services
561600 Investigation & Security Services
561710 Exterminating & Pest Control Services
561720 Janitorial Services
561730 Landscaping Services
561740 Carpet & Upholstery Cleaning Services
561790 Other Services to Buildings & Dwellings
561900 Other Support Services (including packaging & labeling services, & convention & trade show organizers)

Waste Management and Remediation Services
562000 Waste Management & Remediation Services

Educational Services
611000 Educational Services (including schools, colleges, & universities)

Health Care and Social Assistance

Offices of Physicians and Dentists
621111 Offices of Physicians (except mental health specialists)
621112 Offices of Physicians, Mental Health Specialists
621210 Offices of Dentists

Offices of Other Health Practitioners
621310 Offices of Chiropractors
621320 Offices of Optometrists
621330 Offices of Mental Health Practitioners (except Physicians)
621340 Offices of Physical, Occupational & Speech Therapists, & Audiologists
621391 Offices of Podiatrists
621399 Offices of All Other Miscellaneous Health Practitioners

Outpatient Care Centers
621410 Family Planning Centers
621420 Outpatient Mental Health & Substance Abuse Centers
621491 HMO Medical Centers
621492 Kidney Dialysis Centers
621493 Freestanding Ambulatory Surgical & Emergency Centers
621498 All Other Outpatient Care Centers

Medical and Diagnostic Laboratories
621510 Medical & Diagnostic Laboratories

Home Health Care Services
621610 Home Health Care Services

Code

Other Ambulatory Health Care Services
621900 Other Ambulatory Health Care Services (including ambulance services & blood & organ banks)

Hospitals
622000 Hospitals

Nursing and Residential Care Facilities
623000 Nursing & Residential Care Facilities

Social Assistance
624100 Individual & Family Services
624200 Community Food & Housing, & Emergency & Other Relief Services
624310 Vocational Rehabilitation Services
624410 Child Day Care Services

Arts, Entertainment, and Recreation

Performing Arts, Spectator Sports, and Related Industries
711100 Performing Arts Companies
711210 Spectator Sports (including sports clubs & racetracks)
711300 Promoters of Performing Arts, Sports, & Similar Events
711410 Agents & Managers for Artists, Athletes, Entertainers, & Other Public Figures
711510 Independent Artists, Writers, & Performers

Museums, Historical Sites, and Similar Institutions
712100 Museums, Historical Sites, & Similar Institutions

Amusement, Gambling, and Recreation Industries
713100 Amusement Parks & Arcades
713200 Gambling Industries
713900 Other Amusement & Recreation Industries (including golf courses, skiing facilities, marinas, fitness centers, & bowling centers)

Accommodation and Food Services

Accommodation
721110 Hotels (except casino hotels) & Motels
721120 Casino Hotels
721191 Bed & Breakfast Inns
721199 All Other Traveler Accommodation
721210 RV (Recreational Vehicle) Parks & Recreational Camps
721310 Rooming & Boarding Houses

Code

Food Services and Drinking Places
722110 Full-Service Restaurants
722210 Limited-Service Eating Places
722300 Special Food Services (including food service contractors & caterers)
722410 Drinking Places (Alcoholic Beverages)

Other Services

Repair and Maintenance
811110 Automotive Mechanical & Electrical Repair & Maintenance
811120 Automotive Body, Paint, Interior, & Glass Repair
811190 Other Automotive Repair & Maintenance (including oil change & lubrication shops & car washes)
811210 Electronic & Precision Equipment Repair & Maintenance
811310 Commercial & Industrial Machinery & Equipment (except Automotive & Electronic) Repair & Maintenance
811410 Home & Garden Equipment & Appliance Repair & Maintenance
811420 Reupholstery & Furniture Repair
811430 Footwear & Leather Goods Repair
811490 Other Personal & Household Goods Repair & Maintenance

Personal and Laundry Services
812111 Barber Shops
812112 Beauty Salons
812113 Nail Salons
812190 Other Personal Care Services (including diet & weight reducing centers)
812210 Funeral Homes & Funeral Services
812220 Cemeteries & Crematories
812310 Coin-Operated Laundries & Drycleaners
812320 Drycleaning & Laundry Services (except Coin-Operated)
812910 Linen & Uniform Supply
812920 Pet Care (except Veterinary) Services
812920 Photofinishing
812930 Parking Lots & Garages
812990 All Other Personal Services

Religious, Grantmaking, Civic, Professional, and Similar Organizations
813000 Religious, Grantmaking, Civic, Professional, & Similiar Organizations

Form **990-T**

Department of the Treasury
Internal Revenue Service

Exempt Organization Business Income Tax Return
(and proxy tax under section 6033(e))

For calendar year 2000 or other tax year beginning .... , 2000, and ending .... , 20 .....
► **See separate instructions.**

OMB No. 1545-0687

2000

A ☐ Check box if address changed	

B Exempt under section
☐ 501( )( )
☐ 408(e)   ☐ 220(e)
☐ 408A   ☐ 530(a)
☐ 529(a)

Please Print or Type

Name of organization (☐ check box if name changed and see instructions)

Number, street, and room or suite no. (If a P.O. box, see page 7 of instructions.)

City or town, state, and ZIP code

D Employer identification number
(Employees' trust, see instructions for Block D on page 7.)

E New unrelated bus. activity codes
(See instructions for Block E on page 7.)

C Book value of all assets at end of year

F Group exemption number (see instructions for Block F on page 7) ►

G Check organization type ► ☐ 501(c) corporation ☐ 501(c) trust ☐ 401(a) trust ☐ Other trust

H Describe the organization's primary unrelated business activity. ►

I During the tax year, was the corporation a subsidiary in an affiliated group or a parent-subsidiary controlled group? . . ► ☐ Yes ☐ No
If "Yes," enter the name and identifying number of the parent corporation. ►

J The books are in care of ►   Telephone number ► (   )

Part I Unrelated Trade or Business Income

			(A) Income	(B) Expenses	(C) Net
1a	Gross receipts or sales				
b	Less returns and allowances _____ **c** Balance ►	**1c**			
2	Cost of goods sold (Schedule A, line 7)	**2**			
3	Gross profit (subtract line 2 from line 1c)	**3**			
4a	Capital gain net income (attach Schedule D)	**4a**			
b	Net gain (loss) (Form 4797, Part II, line 18) (attach Form 4797)	**4b**			
c	Capital loss deduction for trusts	**4c**			
5	Income (loss) from partnerships and S corporations (attach statement)	**5**			
6	Rent income (Schedule C)	**6**			
7	Unrelated debt-financed income (Schedule E)	**7**			
8	Interest, annuities, royalties, and rents from controlled organizations (Schedule F)	**8**			
9	Investment income of a section 501(c)(7), (9), or (17) organization (Schedule G)	**9**			
10	Exploited exempt activity income (Schedule I)	**10**			
11	Advertising income (Schedule J)	**11**			
12	Other income (see page 8 of the instructions—attach schedule)	**12**			
13	**Total** (combine lines 3 through 12)	**13**			

Part II Deductions Not Taken Elsewhere (See page 9 of the instructions for limitations on deductions.)
(Except for contributions, deductions must be directly connected with the unrelated business income.)

14	Compensation of officers, directors, and trustees (Schedule K)	**14**	
15	Salaries and wages	**15**	
16	Repairs and maintenance	**16**	
17	Bad debts	**17**	
18	Interest (attach schedule)	**18**	
19	Taxes and licenses	**19**	
20	Charitable contributions (see page 11 of the instructions for limitation rules)	**20**	
21	Depreciation (attach Form 4562)	**21**	
22	Less depreciation claimed on Schedule A and elsewhere on return .	**22a**	**22b**
23	Depletion	**23**	
24	Contributions to deferred compensation plans	**24**	
25	Employee benefit programs	**25**	
26	Excess exempt expenses (Schedule I)	**26**	
27	Excess readership costs (Schedule J)	**27**	
28	Other deductions (attach schedule)	**28**	
29	**Total deductions** (add lines 14 through 28)	**29**	
30	Unrelated business taxable income before net operating loss deduction (subtract line 29 from line 13).	**30**	
31	Net operating loss deduction	**31**	
32	Unrelated business taxable income before specific deduction (subtract line 31 from line 30) . .	**32**	
33	Specific deduction (Generally $1,000, but see line 33 instructions for exceptions)	**33**	
34	**Unrelated business taxable income** (subtract line 33 from line 32). If line 33 is greater than line 32, enter the smaller of zero or line 32	**34**	

For Paperwork Reduction Act Notice, see instructions.   Cat. No. 11291J   Form **990-T** (2000)

Form 990-T (2000)   Page **2**

Part III   Tax Computation

35 **Organizations Taxable as Corporations** (see instructions for tax computation on page 12).
Controlled group members (sections 1561 and 1563)—check here ☐ . **See instructions** and:
   a Enter your share of the $50,000, $25,000, and $9,925,000 taxable income brackets (in that order):
      (1) |$_____| **(2)** |$_____| **(3)** |$_____|
   b Enter organization's share of: **(1)** additional 5% tax (not more than $11,750) |$_____|
      (2) additional 3% tax (not more than $100,000) . . . . |$_____|
   c Income tax on the amount on line 34 . . . . ▶ | 35c |

36 **Trusts Taxable at Trust Rates** (see instructions for tax computation on page 12) Income tax on
the amount on line 34 from: ☐ Tax rate schedule or ☐ Schedule D (Form 1041) . . . . ▶ | 36 |

37 **Proxy tax** (see page 13 of the instructions) . . . . ▶ | 37 |

38 Alternative minimum tax . . . . | 38 |

39 **Total** (add lines 37 and 38 to line 35c or 36, whichever applies) . . . . | 39 |

Part IV   Tax and Payments

40a Foreign tax credit (corporations attach Form 1118; trusts attach Form 1116) . | 40a |
   b Other credits (see page 13 of the instructions) . . . . | 40b |
   c General business credit—Check if from:
      ☐ Form 3800 or ☐ Form (specify) ▶.................................. | 40c |
   d Credit for prior year minimum tax (attach Form 8801 or 8827) . . . | 40d |
   e **Total credits** (add lines 40a through 40d) . . . . | 40e |

41 Subtract line 40e from line 39 . . . . | 41 |

42 Recapture taxes. Check if from: ☐ Form 4255 ☐ Form 8611 . . . . . . | 42 |

43 **Total tax** (add lines 41 and 42) . . . . | 43 |

44 **Payments: a** 1999 overpayment credited to 2000 . . . . | 44a |
   b 2000 estimated tax payments . . . . | 44b |
   c Tax deposited with Form 8868 . . . . | 44c |
   d Foreign organizations—Tax paid or withheld at source (see instructions) | 44d |
   e Backup withholding (see instructions) . . . . | 44e |
   f Other credits and payments (see instructions) . . . . . . | 44f |

45 **Total payments** (add lines 44a through 44f) . . . . | 45 |

46 Estimated tax penalty (see page 4 of the instructions). Check ▶ ☐ if Form 2220 is attached . | 46 |

47 **Tax due**—If line 45 is less than the total of lines 43 and 46, enter amount owed . . . . . | 47 |

48 **Overpayment**—If line 45 is larger than the total of lines 43 and 46, enter amount overpaid . . . ▶ | 48 |

49 Enter the amount of line 48 you want: **Credited to 2001 estimated tax** ▶ | Refunded ▶ | 49 |

Part V   Statements Regarding Certain Activities and Other Information (See instructions on page 14.)

		Yes	No
1	At any time during the 2000 calendar year, did the organization have an interest in or a signature or other authority over a financial account in a foreign country (such as a bank account, securities account, or other financial account)?		
	If "Yes," the organization may have to file Form TD F 90-22.1. If "Yes," enter the name of the foreign country here ▶ ---		
2	During the tax year, did the organization receive a distribution from, or was it the grantor of, or transferor to, a foreign trust? If "Yes," see page 14 of the instructions for other forms the organization may have to file.		
3	Enter the amount of tax-exempt interest received or accrued during the tax year ▶ $		

Schedule A—Cost of Goods Sold (See instructions on page 15.)

Method of inventory valuation (specify) ▶

1	Inventory at beginning of year	1		**6**	Inventory at end of year . . .	6	
2	Purchases	2		**7**	**Cost of goods sold.** Subtract line 6 from line 5. (Enter here and on line 2, Part I.)	7	
3	Cost of labor	3					
4a	Additional section 263A costs (attach schedule)	4a		**8**	Do the rules of section 263A (with respect to property produced or acquired for resale) apply to the organization?	Yes / No	
b	Other costs (attach schedule)	4b					
5	**Total**—Add lines 1 through 4b	5					

Please Sign Here
Under penalties of perjury, I declare that I have examined this return, including accompanying schedules and statements, and to the best of my knowledge and belief, it is true, correct, and complete. Declaration of preparer (other than taxpayer) is based on all information of which preparer has any knowledge.

▶ _____ | _____
Signature of officer or fiduciary   Date   Title

Paid Preparer's Use Only

Preparer's signature ▶	Date	Check if self-employed ▶ ☐	Preparer's SSN or PTIN
Firm's name (or yours, if self-employed), address, and ZIP code ▶		EIN ▶	
		Phone no.	( )

Form **5330**
(Rev. August 1998)

Department of the Treasury
Internal Revenue Service

Return of Excise Taxes
Related to Employee Benefit Plans

(Under sections 4971, 4972, 4973(a)(3), 4975, 4976, 4977, 4978, 4978A,
4978B, 4979, 4979A, and 4980 of the Internal Revenue Code)

OMB No. 1545-0575

Filer tax year beginning _____ and ending _____

A Name of filer (see instructions on page 3)

Number, street, and room or suite no. (If a P.O. box, see page 3 of the instructions)

City or town, state, and ZIP code

B Check applicable box and see instructions.

☐ Employer identification number (EIN)
☐ Social security number (SSN)

Filer's identification number
▶

C Name and address of plan sponsor

E Plan sponsor's EIN

F Plan year ending

D Name of plan

G Plan number

H Check here if this is an amended return . . . . ▶ ☐

Part I   Summary of Taxes Due

		FOR IRS USE ONLY		
1	Section 4972 tax on nondeductible contributions to qualified plans (from line 13l). . .	161	**1**	
2	Section 4973(a)(3) tax on excess contributions to section 403(b)(7)(A) custodial accounts (from line 22)	164	**2**	
3	Section 4976 tax on disqualified benefits (from line 23).	200	**3**	
4a	Section 4978 and 4978A tax on certain ESOP dispositions (from line 24a)	209	**4a**	
b	Section 4978B tax on certain ESOP dispositions (from line 24b).	202	**4b**	
5	Section 4979A tax on certain prohibited allocations of qualified ESOP securities (from line 25) . .	203	**5**	
6	Section 4975 tax on prohibited transactions (from line 26c)	159	**6**	
7	Section 4971 tax on failure to meet minimum funding standards (from line 31)	163	**7**	
8	Section 4977 tax on excess fringe benefits (from line 32d)	201	**8**	
9	Section 4979 tax on excess contributions to certain plans (from line 33b)	205	**9**	
10	Section 4980 tax on reversion of qualified plan assets to an employer (from line 36) . .	204	**10**	
11	Section 4971(f) tax on failure to pay liquidity shortfall (from line 41).	226	**11**	
12a	**Total tax.** Add lines 1 through 11 (see instructions)		**12a**	
b	Enter amount of tax paid with Form 5558 or any other tax paid prior to filing this return . . .		**12b**	
c	**Total tax due.** Subtract line 12b from line 12a. Attach check or money order for full amount payable to "United States Treasury." Write your name, identification number, and "Form 5330, Section(s) _____ " on it . . . . ▶		**12c**	

Please Sign Here

Under penalties of perjury, I declare that I have examined this return, including accompanying schedules and statements, and to the best of my knowledge and belief, it is true, correct, and complete. Declaration of preparer (other than taxpayer) is based on all information of which preparer has any knowledge.

▶ _____ Your signature

( ) _____ Telephone number

▶ _____ Date

Paid Preparer's Use Only

Preparer's signature ▶ _____

Date _____

Firm's name (or yours if self-employed) and address ▶ _____

For Privacy Act and Paperwork Reduction Act Notice, see page 6 of the instructions.   Cat. No. 11870M   Form **5330** (Rev. 8-98)

DUE DATE: Taxes listed on this page are due on the last day of the 7th month after the end of the tax year of the filer.

Part II   Tax on Nondeductible Employer Contributions to Qualified Plans (Section 4972)

13a Total contributions for your tax year to your qualified (under section 401(a), 403(a), or 408(k), or 408(p)) plan . . . .

   b Amount allowable as a deduction under section 404 . . . .

   c Subtract line 13b from line 13a . . . .

   d Enter amount of any prior year nondeductible contributions made for years beginning after 12/31/86 . . . .

   e Amount of any prior year nondeductible contributions for years beginning after 12/31/86 returned to you in this tax year or any prior tax year . . . .

   f Subtract line 13e from line 13d . . . .

   g Amount of line 13f carried forward and deductible in this tax year. . . . .

   h Subtract line 13g from line 13f . . . .

   i Tentative taxable excess contributions. Add lines 13c and 13h . . . .

   j Nondeductible section 4972(c)(6) contributions exempt from excise tax . . . .

   k Taxable excess contributions. Subtract line 13j from line 13i . . . .

   l Multiply line 13k by 10%. Enter here and on line 1 . . . . ▶

Part III   Tax on Excess Contributions to Section 403(b)(7)(A) Custodial Accounts (Section 4973(a)(3))

14 Total amount contributed for current year less rollovers (see instructions) . . . .

15 Amount excludable from gross income under section 403(b) (see instructions) . . . . . .

16 Current year excess contributions (line 14 less line 15, but not less than zero) . . . . . .

17 Prior year excess contributions not previously eliminated. If zero, go to line 21 . . . . . .

18 Contribution credit (if line 15 is more than line 14, enter the excess; otherwise, enter -0-). . . . .

19 Total of all prior years' distributions out of the account included in your gross income under section 72(e) and not previously used to reduce excess contributions . . . .

20 Adjusted prior years' excess contributions (line 17 less the total of lines 18 and 19) . . . . .

21 Taxable excess contributions (line 16 plus line 20) . . . .

22 **Excess contributions tax.** Enter the lesser of line 21 or 6% of the value of your account as of the last day of the year. Enter here and on line 2 . . . . ▶

Part IV   Tax on Disqualified Benefits (Section 4976)

23 If your welfare benefit fund has provided a disqualified benefit during your taxable year, enter the amount of the disqualified benefit here and on line 3 (see instructions) . . . . ▶

Part V   Tax on Certain ESOP Dispositions (Sections 4978, 4978A, and 4978B)

24a Enter your section 4978 or 4978A tax on dispositions of employer securities by employee stock ownership plans and certain worker-owned cooperatives here and on line 4a (see instructions) ▶
Check the box to indicate whether the tax applies as a result of the application of
   ☐ Section 664(g)   ☐ Section 4978A   ☐ Section 1042

   b Enter your section 4978B tax on dispositions of employer securities to which section 133 applied here and on line 4b . . . . ▶

Part VI   Tax on Certain Prohibited Allocations of Qualified ESOP Securities (Section 4979A)

25 Enter 50% of the prohibited allocation or the allocation described in section 664(g)(5)(A), here and on line 5 (see instructions) . . . . ▶

Form 5330 (Rev. 8-98)   Page **3**

DUE DATE: Section 4975 taxes are due on the last day of the 7th month after the end of the tax year of the filer.

Part VII   Tax on Prohibited Transactions (Section 4975)

26a Is the excise tax a result of a prohibited transaction that was (check one or more):

☐ discrete   ☐ other than discrete (a lease or a loan)

b Transaction number	**(a)** Date of transaction (see instructions)	**(b)** Description of prohibited transaction	**(c)** Amount involved in prohibited transaction (see instructions)	**(d)** Initial tax on prohibited transaction (multiply each transaction in column (c) by the appropriate rate (see instructions))
(i)				
(ii)				
(iii)				
(iv)				

26c Add amounts in column (d). Enter here and on line 6 . . . . ▶

27 Have you corrected **all** of the prohibited transactions that you are reporting on this return? (See instructions) . . . . ☐ **Yes** ☐ **No**
If "Yes," complete Part IX. If "No," complete Part IX and see instructions.

Part VIII   Schedule of Other Participating Disqualified Persons (See instructions)

28	**(a)** Name and address of disqualified person	**(b)** Transaction number from Part VII	**(c)** Employer identification number or social security number
(i)			
(ii)			
(iii)			
(iv)			

Part IX   Description of Correction (See line 27 instructions.)

29 **(a)** Transaction number from Part VII	**(b)** Nature of correction	**(c)** Date of correction
(i)		
(ii)		
(iii)		
(iv)		

Form 5330 (Rev. 8-98)   Page **4**

DUE DATE: See **When To File** for taxes due under sections 4971, 4977, 4979, 4980, and 4971(f).

Part X   **Tax on Failure To Meet Minimum Funding Standards (Section 4971)**

30 Accumulated funding deficiency in the plan's minimum funding standard account (see instructions)
31 Multiply line 30 by tax rate (see instructions for applicable tax rates). Enter here and on line 7 . ▶

Part XI   **Tax on Excess Fringe Benefits (Section 4977)**

32a Did you make an election to be taxed under section 4977?. . . . . . . ☐ Yes ☐ No
  b If "Yes," enter the calendar year in which the excess fringe benefits were paid ▶ _____
  c If line 32a is "Yes," enter the excess fringe benefits on this line (see instructions) . . . . . .
  d Enter 30% of line 32c on this line and on line 8 . . . . ▶

Part XII   **Tax on Excess Contributions to Certain Plans (Section 4979)**

33a Enter the amount of any excess contributions under a cash or deferred arrangement that is part of
a plan qualified under section 401(a), 403(a), 403(b), 408(k), 501(c)(18) or excess aggregate
contributions described in section 401(m) . . . .
  b Multiply line 33a by 10%. Enter here and on line 9 . . . . ▶

Part XIII   **Tax on Reversion of Qualified Plan Assets to an Employer (Section 4980)**

34 Date reversion occurred ▶ month _____ day _____ year_____
35a Employer reversion amount _____   **b** Excise tax rate _____ %
36 Multiply line 35a by line 35b and enter the amount here and on line 10 (see instructions) . . ▶
37 Explain below why you qualify for a rate other than 50%:
_____
_____
_____
_____

Part XIV   **Tax on Failure to Correct Liquidity Shortfall (Section 4971(f))**

		1st Quarter	2nd Quarter	3rd Quarter	4th Quarter	Total
38	Amount of shortfall . . .					
39	Amount corrected. . . .					
40	Net shortfall amount. . .					
41	Multiply line 40 (total column) by 10%. Enter here and on line 11. . . . . ▶					

Form **5329**

Department of the Treasury
Internal Revenue Service

**Additional Taxes Attributable to IRAs,
Other Qualified Retirement Plans, Annuities,
Modified Endowment Contracts, and MSAs**
(Under Sections 72, 530, 4973, and 4974 of the Internal Revenue Code)
▶ Attach to Form 1040.   ▶ See separate instructions.

OMB No. 1545-0203

2000

Attachment
Sequence No. **29**

Name of individual subject to additional tax. (If married filing jointly, see page 2 of the instructions.)

Your social security number

**Fill in Your Address Only
If You Are Filing This
Form by Itself and Not
With Your Tax Return**

Home address (number and street), or P.O. box if mail is not delivered to your home

Apt. no.

City, town or post office, state, and ZIP code

If this is an amended
return, check here ▶ ☐

If you **only** owe the 10% tax on early distributions, you may be able to report this tax directly on Form 1040 without filing Form 5329. See **Who Must File** on page 1 of the instructions.

Part I   Tax on Early Distributions

Complete this part if a taxable distribution was made from your qualified retirement plan (including an IRA other than an education IRA), annuity contract, or modified endowment contract before you reached age 59½. If you received a Form 1099-R that incorrectly indicates an early distribution (with no known exception to the additional tax) or you received a Roth IRA distribution, you also may have to complete this part. See page 2 of the instructions.

Note: You must include the taxable amount of the distribution on Form 1040, line 15b or 16b.

1	Early distributions included in gross income. For Roth IRA distributions, see page 2 of the instructions	1	
2	Early distributions not subject to additional tax. Enter the appropriate exception number from page 2 of the instructions: _____	2	
3	Amount subject to additional tax. Subtract line 2 from line 1	3	
4	**Tax due.** Enter 10% (.10) of line 3. Also include this amount on Form 1040, line 54	4	

Caution: If any part of the amount on line 3 was a distribution from a SIMPLE retirement plan, you may have to include 25% of that amount on line 4 instead of 10%. See page 3 of the instructions.

Part II   Tax on Certain Taxable Distributions From Education (Ed) IRAs

Complete this part if you had a taxable amount on Form 8606, line 30.
Note: You must include the taxable amount of the distribution on Form 1040, line 15b.

5	Taxable distributions from your Ed IRAs, from Form 8606, line 30	5	
6	Taxable distributions not subject to additional tax. See page 3 of the instructions	6	
7	Amount subject to additional tax. Subtract line 6 from line 5	7	
8	**Tax due.** Enter 10% (.10) of line 7. Also include this amount on Form 1040, line 54	8	

Part III   Tax on Excess Contributions to Traditional IRAs

Complete this part if you contributed more to your traditional IRAs for 2000 than is allowable or you had an excess contribution on line 16 of your 1999 Form 5329.

9	Enter your excess contributions from line 16 of your 1999 Form 5329. If zero, go to line 15	9	
10	If your traditional IRA contributions for 2000 are less than your maximum allowable contribution, see page 3. Otherwise, enter -0-	10	
11	Taxable 2000 distributions from your traditional IRAs	11	
12	2000 withdrawals of prior year excess contributions included on line 9. See page 3	12	
13	Add lines 10, 11, and 12	13	
14	Prior year excess contributions. Subtract line 13 from line 9. If zero or less, enter -0-	14	
15	Excess contributions for 2000. See page 3. Do not include this amount on Form 1040, line 23	15	
16	Total excess contributions. Add lines 14 and 15	16	
17	**Tax due.** Enter 6% (.06) of the **smaller** of line 16 **or** the value of your traditional IRAs on December 31, 2000 (including contributions for 2000 made in 2001). Also include this amount on Form 1040, line 54	17	

For Paperwork Reduction Act Notice, see page 4 of separate instructions.   Cat. No. 13329Q   Form **5329** (2000)

Form 5329 (2000)   Page **2**

Part IV   Tax on Excess Contributions to Roth IRAs

Complete this part if you contributed more to your Roth IRAs for 2000 than is allowable or you had an excess contribution on line 24 of your 1999 Form 5329.

18	Enter your excess contributions from line 24 of your 1999 Form 5329. If zero, go to line 23 . .	**18**	
19	If your Roth IRA contributions for 2000 are less than your maximum allowable contribution, see page 3. Otherwise, enter -0-	**19**	
20	2000 distributions from your Roth IRAs, from Form 8606, line 17 . .	**20**	
21	Add lines 19 and 20	**21**	
22	Prior year excess contributions. Subtract line 21 from line 18. If zero or less, enter -0- . . .	**22**	
23	Excess contributions for 2000. See page 3	**23**	
24	Total excess contributions. Add lines 22 and 23	**24**	
25	**Tax due.** Enter 6% (.06) of the **smaller** of line 24 **or** the value of your Roth IRAs on December 31, 2000 (including contributions for 2000 made in 2001). Also include this amount on Form 1040, line 54 . . .	**25**	

Part V   Tax on Excess Contributions to Education (Ed) IRAs

Complete this part if the contributions to your Ed IRAs in 2000 were more than is allowable or you had an excess contribution on line 32 of your 1999 Form 5329.

26	Enter the excess contributions from line 32 of your 1999 Form 5329. If zero, go to line 31 . .	**26**	
27	If the contributions to your Ed IRAs in 2000 were less than the maximum allowable contribution, see page 3. Otherwise, enter -0- .	**27**	
28	2000 distributions from your Ed IRAs, from Form 8606, line 28 . .	**28**	
29	Add lines 27 and 28	**29**	
30	Prior year excess contributions. Subtract line 29 from line 26. If zero or less, enter -0- . . .	**30**	
31	Excess contributions for 2000. See page 4	**31**	
32	Total excess contributions. Add lines 30 and 31	**32**	
33	**Tax due.** Enter 6% (.06) of the **smaller** of line 32 **or** the value of your Ed IRAs on December 31, 2000. Also include this amount on Form 1040, line 54 . . .	**33**	

Part VI   Tax on Excess Contributions to Medical Savings Accounts (MSAs)

Complete this part if you or your employer contributed more to your MSAs in 2000 than is allowable or you had an excess contribution on line 40 of your 1999 Form 5329.

34	Enter the excess contributions from line 40 of your 1999 Form 5329. If zero, go to line 39 . .	**34**	
35	If the contributions to your MSAs for 2000 are less than the maximum allowable contribution, see page 4. Otherwise, enter -0-	**35**	
36	Taxable 2000 distributions from your MSAs, from Form 8853, line 8 . .	**36**	
37	Add lines 35 and 36	**37**	
38	Prior year excess contributions. Subtract line 37 from line 34. If zero or less, enter -0- . . .	**38**	
39	Excess contributions for 2000. See page 4. Do not include this amount on Form 1040, line 25	**39**	
40	Total excess contributions. Add lines 38 and 39	**40**	
41	**Tax due.** Enter 6% (.06) of the **smaller** of line 40 **or** the value of your MSAs on December 31, 2000. Also include this amount on Form 1040, line 54	**41**	

Part VII   Tax on Excess Accumulation in Qualified Retirement Plans

Complete this part if you did not receive the minimum required distribution from your qualified retirement plan (including an IRA other than an Ed IRA or Roth IRA).

42	Minimum required distribution. See page 4	**42**	
43	Amount actually distributed to you	**43**	
44	Subtract line 43 from line 42. If zero or less, enter -0-	**44**	
45	**Tax due.** Enter 50% (.50) of line 44. Also include this amount on Form 1040, line 54	**45**	

Signature. Complete only if you are filing this form by itself and not with your tax return.

Please Sign Here	Under penalties of perjury, I declare that I have examined this form, including accompanying schedules and statements, and to the best of my knowledge and belief, it is true, correct, and complete. Declaration of preparer (other than taxpayer) is based on all information of which preparer has any knowledge.		
	▶ Your signature		▶ Date

Paid Preparer's Use Only	Preparer's signature ▶	Date	Check if self-employed ☐	Preparer's SSN or PTIN
	Firm's name (or yours if self-employed), address, and ZIP code ▶		EIN	
			Phone no. ( )	

Form **5329** (2000)

Form **SS-4**
(Rev. April 2000)
Department of the Treasury
Internal Revenue Service

Application for Employer Identification Number

(For use by employers, corporations, partnerships, trusts, estates, churches, government agencies, certain individuals, and others. See instructions.)
▶ Keep a copy for your records.

EIN

OMB No. 1545-0003

Please type or print clearly.

1 Name of applicant (legal name) (see instructions)

2 Trade name of business (if different from name on line 1)

3 Executor, trustee, "care of" name

4a Mailing address (street address) (room, apt., or suite no.)

5a Business address (if different from address on lines 4a and 4b)

4b City, state, and ZIP code

5b City, state, and ZIP code

6 County and state where principal business is located

7 Name of principal officer, general partner, grantor, owner, or trustor—SSN or ITIN may be required (see instructions) ▶

8a Type of entity (Check only one box.) (see instructions)

Caution: If applicant is a limited liability company, see the instructions for line 8a.

☐ Sole proprietor (SSN) _____
☐ Partnership ☐ Personal service corp.
☐ REMIC ☐ National Guard
☐ State/local government ☐ Farmers' cooperative
☐ Church or church-controlled organization
☐ Other nonprofit organization (specify) ▶ _____
☐ Other (specify) ▶

☐ Estate (SSN of decedent) _____
☐ Plan administrator (SSN) _____
☐ Other corporation (specify) ▶ _____
☐ Trust
☐ Federal government/military
_____ (enter GEN if applicable) _____

8b If a corporation, name the state or foreign country (if applicable) where incorporated

State

Foreign country

9 Reason for applying (Check only one box.) (see instructions)
☐ Started new business (specify type) ▶ _____
☐ Hired employees (Check the box and see line 12.)
☐ Created a pension plan (specify type) ▶
☐ Banking purpose (specify purpose) ▶ _____
☐ Changed type of organization (specify new type) ▶ _____
☐ Purchased going business
☐ Created a trust (specify type) ▶ _____
☐ Other (specify) ▶

10 Date business started or acquired (month, day, year) (see instructions)

11 Closing month of accounting year (see instructions)

12 First date wages or annuities were paid or will be paid (month, day, year). **Note:** If applicant is a withholding agent, enter date income will first be paid to nonresident alien. (month, day, year) . . . . ▶

13 Highest number of employees expected in the next 12 months. **Note:** If the applicant does not expect to have any employees during the period, enter -0-. (see instructions) . . . . ▶

Nonagricultural	Agricultural	Household

14 Principal activity (see instructions) ▶

15 Is the principal business activity manufacturing? . . . . ☐ Yes ☐ No
If "Yes," principal product and raw material used ▶

16 To whom are most of the products or services sold? Please check one box. ☐ Business (wholesale)
☐ Public (retail) ☐ Other (specify) ▶ ☐ N/A

17a Has the applicant ever applied for an employer identification number for this or any other business? . . . . ☐ Yes ☐ No
Note: If "Yes," please complete lines 17b and 17c.

17b If you checked "Yes" on line 17a, give applicant's legal name and trade name shown on prior application, if different from line 1 or 2 above.
Legal name ▶   Trade name ▶

17c Approximate date when and city and state where the application was filed. Enter previous employer identification number if known.
Approximate date when filed (mo., day, year) | City and state where filed | Previous EIN

Under penalties of perjury, I declare that I have examined this application, and to the best of my knowledge and belief, it is true, correct, and complete.

Business telephone number (include area code)
( )
Fax telephone number (include area code)
( )

Name and title (Please type or print clearly.) ▶

Signature ▶   Date ▶

Note: Do not write below this line. For official use only.

Please leave blank ▶	Geo.	Ind.	Class	Size	Reason for applying

For Privacy Act and Paperwork Reduction Act Notice, see page 4.   Cat. No. 16055N   Form **SS-4** (Rev. 4-2000)

General Instructions

Section references are to the Internal Revenue Code unless otherwise noted.

Purpose of Form

Use Form SS-4 to apply for an employer identification number (EIN). An EIN is a nine-digit number (for example, 12-3456789) assigned to sole proprietors, corporations, partnerships, estates, trusts, and other entities for tax filing and reporting purposes. The information you provide on this form will establish your business tax account.

Caution: *An EIN is for use in connection with your business activities only. Do* **not** *use your EIN in place of your social security number (SSN).*

Who Must File

You must file this form if you have not been assigned an EIN before and:

• You pay wages to one or more employees including household employees.

• You are required to have an EIN to use on any return, statement, or other document, even if you are not an employer.

• You are a withholding agent required to withhold taxes on income, other than wages, paid to a nonresident alien (individual, corporation, partnership, etc.). A withholding agent may be an agent, broker, fiduciary, manager, tenant, or spouse, and is required to file **Form 1042**, Annual Withholding Tax Return for U.S. Source Income of Foreign Persons.

• You file **Schedule C**, Profit or Loss From Business, **Schedule C-EZ**, Net Profit From Business, or **Schedule F**, Profit or Loss From Farming, of **Form 1040**, U.S. Individual Income Tax Return, **and** have a Keogh plan or are required to file excise, employment, or alcohol, tobacco, or firearms returns.

The following must use EINs even if they do not have any employees:

• State and local agencies who serve as tax reporting agents for public assistance recipients, under Rev. Proc. 80-4, 1980-1 C.B. 581, should obtain a separate EIN for this reporting. See **Household employer** on page 3.

• Trusts, except the following:

1. Certain grantor-owned trusts. (See the **Instructions for Form 1041**, U.S. Income Tax Return for Estates and Trusts.)

2. Individual retirement arrangement (IRA) trusts, unless the trust has to file **Form 990-T**, Exempt Organization Business Income Tax Return. (See the **Instructions for Form 990-T**.)

• Estates

• Partnerships

• REMICs (real estate mortgage investment conduits) (See the **Instructions for Form 1066**, U.S. Real Estate Mortgage Investment Conduit (REMIC) Income Tax Return.)

• Corporations

• Nonprofit organizations (churches, clubs, etc.)

• Farmers' cooperatives

• Plan administrators (A plan administrator is the person or group of persons specified as the administrator by the instrument under which the plan is operated.)

When To Apply for a New EIN

New Business. If you become the new owner of an existing business, **do not** use the EIN of the former owner. **If you already have an EIN, use that number.** If you do not have an EIN, apply for one on this form. If you become the "owner" of a corporation by acquiring its stock, use the corporation's EIN.

Changes in Organization or Ownership. If you already have an EIN, you may need to get a new one if either the organization or ownership of your business changes. If you incorporate a sole proprietorship or form a partnership, you must get a new EIN. However, **do not** apply for a new EIN if:

• You change only the name of your business,

• You elected on **Form 8832**, Entity Classification Election, to change the way the entity is taxed, or

• A partnership terminates because at least 50% of the total interests in partnership capital and profits were sold or exchanged within a 12-month period. (See Regulations section 301.6109-1(d)(2)(iii).) The EIN for the terminated partnership should continue to be used.

Note: *If you are electing to be an "S corporation," be sure you file* **Form 2553,** *Election by a Small Business Corporation.*

File Only One Form SS-4. File only one Form SS-4, regardless of the number of businesses operated or trade names under which a business operates. However, each corporation in an affiliated group must file a separate application.

EIN Applied for, But Not Received. If you do not have an EIN by the time a return is due, write "Applied for" and the date you applied in the space shown for the number. **Do not** show your social security number (SSN) as an EIN on returns.

If you do not have an EIN by the time a tax deposit is due, send your payment to the Internal Revenue Service Center for your filing area. (See **Where To Apply** below.) Make your check or money order payable to "United States Treasury" and show your name (as shown on Form SS-4), address, type of tax, period covered, and date you applied for an EIN. Send an explanation with the deposit.

For more information about EINs, see **Pub. 583**, Starting a Business and Keeping Records, and **Pub. 1635**, Understanding Your EIN.

How To Apply

You can apply for an EIN either by mail or by telephone. You can get an EIN immediately by calling the Tele-TIN number for the service center for your state, or you can send the completed Form SS-4 directly to the service center to receive your EIN by mail.

Application by Tele-TIN. Under the Tele-TIN program, you can receive your EIN by telephone and use it immediately to file a return or make a payment. To receive an EIN by telephone, complete Form SS-4, then call the Tele-TIN number listed for your state under **Where To Apply.** The person making the call must be authorized to sign the form. (See **Signature** on page 4.)

An IRS representative will use the information from the Form SS-4 to establish your account and assign you an EIN. Write the number you are given on the upper right corner of the form and sign and date it.

Mail or fax (facsimile) the signed Form SS-4 **within 24 hours** *to the Tele-TIN Unit at the service center address for your state. The IRS representative will give you the fax number. The fax numbers are also listed in Pub. 1635.*

Taxpayer representatives can receive their client's EIN by telephone if they first send a fax of a completed **Form 2848**, Power of Attorney and Declaration of Representative, or **Form 8821**, Tax Information Authorization, to the Tele-TIN unit. The Form 2848 or Form 8821 will be used solely to release the EIN to the representative authorized on the form.

Application by Mail. Complete Form SS-4 at least 4 to 5 weeks before you will need an EIN. Sign and date the application and mail it to the service center address for your state. You will receive your EIN in the mail in approximately 4 weeks.

Where To Apply

The Tele-TIN numbers listed below will involve a long-distance charge to callers outside of the local calling area and can be used only to apply for an EIN. **The numbers may change without notice.** Call 1-800-829-1040 to verify a number or to ask about the status of an application by mail.

If your principal business, office or agency, or legal residence in the case of an individual, is located in:	Call the Tele-TIN number shown or file with the Internal Revenue Service Center at:
Florida, Georgia, South Carolina	Attn: Entity Control Atlanta, GA 39901 770-455-2360
New Jersey, New York (New York City and counties of Nassau, Rockland, Suffolk, and Westchester)	Attn: Entity Control Holtsville, NY 00501 516-447-4955
New York (all other counties), Connecticut, Maine, Massachusetts, New Hampshire, Rhode Island, Vermont	Attn: Entity Control Andover, MA 05501 978-474-9717
Illinois, Iowa, Minnesota, Missouri, Wisconsin	Attn: Entity Control Stop 6800 2306 E. Bannister Rd. Kansas City, MO 64999 816-926-5999
Delaware, District of Columbia, Maryland, Pennsylvania, Virginia	Attn: Entity Control Philadelphia, PA 19255 215-516-6999
Indiana, Kentucky, Michigan, Ohio, West Virginia	Attn: Entity Control Cincinnati, OH 45999 859-292-5467

Form SS-4 (Rev. 4-2000)   Page **3**

Kansas, New Mexico, Oklahoma, Texas	Attn: Entity Control Austin, TX 73301 512-460-7843
Alaska, Arizona, California (counties of Alpine, Amador, Butte, Calaveras, Colusa, Contra Costa, Del Norte, El Dorado, Glenn, Humboldt, Lake, Lassen, Marin, Mendocino, Modoc, Napa, Nevada, Placer, Plumas, Sacramento, San Joaquin, Shasta, Sierra, Siskiyou, Solano, Sonoma, Sutter, Tehama, Trinity, Yolo, and Yuba), Colorado, Idaho, Montana, Nebraska, Nevada, North Dakota, Oregon, South Dakota, Utah, Washington, Wyoming	Attn: Entity Control Mail Stop 6271 P.O. Box 9941 Ogden, UT 84201 801-620-7645
California (all other counties), Hawaii	Attn: Entity Control Fresno, CA 93888 559-452-4010
Alabama, Arkansas, Louisiana, Mississippi, North Carolina, Tennessee	Attn: Entity Control Memphis, TN 37501 901-546-3920
If you have no legal residence, principal place of business, or principal office or agency in any state	Attn: Entity Control Philadelphia, PA 19255 215-516-6999

Specific Instructions

The instructions that follow are for those items that are not self-explanatory. Enter N/A (nonapplicable) on the lines that do not apply.

Line 1. Enter the legal name of the entity applying for the EIN exactly as it appears on the social security card, charter, or other applicable legal document.

Individuals. Enter your first name, middle initial, and last name. If you are a sole proprietor, enter your individual name, not your business name. Enter your business name on line 2. Do not use abbreviations or nicknames on line 1.

Trusts. Enter the name of the trust.

Estate of a decedent. Enter the name of the estate.

Partnerships. Enter the legal name of the partnership as it appears in the partnership agreement. **Do not** list the names of the partners on line 1. See the specific instructions for line 7.

Corporations. Enter the corporate name as it appears in the corporation charter or other legal document creating it.

Plan administrators. Enter the name of the plan administrator. A plan administrator who already has an EIN should use that number.

Line 2. Enter the trade name of the business if different from the legal name. The trade name is the "doing business as" name.

Note: *Use the full legal name on line 1 on all tax returns filed for the entity. However, if you enter a trade name on line 2 and choose to use the trade name instead of the legal name, enter the trade name on all returns you file. To prevent processing delays and errors, **always** use either the legal name only or the trade name only on all tax returns.*

Line 3. Trusts enter the name of the trustee. Estates enter the name of the executor, administrator, or other fiduciary. If the entity applying has a designated person to receive tax information, enter that person's name as the "care of" person. Print or type the first name, middle initial, and last name.

Line 7. Enter the first name, middle initial, last name, and SSN of a principal officer if the business is a corporation; of a general partner if a partnership; of the owner of a single member entity that is disregarded as an entity separate from its owner; or of a grantor, owner, or trustor if a trust. If the person in question is an alien individual with a previously assigned individual taxpayer identification number (ITIN), enter the ITIN in the space provided, instead of an SSN. You are not required to enter an SSN or ITIN if the reason you are applying for an EIN is to make an entity classification election (see Regulations section 301.7701-1 through 301.7701-3), and you are a nonresident alien with no effectively connected income from sources within the United States.

Line 8a. Check the box that best describes the type of entity applying for the EIN. If you are an alien individual with an ITIN previously assigned to you, enter the ITIN in place of a requested SSN.

Caution: *This is not an election for a tax classification of an entity. See "Limited liability company (LLC)" below.*

If not specifically mentioned, check the "Other" box, enter the type of entity and the type of return that will be filed (for example, common trust fund, Form 1065). Do not use N/A. If you are an alien individual applying for an EIN, see the **Line 7** instructions above.

Sole proprietor. Check this box if you file Schedule C, C-EZ, or F (Form 1040) and have a qualified plan, or are required to file excise, employment, or alcohol, tobacco, or firearms returns, or are a payer of gambling winnings. Enter your SSN (or ITIN) in the space provided. If you are a nonresident alien with a nonresident alien with no effectively

connected income from sources within the United States, you do not need to enter an SSN or ITIN.

REMIC. Check this box if the entity has elected to be treated as a real estate mortgage investment conduit (REMIC). See the Instructions for Form 1066 for more information.

Other nonprofit organization. Check this box if the nonprofit organization is other than a church or church-controlled organization and specify the type of nonprofit organization (for example, an educational organization).

If the organization also seeks tax-exempt status, you must file either **Package 1023,** Application for Recognition of Exemption, or **Package 1024,** Application for Recognition of Exemption Under Section 501(a). Get **Pub. 557,** Tax Exempt Status for Your Organization, for more information.

Group exemption number (GEN). If the organization is covered by a group exemption letter, enter the four-digit GEN. (Do not confuse the GEN with the nine-digit EIN.) If you do not know the GEN, contact the parent organization. Get Pub. 557 for more information about group exemption numbers.

Withholding agent. If you are a withholding agent required to file Form 1042, check the "Other" box and enter "Withholding agent."

Personal service corporation. Check this box if the entity is a personal service corporation. An entity is a personal service corporation for a tax year only if:

● The principal activity of the entity during the testing period (prior tax year) for the tax year is the performance of personal services substantially by employee-owners, and

● The employee-owners own at least 10% of the fair market value of the outstanding stock in the entity on the last day of the testing period.

Personal services include performance of services in such fields as health, law, accounting, or consulting. For more information about personal service corporations, see the **Instructions for Forms 1120 and 1120-A,** and **Pub. 542,** Corporations.

Limited liability company (LLC). See the definition of limited liability company in the **Instructions for Form 1065,** U.S. Partnership Return of Income. An LLC with two or more members can be a partnership or an association taxable as a corporation. An LLC with a single owner can be an association taxable as a corporation or an entity disregarded as an entity separate from its owner. See Form 8832 for more details.

Note: *A domestic LLC with at least two members that does not file Form 8832 is classified as a partnership for Federal income tax purposes.*

● If the entity is classified as a partnership for Federal income tax purposes, check the "partnership" box.

● If the entity is classified as a corporation for Federal income tax purposes, check the "Other corporation" box and write "limited liability co." in the space provided.

● If the entity is disregarded as an entity separate from its owner, check the "Other" box and write in "disregarded entity" in the space provided.

Plan administrator. If the plan administrator is an individual, enter the plan administrator's SSN in the space provided.

Other corporation. This box is for any corporation other than a personal service corporation. If you check this box, enter the type of corporation (such as insurance company) in the space provided.

Household employer. If you are an individual, check the "Other" box and enter "Household employer" and your SSN. If you are a state or local agency serving as a tax reporting agent for public assistance recipients who become household employers, check the "Other" box and enter "Household employer agent." If you are a trust that qualifies as a household employer, you do not need a separate EIN for reporting tax information relating to household employees; use the EIN of the trust.

QSub. For a qualified subchapter S subsidiary (QSub) check the "Other" box and specify "QSub."

Line 9. Check only **one** box. Do not enter N/A.

Started new business. Check this box if you are starting a new business that requires an EIN. If you check this box, enter the type of business being started. **Do not** apply if you already have an EIN and are only adding another place of business.

Hired employees. Check this box if the existing business is requesting an EIN because it has hired or is hiring employees and is therefore required to file employment tax returns. **Do not** apply if you already have an EIN and are only hiring employees. For information on the applicable employment taxes for family members, see **Circular E,** Employer's Tax Guide (Publication 15).

Created a pension plan. Check this box if you have created a pension plan and need an EIN for reporting purposes. Also, enter the type of plan.

Note: *Check this box if you are applying for a trust EIN when a new pension plan is established.*

Banking purpose. Check this box if you are requesting an EIN for banking purposes only, and enter the banking purpose (for example, a bowling league for depositing dues or an investment club for dividend and interest reporting).

Changed type of organization. Check this box if the business is changing its type of organization, for example, if the business was a sole proprietorship and has been incorporated or has become a partnership. If you check this box, specify in the space provided the type of change made, for example, "from sole proprietorship to partnership."

Purchased going business. Check this box if you purchased an existing business. **Do not** use the former owner's EIN. **Do not** apply for a new EIN if you already have one. Use your own EIN.

Created a trust. Check this box if you created a trust, and enter the type of trust created. For example, indicate if the trust is a nonexempt charitable trust or a split-interest trust.

Note: *Do not check this box if you are applying for a trust EIN when a new pension plan is established. Check "Created a pension plan."*

Exception. Do **not** file this form for certain grantor-type trusts. The trustee does not need an EIN for the trust if the trustee furnishes the name and TIN of the grantor/owner and the address of the trust to all payors. See the Instructions for Form 1041 for more information.

Other (specify). Check this box if you are requesting an EIN for any other reason, and enter the reason.

Line 10. If you are starting a new business, enter the starting date of the business. If the business you acquired is already operating, enter the date you acquired the business. Trusts should enter the date the trust was legally created. Estates should enter the date of death of the decedent whose name appears on line 1 or the date when the estate was legally funded.

Line 11. Enter the last month of your accounting year or tax year. An accounting or tax year is usually 12 consecutive months, either a calendar year or a fiscal year (including a period of 52 or 53 weeks). A calendar year is 12 consecutive months ending on December 31. A fiscal year is either 12 consecutive months ending on the last day of any month other than December or a 52-53 week year. For more information on accounting periods, see **Pub. 538,** Accounting Periods and Methods.

Individuals. Your tax year generally will be a calendar year.

Partnerships. Partnerships generally must adopt one of the following tax years:
● The tax year of the majority of its partners,
● The tax year common to all of its principal partners,
● The tax year that results in the least aggregate deferral of income, or
● In certain cases, some other tax year.

See the Instructions for Form 1065 for more information.

REMIC. REMICs must have a calendar year as their tax year.

Personal service corporations. A personal service corporation generally must adopt a calendar year unless:
● It can establish a business purpose for having a different tax year, or
● It elects under section 444 to have a tax year other than a calendar year.

Trusts. Generally, a trust must adopt a calendar year except for the following:
● Tax-exempt trusts,
● Charitable trusts, and
● Grantor-owned trusts.

Line 12. If the business has or will have employees, enter the date on which the business began or will begin to pay wages. If the business does not plan to have employees, enter N/A.

Withholding agent. Enter the date you began or will begin to pay income to a nonresident alien. This also applies to individuals who are required to file Form 1042 to report alimony paid to a nonresident alien.

Line 13. For a definition of agricultural labor (farmwork), see **Circular A,** Agricultural Employer's Tax Guide (Publication 51).

Line 14. Generally, enter the exact type of business being operated (for example, advertising agency, farm, food or beverage establishment, labor union, real estate agency, steam laundry, rental of coin-operated vending machine, or investment club). Also state if the business will involve the sale or distribution of alcoholic beverages.

Governmental. Enter the type of organization (state, county, school district, municipality, etc.).

Nonprofit organization (other than governmental). Enter whether organized for religious, educational, or humane purposes, and the principal activity (for example, religious organization—hospital, charitable).

Mining and quarrying. Specify the process and the principal product (for example, mining bituminous coal, contract drilling for oil, or quarrying dimension stone).

Contract construction. Specify whether general contracting or special trade contracting. Also, show the type of work normally performed (for example, general contractor for residential buildings or electrical subcontractor).

Food or beverage establishments. Specify the type of establishment and state whether you employ workers who receive tips (for example, lounge—yes).

Trade. Specify the type of sales and the principal line of goods sold (for example, wholesale dairy products, manufacturer's representative for mining machinery, or retail hardware).

Manufacturing. Specify the type of establishment operated (for example, sawmill or vegetable cannery).

Signature. The application must be signed by (a) the individual, if the applicant is an individual, (b) the president, vice president, or other principal officer, if the applicant is a corporation, (c) a responsible and duly authorized member or officer having knowledge of its affairs, if the applicant is a partnership or other unincorporated organization, or (d) the fiduciary, if the applicant is a trust or an estate.

How To Get Forms and Publications

Phone. You can order forms, instructions, and publications by phone 24 hours a day, 7 days a week. Just call 1-800-TAX-FORM (1-800-829-3676). You should receive your order or notification of its status within 10 workdays.

Personal computer. With your personal computer and modem, you can get the forms and information you need using IRS's Internet Web Site at **www.irs.gov** or File Transfer Protocol at **ftp.irs.gov.**

CD-ROM. For small businesses, return preparers, or others who may frequently need tax forms or publications, a CD-ROM containing over 2,000 tax products (including many prior year forms) can be purchased from the National Technical Information Service (NTIS).

To order **Pub. 1796,** Federal Tax Products on CD-ROM, call **1-877-CDFORMS** (1-877-233-6767) toll free or connect to **www.irs.gov/cdorders**

The time needed to complete and file this form will vary depending on individual circumstances. The estimated average time is:

Recordkeeping	7 min.
Learning about the law or the form	22 min.
Preparing the form	46 min.
Copying, assembling, and sending the form to the IRS	20 min.

If you have comments concerning the accuracy of these time estimates or suggestions for making this form simpler, we would be happy to hear from you. You can write to the Tax Forms Committee, Western Area Distribution Center, Rancho Cordova, CA 95743-0001. **Do not** send the form to this address. Instead, see **Where To Apply** on page 2.

Form **8606**	Nondeductible IRAs	OMB No. 1545-1007
	► See separate instructions.	**1999**
Department of the Treasury Internal Revenue Service (99)	► Attach to Form 1040, Form 1040A, or Form 1040NR.	Attachment Sequence No. **48**

Name. If married, file a separate form for each spouse required to file Form 8606. See page 5 of the instructions.	Your social security number

Fill in Your Address Only if You Are Filing This Form by Itself and Not With Your Tax Return ▷

Home address (number and street, or P.O. box if mail is not delivered to your home)	Apt. no.
City, town or post office, state, and ZIP code	

Part I Traditional IRAs (Nondeductible Contributions, Distributions, and Basis)

Complete Part I If:
- You made nondeductible contributions to a traditional IRA for 1999,
- You received distributions from a traditional IRA in 1999 **and** you made nondeductible contributions to a traditional IRA in 1999 or an earlier year, **or**
- You converted part, but not all, of your traditional IRAs to Roth IRAs during 1999 **and** you made nondeductible contributions to a traditional IRA in 1999 or an earlier year. See the instructions for lines 8, 11, and 15 for special computations.

1	Enter your nondeductible contributions to traditional IRAs for 1999, including those made for 1999 from January 1, 2000, through April 17, 2000. See page 5 of the instructions	**1**
2	Enter your total IRA basis for 1998 and earlier years. See page 5 of the instructions	**2**
3	Add lines 1 and 2	**3**

Did you receive any distributions (withdrawals) from traditional IRAs in 1999?
— **No** ➤ Enter the amount from line 3 on line 12. Do not complete the rest of Part I.
— **Yes** ➤ Go to line 4.

4	Enter only those contributions included on line 1 that were made from January 1, 2000, through April 17, 2000. See page 5 of the instructions	**4**
5	Subtract line 4 from line 3	**5**
6	Enter the total value of **ALL** your traditional IRAs as of December 31, 1999, plus any outstanding rollovers. See page 5 of the instructions	**6**
7	Enter the total distributions you received from traditional IRAs in 1999. **Do not** include rollovers. See page 5 of the instructions	**7**
8	Add lines 6 and 7. (But if you converted part or all of your traditional IRAs to Roth IRAs in 1999, see page 5 of the instructions for the amount to enter.)	**8**
9	Divide line 5 by line 8 and enter the result as a decimal (rounded to at least 3 places). **Do not** enter more than "1.000"	**9** ✕ .
10	Multiply line 7 by line 9. This is the amount of your nontaxable distributions for 1999	**10**
11	Subtract line 10 from line 5. (But if you converted part or all of your traditional IRAs to Roth IRAs in 1999, see page 6 of the instructions for the amount to enter.) This is your basis in traditional IRAs as of December 31, 1999	**11**
12	Add lines 4 and 11. This is your **total basis in traditional IRAs for 1999 and earlier years**	**12**
13	**Taxable distributions from traditional IRAs.** Subtract line 12 from line 7. Enter the result here and include it in the total on Form 1040, line 15b; Form 1040A, line 10b; or Form 1040NR, line 16b	**13**

Part II 1999 Conversions From Traditional IRAs to Roth IRAs

Caution: If your modified adjusted gross income is over $100,000 **or** you are married filing separately and you lived with your spouse at any time in 1999, you **cannot** convert any amount from traditional IRAs to Roth IRAs for 1999. If you erroneously made a conversion, you must recharacterize (correct) the conversion. See page 6 of the instructions for details.

14a	Enter the total amount that you converted from traditional IRAs to Roth IRAs in 1999	**14a**
b	Recharacterizations. (These are corrections of amounts converted from traditional IRAs to Roth IRAs in 1999.) See page 3 of the instructions	**14b**
c	Subtract line 14b from line 14a. This is the net amount you converted to Roth IRAs in 1999	**14c**
15	Enter your basis in the amount you entered on line 14c. See page 6 of the instructions	**15**
16	**Taxable amount of conversions.** Subtract line 15 from line 14c. Enter the result here and include this amount in the total on Form 1040, line 15b; Form 1040A, line 10b; or Form 1040NR, line 16b	**16**

For Paperwork Reduction Act Notice, see page 8.   Cat. No. 63966F   Form **8606** (1999)

Form 8606 (1999)   Page **2**

Part III   **Distributions From Roth IRAs**

TIP There is a worksheet on page 6 of the instructions to help you keep track of your contributions, distributions, and year-end balances in your Roth IRA. You may need these amounts in future years.

17	Enter the total Roth IRA distributions (withdrawals) you received in 1999. **Do not** include rollovers	**17**
18a	Enter your basis in your Roth IRA contributions for **1998**. See page 6 of the instructions **18a**	
b	Enter your Roth IRA contributions for 1999, including those made for 1999 from January 1, 2000, through April 17, 2000. **Do not** include rollovers or amounts converted from traditional IRAs **18b**	
c	Recharacterizations of 1999 contributions to or from Roth IRAs. See page 6 of the instructions **18c**	
d	Combine lines 18a through 18c	**18d**
19	Subtract line 18d from line 17. If zero or less, enter -0- and **do not** complete the rest of Part III	**19**
	Note: If you converted amounts from traditional IRAs to Roth IRAs in **1998** and elected to report the taxable income over 4 years, go to line 20a; otherwise, skip to line 21.	
20a	Subtract the amount from your **1998** Form 8606, line 17, from the amount on line 16 of that form and enter the result **20a**	
b	Enter the amount, if any, from your **1998** Form 8606, line 22 .... **20b**	
c	Enter the 1999 taxable portion of your **1998** Roth IRA conversion. See page 7 of the instructions. Be sure to include this amount on line 27 .... ▶ **20c**	
d	Add lines 20b and 20c	**20d**
e	Subtract line 20d from line 20a. If zero or less, enter -0-	**20e**
21	Enter the **smaller** of line 19 or line 20e. If line 20e is blank, enter -0- .... ▶	**21**
22	Subtract line 21 from line 19. If zero, skip lines 23 through 26 and go to line 27	**22**
23	Enter your basis in your Roth IRA conversions for **1998**. See page 7 of the instructions **23**	
24	Enter the amount, if any, from line 14c of this form **24**	
25	Add lines 23 and 24	**25**
26	Subtract line 25 from line 19. If zero or less, enter -0- .... ▶	**26**
27	**Taxable amount.** Add lines 20c, 21, and 26. Enter the total here and include this amount in the total on Form 1040, line 15b; Form 1040A, line 10b; or Form 1040NR, line 16b	**27**
	Note: You may be subject to an additional 10% tax. See page 7 of the instructions for details.	

Part IV   **Distributions From Education (Ed) IRAs**

Caution: For 1999, a beneficiary can receive total contributions to Ed IRAs of up to $500. See page 7 of the instructions if contributions exceeded $500.

28	Enter the total Ed IRA distributions (withdrawals) you received in 1999. **Do not** include rollovers	**28**
29	Do you elect to waive the exclusion from income for Ed IRA distributions? If you check "No" and exclude from income any portion of an Ed IRA distribution, no Hope or lifetime learning credit will be allowed for your 1999 qualified tuition and related expenses.	
	☐ **Yes.** Enter -0-.	**29**
	☐ **No.** Enter your qualified higher education expenses for 1999.	
30	**Taxable amount.** Is line 28 equal to or less than line 29?	
	☐ **Yes.** Enter -0-; none of your Ed IRA distributions are taxable for 1999. But you should complete the worksheet on page 7 of the instructions to figure your basis in your Ed IRAs. You may need to know your basis in future years.	**30**
	☐ **No.** See the worksheet on page 7 of the instructions for the amount to enter. Also include this amount in the total on Form 1040, line 15b; Form 1040A, line 10b; or Form 1040NR, line 16b.	
	Note: If you have a taxable amount on line 30, you may be subject to an additional 10% tax. See page 8 of the instructions for details, including exceptions to the additional tax.	

Sign Here Only if You Are Filing This Form by Itself and Not With Your Tax Return	Under penalties of perjury, I declare that I have examined this form, including accompanying attachments, and to the best of my knowledge and belief, it is true, correct, and complete.
	▶ _____ ▶ _____
	Your signature Date

Index

60-day rule, 3/17–18, 4/14, 8/20
401 (k) plans
  administrative duties/costs, 2/9, 2/16–17
  contributions
    limits, 2/14–15
    requirements, 2/14–15
    salary reduction, 3/14
  deadlines, for establishing plan, 2/12–13
  defined, 1/18
  distribution requirements/restrictions, 2/18–19
  eligibility restrictions, 2/11
  nondiscrimination rules, 2/9
  with non-owner employees, 2/9, 2/17
  without non-owner employees, 2/5–6
403 (b) plans. *See* Tax-deferred annuity plans
457 plans, 3/14

A

Accrued benefits, defined, G/2
Actuaries, 7/10–11
Adjusted gross income (AGI)
  modified, 9/4
Administrative duties/costs. *See also under specific plans*
  employer plan comparisons, 2/16–17
  as plan selection criteria, 1/6, 1/18, 1/24–25
Affiliated service groups, defined, G/2
After-tax dollars, defined, G/2

Age
  leaving business after age 55
    defined benefit plans, 7/22
    money purchase pension plans, 6/23
    profit sharing plans, 5/24–25
  as plan selection criteria, 2/2, 2/5
  of SEP distribution, 4/13
  of SIMPLE IRA distribution, 3/17, 3/19, 3/23
  still working at 70½
    defined benefit plans, 7/23
    money purchase pension plans, 6/24
    profit sharing plans, 5/26
    SEPs, 4/18
    SIMPLE IRAs, 3/23
    traditional IRAs, 8/8
Anti-alienation rule, 5/21, 6/21, 7/20

B

Beneficiaries, changing
  defined benefit plans, 7/18
  money purchase pension plans, 6/19
  profit sharing plans, 5/19
  Roth IRAs, 9/17
  SEPs, 4/12
  SIMPLE IRAs, 3/16
  traditional IRAs, 8/16
Beneficiaries, naming
  defined benefit plans, 7/7–10
  money purchase pension plans, 6/8–10

profit sharing plans, 5/9, 5/42
Roth IRAs, 9/7–8
SEPs, 4/35–36
SIMPLE IRAs, 3/37
traditional IRAs, 8/7–8
Board of director fees, 1/10
Borrowing from retirement plans, 1/15
   60-day rule, 3/17–18, 4/14, 8/20
   defined benefit plan, 7/19–20
   Keogh plan, 1/15
   money purchase pension plan, 6/21
   profit sharing plan, 5/20
   Roth IRA, 9/23
   SIMPLE IRA, 3/17–18
   traditional IRA, 8/20
Brokers. *See* Money managers
Business termination
   early distribution for, 6/20
   IRS determination of, 5/25

C

Capital gains earned under plan, 1/22
C corporations
   self-employment status and, 1/10, I/2
Charities, as beneficiaries
   of defined benefit plans, 7/10
   of money purchase pension plans, 6/9
   of profit sharing plans, 5/9
   of SEPs, 4/35
   of SIMPLE IRAs, 3/37
   of traditional IRAs, 8/7
Collectibles, using plan assets to purchase
   Roth IRA rules, 9/36
   SEP rules, 4/25–26
   SIMPLE IRA rules, 3/29–30
   traditional IRA rules, 8/27–28
Commonly controlled businesses
   defined benefit plan rules, 7/34–35
   money purchase pension plan rules, 6/38
   profit sharing plan rules, 5/36–38
   SEP rules, 4/32
   SIMPLE IRA rules, 3/34
Compensation. *See also* Net earnings from self-
  employment
   limits on
     money purchase pension plans, 6/11–12

profit sharing plans, 5/12–13
   SEPs, 4/8–9
Comr. v. Keystone Consolidated Industries Inc.,
  6/16, 7/14
Contribution limits. *See also under specific plans*
   employer plan comparisons, 2/14–15
   as plan selection criteria, 1/23–24, 2/2
   for $30,000 vs. $50,000 thresholds, 2/4
Contribution requirements, 1/28–29. *See also*
  under specific plans
   employer plan comparisons, 2/14–15
   flexibility, 2/4
   as plan selection criteria, 1/6, 1/18, 2/2
Contributions, calculating, 1/13
Controlled group of corporations, defined, G/2
Conversion, defined, G/2
Corporations
   C corporations, 1/10, G/2, I/2
   controlled group of, G/2
   S corporations, 1/10, G/5, I/2
   working for, 1/10
Creditor protection, as benefit, 1/6
Custodial accounts. *See also under specific*
  plans
   for IRAs, 1/27
   for Keogh plans, 1/27
Custodians
   for Keogh plans, 1/8, 1/27
   mutual funds as, 1/31
Customized plans, 1/28
   money purchase pension plans, 6/8, 6/20
   profit sharing plans, 5/8, 5/20
   SIMPLE IRAs, 3/6–7

D

Deadlines for establishing plan. *See also under*
  specific plans
   employer plan comparisons, 2/12–13
   as plan selection criteria, 1/6, 1/25–26, 2/2
Death, early distributions
   defined benefit plans, 7/19, 7/21
   money purchase pension plans, 6/20, 6/23
   profit sharing plans, 5/23
   Roth IRA rules, 9/31
   SEPs, 4/15
   SIMPLE IRAs, 3/19
   traditional IRAs, 8/17

Defined benefit plans, 1/19, 2/5, 7/3–35
  actuarial assumptions, 7/13
  administrative duties/costs, 1/24, 2/16–17,
    7/17–18
    tax reporting requirements, 7/16–17, 7/31
  advantages, 7/5–6
  beneficiaries
    changing, 7/18
    naming, 7/7–10
  benefit limitations, 7/12–13
  combining with other plans
    IRAs, 7/35, 8/11
    multiple employer plans, 7/32–35
    SIMPLE IRAs, 5/36
  contributions
    calculating, 7/10–11
    cash or property, 7/14
    excess, 7/25–26
    failure to make, 7/15
    hardship waivers, 7/18
    limits on, 1/19, 2/5, 2/14–15, 7/3, 7/5–6,
      7/11–13
    minimum funding deficiencies, 7/28–29
    in no-profit years, 7/6
    requirements for, 1/19, 2/5, 2/9, 2/14–15,
      7/4–6, 7/13–14
  deadlines
    for contributions, 7/14–15, 7/29
    for establishing plan, 2/12–13, 7/10
  disadvantages, 7/6
  distribution requirements/restrictions,
    2/18–19, 7/18–23
    for divorce payments, 7/20–21
    for hardships, 7/20
    inservice, 7/19
    for loans, 7/19–20
    reporting, 7/18
  early distributions
    after age 55, 7/22
    for death, 7/21
    for disabilities, 7/22
    for federal tax levies, 7/23
    penalties, 7/21, 7/26
    for QDRO payments, 7/22
    for refunds, 7/22–23
  eligibility restrictions, 2/11
  employees
    administrative costs, 7/6
    contributions for, 7/6
    nondiscrimination rules, 7/6
    tax reporting requirements, 7/16
  establishing, 7/6–10
  ideal candidate for, 7/3
  investing plan assets, 7/17
  joint and survivor annuity requirement, 7/9
  key points, 7/4
  mandatory distributions, 7/23, 7/28
  minimum funding requirement, 6/19
  for non-owner employees, 2/9, 2/17
  penalties, 7/23–30
    early distribution, 7/21, 7/26
    infractions, consequences of, 7/24
    mandatory distribution, 7/28
    minimum funding deficiencies, 7/28–29
    nondeductible contributions, 7/24–26
    overstatement, 7/29–30
    pledging account as security, 7/28
    prohibited transactions, 7/26–28
    using assets to purchase life insurance, 7/28
  plan documents, 7/7–8, 7/18
  plan year, 7/10
  tax deductions, claiming, 2/5, 7/15
  terminating, 7/30–32
  trustee/custodial accounts, 7/7
  who may establish, 7/5
Defined contribution plans, 1/16
  401 (k) plans, 1/18
  administrative duties/costs, 1/24
  defined, G/3
  money purchase pension plans, 1/18–19
  profit sharing plans, 1/17–18
Disability, early distributions
  defined benefit plans, 7/19, 7/22
  money purchase pension plans, 6/20, 6/23
  profit sharing plans, 5/23
  Roth IRA rules, 9/31
  SEPs, 4/15
  SIMPLE IRAs, 3/19–20
  traditional IRAs, 8/17–18
Discretionary contributions
Disqualification of plans, 1/30
Disqualified persons
  defined benefit plan rules on, 7/26–28
  money purchase pension plan rules on,
    6/28–29

profit sharing plan rules on, 5/29–30
Roth IRA rules, 9/34–35
SEP rules on, 4/24–25
SIMPLE IRA rules on, 3/27–28
traditional IRA rules on, 8/25–27
Distribution requirements/restrictions. *See also under specific plans*
comparing plans, 2/18–19
exceptions, 1/30
for IRAs, 2/22–23
taxes on, 2/22–25
Divorce payments, distributions for
defined benefit plan rules, 7/20–21
money purchase pension plans, 6/21–22
Qualified Domestic Relations Order (QDRO),
5/21–22, 6/21–22, 7/20–21, 7/22
Roth IRA rules, 9/23
SEPs, 4/14
SIMPLE IRAs, 3/18–19
traditional IRA rules, 8/21

E

Education expenses, early distributions
Roth IRA rules, 9/33
SEPs rules, 4/17
SIMPLE IRAs rules, 3/21
traditional IRAs rules, 8/19
Eligibility restrictions, employer plan comparisons, 2/11
Employees. *See also under specific plans*
adding, as plan selection criteria, 1/6–7, 1/25, 2/6–9, I/2
dual status of sole proprietors, 1/10
Keogh rules for, 1/8, 1/15–16, 1/28
owner vs. nonowner, I/2
rewarding and excluding, 2/7, 2/8
tax reporting requirements, 1/29
Employer plans, 2/3
administrative duties, comparison chart, 2/16–17
contribution rules, comparison chart, 2/14–15
deadlines, comparison chart, 2/12–13
defined, 2/2
distribution rules, comparison chart, 2/18–19
eligibility restrictions, comparison chart, 2/11
IRA deductions, 8/11–15

multiple-employers, 3/31–34
no non-owner employees, 2/3–6, 2/20
with non-owner employees, 2/6–9, 2/21
Executor fees, 1/10–11
Expenses
contribution treated as, 3/8
start-up, 3/7
Experience losses

F

Financial institutions
for customized plans, 1/28
for plan assets, selecting, 1/26
plan documents of, 1/24, 1/27, 1/30
Financial planners. *See* Money managers
Fiscal year
for defined benefit plans, 7/10
for money purchase pension plans, 6/10
for profit sharing plans, 5/11
for SEPs, 4/7
for SIMPLE IRAs, 3/8
Forms and notices, IRS, A/3–36
550-EZ (Annual Return of One-Participant Retirement Plan), A/9–22
for money purchase pension plans, 6/18
990-T (Exempt Organization Income Tax Return), A/23–24
for defined benefit plans, 7/17
for money purchase pension plans, 6/18–19
for profit sharing plans, 5/18
for Roth IRAs, 9/17
for SEPs, 4/12
for SIMPLE IRAs, 3/16
1040 (Individual Income Tax Return), A/3–4
for profit sharing plans, 5/16
for SIMPLE IRAs, 3/15
1065, for SIMPLE IRAs, 3/15
5303-SEP, 4/6–7
5303-SIMPLE, 3/6, 3/7
5304-SIMPLE, 3/35
5305-SA (Individual Retirement Custodial Account Agreement), for SIMPLE IRAs, 3/36, 3/40–41
5305-SEP, for SEPs, 4/34–35, 4/41–42
5305-SIMPLE, 3/36

5305-SIMPLE (Individual Retirement Custodial
  Account Agreement), 3/35–36, 3/38–39
5329 (Additional Taxes Attributable to IRAs,
  Other Retirement Plans, A/29–30
  for profit sharing plans, 5/31
  for SEPs, 4/23, 4/25
  for SIMPLE IRAs, 3/29, 3/30
5330 (Return of Excise Taxes, Employee Benefit Plans), A/25–28
5498, for SIMPLE IRAs, 3/16
5500-EZ
  for defined benefit plans, 7/16
  for profit sharing plans, 5/17–18
8606 (Nondeductible IRAs), A/35–36
Internet resources, 1/11
IRS Publication 533 (sources of self-employment income), 1/11
Notice 89-25 (Question and Answer 12),
  A/7–8
  for SEPs, 4/15
  for SIMPLE IRAs, 3/20
Schedule C, for SIMPLE IRAs, 3/15
Schedule SE (Self-Employment Tax), A/5–6
  for money purchase pension plans, 6/14
  for profit sharing plans, 5/14
  for SIMPLE IRAs, 3/9, 3/12
SS-4 (Application for Employer Identification
  Number), A/31–34

G

Guardian fees, 1/10–11

H

Hardship distributions
  defined benefit plan rules, 7/20
  money purchase pension plan rules, 6/21
  profit sharing plan rules, 5/20–21
  Roth IRA rules, 9/23
  SEP rules, 4/14
  SIMPLE IRA rules, 3/17, 3/18
  traditional IRA rules, 8/21
Hardship waivers, 7/18
Home purchase, early distributions
  Roth IRA rules, 9/33–34
  SEPs, 4/17–18

SIMPLE IRAs, 3/21–22
traditional IRAs, 8/19–20

I

Income tax. See Tax reporting requirements
Individual plans, 2/10–11
  defined, 2/2–3
Individual retirement accounts (IRAs), 1/19–20.
  See Roth IRAs; SIMPLE IRAs; Traditional IRAs
  custodial accounts, 1/27
  disadvantages, 8/5
  excess contribution penalties, 4/23
  income tax on, 1/29
  inservice distributions, 6/20
  prohibited transactions, 1/30
  traditional vs. Roth, 2/10–11, 2/22–23, 2/24–25
  types of, 1/20
Individual retirement annuities, 8/3, 8/5
Information returns, 1/29
Inservice distribution. See also under specific
  plans
Insurance
  plan contributions to purchase, 1/15
    defined benefit plans, 7/28
    money purchase pension plans, 6/29
    profit sharing plans, 5/30–31
    Roth IRAs, 9/32, 9/36
    SEPs, 4/16, 4/25
    SIMPLE IRAs, 3/21, 3/29
    traditional IRAs, 8/19, 8/27
  to protect employee benefits, 7/6
  PS 58 cost, 5/30
Investing plan contributions. See under specific
  plans
  financial institution selection and, 1/26
  in limited partnerships, 3/16, 4/12
  managing, 1/30–31
  money managers, 1/26, 1/31
  mutual funds, 1/31
  tax consequences, 1/29
Investing retirement money, I/3
IRA adoption agreements, 8/6–7, 9/6–7
IRS
  customized plan approval, 1/28, 5/8
  hardship waivers granted, 7/18
  plan document approval, 7/7
  terminology for IRAs, 8/5

J

Joint and survivor annuity requirement
   for defined benefit plans, 7/9
   for money purchase pension plans, 6/9
   for profit sharing plans, 5/10

K

Keogh plans
   choosing, 1/23–26
   contributions, calculating, 3/8
   defined, 1/7
   defined benefit plans, 1/16, 1/19, 1/24
   defined contribution plans, 1/16–19, 1/24
   employees and, 1/15–16
   history, 1/9
   paperwork, 1/27
   prohibited transactions, 1/15, 1/30
   requirements, 1/7–8
   restrictions, 1/12–15, 1/17
   SIMPLE IRAs and, 1/21
   substantially equal periodic payments, 3/20
   tax deductibility, 1/8, 1/21, 1/22
   tax reporting requirements, 1/29
   who qualifies, 1/10–11

L

Letter of determination, 1/28
   confirming qualified plan, 7/7
   to terminate plan, 5/32, 6/31–32, 7/30–31
Limited liability companies (LLCs), Keogh plans
   for, 1/11
Limited liability partnerships (LLPs), Keogh
   plans for, 1/11
Loans. *See also* Borrowing from retirement
   plans
Loans, pledging account as security
   defined benefit plans, 7/28
   money purchase pension plans, 6/29
   profit sharing plans, 5/31
   Roth IRA rules, 9/36–37
   SEPs, 4/26
   SIMPLE IRAs, 3/30
   traditional IRAs, 8/28

M

Medical expenses, early distributions
   profit sharing plans, 5/24
   Roth IRA rules, 9/32
   SIMPLE IRAs, 3/20–21
   traditional IRAs, 8/18–19
Minimum funding standard accounts, for defined benefit plans, 7/13–14, 7/17–18
Money managers, 1/26, 1/31
Money purchase pension plans, 1/18–19, 2/5,
   6/3–47
   administrative duties/costs, 2/8–9, 2/16–17,
     6/5, 6/17–19
     tax reporting requirements, 2/9, 6/6, 6/18,
       6/18–19, 6/32
   adoption agreements, 6/43–47
   advantages, 6/5
   beneficiaries
     changing, 6/19
     naming, 6/8–10
   combining with other plans
     IRAs, 6/38–39
     multiple employer plans, 6/33–38
     profit sharing plans, 5/5, 6/3, 6/35–36
   contributions, 6/10–17
     calculating, 6/12–14
     cash-only, 6/16
     choosing plan rate, 6/15
     excess, 6/12
     flexibility of, 2/4
     limits on, 1/18, 2/14–15, 6/5–6, 6/10–12,
       6/35
     in no-profit years, 6/11, 6/15
     requirements for, 1/18, 2/5, 2/8, 2/14–15,
       6/6, 6/10, 6/15–16
     tax refunds as, 6/17
   deadlines
     for contributions, 6/16–17
     for establishing plan, 2/12–13, 6/10
     minimum funding, 6/16, 6/30–31
   disadvantages, 6/5–6
   distinguished from profit sharing plans, 6/3–5
   distribution requirements/restrictions,
     2/18–19, 6/6, 6/19–24
     on divorce payments, 6/21
     on hardships, 6/21

on loans, 6/21
early distributions, 6/22–24
  after age 55, 6/23
  for death, 6/23
  disability, 6/23
  for federal tax levies, 6/24
  penalties, 6/22
  for QDRO payments, 6/23–24
  for refunds, 6/24
eligibility restrictions, 2/11
employees
  adding, 6/3
  contributions for, 6/6, 6/11
  nondiscrimination rules, 6/6
  restricting participation, 6/39
  tax reporting requirements, 6/18
establishing, 6/6–10
flexibility, 6/35
ideal candidate for, 6/3
inservice distributions, 6/20
investing plan assets, 6/19
joint and survivor annuity requirement, 6/9
key points, 6/4
mandatory distributions, 6/24, 6/30
minimum funding requirement, 6/15–16, 6/30–31
more than one business, 6/5, 6/36–38
nondiscrimination rules, 2/9
for non-owner employees, 2/8–9, 2/17
penalties, 6/25–31
  for early distributions, 6/27
  infractions, consequences of, 6/25
  mandatory distribution, 6/30
  minimum funding deficiency, 6/30–31
  for nondeductible contributions, 6/25–27
  pledging account as security, 6/29
  for prohibited transactions, 6/27–29
  using assets to purchase life insurance, 6/29
plan documents
  amending, 6/15
  customized, 6/8, 6/20
  filling out, 6/39–47
  prototype plan, 6/7
  updating, 6/19
plan year, 6/10
prohibited transactions, 6/16
tax deductions, claiming, 6/17

terminating, 6/31–33
trustee/custodial accounts, 6/6–7
who may establish, 6/5
Mutual funds
  as custodian of plan assets, 1/31
  defined, 1/31

N

Net earnings from self-employment
  calculating contributions, 1/13
  vs. compensation, of Keogh plans, 1/12–14
  estimating, 2/2
Nondiscrimination rules, 2/6–7. *See also under specific plans*

P

Paperwork, to establish plans, 1/26–27
Partnerships. *See also* Limited liability companies
  borrowing from Keogh plans, 1/15
  contribution limit flexibility, 3/32, 4/31–32
  defined, 1/11
  defined benefit plan rules, 7/34–35
  Keogh plans for, 1/11
  limited liability partnerships (LLPs), 1/11
  money purchase pension plan rules, 6/37–38
  profit sharing plan rules, 5/37–38
  SEP rules, 1/20, 4/31–32
  SIMPLE IRA rules, 3/33–34
Penalties. *See also under specific plans*
  for early distribution, 1/3
Profit sharing plans, 2/4, 5/3–48
  administrative duties/costs, 2/8, 2/16–17, 5/16–19
    tax reporting requirements, 5/6, 5/17–18, 5/32–33
  adoption agreements, 5/42, 5/43–48
  advantages, 5/5
  beneficiaries
    changing, 5/19
    naming, 5/9, 5/42
  combining with other plans
    defined benefit plans, 5/35–36
    IRAs, 5/39

money purchase pension plans, 2/4, 2/5, 2/8, 5/5, 6/3
multiple employer plans, 5/33–38
contributions, 5/11–17
    calculating, 5/13–15
    cash-only, 5/15
    limits on, 1/17, 2/14–15, 5/3, 5/5–6, 5/12–13, 5/35–36
    in no-profit years, 5/12
    requirements for, 2/4, 2/14–15, 5/3–5, 5/15
    tax refunds as, 5/16
deadlines
    for contributions, 5/16
    for establishing plan, 2/12–13, 5/11
defined, 1/17–18
disadvantages, 5/6
distinguished from money purchase pension plans, 6/3–5
distribution requirements/restrictions, 2/18–19, 5/19–26
    on divorce payments, 5/21–22
    on hardships, 5/20–21
    inservice, 5/4, 5/5, 5/19–20
    on loans, 5/20
early distributions, 5/22–26
    after age 55, 5/24–25
    for death, 5/23
    disability, 5/23
    for federal tax levies, 5/25
    for medical expenses, 5/24
    penalties, 5/28–29
    periodic payments, 5/23–24
    for QDRO payments, 5/25
    for refunds, 5/25
eligibility restrictions, 2/11
employees
    adding, 5/3, 5/20
    contributions for, 5/4, 5/12
    nondiscrimination rules, 5/6
    restricting participation, 5/5–6
    tax reporting requirements, 5/18
establishing, 5/6, 5/6–7
ideal candidate for, 5/3
investing plan assets, 5/18
joint and survivor annuity requirement, 5/10
key points, 5/4
mandatory distributions, 5/25–26, 5/31
more than one business, 5/5, 5/36–38

for non-owner employees, 2/7–8, 2/17
penalties
    for early distributions, 5/22–23, 5/28–29
    infractions, consequences of, 5/26
    mandatory distribution, 5/31
    for nondeductible contributions, 5/27–28
    pledging account as security, 5/31
    for prohibited transactions, 5/29–30
    using assets to purchase life insurance, 5/30–31
plan documents, 5/8–9
    customized, 5/8, 5/20
    filling out, 5/39–48
    prototype, 5/8
    updating, 5/18–19
plan year, 5/11
tax deductions, claiming, 5/6, 5/16
terminating
    distribution of assets, 5/32–33
    paperwork, 5/32
trustee/custodial accounts, 5/7
who may establish, 5/5
Prohibited transactions, 1/30
    defined benefit plan rules, 7/26–28
    Keogh plan rules, 1/15, 1/30
    money purchase pension plan rules, 6/27–29
    profit sharing plan rules, 5/29–30
    Roth IRA rules, 9/34–35
    SEP rules, 4/23–25
    SIMPLE IRA rules, 3/27–29
    traditional IRA rules, 8/25–27
PS 58 cost, 5/30

Q
Qualified Domestic Relations Order (QDRO), 7/22
    defined benefit plans and, 7/20–21, 7/22
    money purchase pension plans and, 6/21–22, 6/23–24
    profit sharing plans and, 5/21–22, 5/25
Qualified plans, 1/9
    defined, 1/7. *see also* Keogh plans
    distributions, 3/16–17, 6/19–20
    establishing, 7/7
    hardship distributions, 3/18, 4/14
    income tax on, 1/29

multiple, 5/35–36
QDRO rules for, 5/21–22, 6/22
rollovers to IRAs, 8/3

R

Retirement plans. *See also specific plans*
benefits, 1/2–6, I/1–2
choosing, 1/6–26, 2/2–3
combining plans, 1/21, 1/22–23, 2/4, 2/5, 2/8
comparison charts, 2/9–10, 2/11–25
deductibility of contributions, 1/3
disqualification, 1/30
distribution requirements/restrictions, 1/2, 1/30, I/3
establishing, 1/26–27
maintaining, 1/28–29
prohibited transactions, 1/30
updating documents, 1/30
Rollover contributions, 8/3, 8/9
Roth IRAs, 1/22, 9/3–40
administrative duties/costs, 9/16–17
preparing statements, 9/17
tax reporting requirements, 9/16–17
adoption agreements, 9/6–7, 9/38–41
advantages, 9/4–5
beneficiaries
changing, 9/17
naming, 9/7–8
combining with other plans
defined benefit plans, 7/35
money purchase pension plans, 6/38–39
multiple IRAs, 9/37
profit sharing plans, 5/39
SEPs, 4/32–33
SIMPLE IRAs, 3/34
contributions, 9/8–16
after age 70½, 9/12
cash-only, 9/16
deductibility of, 9/3, 9/5
distributing, 9/18, 9/29
limits on, 1/22, 2/23, 2/25, 9/8–11
nondeductible, 2/11
requirements for, 1/22, 9/11–12
tax refunds as, 9/16
conversions
distributing, 9/18, 9/29–30

errors, 9/15–16
of SIMPLE IRAs and SEPs, 9/15
traditional to Roth, 9/8, 9/12–15
deadlines
for contributions, 9/16
for establishing plan, 1/26, 9/8
disadvantages, 9/5
distinguished from traditional, 2/10–11, 9/4–5
distribution requirements/restrictions, 2/25
for contributions, 9/18
for converted amounts, 9/18
for divorce payments, 9/23
for hardships, 9/23
for investment returns, 9/19–21
for loans, 9/23
ordering of, 9/21–22
for rollovers, 9/22
early distributions
exemptions to penalty, 9/31–34
nonqualified, 9/28–31
penalties, 9/15
qualified, 9/28
eligibility restrictions, 2/23, 2/25
establishing, 9/5–8
income limits, 1/22
interest earned, 1/22
investing plan assets, 9/17
distributing returns, 9/19–21, 9/29
mandatory distributions, 9/24, 9/37
penalties, 9/24–37
for early distributions, 9/15, 9/28–34
for excess contributions, 9/25–28
infractions, consequences of, 9/24
mandatory distribution, 9/37
pledging account as security, 9/36–37
for prohibited transactions, 9/34–35
using assets to purchase collectibles, 9/36
using assets to purchase life insurance, 9/36
plan documents, updating, 9/17
rollover contributions, 9/8, 9/12, 9/16
distributing, 9/22
SIMPLE IRAs and, 1/21
for single persons, 2/23
terminating, 9/37
trustee/custodial accounts, 9/6
who may establish, 9/3–4
Royalties, 1/11

S

Salary reduction contributions
  cap on contributions, 5/34
  deadlines, 3/15
  limitations, 3/13–14
Savings Incentive Match Plan for Employees.
  See SIMPLE IRAs
Savings plan, retirement plans as, 1/3
S corporations
  self-employment status and, 1/10, I/2
Self-employed, defined, I/2
Self-employed, multiple businesses
  defined benefit plans, 7/33–35
  money purchase pension plan rules, 6/36–38
  profit sharing plan rules, 5/36–38
  SEP rules, 4/30–32
  SIMPLE IRA rules, 3/33–34
Self-employed, own one business
  defined benefit plans, 7/33
  money purchase pension plan rules, 6/34–36
  profit sharing plan rules, 5/35–36
  SEP rules, 4/28–30
Self-employed, with day job, 1/10
  defined benefit plans, 7/32
  money purchase pension plan rules, 6/34
  profit sharing plan rules, 5/34
  SEP rules, 4/5, 4/28
  SIMPLE IRA rules, 3/13–14, 3/31–32
  and working for corporations, 5/34
Self-Employed Individual Tax Retirement Act.
  See Keogh plans
Self-employment income
  IRS Publication 533, 1/10–11
  sources, 1/10–11
Separate employer rule
  for defined benefit plans, 7/32
  for money purchase pension plans, 6/33
  for profit sharing plans, 5/34
  for SEPs, 4/27
  for SIMPLE IRAs, 3/31
SEPs, 1/20, 2/4, 4/3–42
  administrative duties/costs, 1/24, 2/4,
    2/16–17, 4/5, 4/12
    tax reporting requirements, 1/20, 1/29, 2/7,
      4/12
  adoption agreements, 4/34, 4/39–40
  advantages, 4/5
  beneficiaries
    changing, 4/12
    naming, 4/35–36
  combining with other plans, 4/4
    IRAs, 4/32–33
    multiple employer plans, 4/5, 4/27–32
    SIMPLE IRAs, 4/30
  contribution agreement, sample, 4/37–38
  contributions, 4/8–10
    calculating, 3/8, 4/9–10
    cash-only, 4/10
    excess, 4/9, 4/10, 4/19–23
    limits on, 1/20, 2/14–15, 4/5, 4/6, 4/8–10
    in no-profit years, 4/8
    requirements for, 1/20, 2/14–15, 4/5, 4/10
    tax refunds as, 4/11
  conversion to IRAs, 9/15
  deadlines
    for contributions, 4/10–11
    for establishing plan, 1/26, 2/4, 2/12–13,
      4/7
    for filing tax returns, 4/5
  disadvantages, 4/6
  distinguished from IRAs, 4/3–4
  distribution requirements/restrictions,
    2/18–19, 4/13–18
    on divorce payments, 4/14
    inservice, 4/13–14
  early distributions
    for death, 4/15
    for disabilities, 4/15
    for federal tax levies, 4/18
    for health insurance premiums, 4/16
    for higher education expenses, 4/17
    for medical expenses, 4/16
    penalties, 4/23
    periodic payments, 4/15–16
    to purchase first home, 4/17–18
  eligibility restrictions, 2/11
  employees
    adding, 4/3, 4/6
    contributions for, 4/5, 4/8
    restricting participation, 4/6
  establishing, 2/7, 4/5, 4/6–7
  inservice distributions, 4/13
    for hardships, 4/14
    for loans, 4/13–14

investing plan assets, 4/12
key points, 4/4
mandatory distributions, 4/18, 4/26–27
more than one business, 4/5, 4/30–32
for non-owner employees, 2/7, 2/17
penalties
    for early distributions, 4/23
    for excess contributions, 4/19–23
    infractions, consequences of, 4/19
    mandatory distribution, 4/26–27
    pledging account as security, 4/26
    prohibited transactions, 4/23–25
    using assets to purchase collectibles, 4/25–26
    using assets to purchase life insurance, 4/25
plan documents, 4/6–7
    filling out, 4/33–35
    prototype plan, 4/33–34
    updating, 4/12
plan year, 4/7
SIMPLE IRAs and, 1/21
tax deductions, claiming, 4/12
terminating, 4/27
trustee/custodial accounts, 4/6
who may establish, 4/3, 4/4–5
SIMPLE 401 (k) plans. See 401 (k) plans
SIMPLE IRAs, 1/20–21, 3/3–41
administrative duties/costs, 1/24, 2/6,
    2/16–17, 3/16
    tax reporting requirements, 1/21, 1/29, 2/6,
        3/5, 3/9, 3/15–16
adoption agreements, 3/35, 3/36
advantages, 3/5
beneficiaries
    changing, 3/16
    naming, 3/37
combining with other plans, 2/7, 3/5
    IRAs, 3/4, 3/34
    multiple employer plans, 3/31–34
contributions
    calculating, 3/5, 3/9–13
    cash-only, 3/15
    excess, 3/24–27
    limits on, 1/21, 1/24, 2/3, 2/6, 2/14–15, 3/3,
        3/5, 3/8–13
    matching, 3/10–11, 3/13, 3/15
    nonelective, 3/10, 3/13, 3/15
    requirements for, 2/3, 2/14–15, 3/5, 3/14

salary reduction, 2/6, 3/9–11, 3/13–14
conversion to IRAs, 9/15
deadlines
    for establishing plan, 1/25, 2/7, 2/12–13,
        3/6, 3/7
    for salary reduction contributions, 3/15
disadvantages, 3/5–6
distinguished from traditional IRAs, 3/3
distribution requirements/restrictions,
    2/18–19, 3/16–23
    on divorce payments, 3/18–19
    inservice, 3/17–18
early distributions, 3/19–22
    for death, 3/19
    for disabilities, 3/19–20
    for federal tax levies, 3/22
    for health insurance premiums, 3/21
    for higher education expenses, 3/21
    for medical expenses, 3/20–21
    penalties, 3/19, 3/27
    periodic payments, 3/20
    to purchase first home, 3/21–22
eligibility restrictions, 2/11
employees
    adding, 2/7, 3/4, 3/5
    contributions for, 3/6, 3/14, 3/15
    non-owner, 2/6–7, 2/17
establishing, 3/5–7
ideal candidate for, 3/3, 4/3
inservice distributions
    for hardships, 3/18
    for loans, 3/17–18
investing plan assets, 3/16
key points, 3/4
mandatory distributions, 3/23, 3/30
more than one business, 3/5, 3/33–34
net income of business, 3/8
penalties
    for early distribution, 3/19, 3/27
    for excess contributions, 3/24–27
    infractions, consequences of, 3/23
    mandatory distribution, 3/30
    pledging account as security, 3/30
    for prohibited transactions, 3/27–29
    using assets to purchase collectibles, 3/29–30
    using assets to purchase life insurance, 3/29
plan documents, 3/6–7

filling out, 3/34–41
  updating, 3/16
plan year, 3/7–8
tax deductions, claiming, 3/15
terminating, 3/30–31
transferring, 3/31
trustee/custodial accounts, 3/6
who may establish, 3/4–5
Simplified employee pensions. *See* SEPs
Small Business Jobs Protection Act (1996), 3/3
Social Security taxes (FICA), reporting, 3/9
Sole proprietors
  borrowing from Keogh plans, 1/15
  defined, 1/10
  defined benefit plan rules, 7/34–35
  establishing status as, 1/10–11
  Keogh plans for, 1/10
  money purchase pension plan rules, 6/36–38
  profit sharing plan rules, 5/37–38
  SEP rules, 1/20, 4/30–32
  SIMPLE IRA rules, 3/33–34
Start-up date of business, 3/7
Substantially equal periodic payments
  for profit sharing plans, 5/23–24
  for Roth IRAs, 9/31–32
  for SEPs, 4/15–16
  for SIMPLE IRAs, 3/20
  for traditional IRAs, 8/18

T

Tax benefits, as plan selection criteria, 1/6, 2/2
Tax brackets, 1/2
Tax Code
  IRA rules in, 1/19
  Keogh plan rules in, 1/7
  Section 408A, 9/3
Tax deductions
  for IRAs, 1/21, 1/22, 2/11, 2/22–23, 2/24–25
  for Keogh plans, 1/8
  to reduce current tax bill, 1/2–3
Tax deferrals
  as benefit, 1/2, 1/3–5
  tax-deferred growth inside retirement plan,
    1/5, 1/30–31
  taxed growth outside retirement plan, 1/4
Tax-deferred annuity plans, 3/14

Tax levies, early distributions for
  defined benefit plans, 7/23
  money purchase pension plans, 6/24
  Roth IRA rules, 9/34
  SEPs, 4/18, 5/25
  SIMPLE IRAs, 3/22
  traditional IRAs, 8/20
Taxpayer ID number
  for defined benefit plans, 7/8
  for money purchase pension plans, 6/40
  for profit sharing pension plans, 5/40
Tax refunds, as contributions
  money purchase pension plan rules, 6/17
  profit sharing plan rules, 5/16
  Roth IRA rules, 9/16
  SEP rules, 4/11
  traditional IRA rules, 8/11
Tax reporting requirements, 1/29. *See also*
  Forms and notices, IRS; *specific plans*
Traditional IRAs, 1/21, 8/3–33
  administrative duties/costs
    preparing statements, 8/16
    reporting contributions and deductions,
      8/15–16
    tax reporting requirements, 8/16
  adoption agreements, 8/6–7, 8/30–33
  advantages, 8/4
  beneficiaries
    changing, 8/16
    naming, 8/7–8
  combining with other plans
    defined benefit plans, 7/35
    money purchase pension plans, 6/38–39
    other IRAs, 8/28–29
    profit sharing plans, 5/39
    SEPs, 4/32–33
    SIMPLE IRAs, 3/34
  contributions, 8/8–11
    cash-only, 8/10
    deductibility of, 8/3
    limits on, 1/21, 2/22, 2/24, 8/8–10
    nondeductible, 2/11
    reporting, 8/15
    requirements for, 1/21, 8/10
    rollover, 8/3, 8/9
    tax refunds as, 8/11
  conversions, 9/8
  deadlines

for contributions, 8/10–11
for establishing plan, 1/26, 8/8
deductions, 8/11–15
  calculating, 8/12–15
  with employer plan, 8/11–15, 8/28
  no employer plan, 8/11
  phase-out, married persons, 8/14
  phase-out, single persons, 8/13
  phase-out range after 2007, 8/15
  reporting, 8/15
disadvantages, 8/5
distinguished from Roth, 2/10–11, 8/4, 8/5, 9/4–5
distinguished from SIMPLE IRAs, 3/3
distribution requirements/restrictions, 2/24, 8/16–21
  on divorce payments, 8/21
  on hardships, 8/21
  on loans, 8/20
early distributions
  for death, 8/17
  for disabilities, 8/17–18
  for federal tax levies, 8/20
  for health insurance premiums, 8/19
  for higher education expenses, 8/19
  for medical expenses, 8/18–19
  penalties, 8/25
  periodic payments, 8/18
  to purchase first home, 8/19–20
eligibility restrictions, 2/22, 2/24
establishing, 8/5–8
investing plan assets, 8/16
mandatory distributions, 8/21, 8/28
for married persons, 2/24
penalties, 8/22–28
  for early distributions, 8/17, 8/25
  for excess contributions, 8/22–25
  infractions, consequences of, 8/22
  mandatory distribution, 8/28
  pledging account as security, 8/28
  for prohibited transactions, 8/25–27
  using assets to purchase collectibles, 8/27–28

using assets to purchase life insurance, 8/27
plan documents, updating, 8/16
SIMPLE IRAs and, 1/21
for single persons, 2/22
terminating, 8/29
transferring from SIMPLE IRAs, 3/31
trustee/custodial accounts, 8/5–6
who may establish, 8/4
Trust accounts
  for defined benefit plans, 7/7
  for Keogh plans, 1/27
  for money purchase pension plans, 6/7
  for profit sharing plans, 5/7
  for SEPs, 4/6
  for SIMPLE IRAs, 3/6
  tax reporting requirements, 1/29
Trustee fees, 1/10–11
Trustees
  for Keogh plans, 1/8, 1/27

U

Unemployment
  contributing to IRAs, 8/4, 9/3
  early distributions and, 3/21, 4/16
Unrelated business taxable income (UBTI), 9/3–4
  for defined benefit plans, 7/17
  for money purchase pension plans, 6/19
  for profit sharing plans, 5/18
  for Roth IRAs, 9/17
  for SEPs, 4/12
  for SIMPLE IRAs, 3/16
  for traditional IRAs, 8/16

V

Vesting schedules, 2/7, 2/8

W

Wages, reporting, 3/9 ■

CATALOG

...more from nolo

BUSINESS

	PRICE	CODE
Avoid Employee Lawsuits (Quick & Legal Series)	$24.95	AVEL
⊙ The CA Nonprofit Corporation Kit (Binder w/CD-ROM)	$49.95	CNP
▣ Consultant & Independent Contractor Agreements (Book w/Disk—PC)	$24.95	CICA
▣ The Corporate Minutes Book (Book w/Disk—PC)	$69.95	CORMI
The Employer's Legal Handbook	$39.95	EMPL
Firing Without Fear (Quick & Legal Series)	$29.95	FEAR
▣ Form Your Own Limited Liability Company (Book w/Disk—PC)	$44.95	LIAB
▣ Hiring Independent Contractors: The Employer's Legal Guide (Book w/Disk—PC)	$34.95	HICI
▣ How to Create a Buy-Sell Agreement & Control the Destiny of your Small Business (Book w/Disk—PC)	$49.95	BSAG
▣ How to Form a California Professional Corporation (Book w/Disk—PC)	$49.95	PROF
▣ How to Form a Nonprofit Corporation (Book w/Disk —PC)—National Edition	$44.95	NNP
⊙ How to Form a Nonprofit Corporation in California (Book w/CD-ROM)	$44.95	NON
▣ How to Form Your Own California Corporation (Binder w/Disk—PC)	$39.95	CACI
▣ How to Form Your Own California Corporation (Book w/Disk—PC)	$39.95	CCOR
▣ How to Form Your Own New York Corporation (Book w/Disk—PC)	$39.95	NYCO
⊙ How to Form Your Own Texas Corporation (CD-ROM)	$39.95	TCOR
How to Write a Business Plan	$29.95	SBS
The Independent Paralegal's Handbook	$29.95	PARA
Leasing Space for Your Small Business	$34.95	LESP
Legal Guide for Starting & Running a Small Business, Vol. 1	$29.95	RUNS
▣ Legal Guide for Starting & Running a Small Business, Vol. 2: Legal Forms (Book w/Disk—PC)	$29.95	RUNS2
Marketing Without Advertising	$22.00	MWAD
▣ Music Law (Book w/Disk—PC)	$29.95	ML
Nolo's California Quick Corp (Quick & Legal Series)	$19.95	QINC
Nolo's Guide to Social Security Disability	$29.95	QSS
Nolo's Quick LLC (Quick & Legal Series)	$24.95	LLCQ
⊙ Open Your California Business in 24 Hours (Book w/CD-ROM)	$24.95	OPEN
▣ The Partnership Book: How to Write a Partnership Agreement (Book w/Disk—PC)	$39.95	PART
Sexual Harassment on the Job	$24.95	HARS
Starting & Running a Successful Newsletter or Magazine	$29.95	MAG

▣ Book with disk

⊙ Book with CD-ROM

	PRICE	CODE
Tax Savvy for Small Business	$34.95	SAVVY
Wage Slave No More: Law & Taxes for the Self-Employed	$24.95	WAGE
▣ Your Limited Liability Company: An Operating Manual (Book w/Disk—PC)	$49.95	LOP
Your Rights in the Workplace	$29.95	YRW

CONSUMER

Fed Up with the Legal System: What's Wrong & How to Fix It	$9.95	LEG
How to Win Your Personal Injury Claim	$29.95	PICL
Nolo's Everyday Law Book	$24.95	EVL
Nolo's Pocket Guide to California Law	$15.95	CLAW
Trouble-Free Travel...And What to Do When Things Go Wrong	$14.95	TRAV

ESTATE PLANNING & PROBATE

8 Ways to Avoid Probate (Quick & Legal Series)	$16.95	PRO8
9 Ways to Avoid Estate Taxes (Quick & Legal Series)	$24.95	ESTX
Estate Planning Basics (Quick & Legal Series)	$18.95	ESPN
How to Probate an Estate in California	$39.95	PAE
◉ Make Your Own Living Trust (CD-ROM)	$34.95	LITR
Nolo's Law Form Kit: Wills	$24.95	KWL
▣ Nolo's Will Book (Book w/Disk—PC)	$34.95	SWIL
Plan Your Estate	$39.95	NEST
Quick & Legal Will Book (Quick & Legal Series)	$21.95	QUIC

FAMILY MATTERS

Child Custody: Building Parenting Agreements That Work	$29.95	CUST
Child Support in California: Go to Court to Get More or Pay Less (Quick & Legal Series)	$24.95	CHLD
The Complete IEP Guide	$24.95	IEP
Divorce & Money: How to Make the Best Financial Decisions During Divorce	$34.95	DIMO
Do Your Own Divorce in Oregon	$29.95	ODIV
Get a Life: You Don't Need a Million to Retire Well	$24.95	LIFE
The Guardianship Book for California	$34.95	GB
◉ How to Adopt Your Stepchild in California (Book w/CD-ROM)	$34.95	ADOP
A Legal Guide for Lesbian and Gay Couples	$25.95	LG
◉ The Living Together Kit (CD-ROM)	$34.95	LTK
Nolo's Pocket Guide to Family Law	$14.95	FLD
Using Divorce Mediation: Save Your Money & Your Sanity	$21.95	UDMD

▣ Book with disk

◉ Book with CD-ROM

	PRICE	CODE

GOING TO COURT

Beat Your Ticket: Go To Court and Win! (National Edition)	$19.95	BEYT
The Criminal Law Handbook: Know Your Rights, Survive the System	$29.95	KYR
Everybody's Guide to Small Claims Court (National Edition)	$18.95	NSCC
Everybody's Guide to Small Claims Court in California	$24.95	CSCC
Fight Your Ticket ... and Win! (California Edition)	$24.95	FYT
How to Change Your Name in California	$34.95	NAME
How to Collect When You Win a Lawsuit (California Edition)	$29.95	JUDG
How to Mediate Your Dispute	$18.95	MEDI
How to Seal Your Juvenile & Criminal Records (California Edition)	$34.95	CRIM
Mad at Your Lawyer	$21.95	MAD
Nolo's Deposition Handbook	$29.95	DEP
Represent Yourself in Court: How to Prepare & Try a Winning Case	$29.95	RYC

HOMEOWNERS, LANDLORDS & TENANTS

California Tenants' Rights	$24.95	CTEN
Contractors' and Homeowners' Guide to Mechanics' Liens (Book w/Disk—PC)—California Edition	$39.95	MIEN
The Deeds Book (California Edition)	$24.95	DEED
Dog Law	$14.95	DOG
Every Landlord's Legal Guide (National Edition, Book w/CD-ROM)	$44.95	ELLI
Every Tenant's Legal Guide	$26.95	EVTEN
For Sale by Owner in California	$29.95	FSBO
How to Buy a House in California	$29.95	BHCA
The Landlord's Law Book, Vol. 1: Rights & Responsibilities (California Edition)	$44.95	LBRT
The California Landlord's Law Book, Vol. 2: Evictions (Book w/CD-ROM)	$44.95	LBEV
Leases & Rental Agreements (Quick & Legal Series)	$24.95	LEAR
Neighbor Law: Fences, Trees, Boundaries & Noise	$24.95	NEI
The New York Landlord's Law Book (Book w/CD-ROM)	$39.95	NYLL
Renters' Rights (National Edition—Quick & Legal Series)	$19.95	RENT
Stop Foreclosure Now in California	$34.95	CLOS

HUMOR

29 Reasons Not to Go to Law School	$12.95	29R
Poetic Justice	$9.95	PJ

Book with disk

Book with CD-ROM

	PRICE	CODE

IMMIGRATION

	PRICE	CODE
How to Get a Green Card	$29.95	GRN
U.S. Immigration Made Easy	$44.95	IMEZ

MONEY MATTERS

	PRICE	CODE
▣ 101 Law Forms for Personal Use (Quick & Legal Series, Book w/Disk—PC)	$29.95	SPOT
Bankruptcy: Is It the Right Solution to Your Debt Problems? (Quick & Legal Series)	$19.95	BRS
Chapter 13 Bankruptcy: Repay Your Debts	$29.95	CH13
▣ Credit Repair (Quick & Legal Series, Book w/Disk—PC)	$18.95	CREP
▣ The Financial Power of Attorney Workbook (Book w/Disk—PC)	$29.95	FINPOA
How to File for Chapter 7 Bankruptcy	$29.95	HFB
IRAs, 401(k)s & Other Retirement Plans: Taking Your Money Out	$24.95	RET
Money Troubles: Legal Strategies to Cope With Your Debts	$24.95	MT
Nolo's Law Form Kit: Personal Bankruptcy	$16.95	KBNK
Stand Up to the IRS	$29.95	SIRS
Surviving an IRS Tax Audit (Quick & Legal Series)	$24.95	SAUD
Take Control of Your Student Loan Debt	$24.95	SLOAN

PATENTS AND COPYRIGHTS

	PRICE	CODE
⊙ The Copyright Handbook: How to Protect and Use Written Works (Book w/CD-ROM)	$34.95	COHA
Copyright Your Software	$24.95	CYS
Domain Names	$24.95	DOM
▣ Getting Permission: How to License and Clear Copyrighted Materials Online and Off (Book w/Disk—PC)	$34.95	RIPER
How to Make Patent Drawings Yourself...	$29.95	DRAW
The Inventor's Notebook	$34.95	INOT
Nolo's Patents for Beginners (Quick & Legal Series)	$29.95	QPAT
▣ License Your Invention (Book w/Disk—PC)	$39.95	LICE
Patent, Copyright & Trademark	$29.95	PCTM
Patent It Yourself	$49.95	PAT
Patent Searching Made Easy	$29.95	PATSE
The Public Domain	$34.95	PUBL
⊙ Software Development: A Legal Guide (Book w/ CD-ROM)	$44.95	SFT
Trademark: Legal Care for Your Business and Product Name	$39.95	TRD
The Trademark Registration Kit (Quick & Legal Series)	$19.95	TREG

▣ Book with disk

⊙ Book with CD-ROM

	PRICE	CODE

RESEARCH & REFERENCE

Legal Research: How to Find & Understand the Law .... $34.95 — LRES

SENIORS

Beat the Nursing Home Trap: A Consumer's Guide to Assisted Living and Long-Term Care $21.95 — ELD

The Conservatorship Book for California .... $44.95 — CNSV

Social Security, Medicare & Pensions .... $24.95 — SOA

SOFTWARE

Call or check our website at www.nolo.com
for special discounts on Software!

⊙ LeaseWriter CD—Windows/Macintosh .... $129.95 — LWD1
⊙ Living Trust Maker CD—Windows/Macintosh .... $89.95 — LTD3
⊙ LLC Maker—Windows .... $89.95 — LLPC
⊙ Patent It Yourself CD—Windows .... $229.95 — PPC12
⊙ Personal RecordKeeper 5.0 CD—Windows/Macintosh .... $59.95 — RKD5
⊙ Small Business Pro 4 CD—Windows/Macintosh .... $89.95 — SBCD4
⊙ WillMaker 8.0 CD—Windows .... $69.95 — WP8

Special Upgrade Offer

Get 35% off the latest edition off your Nolo book

It's important to have the most current legal information. Because laws and legal procedures change often, we update our books regularly. To help keep you up-to-date we are extending this special upgrade offer. Cut out and mail the title portion of the cover of your old Nolo book and we'll give you 35% off the retail price of the NEW EDITION of that book when you purchase directly from us. For more information call us at 1-800-992-6656. This offer is to individuals only.

🖫 Book with disk

⊙ Book with CD-ROM

Order Form

Name _____

Address _____

City _____

State, Zip _____

Daytime Phone _____

E-mail _____

Our "No-Hassle" Guarantee

Return anything you buy directly from Nolo for any reason and we'll cheerfully refund your purchase price. No ifs, ands or buts.

☐ Check here if you do not wish to receive mailings from other companies

Item Code	Quantity	Item	Unit Price	Total Price

Method of payment

☐ Check   ☐ VISA   ☐ MasterCard

☐ Discover Card   ☐ American Express

Subtotal	
Add your local sales tax (California only)	
Shipping: RUSH $8, Basic $3.95 (See below)	
"I bought 3, Ship it to me FREE!"(Ground shipping only)	
TOTAL	

Account Number _____

Expiration Date _____

Signature _____

Shipping and Handling

Rush Delivery-Only $8

We'll ship any order to any street address in the U.S. by UPS 2nd Day Air* for only $8!

* Order by noon Pacific Time and get your order in 2 business days. Orders placed after noon Pacific Time will arrive in 3 business days. P.O. boxes and S.F. Bay Area use basic shipping. Alaska and Hawaii use 2nd Day Air or Priority Mail.

Basic Shipping—$3.95

Use for P.O. Boxes, Northern California and Ground Service.

Allow 1-2 weeks for delivery. U.S. addresses only.

For faster service, use your credit card and our toll-free numbers

Order 24 hours a day

Online	www.nolo.com
Phone	1-800-992-6656
Fax	1-800-645-0895
Mail	Nolo.com 950 Parker St. Berkeley, CA 94710

Visit us online at
www.nolo.com

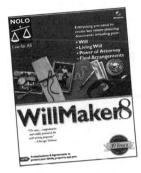

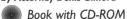

Take 2 minutes & Give us your 2 cents

Your comments make a big difference in the development and revision of Nolo books and software. Please take a few minutes and register your Nolo product—and your comments—with us. Not only will your input make a difference, you'll receive special offers available only to registered owners of Nolo products on our newest books and software. Register now by:

PHONE	FAX	EMAIL	or **MAIL** us
1-800-992-6656	1-800-645-0895	cs@nolo.com	this registration card

REMEMBER:
Little publishers have big ears. We really listen to you.

fold here

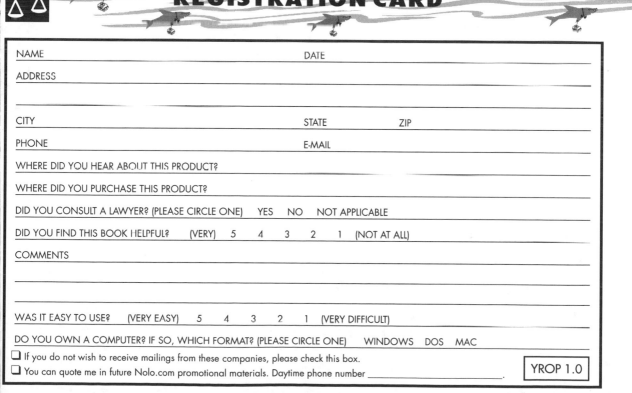

REGISTRATION CARD

NAME _____ DATE _____

ADDRESS _____

CITY _____ STATE _____ ZIP _____

PHONE _____ E-MAIL _____

WHERE DID YOU HEAR ABOUT THIS PRODUCT? _____

WHERE DID YOU PURCHASE THIS PRODUCT? _____

DID YOU CONSULT A LAWYER? (PLEASE CIRCLE ONE)   YES   NO   NOT APPLICABLE

DID YOU FIND THIS BOOK HELPFUL?   (VERY)   5   4   3   2   1   (NOT AT ALL)

COMMENTS _____

WAS IT EASY TO USE?   (VERY EASY)   5   4   3   2   1   (VERY DIFFICULT)

DO YOU OWN A COMPUTER? IF SO, WHICH FORMAT? (PLEASE CIRCLE ONE)   WINDOWS   DOS   MAC

❑ If you do not wish to receive mailings from these companies, please check this box.

❑ You can quote me in future Nolo.com promotional materials. Daytime phone number _____.

YROP 1.0

NOLO IN THE NEWS

"Nolo helps lay people perform legal tasks without the aid—or fees—of lawyers."

—USA TODAY

Nolo books are ..."written in plain language, free of legal mumbo jumbo, and spiced with witty personal observations."

—ASSOCIATED PRESS

"...Nolo publications...guide people simply through the how, when, where and why of law."

—WASHINGTON POST

"Increasingly, people who are not lawyers are performing tasks usually regarded as legal work... And consumers, using books like Nolo's, do routine legal work themselves."

—NEW YORK TIMES

"...All of [Nolo's] books are easy-to-understand, are updated regularly, provide pull-out forms...and are often quite moving in their sense of compassion for the struggles of the lay reader."

—SAN FRANCISCO CHRONICLE

fold here

- -

nolo
950 Parker Street
Berkeley, CA 94710-9867

Attn: | **YROP 1.0** |